TROTSKYISM IN THE UNITED STATES

TROTSKYISM IN THE UNITED STATES

Historical Essays and Reconsiderations

Second Edition

GEORGE BREITMAN,
PAUL LE BLANC, AND
ALAN WALD

Haymarket Books
Chicago, Illinois

This edition published in 2016 by
Haymarket Books
P.O. Box 180165
Chicago, IL 60618
773-583-7884
www.haymarketbooks.org
info@haymarketbooks.org

ISBN: 978-1-60846-685-6

Trade distribution:
In the US, Consortium Book Sales and Distribution, www.cbsd.com
In Canada, Publishers Group Canada, www.pgcbooks.ca
In the UK, Turnaround Publisher Services, www.turnaround-uk.com
All other countries, Publishers Group Worldwide, www.pgw.com

This book was published with the generous support of Lannan Foundation
and Wallace Action Fund.

Cover design by Eric Kerl.

Printed in Canada by union labor.

Library of Congress Cataloging-in-Publication data is available.

10 9 8 7 6 5 4 3 2 1

RECYCLED
Paper made from
recycled material
FSC® C103567

To the memory of
George Novack,
who sought to extend and deepen
our understanding of philosophy and history
so that we might be better able to change the world

Contents

Preface to the 2016 Edition

It is good to see this set of essays—authored by my mentor, the late George Breitman, my friend Alan Wald, and myself—being made more generally available for scholars and activists, especially those engaging with the vibrant traditions of revolutionary socialism. These essays seek, each in their own way, to advance an understanding of the history of an important current in that movement.

When I was young, I was taught to see "the Trotskyites" as a joke at best, and perhaps something more sinister (phonies, inveterate sectarians, manipulators, splitters, wreckers) at worst. Based on my own activism, my own study of diverse historical accounts and points of view, and a series of experiences over a number of years from the early 1960s through the early 1970s, I came to a different conclusion. I became a Trotskyist.

Some may wonder about the two different appellations—Trotsky*ite* and Trotsky*ist*. At times they are seen as synonyms, but sometimes there is really something deeper involved. To be a Trotskyist is to be in agreement, more or less, with the basic ideas and perspectives of Leon Trotsky. "Trotskyite," however, originated as a term of denigration and abuse, and when applied to a person, it is meant to convey the notion of someone who is simply and rigidly in orbit around the very terrible ideas and personality of a pseudo-revolutionary fly-by-night figure named Leon Trotsky. I have never considered myself to be *that*—but my Trotskyism has certainly evolved over the years, impacted by ongoing experience, study, and reflection. Each of the authors of this book—each in his own way—experienced a shifting (perhaps deepening) understanding of what happened in history, and that is reflected in these presentations and reflections on U.S. Trotskyism.

1

Leon Trotsky was one of the revolutionary socialist tradition's central figures. Readers can find presentations of his perspectives in a number of works by and about him, including my own *Leon Trotsky* (Reaktion Books, 2015) and a collection of Trotsky's writings that I coedited with Kunal Chattopadhyay, *Leon Trotsky: Writings in Exile* (Pluto Press, 2012). These perspectives provided the basis for the global network of revolutionary Marxists (often referred to as "Trotskyists") that organized itself formally in 1938 as the Fourth International. The present volume focuses on the U.S. section of this world organization, starting off as the Communist League of America and ending as the Socialist Workers Party (SWP).

The U.S. Trotskyists traced their beginnings to the heroic years of the early Communist movement, inspired by the Russian Revolution in which Lenin, Trotsky, and the Russian Bolsheviks led a workers' and peasants' upsurge for the purpose of establishing rule by democratic councils (soviets) of the toilers all across the former tsarist empire, and sparking a global set of popular insurgencies that would overturn domination by capitalists and kings and establish a genuine common-wealth of the world's working people. Betraying this vision was a layer of "practical-minded" leaders in the labor and socialist movement—social democrats—who opposed revolution and sought more limited improve-ments in compromise and partnership with the lords of capital and the powers that be. An even deeper, and ultimately more murderous, betrayal crystallized with a deradicalization of Russia's postrevolutionary regime, and of the world Communist movement, under a bureaucratic dictator-ship headed by Joseph Stalin. Those who gathered around Trotsky, in Russia and around the world, stood in opposition to such betrayals, with revolutionary socialist commitments intact.

The U.S. Trotskyists were also rooted in the native traditions of American radicalism, which I trace in my new collection *Left Americana* (2017) and whose story is told in a number of other works—most famously Howard Zinn's *A People's History of the United States*, with somewhat different takes in Sidney Lens's *Radicalism in America* (1966) and Michael Kazin's *American Dreamers* (2013), and other accounts. It includes Tom Paine and other radicals of 1776; Frederick Douglass and others who later fought uncompromisingly against slavery; early femi-nists such as Frances Wright and Sojourner Truth and Elizabeth Cady

Stanton; such labor radicals as Mary "Mother" Jones, Albert and Lucy Parsons, Eugene V. Debs, and "Big Bill" Haywood, all of whom saw the realization of a socialist democracy as an ultimate goal of workers fighting for a better life in the here and now.

After their ejection from the Communist mainstream in 1928, the pioneer Trotskyists of the United States worked hard—in the context of the Great Depression—to double and triple and quadruple their numbers, spread their ideas, and set an impressive fighting example. By 1938 they had formed the SWP. Each of the authors of this volume was a member of that organization—one a founding member, one a recruit in the late 1960s, and one a recruit in the early 1970s.

In the 1980s, after U.S. Trotskyism's impressive half-century record of engagement in struggles of workers and the oppressed, the SWP suffered a shattering crisis. George Breitman composed the talks reproduced here before that crisis hit, at a time when the party to which he had committed his life seemed to him to be doing fairly well—although several years later it would expel him (and many others, including Alan and myself) from its ranks. Some formulations in the contributions I wrote for this book are marked by my hopes, at the time of writing, that the fragments of the SWP might somehow come together to rebuild a revitalized and strong section of the Fourth International in the United States. That was not to be. Alan Wald seems now to have been most accurate in perceiving the end of the U.S. Trotskyism of which the three of us had been part. Yet there is much in that tradition, both positive and negative lessons, for activists seeking to build a revolutionary movement dedicated to a better tomorrow. Some of that is presented here.

One of the many limitations of this volume is the restriction of focus to what might be termed the U.S. Trotskyist "mainstream"—which means a failure to give adequate examination of a rich variety of split-offs, offshoots, and so on that had a vibrant life of their own, and in some cases made important contributions to U.S. radicalism and social struggles.

Before 1938 these offshoots included clusters of people associated with Albert Weisbord, B. J. Field, Hugo Oehler and Tom Stamm, George Marlen (Spiro), and others. From 1940 onward, there were those associated with Max Shachtman, Albert Goldman and Felix Morrow, C. L. R. James and Raya Dunayevskaya, Bert Cochran, Sam Marcy, Clara and Richard Fraser, James Robertson, Tim Wohlforth, and others. The beginnings of such a comprehensive history are offered in Robert J. Alexander's useful 1,100-page compendium, *International Trotskyism, 1929–1985: A Documented Analysis of the Movement* (Duke University Press, 1991), with several hundred pages on various U.S. groups and grouplets. There are also many individual collections and accounts (in some cases, quite rich and substantial) related to one or another of the various dissident-Trotskyist and former-Trotskyist streams and tributaries.

The fact remains that this book of materials by George Breitman, Alan Wald, and myself is the first approximation of a single, readable account of U.S. Trotskyism from its early beginnings in the 1920s to its disintegration in the 1980s, with at least some attention to detail, nuance, complexity, and with an allowance for different interpretations whose interplay may help define issues and deepen understanding.

II

Someone once told me that the very conception of *American* Trotskyism is a "nationalist conceit" because Trotskyism is a quintessentially *internationalist* orientation. And, of course, the same could be said about Marxism as such. But in both cases, this strikes me as quite wrong. The life of these "-isms" has come from the people who embraced them, made use of them, lived them, contributed to them. These people—each of them, all of them—are embedded in, reflect, and interact with specific cultural contexts and national experiences that indelibly mark their particular Marxism or Trotskyism. Sometimes distinctive contributions can result.

In any event, U.S. Trotskyism cannot be adequately understood divorced from the specific contexts and experiences of U.S. Trotskyists. Scholars and activists who wish to understand U.S. Trotskyism must also connect with the history of the United States, and especially with the distinctive complexities of the struggles of the U.S. working class and the broader U.S. Left. Naturally, the dynamic and fertile interplay of the national with the international are part of what both Marxism and the authentically revolutionary socialist project are all about.

As noted above, Trotskyists have often been tagged by critics as being—almost by definition—hopeless sectarians determined to take over, split, or wreck those they perceive as opponents. A recent example can be found in Leilah Danielson's *American Gandhi: A. J. Muste and the History of Radicalism in the Twentieth Century* (2014). Muste was a genuinely great human being who, blending Christianity with Marxism and much else, played an important role in labor, antiwar, and civil rights struggles. He is someone who has influenced me profoundly in the course of my life. In my opinion (argued in a forthcoming documentary history of U.S. Trotkyism, to be published by Brill in three volumes and later by Haymarket Books), Danielson presents a faulty interpretation of the merger of the American Workers Party led by Muste in the early 1930s with the Trotskyist-oriented Communist League of America. In the course of doing that she also misrepresents something I say in the present book: "Paul Le Blanc disputes the notion that there was 'a sectarian impulse within the tradition of American Trotskyism'. . . but my research has suggested otherwise."[1]

The idea attributed to me is one that I do not hold. The passage from which Danielson wrenches the quote-fragment involves a somewhat different point. In one of Alan's essays in this book, a particular quote by U.S. Trotskyist Morris Lewit (whom I knew and had affection for) is presented as "a dramatic illustration of a sectarian impulse within the tradition of American Trotskyism." In my introduction I disagree with Alan's interpretation of that quote, offering a different interpretation (which may be right or wrong, but that is another matter).

As one reads through my two essays in this book, however, one will find that I touch on and discuss more than one sectarian impulse cropping up among U.S. Trotskyists. The same is true of the remarkable historical excavations of George Breitman that are presented here, as well as of Alan's essays. My own view is that such sectarian impulses are all too common among many political tendencies (left, right, and center). Danielson's account, in contrast, seems to indicate that Trotskyists are sectarian simply *because they are Trotskyists*. The point is, I think, that we must move beyond a "good guys versus bad guys" conceptualization as we seek to understand the history of the U.S. Left and the conflicts within it—approaching the contending elements both critically and with respect. That is how we can learn the most. Certainly the history of U.S. Trotskyism calls out for that approach, which I think is manifest in all the essays that make up this volume.

---

[1] Danielson, *American Gandhi*, 403.

III

Trotskyism in the United States is one of the possible entry points into a vibrant tradition that can contribute much to the understanding of scholars, to be sure, but also to activists. Though devoid of a bibliography, contributions in this volume offer extensive endnotes in which references to essential sources can be found. In our new century, many sources have appeared containing additional detail and insight—and sometimes different interpretations of significant matters. First of all, there is the important work of Bryan Palmer, particularly his biography of James P. Cannon, only the first volume of which has appeared at the time of this writing—*James P. Cannon and the Origins of the American Revolutionary Left, 1890–1928* (University of Illinois Press, 2007). Worth consulting, as well is his *Revolutionary Teamsters: The Minneapolis Truckers' Strikes of 1934* (Haymarket Books, 2014). Efforts among other scholars are beginning to generate additional works of value.

Writings by and about two leading activists from the early 1930s to the 1980s can be found in *Revolutionary Labor Socialist: The Life, Ideas, and Comrades of Frank Lovell*, edited by Paul Le Blanc and Thomas Barrett (Smyrna Press, 2000) and *Malcolm X and the Third American Revolution: The Writings of George Breitman*, edited by Anthony Marcus (Humanity Books, 2005), the latter due to be republished in a revised edition by Haymarket Books. Scholars may want to explore the Breitman and Lovell papers, housed in the Tamiment Library at New York University's Bobst Library (along with the papers of many others on the Left, as well as an amazing repository of other materials of the U.S. Left). The Holt Labor Library in San Francisco and the Prometheus Research Library in New York are also significant repositories on U.S. Trotskyism.

Knowledgeable participants have also been making important contributions on the period of the 1960s to 1970s. These include: Barry Sheppard, *The Party: The Socialist Workers Party 1960–1988, A Political Memoir*, Volume 1 (Resistance Books, 2005) and Volume 2 (Resistance Books, 2012); Peter Camejo, *North Star: A Memoir* (Haymarket Books, 2010); Leslie Evans, *Outsider's Reverie: A Memoir* (Boryana Books, 2009); and the fine memoir by Canadian comrade Ernest Tate, *Revolutionary Activism in the 1950s & 60s*, 2 volumes (Resistance Books, 2014).

A multivolume series, "Dissident Marxism in the United States," is already in progress, and will include a documentary trilogy (scheduled to be published by Brill in 2017) on U.S. Trotskyism from 1928 up to the mid-1960s, which I have been composing and editing with Tom Bias, Bryan Palmer, and Andy Pollack. In addition, a treasure trove of materials can be found online at the Marxists Internet Archive and its Encyclopedia of Trotskyism On-Line (ETOL).

All of this will be helpful, hopefully, for those who wish to learn about and/or do research on the history of U.S. Trotskyism—and perhaps for those who intend to make some history of their own.

PAUL LE BLANC
June 17, 2016

Acknowledgments

Neither my collaborator Alan Wald nor I are satisfied with the modest collection of photographs provided here—a larger selection we had planned was precluded by space limitations, and there are even many more wonderful photos and illustrations which we hope will be gathered and made available in the future.

The following should be credited for specific items: Archives of Labor and Urban Affairs at Wayne State University (photo of Leon Trotsky, Natalia Sedova, Joe Hansen, Jean Van Heijenoort, Raya Dunayevskaya); Glen Boatman (photos of Diego Rivera mural and of James P. Cannon with Wong); Miriam Braverman (photo of Harry Braverman); Dorothea Breitman (photos of herself and George Breitman); Alexander Buchman (photo of Natalia Sedova, Leon Trotsky, Farrell Dobbs, Marvel Scholl Dobbs); Sol Dollinger (photo of Genora Johnson Dollinger); Edmund Kovacs (photos of Murry Weiss and of Myra Tanner Weiss); Jill Krementz (photo of Bert Cochran); Morris Lewit (photos of himself and Sylvia Bleecker); Frank Lovell (photos of himself, Sarah Lovell, and V. R. Dunne); Scott McLemee (photo of C. L. R. James); the Minnesota Historical Society (photo of Max Shachtman with James P. Cannon); Della Rossa (photos of George Novack, Tom Kerry, Karolyn Kerry, Evelyn Reed, Fred Halstead, Joe and Reba Hansen); Prometheus Research Library (photos of Martin Abern, Antoinette Konikow, and of group including James P. Cannon, Rose Karsner, Arne Swabeck, Carl Skoglund, Oscar Coover, Sr.); Evelyn Sell (photo of herself); Tamiment Institute Library, New York University (photos of Max Shachtman with Ernest Rice McKinney, and of group—taken by Ethel Lobman—with Tom Kerry, Laura Gray, Carl Skoglund, Dick Garza). Especially valuable are resources on American Trotskyism at Tamiment Institute Library/Robert Wagner Labor Archives (70 Washington Square South,

New York, NY 10012) and Prometheus Research Library (P.O. Box 185, Canal Street Station, New York, NY 10013).

Alan and I are keenly aware that this book would not be a book without the staff associated with the operations of Humanities Press, of central importance being our production editor Nancy Stutesman who endured delays with patience and good humor, and deserves much thanks. Among others at Humanities who helped with this project were Cindy Kaufman-Nixon and, of course, Keith Ashfield, whose commitment to making such works available should have a significant impact for scholars and activists for some time to come. I would once more like to thank and express love to my companion Carol McAllister for her supportiveness, and her courageous example, in a hard year.

—PAUL LE BLANC

Introduction

PAUL LE BLANC

The essays in this volume deal with various aspects of the history of the political current in the United States that came to be known as "American Trotskyism." This was one of the most dynamic currents on the U.S. Left from the late 1920s up to the 1980s—seeking to bring about a socialist society by means of a critical-minded Marxist activism deeply committed to working-class democracy and revolutionary internationalism—which had an intellectual and political impact far beyond its small numbers.

To date there is no definitive history of that movement, although the material offered here by three different authors provides a starting point for those who want essential information about U.S. Trotskyism.[1] The ample references can be useful for those who wish to carry out further research. More than this, the authors develop interpretations that confront the meaning of revolutionary politics in the United States. The authors write from somewhat different standpoints.

George Breitman (1916–86) was, for many years, one of the leaders of the U.S. Trotskyists—a branch organizer in Newark and Detroit; an editor of the weekly *Militant*; a member of the National Committee of the Socialist Workers Party (SWP) and at certain points a member of its Political Committee; an early and perceptive analyst of the ideas of Malcolm X and an architect of the SWP's approach to Black nationalism; the editor of a multivolume collection of Leon Trotsky's writings; a director of Pathfinder Press. In important ways, George was one of those—along with many seasoned comrades of the 1930s through the 1970s—who *created* the movement that is dealt with in this volume. Yet he had also earned widespread respect for the uncompromising

1

critical-mindedness and intellectual integrity in his considerable efforts to recount the history of that movement. George could have said of himself what the radical sociologist C. Wright Mills once wrote: "I have tried to be objective. I do not claim to be detached." George's meticulousness and objectivity, and his deep commitment to the movement to which he dedicated his life, shine through in his contribution to this volume—first presented as three classes for his comrades at the 1974 summer educational conference of the SWP—"The Liberating Influence of the Transitional Program."

The other two authors have been profoundly influenced by Breitman's work and example, and yet our work is different from his in more ways than one. Born three decades after him, we were shaped by different experiences, and although we had the good fortune to be George's friends and political comrades, we were relative latecomers to the Trotskyist movement. Neither of us could pretend to be his "most faithful disciple," let alone his successor (nor was George interested in such stuff). At the same time, each in our own way, we seek to continue the work in which he was engaged.

Alan Wald became part of the Young Socialist Alliance (YSA) and the SWP in the late 1960s, after some experience in the New Left organization Students for a Democratic Society (SDS). Alan has become a distinguished cultural historian and biographer of left-wing writers. His initial focus was on the so-called "Trotskyist intellectuals" of the 1930s and 1940s, who are dealt with in such works as *James T. Farrell: The Revolutionary Socialist Years* (1978), *The Revolutionary Imagination: The Poetry and Politics of John Wheelwright and Sherry Mangan* (1983), and the massively researched volume *The New York Intellectuals: The Rise and Decline of the Anti-Stalinist Left from the 1930s to the 1980s* (1987). As a rank-and-file activist in the SWP, Alan took a more or less oppositional position fairly early on (much influenced by Ernest Mandel and by the British journal *New Left Review*). This perhaps contributes to the critical edge in some of his interpretations.

I also was very much a part of SDS and the New Left experience of the 1960s, joining the YSA and the SWP in the early 1970s. My own studies have focused on the history of the labor and socialist movements—reflected in my first book *Lenin and the Revolutionary Party* (1990); my contributions to the *Encyclopedia of the American Left* (1991), edited by Mari Jo Buhle, Paul Buhle, and Dan Georgakas; and the volume I edited with Scott McLemee, *C. L. R. James and Revolutionary Marxism* (1993). I think that one could find either positive or negative reasons (perhaps both) for the fact that I do not share all of Alan's critical judgments in regard to the history of American Trotskyism. (Also, my own oppositional position in the SWP began more than a decade after Alan's.) At any rate, the interpretive differences are there—some of them quite sharp—and it seems to me that they are useful in shedding light on different facets of a complex reality and in generating deeper questions about the politics and history related to the phenomenon of U.S. Trotskyism.

It may be worthwhile to give the reader some sense of these interpretive differences. The first essay of this volume approvingly cites U.S. Trotskyist leader James P. Cannon's 1946 call "to build up the [Socialist Workers] party which believes in the unlimited power and resources of the American workers, *and believes no less in its own capacity to lead them to storm and victory.*" This grates against the method of embracing political rivals urged at the conclusion of the final essay in this volume by Alan Wald.

Alan is similarly critical of another leader of the SWP, Morris Lewit (under the party name of "Stein"), who—in the midst of a sharp polemical exchange with an internal oppositional current in 1944—also argued for a single, self-confident revolutionary party: "We are monopolists in politics and we operate like monopolists. Either through merger or irreconcilable struggle. We have proved this by the whole history of our movement." Lewit went on to discuss the experience with A. J. Muste's American Workers Party and the left wing of the Socialist Party (both of which led to "mergers"), and with rightward-moving Communist dissidents led by Jay Lovestone, as well as with the opposition in and split from the SWP led by Max Shachtman (both of which involved "irreconcilable struggle").[2]

Alan sees this as a dramatic illustration of a sectarian impulse within the tradition of American Trotskyism. To extend the debate between Alan and myself, I think that (1) the primary rivals of the SWP in the 1940s were Stalinists and social democrats, who could not have been embraced by revolutionary socialists in the way Alan suggests; (2) the SWP *was* prepared to consider reunification with the Workers Party led by Shachtman (a reunification that failed to occur, in large part, due to differences on cold war anticommunism—unity negotiations being torpedoed by Shachtman precisely over this question); and (3) at the same time, the SWP always defended the political rights of all others on the Left and sought united fronts with them on specific issues.[3]

Alan sees such a line of argument as simply sugarcoating the sectarianism he is criticizing, a view that undoubtedly could be capably elaborated by him—drawing a further response by me, and so on. Our failure to see eye to eye on everything is hardly disturbing, since it is alien to the tradition of revolutionary Marxism (with which each of the authors in this volume has identified) to consider that any "orthodox" history of such a topic as ours is desirable, or that any one standpoint has a monopoly on "truth." Related to this is a point made in George Breitman's 1974 essay reprinted in this volume:

> There has been much change and considerable progress since the founding of the SWP. Much of this we owe to the pioneers, without whom we couldn't have done half of what we did. But we would have perished if we hadn't gone beyond the pioneers, and we have gone beyond them, learning how to sharpen the ideas and improve the practice that they initiated or developed. And this is good because the time is coming when we shall have to storm revolutionary heights that the conditions of their time prevented them from reaching.

One could argue that this is overly optimistic in more than one way. The possibility of "storming the revolutionary heights" seemed closer to many in 1974 than it does in 1996. Worse than that, certain of Breitman's younger comrades ended up "going beyond the pioneers" in ways that appalled him, in fact falling far short of the revolutionary insights, achievements, and integrity represented by earlier generations (including Breitman's own). Yet the approach that Breitman insists on remains valid—learning from (but not worshipping) the revolutionary pioneers, maintaining one's own critical intelligence in order to appreciate their accomplishments and transcend their limitations. It is only in this way that one can move forward.

Although this volume stands as a tribute to our coauthor George Breitman, Alan and I decided that it would be appropriate to dedicate this book to another veteran of American Trotskyism who was important to us: George Novack, who was one of the best-known Trotskyist intellectuals in the United States. A widely respected Marxist philosopher and historian, with a special inclination toward popularization, he profoundly influenced us through his example and writings, and through personal assistance and kindness—which continued to transcend the political and organizational estrangement that separated us from him in his final decade. In an autobiographical note, Novack gives a sense of some of the better qualities that marked him and the movement to which he belonged:

> I followed Marx's injunction that it is not enough for thinkers to interpret the world in one way or another; they must work collectively to change it along socialist lines. . . . Theorists are not privileged to abstain from all the chores of party building and shuffle them off onto the lowly activists. They are called on to participate directly in the everyday struggles of the people, taking due account of the value of their specialized capacities in the overall allocation of functions.
>
> This was the model set by the personalities who most admirably exemplified the aims and ideals of scientific socialism, and I tried to emulate them to the measure of my abilities. I was fortunate enough to collaborate with two of them during their lifetimes: Leon Trotsky and James P. Cannon, founder of the American Trotskyist movement. . . .
>
> After 1940, living in the stronghold of imperialism, it was difficult to keep faith in the prospects of socialism and hold fast to its principles without a long view of history and a worldwide outlook. I had to watch most of my generation fall by the wayside and conclude a separate peace with the ruling powers in the universities, the publishing field, the professional and business worlds. Today, at the age of seventy, I am one of a very few: an unrepentant Marxist and full-time professional in the revolutionary movement.[4]

The example of the lifelong commitment to socialism provided by such people as Novack and Breitman, and the important work that they have left behind, stand as a challenge to and a resource for those who want a world in which the free development of each person is the condition for the free development of all.

Notes

1.   The essays gathered here were published elsewhere in some form. George Breitman's "The Liberating Influence of the Transitional Program," originating as three talks given in 1974, was first published in *SWP Discussion Bulletin* 33, no. 5, in June 1975; it was later serialized in the *Bulletin in Defense of*

Marxism, (nos. 34–40, from October 1986 through April 1987, and later reprinted—in revised form, according to the author's notes—in Paul Le Blanc, ed., *Revolutionary Traditions of American Trotskyism* (New York: Fourth Internationalist Tendency, 1988). It is reproduced here with permission of Dorothea Breitman.

Paul Le Blanc's "The First Fifty Years of American Trotskyism" first appeared in 1987 as the pamphlet *Trotskyism in America, the First Fifty Years*, published by the Fourth Internationalist Tendency in New York; the present version has been substantially revised and expanded. "Leninism and the Decline of U.S. Trotskyism" first appeared in Paul Le Blanc, ed., *Revolutionary Principles and Working-Class Democracy* (New York: Fourth Internationalist Tendency, 1992); it is reproduced here with relatively minor corrections and revisions.

Alan Wald's "George Novack, 1905–92—Meaning a Life," first appeared in *Bulletin in Defense of Marxism*, no. 100 (October–November 1992). His essay "From the Old Left to the New Left and Beyond" first appeared in *International Marxist Review*, no. 14 (Winter 1992). "The End of American Trotskyism?" originated as a talk given at the 1993 national education conference of Solidarity, held in St. Louis, Missouri, and was first published in somewhat different form in *Against the Current*, nos. 53 (November/December 1994), 54 (January/February 1995), and 55 (March/April 1995).

I would like to thank Donna McKee, secretary to the History Department at Slippery Rock University, for generously offering to retype the material on George Breitman for the appendix of this book.

2.   M. Stein, "The Internal Party Situation," *Internal Bulletin* 6, no. 13 (December 1944): 10–11; portions of this are reprinted as Morris Lewit, "The Internal Functioning of a Revolutionary Party," *Bulletin in Defense of Marxism*, no. 120 (November 1994): 30–31.

3.   Points one and three here should not be particularly controversial. Brief discussion of the unity negotiations between the SWP and Shachtman's group can be found in Peter Drucker, *Max Shachtman and His Left, a Socialist's Odyssey through the "American Century"* (Atlantic Highlands, NJ: Humanities Press, 1994), pp. 212–13, with an interpretive tilt in Shachtman's direction; more extensive material, with a different point of view, can be found in James P. Cannon, *The Struggle for Socialism in the "American Century"* (New York: Pathfinder Press, 1977), pp. 323–90, 408–21.

4.   George Novack, *Polemics in Marxist Philosophy* (New York: Monad Press, 1978), pp. 33, 36–37.

PART 1

Outlines and Essentials

1

Trotskyism in the United States: The First Fifty Years

PAUL LE BLANC

This is an account of the revolutionary socialist current in the United States known as "American Trotskyism," which existed with some measure of continuity from 1928 until the early 1980s—first as the Communist League of America (CLA), then as the Workers Party of the United States (WPUS), then briefly as a left-wing current inside the Socialist Party (SP) of America, and beginning in 1938 as the Socialist Workers Party (SWP).

In 1978 one of the SWP's most respected veterans, George Novack, wrote a brief history in the November issue of *International Socialist Review* entitled "Fifty Years of American Trotskyism." Novack hoped to explain "the capacity of this relatively small revolutionary socialist formation to influence the course of broad social struggles."[1] His clear, succinct article offered much information in a coherent chronological narrative.

At the same time, however, Novack's effort had serious limitations. It restricted itself to noting some of U.S. Trotskyism's primary accomplishments and some of its most salient internal conflicts—all in a somewhat self-congratulatory tone that was apparently designed to instruct and encourage younger comrades. It in no way prepared the reader for the fact that the SWP would soon explicitly abandon Trotskyism, proclaim itself to be a "sister party" of the Cuban Communist Party, and experience a demoralizing decline.

The fact remains that, in order to develop an in-depth historical materialist analysis, one must begin with at least the basic outline of the story. What follows is little more than an introduction that retraces what Novack offered in 1978, although drawing on additional sources. Another limitation: the present essay is an account of the first fifty years of American Trotskyism, so its focus is on the late 1920s to the late 1970s. In another essay reproduced in this volume, I attempt a more adequate analysis—more seriously connecting party history with broader social realities, and also dealing with developments of the 1980s, which help illuminate the earlier history.

Novack's account of U.S. Trotskyism was limited to an exclusive focus on the majority currents within the CLA, the WPUS, the Trotskyist faction in the SP, and the SWP. In his opinion, those breaking from this majority broke from "real Trotskyism." I have come to believe that reality is more complex, more interesting than this, but the focus of the present account is also on the "mainstream" of the U.S. Trotskyist movement, with which I identify.

In this account I mention the names of many people who were active in the revolutionary movement. I only regret that I have not been able to describe all these people and to offer names and descriptions of even more people—their personal backgrounds as well as political experiences, ideas, and passions. The history of the Trotskyist movement was not made by theoretical abstractions or impersonal forces or interchangeable beings. This history was made by actual people with names, with faces and bodies, with interesting and often complex lives. Mentioning so many names is my way of indicating this personal involvement in the making of history. It would be good if other historians sought to find the life stories connected with these names, and to trace the interconnections of these life stories with one another and with the larger social reality, in order to provide a more adequate account of the history that is sketched here. Readers should use their critical imaginations and powers of empathy to infuse this historical outline with the vibrant humanity that was essential to the actual Trotskyist movement.

Origins

A vital stream of labor radicalism arose after the American Civil War ended in 1865, contributing substantially to the organization and sometime successes of the National Labor Union, the Knights of Labor, the

Eight Hour Leagues, and many other major expressions of trade unionism and labor reform. Among the Marxist-influenced organizational forms through which U.S. socialists functioned in the nineteenth century were the American sections of the International Workingmen's Association (the First International), the Workingmen's Party of the United States, the Socialist Labor Party, and the semianarchist International Working People's Association.[2]

By 1901, many of the remnants and continuations of this labor-socialist tradition combined with other elements (former Populists, Christian socialists, radicalized feminists, leftward-moving intellectuals, battle-scarred trade unionists, and so on) to form the Socialist Party of America. Christopher Lasch has summarized some of the significant facts:

> In the years immediately preceding the First World War, the socialist movement laid down deep roots in the United States, in spite of many obstacles. . . . At its numerical peak in 1912, the party had 118,000 members well distributed throughout the country. It claimed 323 English- and foreign-language publications with a total circulation probably in excess of two million. The largest of the Socialist newspapers, *The Appeal to Reason*, of Girard, Kansas, had a weekly circulation of 761,747. In 1912, the year Eugene V. Debs polled six percent of the presidential vote, Socialists held 1,200 offices in 340 cities, including 79 mayors in 24 states. As late as 1918, they elected 32 state legislators. In 1916, they elected Meyer London [from New York City] to Congress and made important gains in the municipal elections of several large cities. [Victor Berger from the Socialist stronghold of Milwaukee was also elected to Congress during this period.][3]

More than this, approximately one-third of the unions in the American Federation of Labor (AFL) were led and strongly influenced by Socialists. Many Socialists played a central role in establishing the militant and vital Industrial Workers of the World (IWW). They also were a major force in the early National Association for the Advancement of Colored People (NAACP), in numerous feminist efforts, and in much of the radical and reform ferment that characterized the so-called Progressive era of 1900–18.

Indeed, many of the Progressive reforms were generated by fear among upper-class political figures, who were feeling the pressure of the rising socialist challenge. As Theodore Roosevelt put it in 1906: "I do not like the social conditions at present. The dull, purblind folly of the very rich men, their greed and arrogance . . . and the corruption in business and politics, have tended to produce a very unhealthy condition of excitement and irritation in the popular mind, which shows itself in the great increase in the socialistic propaganda." Politicians such as Teddy Roosevelt and Woodrow Wilson aggressively pushed for reforms that would force the so-called robber barons—the industrial capitalists who had transformed the U.S. economy in the decades following the Civil War—to "clean up their act," in order to preserve capitalism. At the same time they attempted to work with conservative (or conservatized) labor figures such as AFL president Samuel Gompers, who symbolized a "reasonable" alternative to militant socialism. Future capitalist politicians—most successful of whom was Franklin D. Roosevelt in the 1930s and 1940s—were to utilize this gambit with great success.[4]

In the early 1900s a divergence opened in Socialist Party ranks between moderates led by Victor Berger and Morris Hillquit, who rejected revolutionary socialism in favor of a more gradualist reform orientation, and those inclined to hold firm to a more militant class-struggle perspective. Representing the left wing of the party were such figures as Eugene V. Debs and the even more intransigent IWW leader "Big Bill" Haywood. The SP has sometimes been idealized (in the words of Lasch, summarizing the account of historian James Weinstein) as "inclusive, nonsectarian, and given to searching and open debate," and the party's structure *was* quite open and loose. The fact remains, however, that—as with social democratic parties generally—the moderate elements dominated the party apparatus, often using their power undemocratically to undercut, or sometimes even repress or expel, left-wing influence.

In the face of the patriotic hysteria and fierce government repression unleashed by World War I, the bulk of the SP held to an antiwar position. Yet the party's left wing increasingly came to feel that this position was being soft-pedaled by the moderates. When the Bolshevik Revolution of 1917 created the world's first workers' state in Russia, the Socialist Party as a whole greeted it with enthusiasm, but the moderates were adamant that this should in no way affect "business as usual" for the party. The left wing, however, argued that there were important lessons to be learned from the Bolsheviks and that the Socialist Party must develop a consistently revolutionary approach to American and world realities. When it became clear in 1919 that the left wing was winning over a party majority, the moderates engineered massive expulsions, eliminating the bulk of the left wing and over half the membership.

Some of the most committed and capable activists from the SP went on to form the core of the new Communist movement in 1919, soon to be joined by other Socialist Party veterans in the early 1920s. There were also left-wing trade union activists from the IWW and AFL. Especially significant in this period was the adherence to communism by a cluster of Black socialists associated with an important radical group called the African Blood Brotherhood led by Cyril Briggs.

At first the new movement was fragmented, riddled with naively utopian hopes and organizational immaturity. Ultra-leftism and government repression reinforced each other, creating an atmosphere incapable of attracting or retaining even a majority of those pro-left forces driven out of the SP, not to mention new recruits from broader working-class layers. By the early 1920s, however, a unified Communist Party was forged that more effectively reflected U.S. radical traditions, blending with the principles of Russian Bolshevism and the experience of the international revolutionary workers' movement.[5]

On the trade union front, the Communist Party created an influential network of leaders and activists in the AFL through the Trade Union Educational League, led by the famed leader of the 1919 steel strike William Z. Foster. It played a major role in the realm of defending civil liberties, largely through the International Labor Defense (ILD), headed by James P. Cannon, as well as through working relationships with such people as Roger Baldwin of the recently formed American Civil Liberties Union. This role was especially important in the face of the fierce government repression that devastated the radical movement in the wake of World War I. The ILD assisted "class-struggle prisoners" regardless of political affiliation—most famous being the Italian anarchists Nicola Sacco and Bartolomeo Vanzetti, as well as militant socialist trade unionists Tom Mooney and Warren K. Billings. The Communists coordinated an impressive array of immigrant fraternal and social organizations and sought to help protect the rights of immigrants through the National Committee for the Protection of the Foreign Born. (It is worth remembering that a majority of U.S. workers in many areas during this period were first- and second-generation immigrants.) Especially due to the insistence of the Communist International, the American Communist Party began to give more consistent and careful attention to the problem of racism and the plight of African Americans than had ever been the case among U.S. left-wing organizations. A small but important core of Black intellectuals and workers came to see, in the words of Harry Haywood, "the elimination of racism and the achievement of complete equality for Blacks as an inevitable byproduct of a socialist revolution in the United States." Attention was also given to the need for a farmer-labor alliance, and to what was then called "the woman question." Through the innumerable books and pamphlets published by International Publishers and Workers Library Publishers, through the *Daily Worker* and a variety of English- and foreign-language periodicals, through classes and lectures and special schools, through marches and rallies and Communist electoral campaigns, the Communist Party sought to spread Marxist ideas and deepen socialist consciousness. Although party membership figures fluctuated between 7,000 and 12,000, many thousands more were drawn to its activities and influenced by its efforts.[6]

Problems will inevitably develop in any movement composed of human beings, and the Communist Party of this period was no exception. But as James P. Cannon put it some years later: "It was composed of thousands of courageous and devoted revolutionists willing to make sacrifices and take risks for the movement. In spite of all their mistakes, they built a party the like of which had never been seen in this country before; that is, a party founded on a Marxist program, with a professional leadership and disciplined ranks."[7] During the decade of relative prosperity and conservatism in the Roaring Twenties, it held to the line of class struggle, political independence of the working class, and revolutionary socialism, gathering and preparing its cadres for the great labor battles that would erupt in the 1930s.

An important quality of the Communist Party was its revolutionary internationalism. This meant opposing imperialism; seeking solidarity with, as well as aiding and learning from, workers' and oppressed peoples' struggles in other lands; rejecting chauvinism, militarism, and capitalist wars. It also meant a loyalty to the ideals of the Russian Revolution and to the working-class Soviet Republic. John Reed, one of the founders of American Communism, had written a classic eyewitness account called *Ten Days that Shook the World*, and the Communist Party continued to educate broadly about the accomplishments, problems, and immense struggles of the Soviet Republic. More than this, the American party saw itself as a loyal section of the Communist International (or

Comintern) led by such Russian Bolsheviks as Lenin, Trotsky, Zinoviev, and Bukharin. This Third International—in contrast to the Second International (or Socialist International), which now represented the moderate socialist parties—was designed to coordinate the work of Communist parties throughout the world for the purpose of achieving the revolutionary overthrow of capitalism.[8]

As the 1920s wore on, however, things began to change. Lenin died in 1924, and factional disputes flared up among the Russian Communists. The new general secretary of the Russian party, Joseph Stalin, allied himself first with Zinoviev and Kamenev against Leon Trotsky, then with Bukharin against the other three, and finally came out against Bukharin as well—and his successive victories reflected the consolidation of power and privilege among the Soviet bureaucracy. This bureaucratic layer tightened dictatorial controls and adopted a "Russia comes first" conservatism, which warped the policies and practices of the Comintern. The Comintern's now-Stalinist leadership increasingly intervened in the life and internal conflicts of Communist parties throughout the world in order to establish its domination. In the U.S. party, for example, a bloc had formed led by Foster and Cannon to push for an orientation that was more in harmony with distinctly American labor-radical traditions, against a faction led by Jay Lovestone, Benjamin Gitlow, and Bertram D. Wolfe, whom the former considered to be opportunistic. The Comintern intervened to ensure the dominance of the Lovestoneites (whom they later expelled in 1929). As Peggy Dennis later commented, "in our political naivete . . . we younger comrades did not particularly connect our own internal struggle with that which had raged in the Comintern and the Soviet Communist Party," nor did many U.S. Communists comprehend that the Comintern's interventions into the affairs of the American Communist Party were "part of Stalin's consolidation of his leadership within the Soviet Party and the international movement, less than five years after Lenin's death." She added, "we eloquently echoed Stalin's published denunciations of Bukharinism and Trotskyism without even objecting to the fact that we were not allowed to read what Bukharin or Trotsky had said or written."[9]

There were some, however, who did not allow their loyalty to the Russian Revolution and the USSR to be turned into intellectual blinders, who were unwilling to become uncritical enthusiasts precisely because they wanted to remain good revolutionists. Among these was

James P. Cannon, who *did* read Trotsky's early critique of Stalinism (later contained in the work *The Third International after Lenin*). He found himself in agreement with the critique, and he quietly began to share the document with other comrades. This was incompatible with the new Stalinist orthodoxy, and it resulted in the expulsion of Cannon, Max Shachtman, Martin Abern, and Rose Karsner in November 1928. Anyone who questioned the expulsions was also expelled—which resulted in such veteran cadres as Arne Swabeck, Albert Glotzer, Carl Skoglund, Vincent Raymond Dunne, and others joining the ranks of the Trotskyists. Even before this wave of expulsions, the veteran revolutionary and socialist-feminist Antoinette Konikow, along with several others, had been expelled from the Communist Party in Boston for defending Trotsky and protesting against the bureaucratization of the Comintern, and they had set up the Independent Communist League of Boston. These modest forces came together to form what was first called the Communist League of America, Left Opposition of the Communist Party. It was formally constituted in May 1929, with about a hundred members in twelve cities.[10]

Cannon and Shachtman

Since Cannon and Shachtman were the most influential leaders of early U.S. Trotskyism, it is worth considering aspects of their political and personal lives that helped shape the movement.

James Patrick Cannon (1890–1974) was born in Rosedale, Kansas, and grew up in a working-class family in which his mother's Catholic religious convictions coexisted uneasily with his father's deep-rooted labor radicalism (from the Knights of Labor and the Populist movement to the Socialist Party of Eugene V. Debs). Cannon became an organizer for the Industrial Workers of the World, trained by IWW leaders "Big Bill" Haywood and especially Vincent St. John in militant strikes, revolutionary agitation, free-speech fights, and patient working-class organizing. A midwestern leader of the Socialist Party's left wing after Russia's 1917 revolution, he helped establish the early Communist movement, serving as the first national chairman of the unified Communist Party—which at the time called itself the Workers Party of America—in 1921. Cannon was a U.S. delegate to the Communist International on five occasions, once spending eight months in Moscow on the Comintern's executive committee. His teachers were Lenin, Trotsky, Zinoviev,

Bukharin, Radek, and other leading representatives of Bolshevism in its heroic years, ensuring a substantial grounding in the principles of revolutionary internationalism and revolutionary Marxist politics. In the late 1920s, when these principles were being fundamentally undermined by the Stalinist bureaucracy, Cannon—who had a reputation as a highly capable organization man and a masterful infighter in the Communist Party's factional jungle—"destroyed" his career in the top echelons of the party by embracing the Bolshevik-Leninist opposition led by Leon Trotsky.

Max Shachtman (1904–72) was part of a Jewish working-class family that immigrated to the United States from Poland one year after he was born. Growing up within the socialist subculture in which much of the Jewish working class was steeped at that time, he became part of the early Communist Party and in the early 1920s became a national leader in the Young Workers League, where he began to develop his skills as a writer, orator, and editor. These skills were further developed when he worked in the International Labor Defense with Cannon, editing the magazine *Labor Defender*. Shachtman's contributions to the Trotskyist movement would be substantial thanks to his intellectual brilliance and eloquence, his tremendous warmth, and his capacity for doing immense amounts of work. Alan Wald notes that "he could be maddeningly irresponsible—not keeping appointments or completing articles by deadlines. He tended to rush to the office and dash off an article for the party's newspaper or fulfill some other assignment at the very last minute."[11] Despite such faults, his authority among the Trotskyists was considerable. Julius Jacobson, a young member of the Trotskyist movement in New York during the 1930s who was especially close to Shachtman, offers this recollection:

> How we admired and respected Max! . . . We respected James P. Cannon, too. But we knew him as Cannon. Shachtman was Max. We could joke and banter with him. And when Max spoke at a "big meeting" at Irving Plaza or Webster Hall we were always there. It was not merely that we were entertained by his razor-sharp wit, his polemical skills, his sense of irony, his robust humor but primarily because we were clearly in the presence of an exceptional political intelligence. Even back then, in his ability to integrate Marxist theory, political history and specific events, he had few peers in the American socialist movement. . . . Max was the theoretician, the writer, the one with greater appeal to the young and the

intellectuals within the Party and its periphery; Cannon was the organizational man, the proletarian oriented leader and magnificent orator. Of the two, Shachtman was clearly the more thoughtful and independent personality.[12]

Proof of Shachtman's greater thoughtfulness and independence, for Jacobson, can be found in his later break with Trotsky (in which Jacobson also participated)—though it is possible that Cannon was thoughtful in ways that Jacobson could not observe. "Jim was complex and many-sided, a very human being with a tremendous sense of humor, both subtle and broad," comments one of his many friends in the movement, Anne Chester. "He had a real feel for and a sensitivity to people to an extraordinary degree." She felt that this was related to Cannon's capacities as a political leader. "These characteristics, together with his highly developed political acumen and conviction that an enduring revolutionary party could not be built on anything less than a collective leadership based on a firm body of revolutionary principles and program," Chester wrote at the time of Cannon's death, "enabled him to unite people of varied abilities, strengths and weaknesses that has stood the test of forty-six years."[13]

This contrasts with Jacobson's views on some of Shachtman's shortcomings: "He was not a candid man nor was he a generous man. Indeed, in politics he possessed a sort of vindictiveness belied by his surface bonhomie. When he felt 'crossed,' even on a relatively minor issue, he often retaliated with a kind of meanness that could shock his closest supporters. He was a combination of callous bureaucrat and sentimentalist."[14]

Cannon had shortcomings of his own. George Novack has referred to his "having had some losing bouts with John Barleycorn until he broke the habit late in life" (novelist James T. Farrell once referred to him cruelly as "the Lenin of America if he hadn't drunk whiskey"), and Novack also asserts that "he was somewhat self-indulgent and not as industrious as he might have been." To many of his factional and political opponents, Cannon was the classic example of a narrow-minded sect leader. Thus Lewis Coser used him as a "case study" in exploring "the sociology of the sect," asserting, among other things, that he had "a fear of 'petty-bourgeois' interests in art, literature, philosophy, or sociology" and was "a true-believer," constantly seeking to purge "traitors" and "heretics" in order to preserve the purity of his tiny revolutionary group. Dwight Macdonald characterized him in a similar manner: "Like the shaman of a tribe, the party boss preaches distrust of and disdain for all outsiders simply because they *are* outside the in-group. . . . They make a principle out of not learning anything from anybody." Such impressions are belied by much material: Cannon's *Letters from Prison* of the mid-1940s (which reveal an intelligence actively engaged with works by a wide range of people on art, literature, philosophy, sociology, and much else), his perceptive and humane reminiscences on *The First Ten Years of American Communism* written in the 1950s, and his positive reactions to radical sociologist C. Wright Mills and the Cuban Revolution.[15] This suggests the truism that deeper qualities are sometimes obscured by superficial impressions. Another factor obscuring these deeper qualities is that they were intertwined with Cannon's passionate *revolutionary Marxist commitments* (which Coser and Macdonald had ceased to share, and which therefore were absent from the manner in which they chose to focus on this complex person). This comes through in the account of Morris Chertov, who recalled that his own first impressions of Cannon had been disappointing: "he came through as 'gray,' his surface appearance at odds with the picture evoked by his record" as an experienced revolutionary with a colorful past in the U.S. radical movement. Chertov's first impression changed during a factional debate within the Trotskyist movement in the mid-1930s. Cannon was "now no longer 'gray,' undefined. Gone was the dour expression. He became avidly alive." A vibrant recollection remained with Chertov forty years later:

> His eyes now looked straight out at us, reading us. We were, under the banner of Trotskyism, the authentic heirs to a hundred years of Marxist struggle against forces seeking its destruction, often internal forces, that sought its end through attempts at corruption of the doctrine. We were heirs to great traditions, which, if absorbed in our blood and bone, would ennoble our lives. We were heirs to great conquests in the realm of theory—our theory was the generalization of hard and bloodily bought revolutionary experience, which, if properly applied, would illuminate our problems. The historic revolution of 1917 was ours, its defense from internal and external attack our proud heritage.[16]

Shachtman's capacities as a speaker capable of inspiring his audience were also great. A recollection by Michael Harrington of Shachtman, some years after he left Trotskyism, conforms to similar accounts of his earlier years:

When Max gave a speech, which sometimes lasted for about three hours, his presentation of socialist theory was usually suffused with personal emotion and experience. In 1956 during the upheaval in Poland I heard him speak to an audience primarily composed of students. None of us, not even those who had been working with Shachtman for some years, knew the names of the Polish Communists reviled, and sometimes murdered, by Stalin when he purged the party in Poland in the thirties. Yet as Max recited their names, sometimes with just an identifying tag—"a trade unionist, a working-class militant"—it was like hearing the roll call of revolutionary martyrs who were bone of our bone, flesh of our flesh.[17]

Shachtman's abilities as a speaker, writer, translator, editor, and theorist, and as an engaging personality with genuine leadership capabilities, were crucial for the advances made by the Trotskyist movement. Remembering the early days of working with Shachtman, Emanuel Geltman, an editor of the Trotskyist youth newspaper *Young Spartacus*, commented that "life [in the early Trotskyist movement] was very intense and close." Peter Drucker, Shachtman's biographer, has added: "Shachtman fed this sense of intensity and closeness by his physical affection for his followers. He would hug them and kiss them. He would pinch their cheeks, hard, in a habit that some felt blended sadism with affection." Drucker emphasizes that—concerned as much with the mind as with the heart—Shachtman helped young comrades around him learn an enormous amount about Marxist theory and history, often by sharply challenging them. A latter-day comrade, Tom Kahn, offered this snapshot of his style: "Max would say, 'You stupid son of a bitch. Are you listening to what you're saying?' Then he would sit down and explain it to you point by point." According to Drucker, "he taught his followers to value intellectual discipline and to delight in catching obscure historical references in his speeches." Drucker adds, however, that although Shachtman encouraged his young followers to write, he had little patience for working with those struggling to develop their writing and editing skills. Consequently, young editor Geltman remembered that he "was closer to Shachtman but . . . learned more from Cannon."[18]

Many years after the fact, four ex-Trotskyists who were former followers of C. L. R. James (James Boggs, Grace Lee Boggs, Lyman Paine, and Freddy Paine) reflected on the two leaders of the movement to which they had once belonged. From a critical distance, it was Cannon who loomed larger for them. Recalling that "polemics in those days [of the 1930s and 1940s] were really . . . murderous," they commented that "Shachtman was a genius at this kind of slaughter because he was bright as hell—he could demolish you with a crack—and he had no moral standards at all." They remembered Cannon differently, although not uncritically: "Cannon believed almost explicitly in everything Trotsky said, including Trotsky's almost mechanical notion of the role of the proletariat in the class struggle which he had taken from the October Revolution." While insisting that "Cannon was an utterly forthright and courageous man," they complained that he knew little about African Americans or other racial minorities, lacked theoretical breadth, and in general "didn't know anything about complexities." At the same time, they noted, "he was not an insecure person." He was able to be a leader "who could sit back and not have to interfere with everything going on." Relatively free from egocentricity, "Cannon never tried to ballyhoo Cannon," and he favored "a great deal of freedom" in allowing comrades (including dissident minorities) to develop their own ideas. They elaborated:

> He represented a proletarian quality which we could never have absorbed through, for example, someone like William Z. Foster. Because, although Cannon was a proletarian type, he was the kind of proletarian who could co-exist with a Max Shachtman or an intellectual like [James] Burnham as long as these intellectuals did not become too flighty. Cannon was not a small or a mean man; he had a basic faith in the proletariat, but he sensed that there was much more to life, to history, to politics and to revolution than just the proletariat. He welcomed intellectuals as long as they did not go off in all directions. C. L. R. James used to say of Cannon that he was not the kind of man who would trample on a minority. He would not line up his majority against you unless you got too far out of line and forced him to do it. Everybody who has a political party has to do that at a certain point. You can't let it be torn apart from whim. So Cannon was a man who had a great deal to teach about how to live within a party.[19]

"Jim was always trying to draw into the revolutionary team every individual who was willing to serve," Farrell Dobbs has observed. "He also had a quality of watching tendencies and trends inside a movement, of thinking always in the largest possible terms with respect to the recruitment of cadres." Dobbs's elaboration of this point has relevance to the first years of the Trotskyist movement:

He recognized, as all serious revolutionaries must, the importance of cadres, and what a crime it is when people cavalierly destroy cadres, or ignore cadres, or let them wither on the vine, or wander down a bypass without really trying to help them find the revolutionary main road.

Jim had a sense of this. And with the help of Trotsky, he played a major role in this country toward concentrating first on trying to win every possible member of the Communist Party who might begin to see the truth and develop toward support of the Trotskyist movement.[20]

The First Five Years

The program of the CLA in no way represented a break from the principles of Bolshevism or from the heritage of American Communism as it had come into its own by the mid-1920s. Rather, it stood for a return to that orientation by the Communist movement as a whole. For this very reason, it took a strong stand against the current manifestations of Stalinism, especially opposing the bureaucratic-conservative degeneration of the USSR, where an increasingly totalitarian regime not merely persecuted dissident revolutionaries but choked the intellectual life of the entire USSR, carrying out a brutal superexploitation of the working class and murderous policies against much of the peasantry. The CLA also opposed the surge of ultra-left sectarianism in the parties of the Comintern, which, beginning in 1929, was isolating Communists in the labor movement. In this period, Communists in the Stalin-dominated mainstream were recklessly denouncing all others on the left as "social fascists" and refusing to build a working-class united front against the capitalists and the real fascists. And the CLA denounced the elimination of genuine democracy in the Communist movement. Week after week, the American Trotskyists focused on these and related questions in their newspaper the *Militant*. The CLA did not seek to establish a new political movement but rather, along with the exiled Leon Trotsky and his supporters throughout the world, to reform the USSR and the Communist mainstream. They sought not to replace but to regenerate the American Communist Party. Cannon later explained:

Just imagine, here was a party with a membership and periphery of tens of thousands of people, with not one daily but no less than ten daily papers in their arsenal, with innumerable weeklies and monthlies, with money and a huge apparatus of professional workers. This relatively formidable power was arrayed against a mere handful of people without means, without connections—without anything but their program and their will to fight for it. They slandered us; they ostracized us, and when that failed to break us, they tried to beat us down physically. They sought to avoid having to answer any arguments by making it impossible for us to speak, to write, to exist.

Our paper was aimed directly at the members of the Communist Party. We didn't try to convert the whole world. We took our message first to those whom we considered the vanguard, those most likely to be interested in our ideas. We knew that we had to recruit at least the first detachments of the movement from their ranks. . . . Our task in that difficult time was to hold on, to clarify the great questions, to educate our cadres in preparation for the future, when objective conditions would open up possibilities for an expansion of the movement. Our task also was to test out to the very end the possibilities of reforming the Communist parties and the Communist International, which up to that time had embraced practically the whole workers vanguard in this country and throughout the world.[21]

The consequent recruitment "in ones and twos" of individuals in and around the Communist movement was vitally important. Among those who either helped found the CLA or joined the CLA in these early years were Sam Gordon, Oscar Coover, Joseph Carter, Charlie Curtiss, George Clarke, Murry and David Weiss, Nathan Gould, Max Geldman, Goldie Geldman, Morris Lewit, Sylvia Bleeker, Bert Cochran, Rae Spiegel (Raya Dunayevskaya), Hugo Oehler, Jack Weber, Sara Weber, George Novack, Felix Morrow, Albert Goldman, Lydia Beidel, Joseph Vanzler (John G. Wright), Fannie Curran, Joseph Hansen, Reba Hansen, and others. Harold R. Isaacs, a left-wing American journalist in China, also came over to Trotskyism in this period, joining the U.S. Trotskyists upon returning to his native land in 1936, and writing the classic *Tragedy of the Chinese Revolution*.

The reminiscences of Max Shachtman give a vivid sense of the organization's life and scope in the early years of the Great Depression;

The organization grew very slowly. Material resources were exceedingly scanty, and after six years of existence it was still short of 500 members throughout the country. Not every member had a job; unemployment in the country was still running ten to twelve million or more, and those who were working had modest incomes and little to spare. Many, perhaps most, of its members were young people, sons and daughters of working-class families, part and parcel of what was so truly called the locked-out generation. . . . It succeeded in getting out a weekly newspaper . . . and a presentable theoretical review [*New International*]. Its small but compact youth organization [the Spartacus Youth League] managed with some irregularity to put out a monthly paper of its own [*Young Spartacus*], In addition it published at certain periods of time little newspapers in the Yiddish language [*Unser Kampf*], in Greek [*Communistes*], and even a few issues in the Polish language. Most important to it, however, were the writings of Trotsky, which it translated and published—a whole series of them in pamphlet form and another series in book form. All this took Herculean efforts. . . . That it was done year in and year out is an indication of the extent of the dedication, the capacity for work and personal sacrifice, and the confidence of its membership.

The overriding concern of the Trotskyists was a complex of questions of communist theory, principle, and tactics, and these can be very complex. It would be a mistake to suppose that they confined themselves to a study of sacred texts and abstruse polemics. . . . Every member, young or old, was constantly urged—it would not be wrong to say he was required—to join and be constantly active in wider organizations.

Workers who were not already in trade unions were called upon to enter one for which they were eligible. Unemployed, including those who were too young to have ever held a job, were prodded, whenever that proved necessary, to find a job, and to join the labor movement, for the Trotskyists always felt a deep commitment to the trade union movement, to its struggles and to its political advancement.

Unemployed who could find no jobs at all were all in one or another of the many councils or other organizations of the out-of-work. Others, who had to subsist on relief, were active in organizations of relief recipients that then existed. Or they belonged to one or another of the tenants' organizations, active among other things in challenging the authorities who evicted tenants from their homes for nonpayment of rent by moving back the pitiful sticks of furniture that were put out on the streets by the marshals.

Students were active night and day in various radical and left-wing student organizations that experienced a considerable growth in the thirties. And the Trotskyist youth, who was generally far better schooled and skilled in matters of Marxist theory, history, and tactics than the student of any other group, was a factor to be contended with by the other political faiths. In unending debates, he rarely took as much as he gave.

A good deal of the modest recruitment attained by the Trotskyist movement came from workers active in the trade unions, many of them

with a background of experience in the radical political movements. . . .
The Trotskyists, young and old, were students of serious problems, and
even those problems that might seem remote or irrelevant to others were
never treated lightly or scoffingly by them.[22]

Not only did the American Trotskyists give in-depth attention to
the history of the Russian Revolution and the more recent problems
of bureaucratic degeneration, but they attempted to comprehend and
explain revolutionary and counterrevolutionary developments throughout the world—especially in China (where a promising working-class
upsurge and a large urban Communist movement were smashed thanks
to the disorienting policies of the Comintern in the late 1920s) and in
Germany, where Stalin's theory of "social fascism" mightily contributed
to the failure of the massive German Communist Party to join with
Social Democratic Party and others in resisting the rise of Hitler. When
Nazism triumphed in 1933 (destroying the German workers' movement), and the Stalinist Comintern refused to question the errors that
had helped lead to this devastating defeat, Trotsky and his cothinkers
were forced to conclude that the Third International had become bankrupt as a revolutionary force.[23]

Consequently, the Trotskyists began preparing for the creation of a
revolutionary Fourth International. Trotskyist organizations throughout
the world turned their attention toward the increasing mass struggles
of the 1930s. They now sought to attract and recruit the new layers of
workers and the oppressed who were being radicalized in these struggles,
and to begin building parties that could provide a revolutionary alternative to the Stalinist movement.

"The new course promptly provided an occasion for a small but highly
educational conflict with opportunism," according to George Novack,
"when the free-lancing B. J. Field opposed the party's class-struggle
policies while playing a leading role in a strike of New York City hotel
workers." Field was a talented intellectual who had independently established his own relationship with Trotsky. Trotsky valued Field's abilities,
which were also demonstrated when he became secretary of the hotel
workers' union. But then Field consistently refused even to discuss with
the CLA leadership some questionable policies that he was carrying out
as leader of an important strike in the early months of 1934. As a result,
he was expelled from the CLA, creating what was to become an oft-
cited example among U.S. Trotskyists of the importance of discipline

and collective functioning and the pitfalls of "free-lancing." (Field went on to form his own small group, the League for a Revolutionary Workers Party, which, according to Sidney Lens, "left no enduring mark but did provide a number of interesting personalities for the post—World War II period—including an Eastland Committee spy [i.e., an informant for the "antisubversive" Senate Internal Security Subcommittee, chaired by Mississippi Senator James O. Eastland], a Rand Corporation theorist . . . among the leading exponents of the nuclear arms race, and on the other side the late Paul Jacobs, a writer of some prominence who once edited *Ramparts* magazine and was part of a group that launched *Mother Jones*, another leftist publication.")[24]

A dramatic contrast to the Field experience was what happened in Minneapolis, where, in 1934, to use the words of radical commentator David Milton, "there occurred a fusion of native-born and immigrant labor militancy around the issue of industrial unionism and once again the workers chose socialist leaders to design strategies of class warfare over economic issues. Vincent Raymond Dunne and Carl Skoglund, leaders of the great truckers' organizing drive, symbolized this unity." Both were veterans of the IWW, the left wing of the Socialist Party, and the early Communist Party. Both were founding members of the CLA. They drew together a core of militants (which included Dunne's brothers Miles and Grant, plus the newly radicalized Farrell Dobbs). This core became the decisive influence in Teamsters Local 574, which sparked the Minneapolis general strike. Writes labor historian Thomas Brooks: "A natural leader, Ray Dunne had the confidence of the Minneapolis drivers. His talent for union generalmanship evidenced itself as he and his aides deployed their forces in the truckers' conflict with the employers. . . . The union, which had its own newspaper, sound trucks, and its own hospital, struck on May 12, 1934. When the city's 'better' elements volunteered to be sworn in as 'special officers' and were armed with badges and guns, the truckers collected iron pipes and baseball bats." James P. Cannon later noted: "Our people didn't believe in anybody or anything but the policy of the class struggle and the ability of the workers to prevail by their mass strength and solidarity." In the ensuing struggle, the entire labor movement of Minneapolis—plus allies among the surrounding small farmers, the city's unorganized workers and unemployed organizations, as well as working-class women and children, sympathetic professionals, and others—entered the fray. A four-month struggle culminated, as Dunne commented, in the workers winning "substantially what we have fought and bled for since the beginning."[25]

Not only did the Minneapolis victory change the city into a solid union town, but—along with the general strikes in Toledo and San Francisco the same year—it helped set the stage for the rise of the Congress of Industrial Organizations (CIO), which broke with the conservative, craft-oriented AFL to organize millions of unskilled industrial workers. "Under its radical leaders Local 574 would push on in the next few years," David Milton records, "to organize the over-the-road drivers throughout the Northwest and contribute to making the Teamsters one of the most formidable of the new industrial and semi-industrial unions." The Trotskyist stronghold in the teamsters' union was broken only in the early 1940s, when goon squads led by Jimmy Hoffa, the lieutenant of the international union's conservative and corrupt president Dan Tobin, joined forces with the U.S. government (directed by Tobin's friend Franklin D. Roosevelt) to smash what Tobin called "these disturbers who believe in the policies of foreign, radical governments" during a time when "our country is in a dangerous position."[26]

The 1934 Minneapolis strike was profoundly important for the CLA. As Cannon commented, "with this opportunity presented in Minneapolis to participate in the mass movement, American Trotskyism was put squarely to the test. It had to demonstrate in action whether it was indeed a movement of good-for-nothing sectarian hairsplitters, or a dynamic political force capable of participating collectively in the mass movement of the workers." The verdict seemed clear, as the entire CLA threw itself into the Minneapolis battles, sending key leaders such as Cannon and Shachtman, plus capable organizers and publicists, to help in winning the strike. Not only did this attract new individual recruits to the CLA, but it also created conditions under which the American Workers Party (AWP)—a revolutionary-minded group of working-class socialists and radical intellectuals led by A. J. Muste—decided to merge with the Trotskyists. Rejecting the sectarianism and dogmatism prevalent in the U.S. Left and calling for a practical activist approach to the problems of American workers, the AWP had played a leadership role in the militant Toledo Auto-Lite strike, in a number of industrial union efforts, and in the Unemployed Leagues. The AWP and CLA fused at the end of 1934 to form the Workers Party of the United States.[27]

A. J. Muste had come from a religious and radical pacifist background, opposing World War I and at the same time gravitating to socialist ideas and the labor movement. A leader of the 1919 Lawrence textile strike, he soon headed up the left-of-center Brookwood Labor College, which played an important role in training many of the radical organizers who would help lead the 1930s labor upsurge. In the Conference for Progressive Labor Action, which evolved into the AWP, Muste had favored sidestepping sectarianism and blending radical ideas with practical organizing. As a leader of the newly formed Workers Party of the United States, he noted in late 1934 that "a number [of labor and left-wing activists] have asked the question, why is it precisely that the group which has been most concerned about theory, and on the other hand, the group which has been most 'activist' have got together?" His answer is worth recording:

> A group which devotes itself to theory in the Marxian sense does not do it for the sake of agreeable mental exercise, as an alternative perhaps to working cross-word puzzles. It is concerned with theory because it needs to know how to act and will not act on a merely opportunistic basis. Elaboration of theory leads, therefore, to practical work in the labor scene. On the other hand, a group which seeks to act in a responsible and not an adventurist spirit in the revolutionary movement, which is concerned about ultimate and not merely about immediate aims, may indeed scorn Talmudic theologizing and debates which lead simply to more debates; but it cannot be indifferent to theory. It can render a service which the trade union bureaucrats, for example, cannot render, not merely because its members may individually be more honest and self-sacrificing, but chiefly because it has a clear conception of the economic and political system, the role of the working class, etc. and therefore can thread its way through the complex maze of events. That is to say, it must fall back on theory. . . . Thus the fusion of the CLA and the AWP was not accidental. Moreover, the fusion will bear fruit which neither group by itself could have produced.[28]

Muste soon left the Trotskyist movement—drawn back to his own earlier religious-based pacifist radicalism, although never entirely abandoning important aspects of the revolutionary Marxism that he had embraced, and he continued to play an important and admirable role on the U.S. Left. The fusion of his group with the CLA has always been viewed by U.S. Trotskyists as a healthy development, and it can be argued that the truth of Muste's positive 1934 remarks was borne out by subsequent events. Some latter-day commentators have asserted that the fusion was simply a crass "Trotskyite" takeover and that most members of the AWP were even less inclined than Muste to embrace Trotskyism. It is true that certain prominent "Musteites" (Louis F. Budenz, Arnold Johnson, J. B. S. Hardman, Benjamin Mandel, Oliver Carlson) opposed the fusion and bolted, but a decisive majority favored it. Among those Musteites who became important in the Trotskyist movement over the coming years were Art Preis, James Burnham, Ernest Rice McKinney, Sam Pollack, Ted Selander, Morris Chertov, Anne Chester, and Ruth Querio. New forces were attracted to the unified organization, including some who were to play leading roles in future years, such as Tom Kerry, Grace Carlson, George Breitman, Milt Alvin, Frank Lovell, Myra Tanner, Richard Fraser, and Jules Geller.

In 1935, however, a debate opened up in the newly unified organization over whether Trotskyists in some countries, particularly France, should seek to join mass social democratic parties, which were attracting some leftward-moving forces. A faction headed by Hugo Oehler and Tom Stamm argued strenuously that this was a violation of revolutionary principle, and they received some support from Muste and Martin Abern. The Oehler-Stamm group became so destructively factional, however, that even Abern and Muste felt compelled to criticize it. By November 1935, this undisciplined faction[1] was expelled—going on to form the Revolutionary Workers League, which soon suffered splits of its own and eventually faded away. The split represented a loss for the

---

[1] A *faction* in the U.S. Trotskyist movement was a grouping formally organized around a fairly deep and far-reaching set of disagreements existing within the larger organization on major political questions. Less far-reaching disagreements could give rise to a more loosely organized entity sometimes referred to as a *tendency*. Factions and tendencies were expected to function in a *disciplined* manner, expressing their differences fully at appropriate times and in appropriate contexts, but refraining from actions that would disrupt the work of the larger organization; if in a minority, they were expected to respect the will of the majority—although at appropriate times they would have an opportunity to try to win a majority to their positions. Those acting in an undisciplined, disruptive manner might be formally reprimanded or—in extreme cases—brought up on charges and subject to expulsion from the organization. Comrades were expected to function according to the Leninist principle of *democratic centralism:* "full freedom in discussion, complete unity in action."

Trotskyist movement. Oehler and some of his cothinkers (such as Sidney Lens, who was to play a significant role on the Left in future years) were talented activists. Yet the political debate among the Trotskyists had been a thoroughgoing one that contributed substantially to the political education and clarification of perspectives among the party's militants. Despite the loss of some members, the Trotskyist majority was about to move forward to new gains over the second half of the decade.[29]

Creation of the Socialist Workers Party

This was to be, in its own way, a difficult period for revolutionary socialists. In line with a fundamental shift in Stalin's Comintern, the American Communist Party veered sharply away from its previous ultra-leftism and adopted a "People's Front" orientation. The thrust of this perspective was that fascism and war could be overcome if communists, socialists, and other currents in the labor movement joined together with liberal capitalist forces for the purpose of establishing left-liberal governments that would foster domestic social reforms combined with a foreign policy aligned with the USSR and against Germany, Italy, and Japan. As it turned out, fascism was not averted in the countries that experienced the most successful People's Fronts—Spain (where a fascist-initiated civil war brought Generalissimo Francisco Franco to power by 1939) and France (where a fascistic Vichy regime was established in 1940, after a successful German invasion). Nor did the People's Front prevent the Second World War.[30]

From the mid to late 1930s, however, the bulk of the Left and labor movements, as well as many left-leaning liberal intellectuals and others, flocked to the "People's Front" banner. The Trotskyists' demand for the political independence of the working class, their insistence on the primacy of class struggle, and their call for socialist revolution as the only real defense against fascism and war—although consistent with the traditions of Bolshevik-Leninism (and also with the heritage of Rosa Luxemburg, Eugene V. Debs, and others of the historic revolutionary Left)—were brushed aside by many as "sectarian." The Communist Party played a "vanguard" role in leading innumerable potential revolutionaries into support for President Franklin D. Roosevelt's New Deal. Armed, as it were, with this orientation as well as with impressive numbers of dedicated and idealistic members, the Communist Party became solidly entrenched in the CIO; it also built significant influence in the Black community, among youth, and in intellectual circles. American membership in the party grew to over 50,000 by the late 1930s.

Within the USSR during this period, vast and bloody purges were begun against actual, potential, former, and imagined opponents of the Stalin leadership. Thousands were shot, and many more thousands were imprisoned, tortured, and sent to labor camps. The exiled Trotsky and his son Leon Sedov were tried in absentia and sentenced to death for masterminding the "terrorist plot" that was alleged to have been organized to overturn the 1917 revolution and hand the USSR over to fascism. Along with this, a worldwide campaign of slander and violence was orchestrated throughout the Comintern against "counterrevolutionary Trotskyism."[31]

Under the impact of the Great Depression and the rise of fascism, significant numbers of workers and youth in many countries were moving leftward, in some cases rallying to and forming a militant left wing within the social democratic parties of the Second International. The Stalinists were reaching out to these forces, but this development also seemed to create the possibility for winning radicalized layers of workers and youth to the revolutionary Marxist politics represented by the Trotskyists. Within the small but vital world Trotskyist movement, it was decided—initially in France—to enter and help form a revolutionary current within the social democratic parties. There seemed to be an opening for this small band of revolutionary dissident communists to break out of their isolation, effectively challenge Stalinism, and win a mass base for the perspectives of working-class revolution. George Novack has discussed "the French turn" as it was applied in the United States:

> When the right wing quit Norman Thomas's Socialist Party in 1935 and he invited other radicals to join his purportedly all-inclusive formation, Trotskyists decided to join it. Their goal was to win the more militant members of its left wing and youth movement to revolutionary ideas.
>
> During the Trotskyists' short sojourn in the Socialist Party [from the spring of 1936 to the late summer of 1937, organized around the newspaper *Socialist Appeal*], Stalin launched the Moscow frame-up trials. We organized a campaign to secure asylum for Trotsky in Mexico (he was expelled from France and Norway under Stalinist pressure) and worked with others in the Trotsky Defense Committee to expose Stalin's monstrous frame-ups. The latter effort culminated in the commission of inquiry headed by philosopher John Dewey. The commission exonerated

Trotsky and his son Leon Sedov and declared Stalin's charges to be baseless. This undertaking was a landmark in the long and honorable Trotskyist record of defending victims of government frame-ups.

The SP officialdom feared the spread of Trotskyist influence. Thomas and his ilk felt threatened by revolutionary socialist criticism of the SP leaders' support to the Popular Front government in Spain during the Spanish Civil War. (The left wing favored militarily defending the Republic against the fascists while giving no political support to the bourgeois government.) When the left objected to SP endorsement of New York's Republican-Fusion Mayor LaGuardia, the SP tops responded with mass expulsions of their left-wing critics.

The balance sheet of entry showed positive results: (1) The majority of the Socialist youth [in the Young People's Socialist League] and those really interested in working for a socialist revolution were won to the Trotskyist current; (2) the cadres accumulated valuable political experience; (3) entry increased Trotskyist forces in the unions, enhancing our proletarian orientation; and (4) by expelling its left wing the SP cut itself off from the radicalized youth and union militants, dealing itself crippling blows from which it never recovered.[32]

The Socialist Workers Party was established after the expulsions. It was founded on New Year's Day 1938 (in the same year that the Fourth International was formally established), with a membership of more than 1,000 and a spirit described by one of the delegates, George Breitman, in a 1977 interview: "The convention represented a milestone in the history of the American revolutionary movement. I am sure most of the delegates shared my conviction that we had participated in something truly significant: the launching—at last!—of the party that would lead the American workers in their coming socialist revolution." Especially important to the SWP, therefore, was its impressive base in the trade union movement: the stronghold in the Minneapolis teamsters led by Skoglund and Dunne, of course, but also the strong presence in the maritime industry, starting on the West Coast, headed by Tom Kerry, and significant forces in the new CIO unions—steel, auto, electrical, and so on.[33]

Shortly after the founding of the SWP, C. L. R. James arrived from Britain to join its ranks. A brilliant West Indian intellectual, James was already author of two marxist classics: *Black Jacobins* and *World Revolution*. He became one of the foremost writers and orators among the U.S. Trotskyists, but he also made a distinctive theoretical contribution. Quickly absorbing essential aspects of the African American reality, and carrying on searching discussions with Trotsky, James formulated a pathbreaking approach to the Black liberation struggle and the issue of self-determination for Black Americans. In addition to stressing the traditional need to oppose all forms of racist discrimination against Blacks, James posited the centrality of the Black struggle to the U.S. class struggle, highlighted the importance of all-Black organizations and movements, and raised the idea that self-determination for African Americans—up to and including the creation of an independent nation, if that is what they chose—was an appropriate perspective for revolutionary Marxists. Not all SWPers accepted James's views (for example, the other influential Black Trotskyist, Ernest Rice McKinney, insisted on an integrationist approach that subordinated race to class), but these were ideas that altered the way many Marxists understood the intersection of race and class.[34]

Throughout the 1930s, the Trotskyists had significant influence among some of the most important elements within the radicalized intelligentsia. Max Shachtman reminisced:

> It is gratifying to recall that among the skilled intellectuals many of the finest minds and talents, the warmest hearts, defied the abuse and the calumny heaped upon them by the Communists and joined in the defense of Trotsky's revolutionary honor, or at the very least, his right to be heard in his own name. They included men and women like James T. Farrell, Edmund Wilson, John Dos Passos, Max Eastman, Sidney Hook, Phillip Rahv and William Phillips and Lionel Abel (the editors of *Partisan Review*, who at that time broke away from the Communists). Also Mary McCarthy, Suzanne LaFollette, Ben Stolberg, Charles Yale Harrison, Meyer Schapiro, Lionel Trilling, James Rorty, James Burnham, John Chamberlain, Dwight Macdonald, and scores of others.[35]

Not all these people actually became Trotskyists—most did not—although James Burnham did become a leader in the SWP, with a reputation perhaps second only to Cannon and Shachtman. And particularly among many of the younger student members, described by Irving Howe as searching for "a language of gesture and response" that signified "a privileged relation to History" and a "critical superiority," the attraction of this intellectual milieu to Trotskyism was important. "Trotskyism was marked by an abundance of intellectual pride," one of these young members (Howe) was to put it many years later.[36] Yet as George Novack's account suggests, this all contributed to a severe crisis for the new SWP:

The shadow of the oncoming war, following upon the horror of the Moscow Trials and the defeat of the Spanish masses, led to a retreat of the formerly prosocialist intellectuals and a dampening of radicalism. Then the Stalin-Hitler Pact, which ushered in the Second World War in August 1939, hit the party. These intertwined events brought out latent weaknesses and precipitated the most thoroughgoing internal struggle in the movement since its inception.

An opposition emerged reflecting the changed mood among the radical intellectuals. Led by Burnham, Shachtman, and Abern, it began its assault on the program of the Fourth International by opposing defense of the Soviet Union from imperialist attack and by challenging the Trotskyist analysis of the Soviet Union as a degenerated workers' state.

The conflict soon involved most of the basic tenets of Marxism— from the validity and value of dialectical materialism to the character of the party. Trotsky described the aim of this opposition as an "attempt to reject, disqualify, and overthrow the theoretical foundations, political principles, and organizational methods of our movement."[37]

The initial dispute was over the question of whether the USSR was, as Trotskyists had traditionally argued, a degenerated workers' state (with a collectively owned economy worth defending in the face of imperialism, although requiring a political revolution to overturn the reactionary dictatorship of the bureaucracy), or whether it was a new form of oppressive class society—which Burnham and Shachtman termed "bureaucratic collectivism"—that must in no way be defended by revolutionaries. In the course of this struggle, two major works were produced: Trotsky's *In Defense of Marxism* and Cannon's *The Struggle for a Proletarian Party*.

Failing to win a majority to its positions, the Shachtman-Burnham faction split away to establish itself as the Workers Party (taking with them the magazine *New International*). In less than two months, Burnham openly abandoned Marxism and shifted rapidly to the right. In 1949 the Workers Party changed its name to the Independent Socialist League, and by 1958 it had deradicalized sufficiently to dissolve into the Socialist Party—Shachtman himself becoming a beacon of cold war anticommunism and labor reformism tied to the Democratic Party, supportive of what he himself would once have denounced as "vicious U.S. imperialism" in Latin America, Southeast Asia, and elsewhere. A left-wing current around Hal Draper (whose important scholarship on Marxism gained him an international reputation) and Phyllis and Julius Jacobson maintained elements of the original Shachtmanite perspective into the 1960s and 1970s through the Independent Socialist Clubs (later called the International Socialists) and the magazine *New Politics*. Others—such as Herman W. Benson, who edited the publication *Union Action and Democracy*, the dissident union activist Stan Weir, and the writer Harvey Swados—also continued to make important contributions to the labor and socialist movements.

In the opinion of Novack, "American Trotskyism gained more than it lost from the struggle and split with the petty-bourgeois opposition [i.e., the Shachtmanites]. The struggle tempered the party majority, which proved its fidelity to Marxism, its ability to defend its program under fire, and its determination to be a genuinely Leninist and working-class organization."[38] Such qualities would be important as the SWP faced the challenges of World War II and then the years of cold war and McCarthyism in the 1940s and 1950s.

From World War II to the Cold War

The basic attitude of the SWP toward the Second World War was outlined by James P. Cannon in this way:

> A war waged by the present government of the United States is a capitalist war because America today is a capitalist nation. It is different from the others only in that it is stronger than the others and bigger. We do not believe in capitalist policy. We do not want to gain any colonies. We do not want bloodshed to make profits for American capital. . . .
>
> We say that the claim that the war against Hitler is a war of democracy against fascism is a subterfuge, that the conflict between American imperialism and German imperialism is for the domination of the world. It is absolutely true that Hitler wants to dominate the world, but we think it is equally true that the ruling group of American capitalists has the same idea, and we are not in favor of either of them.
>
> We do not think that the Sixty Families who own America want to wage this war for some sacred principle of democracy. We think they are the greatest enemies of democracy here at home. We think they would only use the opportunity of a war to eliminate all civil liberties at home, to get the best imitation of fascism they can possibly get.[39]

This was certainly a minority position in the United States in 1941 as the country entered the war (although it won serious activists such as Jean Tussey from the Socialist Party, Haskell and Naomi Berman from the left-Zionist Hashomer Hatzair, and others). As the SWP analysis indicated, U.S. policymakers saw the war in terms of establishing an "American Century" in which U.S. business interests would combine with the U.S. government to establish economic and political hegemony on a global scale. U.S. victory over Germany, Italy, and Japan set the stage for a new conflict with all forces that actually or potentially threatened the realization of this "American Century"—the USSR; the postwar radical upsurge; the anticolonial and national liberation upheavals in Asia, Africa, and Latin America. Combined with this foreign policy orientation was the anticommunist, anti-Left hysteria and repression that was later labeled "McCarthyism" (after Senator Joseph McCarthy) but was really initiated under the liberal Democratic auspices of Franklin D. Roosevelt's running mate and chosen successor Harry S. Truman.[40] The Trotskyists of 1941 were able to anticipate such later developments and avoided some of the disorientation that afflicted many on the Left.

One of the major pieces of reactionary legislation facilitating the future anticommunist crusade was the Smith Act, which made it a crime to advocate the overthrow of the U.S. government. This law was passed in 1940 and was first used against the Socialist Workers Party in 1941, on the eve of the U.S. entry into World War II. Indicted were the principal leaders of the SWP and of the Minneapolis teamsters union. A Civil Rights Defense Committee was established, headed up by novelist James T. Farrell, which secured broad support for the indicted Trotskyists. The defendants used the courtroom to explain and popularize their revolutionary socialist views. A by-product of the trial is the official court testimony given by James P. Cannon, published as *Socialism on Trial*, which remains a minor classic of socialist education. This and SWP lawyer Albert Goldman's final speech to the jury, given the title *In Defense of Socialism*, were widely circulated in inexpensive editions to win people to socialist ideas. Ultimately, however, Cannon, Goldman and sixteen other prominent Trotskyists were sent to prison. Although the Trotskyist leadership of the Minneapolis teamsters union was eliminated, however, the SWP itself endured and even made gains.[41]

As World War II wore on, increasing numbers of industrial workers challenged the no-strike pledge that had been forced on them by the government and their own union leaders, because—as labor historian James Green has summed it up—"they simply refused to allow management to abuse them by taking advantage of the war situation." There were thousands of "wildcat strikes" involving millions of workers against the wartime wage freeze and various on-the-job indignities. In some unions—the United Auto Workers in particular—there was also openness to the idea of forming a labor party based on the union movement. Along with this widespread working-class militancy was an increased militancy in the Black community. This was reflected in demands for fair employment practices and civil rights pressed by W. E. B. Du Bois, the NAACP, and Black trade union leader A. Philip Randolph. In some cases this sentiment involved a more militant rejection of the oppressive, racist domination of white society—and, among a significant Black nationalist current, a rejection of white society itself.[42]

While the top SWP leaders were still in prison, the party was able to take advantage of many of these opportunities. The man who assumed Cannon's position as national secretary in this period was a seasoned activist named Morris Lewit, whose party name was Morris Stein. As a youthful immigrant, he had played a role in the early Communist movement in the United States and had early taken his place in the ranks of the Left Opposition against bureaucratic degeneration. As were so many of the initial revolutionaries of the labor movement, Lewit/Stein was a skilled worker (a plumber by trade), a worker-intellectual who had been shaped by the revolutionary socialist subculture that was so important within the Russian and Jewish proletariat. Initially identified with the Shachtman current in the early Trotskyist movement, he became one of Cannon's most trusted confidants and was an obvious choice to fill in as national secretary during the World War II crisis. A shrewd political thinker and capable administrator, Lewit was backed up by other comrades who moved forward in the face of the imprisonment of the SWP's central leadership. The editorship of the *Militant* was assumed by Frank Graves, also sometimes known as John Liang; his real identity was Cecil Glass, a South African revolutionary (a founding member of the South African Communist Party) who had spent many years in China assisting the Trotskyist movement there under the name Li Fu-jen. Karolyn Kerry, who transferred with her husband into New York to strengthen the national office, was one of many women comrades who shouldered special responsibilities to keep the party functioning as many male party members were drafted into military service.

Despite war and repression, the party flourished, Novack recalls: "The national convention in November 1944 already recorded appreciable signs of progress in various fields: increased sales and subscriptions of *The Militant*, stepped-up recruitment of workers and Afro-Americans, greater influence in key union locals, and a burst of optimism in the membership." By its 1946 convention in Chicago, SWP membership stood at almost 1,500. In this period, many SWP members took industrial jobs, some industrial workers were recruited, and a substantial presence was established in several industrial unions: auto, steel, rubber, aircraft, and maritime. Active in movements for racial equality, the SWP drew hundreds of Black militants into its ranks and established a base of support in some Black communities. Among the African American members of this period who became prominent in the SWP, or well known in later years after leaving the SWP, were Dr. Edgar Keemer (who wrote a *Militant* column under the name of Charles Jackson), Larry Stewart, Milton Richardson, Joe Morgan, Ernie Dillard, Louise Simpson, James Boggs, Charles Denby, and—slightly later—Clifton DeBerry. Also during this period, some white SWPers became quite prominent in civil rights activities, gaining substantial credibility as consistent opponents of racism and partisans of African American rights. (One white SWP member, Herbert Hill, was to leave the party and assume an important national position in the NAACP.)[43]

In 1945 the imprisoned Trotskyist leaders emerged to take their places in the revitalized party. Most of them were hopeful that Trotsky's optimistic prediction—that World War II would bring a global revolutionary upsurge, drawing masses of workers and others to the banner of the Fourth International—was about to be realized. Yet reality proved to be more complex, and a new factional fight soon developed. It was precipitated in part by the difficulties facing the Trotskyist movement in Europe, where the Stalinist and social democratic movements proved to be far more resilient than expected. In Eastern Europe the Soviet Red Army established Stalinist hegemony as it pushed the Nazi armies back to Germany. In Western Europe, which constituted a diplomatically prearranged capitalist sphere of influence, the Communist parties (following Stalin's commands) and the social democratic parties (following their own reformist impulses) were able to channel the postwar radical working-class ferment and energy away from revolutionary socialism. The Trotskyists were unable to rally the masses to the banner of the Fourth International. Albert Goldman and Felix Morrow, two of the eighteen imprisoned in the Smith Act trial, and among the party's most capable intellectuals, were the first to insist that reality required a more pessimistic analysis. Yet their pessimism slid into demoralization and resulted in a deeper questioning of the SWP's revolutionary program and orientation. They became partisans of reunification with the Shachtmanites, organizing a small faction (also influencing such people as SWP sympathizer James T. Farrell) that challenged the majority not only through internal discussion but also through violation of party discipline. After the consequent expulsions, Goldman and some of his cothinkers joined Shachtman's organization, although he soon resigned from it. Both Goldman and Morrow abandoned Marxism and became cold war anticommunists.[44]

A majority of SWP members did not feel such demoralization, in part because of their experience in the exciting post-World War II working-class struggles sweeping the United States. This was the period of what veteran Trotskyist labor reporter Art Preis called "American labor's greatest upsurge." As he put it:

> The tremendous advance of the class struggle during the postwar period can be seen by a comparison of the strike statistics for 1937 and 1945–46. In 1937, the epic year of the CIO's rise, there were 4,740 strikes involving 1,861,000 strikers, for a total loss of 28,425,000 man-days of work. In 1945 the number of strikes was 4,750, with 3,470,000 on strike, almost double the 1937 figure, and a loss of 38,000,000 man-days. In 1946 the number of strikes reached 4,985 with 4,600,000 strikers and 116,000,000 man-days lost.[45]

The great victories that workers won through these struggles were accompanied by an exhilaration over the new possibilities that seemed to reflect a dissatisfaction with "politics as usual" and an openness, on the part of many, to new ideas. There was a similar but even greater ferment throughout the postwar world, even though it was not developing under the banner of the Fourth International. For some party militants, it seemed that a Trotskyist advance in the United States might facilitate similar advances elsewhere. "For a brief time," recalls Novack, "it appeared that the SWP was on the way to transforming itself from a small and restricted propaganda group into an organization of mass agitation and action. Its expanding influence in the left wing of the industrial unions and among the Black militants placed that almost within reach. The ranks were poised and ready to realize this objective."

Growing in size and influence, the party membership had a magnetic optimism that caused a group around C. L. R. James to break away from the Shachtmanites and rejoin the SWP in 1947. The tone for this conjuncture had been set by James P. Cannon and his cothinkers in the SWP leadership, who in the autumn of 1946 had written an important document, "Theses on the American Revolution" (also known as *The American Theses*), which first of all expressed a resounding confidence in the revolutionary capacities of the U.S. working class and argued that "the workers' struggle for power in the U.S. is not a perspective of a distant and hazy future but the realistic program of our epoch." The theses added: "The Russian revolution raised the workers and the colonial peoples to their feet. The American revolution with its hundredfold greater power will set in motion revolutionary forces that will change the face of our planet." In the SWP, the theses argued, "the fundamental core of a professional leadership has been assembled and trained in the irreconcilable spirit of the combat party of the socialist revolution." Defending this proposition, Cannon asserted: "Nothing condemns a party more than a lack of faith in its own future. I don't believe it is possible for any party to lead a revolution if it doesn't even have the ambition to do so." He concluded his classic pamphlet *The Coming American Revolution:* "Our part is to build up this party which believes in the unlimited power and resources of the American workers, and believes no less in its own capacity to lead them to storm and victory."[46]

But the powerful defenders of the capitalist status quo had other ideas of what should happen. A reactionary counteroffensive was launched in the United States and throughout the world. In the United States the Taft-Hartley Act was passed to prevent further upsurges of labor militancy. In the southern portion of the country and elsewhere, a resurgence of racism was generated, and the Ku Klux Klan used terror, beatings, and killings to keep Blacks "in their place." Nationwide, a new "red scare" was whipped up by employers, politicians, and the mass media—with witch-hunting investigating committees, compulsory loyalty oaths and hearings, highly publicized trials of alleged "Communist subversives," anti-"Red" mob violence, blacklists, and so forth. The main target was the Communist Party, with its more than 60,000 members and broad periphery, but Trotskyists and other radicals were targeted as well. The majority sectors of the AFL and CIO bureaucracy also participated. In 1949 and 1950 the CIO expelled eleven so-called left-wing unions from labor's mainstream, and leaders of both the AFL and the CIO joined government and business forces in seeking to destroy what they called "those Commie outfits." Within a few years, all significant radical influence in the unions, and in other areas of American life, was effectively crushed. Party membership declined to less than 20,000.[47]

Although in no way diluting its revolutionary critique of Stalinism, the SWP was in the forefront of those who defended the democratic rights of the Communist Party (which, sadly, did not reciprocate). They fought against the reactionary onslaught in defense of their own rights as well. Central to this battle was the seven-year fight against the victimization of James Kutcher, a World War II veteran who had lost his legs in the Italian campaign and then taken a clerical job with the Veterans Administration after the war—only to be fired in 1948 for his revolutionary beliefs and membership in the SWP. Widespread sympathy and support were mobilized in his behalf throughout this period of anticommunist hysteria. After eleven hearings, Kutcher got his job back, which constituted a major victory against the "witch-hunting" and blacklisting policies of the government. One of the products of this was Kutcher's own account, *The Case of the Legless Veteran*.[48]

Meanwhile, U.S. policymakers were concentrating their considerable resources on the ways and means of containing, undermining, and rolling back the revolutionary and anticapitalist upsurges of the post–World War II period. They faced Communist victories in Yugoslavia and China; additional Communist advances in Korea, Greece, and Vietnam; and radical nationalist upsurges throughout the world. Their response took a variety of forms—including the generous Marshall Plan designed to undercut the economic bases of working-class revolution and to reconstruct Europe on a sound capitalist footing, military alliances such as the North Atlantic Treaty Organization and the building of nuclear weapons, Central Intelligence Agency "dirty tricks" and coups (helping to set up reactionary dictatorships in such places as South Vietnam, Iran, and Guatemala), and a well-oiled anticommunist propaganda crusade; in 1950 it also took the form of massive military intervention in the Korean War. The global economic hegemony that U.S. corporations were establishing, combined with a continuing high level of military spending, contributed to an economic prosperity in the United States that enhanced the confidence of the capitalists while helping to generate an acceptance of the status quo by significant sectors of the working class.

The combination of cold war "patriotism," repression, and prosperity resulted in a general decline of the radical movement.

"With the workers increasingly unresponsive to socialist ideas and proposals," Novack writes, "virtually the entire membership of the SWP fractions in auto, aircraft, steel and maritime were driven from their jobs and blacklisted. Many fine worker militants, seeing little chance for effective opposition to the ascendant labor bureaucracy, drifted out of the party, as did many Black members who had expected the party to mobilize wide support for their demands. Party branches withered and disappeared." An additional obstacle to retaining a significant number of African American recruits was the lack of understanding and sensitivity of some white SWPers regarding the dynamics of racism, including how they themselves had been affected by those dynamics. Yet the growing frustrations of a small revolutionary organization in the United States during the early 1950s would inevitably have caused many to fall away, even under ideal circumstances. The difficult situation also fueled new splits. The Johnson-Forest tendency, led by C. L. R. James and Raya Dunayevskaya (whose party names were J. R. Johnson and F. Forest), left in 1951, in part due to differences on how to analyze the USSR, China, and other such countries (which the Johnson-Forest tendency viewed as "state-capitalist"), but perhaps even more out of a frustrated sense that life in the SWP was preventing them from reaching out to masses of working people who would, they believed, respond more readily to the insights and approaches being developed by James, Dunayevskaya, Grace Lee, Martin Glaberman, and others in the tendency. As it turned out, the Johnson-Forest group—organized as the *Correspondence* committees—itself was unable to grow and soon split into two groups: those aligned with James (from which a group led by James Boggs and Grace Lee Boggs soon split away), and Dunayevskaya's *News and Letters* committee of "Marxist-Humanists"—each of which continued to dwindle.[49]

The SWP proved more durable, although from 1952 to 1953 it was wracked by an even more serious factional dispute, affecting what Novack termed "the inner core of the party." The new opposition was led by Bert Cochran, George Clarke, Mike Bartell (Milton Zaslow), Harry Braverman, and other tested cadres. The "Cochranites," as they were called, were a somewhat heterogeneous grouping. Some of them had an analysis that has been summarized in this way: "The party should not be trying to build branches, running election campaigns, or even trying to recruit members in this period. The country was facing the triumph of fascism and there wasn't a damn thing we could do about it because of the conservatism of the workers and our party's weakness." A few favored entering the Communist Party because it was thought to have a greater chance of survival as a socialist force connected with the overturn of capitalism elsewhere; eventually Trotskyists and others could help democratize it. Others believed that the SWP should orient itself toward independent radical elements that had been influenced by Stalinism—the remnants of Henry Wallace's ill-fated Progressive Party, the weekly *National Guardian*, Paul Sweezy's and Leo Huberman's independent socialist magazine *Monthly Review*, and so on. Still others felt that if Trotskyists refrained from exposing themselves, conducting only the most modest public activities, they would be able to survive in some of the unions and other institutions in the labor and liberal wing of the American mainstream. They were all agreed, however, that—as one of the 1953 documents put it—the SWP was suffering from "a six-year-old disorientation in the face of unexpected changes in the world and at home, . . . disappointment over the collapse of exaggerated hopes, . . . an inability to cope soberly and analytically with the new reality created by the deepening reaction and coming war." The expectation of fascism and a third world war was shared by many on the Left at the time, but the SWP majority was not inclined to accept the prescriptions of the Cochran faction, prescriptions that they viewed as moving toward "liquidation" and conciliation with Stalinism and the labor bureaucracy of the CIO. The Cochranites accused the majority of "vulgar anti-Stalinism" and "sectarian ossification." The conflict was further complicated because it became entwined with a larger factional dispute that wracked the Fourth International.[50]

In 1953, after a two-year factional battle, the Fourth International split into two groups claiming the mantle of the world organization. One—headed by an International Secretariat—was led by Michel Pablo (Raptis), Ernest Mandel, Pierre Frank, Livio Maitan, and others who favored a strategy of deep "entryism" by Trotskyists into the mass Stalinist or social democratic movements. The other—headed by an International Committee—was led by Cannon, Gerry Healy of Britain, Pierre Lambert of France, and others who favored a more "orthodox" orientation of maintaining and building Trotskyist parties. This destructive fissure was partially healed in 1963, but in the early 1950s it helped deepen the division among the U.S. Trotskyists.

After a definitive split from the SWP, the Cochran group for a few years published an interesting and well-edited magazine called *American Socialist*, but then it disintegrated, although some of the Cochranites continued to make contributions to left-wing politics. Cochran himself wrote several useful books on recent U.S. history and politics but drifted increasingly away from his initial revolutionary socialist commitments. Irving Beinin became the business manager for the *National Guardian* and active in independent radical politics. Jules Geller and Harry Braverman played distinguished roles among those involved with *Monthly Review* and Monthly Review Press, and Braverman authored the Marxist classic *Labor and Monopoly Capital*. Genora Dollinger, who had organized the colorful Women's Emergency Brigade during the 1930s struggles of the United Auto Workers, became a central figure in the splendid 1970s documentary "With Babies and Banners," which linked working-class and feminist struggles. David Herreshoff combined radical scholarship and activism, authoring the study *The Origins of American Marxism, from the Transcendentalists to De Leon*. Contributions were made by others as well—but not as part of a coherent organization.[51]

The SWP did endure as a coherent organization and sought recruits, keeping alive as best it could the Trotskyist heritage—a heritage that it hoped would be absorbed and utilized by working-class activists in future upsurges. A sense of those in whom some SWP hopes were invested comes through in a memoir of the late 1940s and early 1950s by radical Youngstown steelworker Ed Mann, who became a major figure in progressive union and community struggles. At the same time, Mann's account gives a sense of something that was lost by the Trotskyist movement in this period:

> There was also a group of Trotskyists at U.S. Steel's Ohio Works. They had a core of maybe ten people who belonged to the Socialist Workers Party. They also had a meeting place on East Federal Street in downtown Youngstown, over a bar. I went to some of their meetings.
>
> I was political, but my role for many years was passive. I went to demonstrations. I didn't understand much of the speeches. I never read Marx. I felt very strongly about peace and freedom, and I felt very comfortable with socialism. I knew about the Socialist Workers Party and the Communist Party, but I wasn't a joiner. I did know that they were decent people.
>
> These guys talked sense, in my estimation. They had ideas. They did things. I felt comfortable with them.

They built a strong union at the Ohio Works. There were Blacks and whites. They had a good literate [local union] newspaper. Ted Dostal [at the time an SWP member] was editor, I think. . . . They ran the local like it was supposed to be run.

In the 1950s the Socialist Workers Party started splitting. It was like the Protestant Church. When there are splits and you don't understand why, you become disillusioned. It gave some of them the opportunity to get out and become respectable. They became staff men for the international union. Ted Dostal didn't.

Another member of that group was Merlin Luce. . . . He's not a know-it-all kind of guy who jumps in and creates more problems than there were before. He's really calm. I like the way he treats people.[52]

This description suggests that the revolutionary working-class faith of *The American Theses* was based on a reality that persisted through the 1950s in a fragmented form. It also suggests why in this same period, with the drifting away of such supporters, American Trotskyism was at its lowest ebb.

Years of Resurgence

The 1950s saw a number of dramatic events that were to contribute to the revitalization of the Trotskyist movement. First of all, there was the steady advance in the struggle of African Americans for civil rights, dignity, and liberation. In 1954, the NAACP won a suit before the U.S. Supreme Court calling for school desegregation, and the following year Rosa Parks sparked the Montgomery bus boycott in Alabama, which catapulted Martin Luther King Jr. to national prominence and accelerated the struggle against racist Jim Crow laws segregating Blacks and whites.[53]

Then there were mortal wounds inflicted on Stalinism in 1956. Growing problems and ferment in the USSR and Eastern Europe caused the bureaucracy there to shift to a "liberal" and reforming mode, which was reflected in Nikita Khrushchev's devastating report confirming Stalin's crimes in the USSR. The effects of this report were to be felt for years to come. Several months later, masses of students and workers in Hungary rose up against the oppressive bureaucratic dictatorship there—only to be brutally crushed by Russian military might. Thousands of Communists experienced a bitter disillusionment, which made it impossible for them to remain in their party. The world Stalinist movement began a process of decomposition that could never be reversed. The Trotskyist movement, in contrast, stood vindicated by its proud record of proletarian internationalism in the face of bureaucratic dictatorship. What's more, through Trotsky's *The Revolution Betrayed* and other works, it was possible to provide a clear revolutionary Marxist understanding of the difference between Bolshevik goals and Stalinist practice, and of how the latter had triumphed in the USSR.[54]

There was also the rising tide of the anticolonial revolution in Asia, Africa, and Latin America. Particularly important was the victory of the Cuban Revolution in 1959, which, under the leadership of Fidel Castro, Ernesto "Che" Guevara, and others, was to show—for the first time since 1917—that revolutionaries independent of Stalinism could achieve the overturn of capitalism in the struggle for liberation. This experience was to demonstrate, once again and most strikingly, the dynamic of permanent revolution, which Trotsky had formulated years before: a democratic revolution radicalizing as it bases itself on the mobilization of the working masses, growing over into a socialist revolution with international ramifications. SWP veteran George Lavan Weissman in this period edited the first English-language anthology of Che's writings, *Che Guevara Speaks*. Joseph Hansen developed a penetrating interpretation of the Cuban Revolution, which was later reprinted in his *Dynamics of the Cuban Revolution, the Trotskyist View*.[55]

Hansen, who served as Trotsky's secretary in Mexico, had in the late 1940s and early 1950s developed innovative analyses of Eastern Europe and China by extending and developing Trotsky's analysis of the USSR as a *degenerated workers' state* (i.e., in the USSR, working-class political rule had been displaced by the bureaucracy, but the achievement of a nationalized planned economy remained). Hansen argued that countries such as China, Yugoslavia, Poland, and Hungary were "deformed workers' states": they had nationalized planned economies based on the needs of the working class, but from the beginning they were deformed—thanks to Stalinism—by bureaucratic dictatorships that must be replaced, through political revolutions, by institutions of workers' democracy. Hansen had gone on to develop a conception of *workers' and farmers' governments:* transitional regimes created through popular revolutionary struggles, which would either betray the hopes of the masses by making peace with capitalism or base themselves on the needs and support of the masses by moving beyond being capitalist states (based on privately owned market economies) and becoming fully fledged workers' states (based on nationalized planned economies). Cuba had moved in such a revolutionary direction, Hansen argued, but must avoid bureaucratic degeneration by establishing institutions of workers' democracy.[56]

These became major points of debate within the Trotskyist movement. Most immediately, one current inside the SWP led by Sam Marcy—alarmed by "Khrushchevite revisionism" and by the perceived "counterrevolutionary" and "capitalist restorationist" implications of the Hungarian revolt, and partially attracted by Maoism—broke away from the SWP to form the Workers World Party in 1959 (taking with them some valuable cadres, such as Ted and Fran Dostal). In contrast to this, most SWP members believed that world events confirmed the fundamental Trotskyist outlook.

The upsurge of the Black liberation struggle, the crisis of Stalinism and ferment in Eastern Europe, and the explosion of anticolonial and radical-nationalist revolutions in third world countries—all this contributed to a radical resurgence among students and youth in the United States. In modest but increasingly significant numbers, they began to throw themselves into the civil rights movement, to protest against nuclear weapons, to defend civil liberties, and to challenge U.S. foreign policy.

"The radical movement as a whole lost virtually an entire generation of recruitment to the Cold War and witch-hunt," Novack observed. "Relative to other currents, the SWP came out of that ordeal with the best morale, since world events had substantiated its basic ideas." In the period of ferment and reevaluation of the late 1950s and early 1960s— when the SWP made special efforts to enter into dialogue and united-front efforts with many older and younger radicals—it was able to draw new recruits to its banner. In the late 1950s, Murry Weiss in particular worked to draw together elements from the Shachtmanite youth group, breakaways from the Communist Party, elements around the *National Guardian*, and so forth. There were joint forums, broad collaboration on publications, even joint electoral efforts. This was qualitatively different from the earlier "regroupment" effort proposed by the Cochranites, because the objective situation was new—the crisis and partial collapse of the Stalinist movement, and the modest but significant radical upsurge among youth. Novack writes that this "revival of radicalism . . . was manifested within our own movement by the reconstitution of a Trotskyist youth organization for the first time in twenty years. The Young Socialist Alliance became the prime vehicle for the regeneration of the SWP."[57]

In the 1950s, the first generation of Trotskyist leaders—Cannon, Dunne, Skoglund, Swabeck—had given way to a second generation, which was represented by Farrell Dobbs and Tom Kerry, along with Joseph Hansen, George Novack, and George Breitman. At the same time, Cannon and other prominent members of the National Committee concentrated in California had such authority within the SWP that they constituted a sort of "dual center" within the party throughout the 1950s and 1960s, often operating as a counterweight and at times forcing shifts in the course advanced by the Dobbs-Kerry leadership in the New York national headquarters. This generated tensions within the organization, worsened by a rift between the Dobbs-Kerry leadership and Murry and Myra Tanner Weiss (who had transferred from California to the national center in New York). Yet there was unanimity over the need to prepare for a leadership transition that would incorporate younger cadres. "Our party did its utmost to recruit and integrate young rebels from the campuses into its depleted ranks and bring them into the leadership," Novack recounts. "This was imperative if the party was to cope with the enlarged opportunities presented to it."[58]

The heightened concern over ensuring a transition in leadership meant helping to consolidate a younger team that would be steeped in the traditions of American Trotskyism while having the boldness to forge new paths into the future—this became the primary goal as energetic young forces began to rejuvenate the movement. Frank Lovell noted that "a levy of wartime and postwar recruits [of the mid-1940s through early 1950s] remained to become prominent party builders—Evelyn Sell, Catarino (Richard) Garza, Nat Weinstein, Lynn Henderson, Ed Shaw, Fred Halstead, Al Hansen, and others of their generation who sustained the SWP during the 'dry period' of the 1950s." Carl Feingold was another young militant recruited during this period who played a significant role in the SWP until the early 1960s. In the late 1950s and early 1960s, a new layer was drawn in, including leftward-moving Shachtmanite youth (such as Tim Wohlforth, James Robertson, Shane Mage, and Barry Sheppard), young activists pulling away from the Stalinist milieu (such as Hedda Garza and Peter Camejo), and others new to the Left who were attracted to radicalism by the broader social ferment. The formal launching of the Young Socialist Alliance (YSA) in 1960 (after a "regroupment" process in the late 1950s) represented an organized expression of radicalized youth who had embraced Trotskyism and identified with the SWP. Among those prominently involved in 1960 were James Petras, Suzanne Weiss, Marvin Garson, Martha Curti, Jim Lambrecht, Peter Allan, Nora Roberts, Sherry Finer, and Eva Chertov. A growing number were soon attracted to this small but dynamic group, including a bright, strong-willed, talented economics student from Carleton College named Jack Barnes, who joined the Trotskyist movement in 1961 and was to play a decisive role in its later development.[59]

There were important internal conflicts in this period, revolving around key political questions. For example, the bulk of U.S. Trotskyists hailed the Cuban Revolution, were impressed with its leadership, and helped organize the Fair Play for Cuba Committee, not only to protest the policies of hostility and aggression of the U.S. government but also to educate about and generate support for what they saw as the positive, radicalizing direction of the revolution. Yet an important current within the YSA and SWP (and also in the British group headed by Gerry Healy and the French group headed by Pierre Lambert inside the International Committee of the Fourth International) rejected the Fidelistas as mere petit bourgeois nationalists or as Stalinists in the making. This related to another contentious issue: the reunification of the Fourth International. In defending the Cuban Revolution from U.S. imperialism, and earlier in supporting the anti-Stalinist Hungarian revolt of 1956, both fragments of the Fourth International had advanced similar positions. Impressed by this convergence, Cannon and other SWP leaders favored the reunification of the two fragments (one headed by the International Secretariat and the other headed by the International Committee), although Healy and Lambert opposed such unity. The SWP and some other forces in the International Committee—but not the Healyites and Lambertists—finally effected a reunification in 1963 (creating a new leadership body known as the United Secretariat).[60]

Bitterly opposed to the SWP position on Cuba as developed by Joseph Hansen, bitterly opposed to reunification with the so-called "Pabloite revisionists" in the Fourth International, and increasingly critical of other aspects of the majority's political perspectives, some of the initial founders and leaders of the Young Socialist Alliance, such as James Robertson and Tim Wohlforth, organized a factional struggle inside the SWP. Developing differences with each other, the Robertson and Wohlforth tendencies left the party under somewhat different circumstances, although both were seen as being "disloyal" by the majority of the party leaders and membership. The expulsion of the Robertsonites, on grounds that were protested even by some party members who disagreed with their politics, occasioned a tightening of organizational norms that were codified in a 1965 resolution, "The Organizational Character of the Socialist Workers Party." By the mid-1960s, both the Robertson and Wohlforth groups were busily building their own small organizations—the Spartacist League and the Workers League.[61]

There were some other losses. A number of dissatisfied party veterans—such as Murry and Myra Tanner Weiss, Art and Edie Fox, Steve and Barbara Zeluck, Carl Feingold, and Art Felberbaum—either resigned or, running afoul of tightening organizational norms, were forced out. In 1964–66 a group in Seattle centered around Clara Kaye and Richard Kirk (party names for Clara and Richard Fraser) developed deep differences and broke away to establish the Freedom Socialist Party. They argued that the SWP was insufficiently feminist, that SWP support for Black nationalism—as opposed to Dick Fraser's conception of "revolutionary integrationism"—was reactionary, that conservative Republican Barry Goldwater represented an outright fascist threat, and that the Chinese Communist Party under Mao Tse-tung had "avoided both the economic pitfalls of Stalinism and the political degeneration accompanying it," instead representing a "Leninist approach to the class struggle." Another prominent founder of American Trotskyism, Arne Swabeck, developed a similar view on China, and some of his undisciplined actions around this question resulted in Swaback's expulsion in 1967 (a measure opposed by Cannon and several others).[62]

It is not merely because it was an issue in some internal party disputes that it is worth noting the role of women in the SWP and the role of the SWP in the women's liberation movement. Rather, it sheds considerable light on the relationship between the Left and feminism, as well as on the role of women in the U.S. Trotskyist movement. It is important to recall that in the twentieth century there were two waves of feminism, one in the first two decades (which very much interacted with the socialist movement), and another beginning in 1969 and gathering force in the 1970s. The absence of a strong, independent feminist movement from the 1920s through the 1960s had a negative impact on the Trotskyist movement, the entire Left, the working class, and society in general—reinforcing patriarchal traditions and male chauvinist attitudes, in various ways subordinating women, and limiting the contributions they could make, including in the Trotskyist movement.

Describing the Socialist Workers Party of the late 1930s, Irving Howe remembered some young female comrades "who were seriously interested in politics and culture, intent upon battling for place and definition, and trying also to be sexually attractive in the styles mandated, more or less, by American society." He noted that "they typed stencils, gave out leaflets, became organizers, spoke with a flaring eloquence," and "they seldom complained, at least openly" about "discrimination within the movement" or about many of their male comrades falling back "onto the modes of condescension [toward women] that prevailed in the outer world." Howe mused: "They must already have been encountering the problems that the 'advanced' young women would be struggling with a few decades later, but they didn't yet have the feminist vocabulary or sense of solidarity that might get them through rough times."[63]

Yet a number of women joining the Trotskyist movement in its earlier years had been formed, in part, by that earlier wave of feminism. "There were occasional discussions of the 'woman question' in our organization from the very beginning," recalled Sam Gordon. "I remember Rose [Karsner] and Sylvia Bleeker as among the most fiery reporters or contributors. They minced no words. Rose especially had, I believe, early on been a supporter of the suffragists." Karsner was a longtime activist in the Socialist Party (her former husband had written the first biography of Eugene V. Debs), a founding member of the Communist movement, especially active in the International Labor Defense, and one of the first U.S. Trotskyists (although overshadowed by her companion, James P. Cannon).

Sylvia Bleeker, a youthful participant in the Russian Revolution and a refugee from the murderous White armies during the Russian civil war, was a veteran of the Communist Party (she was a CP candidate for Congress in 1930, when she was expelled for supporting the Left Opposition) and a popular figure in the needle trades unions—serving as secretary-treasurer of Millinery Hand Workers Union, Local 43. (Composed predominantly of young women under the age of twenty-five, this was the largest local of female workers in the United States and the second-largest local in the

International Ladies Garment Workers Union, which in 1928 broke away to become part of the Needle Trades Workers' Industrial Union.) Bleeker also helped produce, with her companion Morris Lewit and others, the Yiddish-language Trotskyist newspaper *Unser Kampf* serving as the fortnightly's business manager.

There were others, such as Dr. Antoinette Bucholz Konikow, who had been a participant in the early Russian Marxist movement before moving to the United States in 1893 and became a leading activist in the Socialist Labor Party, the Socialist Party, and the Communist Party (where she became the first open defender of Trotsky and his ideas). Konikow, who had served on the five-member Women's Commission of the Socialist Party, was a lifelong feminist and a prominent figure in the semilegal birth control movement (author of *Voluntary Motherhood* and *Physician's Manual of Birth Control*, and an opponent of the more conservative "population control" approach developed by Margaret Sanger). Along with Rose Karsner, Konikow was a prominent figure in the American Committee for European Workers Relief, which sent food, clothing, and medicine to antifascist workers who had been in prisons and concentration camps during World War II.[64]

Ernestine Hara Kettler, a militant in the women's suffrage movement, also had a background in the Socialist Party and the IWW, as well as the fringes of the Communist movement, before coming over to Trotskyism in the 1930s. (She later became a Shachtmanite.) Her comments capture a common attitude of the time:

> As for feminism, that wasn't really an issue. After all, Socialists were supposed to have a notion of equality between all people and naturally that equality would extend to women as well; they certainly believed in equality for women in industry and politics. They claimed that so long as you live in a capitalist country you're not going to get that equality. Except that we couldn't turn the society overnight into a socialist one, so therefore you have to fight for it individually, or piecemeal. Whenever I did have an argument it was short and not bitter.[65]

Yet in the 1940s and 1950s, some arguments on "the woman question" in the party became more extended and cut deeper. The issue of the subordination of women became a focus of factional conflict when it was taken up by the Johnson-Forest tendency. Some of the SWP's more prominent female activists such as Myra Tanner Weiss and Clara Kaye

(Fraser) also became strongly identified with fighting "male chauvinism" in the party—although some male comrades, Cannon in particular, were also inclined to take the issue seriously. A sharp internal controversy in the 1950s over the "political correctness" or "incorrectness" of women using cosmetics (a male comrade had written a column in the *Militant* mocking such use) suggested that strong feelings existed just below the surface around gender issues. There was an early enthusiasm in the SWP for such works as Betty Friedan's *The Feminine Mystique* (1963) and Kate Millett's *Sexual Politics* (1969). SWP veteran Evelyn Reed, in a set of essays of the 1950s and 1960s collected into the pamphlet *Problems of Women's Liberation*, made a widely recognized contribution to the new women's liberation movement. The impact of the new wave of feminism on the SWP and YSA resulted in what George Breitman called "a big leap" in the SWP regarding "both the theory and practice of the women's struggle," which included a significant infusion of women into the membership and leadership positions of the Trotskyist movement.[66]

According to George Novack, the attention of both male and female Trotskyists during the 1960s "was not directed toward internal discussions, but outward to the social struggles agitating the country." More than this, worldwide events in 1968 seemed a dramatic confirmation of the revolutionary internationalism for which the Trotskyists stood. The remarkable Tet offensive in Vietnam provided a powerful example of a national liberation movement challenging imperialism. The martyred Che Guevara's call for "two, three, many Vietnams" still reverberated throughout Latin America, where guerrilla fighters, left-wing workers movements, and revolutionary students and youth continued to fight against oppressive regimes allied to the United States. The explosion of social protest in France during May and June, bringing a mass student radicalization together with a general strike of the working class, came close to bringing down de Gaulle's government, showing that workers in the "advanced capitalist West" still had revolutionary potential capable of combining with the energy of radical youth. Students and workers in Czechoslovakia also joined in the massive upsurge of the Prague Spring, pushing to replace Stalinism by a hopeful "socialism with a human face," resisting nonviolently but heroically when Warsaw Pact military forces crushed their efforts in August. The United States experienced massive antiwar protests, radical student strikes on major college campuses, and spontaneous nationwide uprisings in African American communities sparked by the assassination of Martin Luther King Jr. It seemed that a global tidal wave was confirming the assertion made by the Peruvian Trotskyist Hugo Blanco that "we live in the age of permanent revolution."[67]

The SWP's principal areas of activity from the early 1960s to the early 1970s were the defense of the Cuban Revolution, the Black liberation struggle, and the anti—Vietnam War movement. Beginning in the late 1960s, involvement in the women's liberation movement (particularly the abortion rights struggle) became another major area of activity. It is not possible to offer a detailed account of these and related activities. A sense of them can be communicated, however, through Novack's summary comments. Regarding the Black liberation struggle, he writes:

> While the SWP supported every action against racism, it was especially concerned to establish collaboration with the most combative and progressive forces in the Black liberation struggle, as Robert F. Williams, the leader of the Monroe, North Carolina, NAACP, who organized Blacks to defend themselves against Klan terror; Malcolm X, the Black Muslim leader who broke with the religious sect in a revolutionary nationalist direction; the Student Non-Violent Coordinating Committee, which organized antisegregation struggles in the southern communities and first raised the slogan of "Black Power"; and the militant caucuses of Black workers.
>
> Through our solidarity with these militants and the publication of our resolutions, books, and pamphlets on their problems—particularly through the contributions of George Breitman—the SWP won a hearing and respect for its ideas. The SWP was the first radical group to recognize and explain the progressive nature [and] the revolutionary implications of Black nationalism, particularly as expounded by Malcolm X.[68]

Indeed, Breitman's *The Last Year of Malcolm X: Evolution of a Revolutionary* and the collection he edited entitled *Malcolm X Speaks* were read by and had an impact on hundreds of thousands, perhaps millions, of people in the United States and elsewhere. Building on earlier positions developed by Lenin, Trotsky, and C. L. R. James, in light of the evolving realities around him, Breitman was able to grasp the revolutionary importance of independent African American movements and of the centrality for African Americans of the demand for self-determination (control of one's own community, one's own future) rather than integration (assimilation into white society). He explained in books, pamphlets, and articles that Black liberation was central to the larger struggle to challenge and overturn capitalist power, that a "combined revolution" would bring socialism to the United States. In large measure through such writings as these, through sensitive work that Breitman coordinated when he was the organizer of the Detroit branch of the SWP during the 1960s, and through dynamic work of the party as a whole throughout the country, a new layer of thoughtful and energetic Black activists was drawn into the Trotskyist movement.

Regarding the anti-Vietnam War movement, Novack writes:

> From its inception the YSA sought to establish itself on the campuses as the chief voice and organizer of socialist-minded students. The YSA's success was largely attributable to the role it played in the anti-Vietnam War movement, which was based upon student activists.
>
> The SWP was the only working-class current to run against [Lyndon Baines] Johnson in the 1964 presidential campaign and warn against his warlike intentions in Indochina. The SWP and YSA threw their full force into the antiwar protests that mounted after Johnson began a full-scale air war, supplemented by massive troop landings in South Vietnam, in February 1965. This gave the party its first opening in many years to participate in extensive mass action on a nationwide scale.
>
> The SWP consistently strove to build an antiwar coalition of diverse forces aimed at the mobilization of the largest body of protest around the issue of getting the United States out of Vietnam. Within the broad movement, party and YSA members fought—with considerable success—for adoption of the slogan of immediate, unconditional withdrawal from Vietnam. They combated tendencies that sought to derail the movement by disorienting it to Democratic Party election campaigns. The experience of working within the antiwar movement from 1964 on was an immensely educative one for young Trotskyist cadres.[69]

More than this, through their sustained and effective work in a number of formations—the National Mobilization Committee to End the War in Vietnam, the Student Mobilization Committee, the National Peace Action Coalition, and others—American Trotskyists, young and old, made a difference. They helped draw together and mobilize popular opposition to the war, helped make U.S. policymakers feel the growing antiwar pressure, and thus helped bring the war to an end. A magnificent account of this is provided in Fred Halstead's *Out Now! A Participant's Account of the American Movement against the Vietnam War*, written by the best known and perhaps the most perceptive of the Trotskyists playing a leadership role in the antiwar movement.[70]

One non-Trotskyist historian with New Left inclinations, Jim O'Brien, later recounted: "The SWP-YSA threw itself wholeheartedly into the movement from the start; its members became (and recruited) the foot-soldiers of singleissue end-the-war committees all across the country. In time its ability to keep these committees active and to build demonstrations had made it the most influential single group in the coalitions that called the giant peace rallies of the late '60s and early '70s."[71] Many activists in the much larger New Left movement of the time were quite critical of "the Trots," as indicated in the recollections in the mid-1970s of Carl Oglesby, former president of the once-massive New Left group Students for a Democratic Society (SDS): "Our attitude toward the Trotskyists was frequently one of irritation at their political stance. It seemed that their foot-dragging at certain moments kept us from being militant when we should have been. I remember associating YSA with milquetoast radicalism that constantly put theory before reality." Yet Oglesby, "reminded gently that SDS is now [i.e., in 1976] a faint memory whereas the Socialist Workers Party is alive and well," felt compelled to add: "Well, I've got to give them credit for that—they were able to endure. I think many of the shortcomings of SWP and YSA were, in another perspective, strengths. Their terrific caution, their insistence on institutional tightness, these characteristics made it difficult for them to respond spontaneously in the 1960s—when spontaneity was crucial. But they also enabled them to endure the 1960s, whereas others of us got knocked off."[72]

The fact remains that the SWP and YSA gained a very negative reputation in some circles. In some cases this might have been brought on by specific instances in which SWP or YSA members were insufficiently tactful, modest, or open. In other cases it might have been brought about simply because they dared to disagree with someone, and then went on to prove their own effectiveness. Consider this early 1972 account by SWP activist Carol Lipman:

> An undated issue (Vol. 1, No. 4) of *Womankind*, a Detroit women's liberation newspaper, carried an article by the Detroit Women's Liberation Movement that charged the SWP with "making a concerted effort in city after city of the country to manipulate and control the women's liberation movement."

As alleged proof, they present a "list of tactics that have appeared in take-over after attempted take-over," including among others:

"1. Come to a women's liberation meeting with a plan for what should be done.

"2. Pack the meeting with members of the SWP and its 'youth' group the YSA.

"3. Set up a structure with a chairwoman (usually in the SWP) who knows Roberts Rules. . . .

"5. Decide to 'build' for a mass demonstration. . . .

"7. Set up a coordinating committee with party members and sympathizers.

"8. Write a leaflet that is always characterized by endorsements. . . ."

Thus, YSA and SWP members are supposed manipulators because they bring ideas to meetings; a lot of YSA and SWP women are interested in building the women's liberation movement and come to meetings; they like orderly meetings and democratic structures; they get broad endorsements for women's actions and programs. What more proof do you need?[73]

In fact, a number of New Left activists were positively impressed by what the SWP and YSA were able to accomplish in this period. Even a hostile commentator, Kirkpatrick Sale, in his valuable history *SDS*, surveying the activist groups that moved forward as the New Left of the 1960s disintegrated, wrote: "The YSA . . . fared the best of all these groups, in part because it was not very demanding in its membership requirements ('general agreement with the organization's program') and in part because it operated with a certain seriousness and discipline that seemed attractive after the *laissezaller* [do your own thing] of SDS (in December [1969], for example, fifteen former SDS chapter heads announced that they were joining YSA to escape SDS's 'personality cliques, based on personal alliances rather than political orientation')."[74]

In a feature article for the *Nation*, Walter and Miriam Schneir commented:

Membership in this cadre-type party is not at all a casual matter; it represents a deep personal commitment. The constitution of the SWP mandates democratic control of its governing bodies, and party democracy is a fundamental principle. But once a decision is reached, it is "binding upon members." Socialist Workers [members] agree to submit to party discipline. . . . The SWP is clearly a way of life, and those who enter it believe profoundly in its mission, which is stated succinctly in the SWP constitution: "The purpose of the Party shall be to educate and organize the working class for the abolition of capitalism and the establishment of a Workers Government to achieve socialism."[75]

In fact, the SWP was preparing to do just that. By 1973 the SWP had close to 1,200 members, many of whom were relatively young: at its national convention that year more than half were under twenty-five years old. The professional-looking weekly *Militant* increased in size and circulation—17,000 in 1970 and 31,000 by 1973. Noting the extent of the party's resources and staff, O'Brien commented that it "was in a position to take an active role when new struggles would emerge in the future." The Schneirs, describing the SWP's five-story national headquarters in New York City, wrote: "It is a hive of activity staffed by about 120 persons (most of them paid employees) and has ample space for far more." They also related: "Seventy-year-old SWP theoretician George Novack, who remembers the party when it could barely afford one telephone, notes with pride: 'We have an infrastructure for a party of about 100,000.'"[76]

Far more important to the infrastructure than an impressive national headquarters was a network of party branches in roughly two to three dozen cities across the country. Each generally supported at least one paid organizer, maintained a combination office—meeting hall-bookstore, and through weekly branch meetings coordinated the work of local party fractions that participated in broader organizations and also local party committees that oversaw finances and other party institutions.[1]

---

[1] In the SWP, *fractions*—not to be confused with factions—were groups of comrades who were involved in a trade union, in a mass movement organization, or in some other entity external to the party. For example, those involved in a local antiwar coalition would be organized in an antiwar fraction that would meet to discuss issues and alternatives facing the coalition, to think through collectively what SWP comrades should do to help build the coalition, to develop a common position on complex and controversial questions, and so on. Sometimes there would also be *national fractions* to coordinate the work of local fractions and organize participation in national conferences and demonstrations. *Committees* consisted of groups of comrades organized around internal assignments having to do with party finances, forums, education, literature sales, and the like.

Institutions of American Trotskyism

Over the years a number of important activities became "institutions" of American Trotskyism. Among these were the energetic election campaigns for national, state, and local office for which the SWP became famous—laboring to overcome undemocratic election laws, to obtain many thousands of signatures needed to get "minor party" candidates on the ballot, and then running vigorous campaigns for the purpose of spreading socialist ideas, drawing people into struggles for social change, and giving voters an opportunity to cast their ballots *against* capitalist politics and for a working-class socialist program.

The first national election campaign of the SWP took place in 1948, with Farrell Dobbs and Grace Carlson running for president and vice president. In 1953, 1956, and 1960, Dobbs and Myra Tanner Weiss were the party's standard-bearers. The 1964 SWP presidential campaign advanced the first African American presidential candidate in U.S. history, Clifton DeBerry, whose running mate was Ed Shaw. The widely respected antiwar leader Fred Halstead led the SWP ticket in 1968, with Black activist Paul Boutelle as the vice presidential candidate. In 1972, Linda Jenness was the party's first female candidate for president, running with Andrew Pulley, a Black ex-GI who had helped lead a much-publicized antiwar protest inside Fort Jackson, South Carolina. Perhaps the most energetic and effective campaigner was the 1976 candidate Peter Camejo, whose running mate was Willie Mae Reid. Andrew Pulley and Mathilde Zimmerman were the 1980 candidates.

Another party institution that became important during the 1960s and 1970s was the "Militant Forum" or "Militant Labor Forum," held—often on a weekly basis—in cities throughout the country. These would offer a variety of speakers, sometimes panels, debates, or films, on a broad range of questions of interest to workers, students, and others in and near the radical movement. More often than not, the forum would be held at the same location that housed the local SWP bookstore, another important institution.

The press of the Trotskyist movement was a vital resource: the weekly newspaper the *Militant* (for a short period in the 1930s called the *Socialist Appeal*); the theoretical magazine, first called *New International*, then called *Fourth International*, finally *International Socialist Review*; the sophisticated analytical newsweekly put out under the supervision of Joseph Hansen, *Intercontinental Press*; and—whenever it came out (sometimes regularly and quite professional looking, sometimes not), with varying formats—the *Young Socialist* of the YSA. By the late 1970s, there was also the Spanish-language *Perspectiva Mundial*. In addition, there was an increasingly rich array of books and pamphlets published by Pioneer Publishers, Merit Publishers, and finally Pathfinder Press.

Another important "institution" involved actually organizing sales of the press—setting up literature tables at meetings, rallies, and demonstrations on campuses and in communities; going out on the streets, into communities, and to factory gates to sell the *Militant* and other materials, while also giving out forum leaflets, socialist election materials, and flyers on upcoming demonstrations. In addition, there were periodic subscription campaigns, mobilizing the entire party membership and organizing special traveling teams, to sell thousands of introductory subscriptions.

Essential for the party's very survival, of course, was the creation of a sound financial base. During the 1970s, each member was required to pay monthly dues of $2, but then all were urged to give a more substantial weekly sustainer, which most did (sometimes less, sometimes more, but for the most part between $5 and $50 per week)—generating substantial income in each branch every month. Out of this would be paid rent and utilities for the local headquarters, all local staff expenses, costs of printing local leaflets, and so forth. Everything else would be sent to the National Office to help meet the expenses of the organization as a whole. In addition, there were important supplements: periodic fund drives; the soliciting of financial contributions from well-to-do sympathizers; and the utilization of the party printshop in New York to take on "outside" commercial printing jobs, which could be especially profitable thanks to the minimal labor costs made possible through the hard work of very dedicated but low-paid SWP printshop workers.

One of the most important of the party's institutions involved education—ranging from the specifics of Marxist theory and the history of the revolutionary movement to the most current political developments of the moment. There would frequently be special educational offerings at party branch meetings, sometimes a class series or a weekend educational conference, often utilizing study guides, class outlines, and other materials produced by the SWP National Education Department. Throughout the 1970s and 1980s, in Oberlin, Ohio, there was a multifaceted, weeklong national educational gathering, the Socialist Activist and Educational Conference, attended by most members as well as many sympathizers and contacts of the party (generally over 1,000 participants). This was based on the "vacation school" concept, which originated in the West Coast Vacation School, held in California from 1935 until 1967. Evelyn Sell recounts:

> A camp was rented for the exclusive use of the school which usually ran for one full week. There were classes in the morning and in the afternoon plus a lecture at night featuring talks by well-known leaders such as James P. Cannon. (Cannon's talks on "Socialism and Democracy" were given at the school in 1957 and were then published as a pamphlet.) Socials and entertainment were organized as well. The school provided an intense educational experience for members and contacts and, at the same time, offered relaxation from day-to-day pressures.
>
> A Mid-West Vacation School was held at a camp in central Michigan during the summer of 1944. Fifteen branches participated over the two-week period. Attendance included 132 members, party supporters and children. People came from seventeen cities: Detroit, Chicago, Toledo, Buffalo, Flint, Cleveland, St. Paul, New York, Newark, Youngstown, Dayton, Akron, Minneapolis, Ann Arbor, Milwaukee, Philadelphia and Allentown. The majority of the adults were workers from auto, aircraft, steel, longshore, rubber, rail and seamen unions. The program covered: History of American Trotskyism, Lenin's *Imperialism*, Marx's *Wage-Labor and Capital*, the Italian events, Perspectives for the American Labor Movement, Democratic centralism, and Colonial Struggles. Three classes a day were held (morning, afternoon, evening). A number of social and recreational activities were included in the two weeks of this vacation school (as in California's).

In addition, there was from 1950 to 1963 the Trotsky School, located at the SWP's Mountain Spring Camp seventy-five miles outside of New York City. This was a full-time educational institution designed to train up to a dozen actual and potential party leaders for six-month periods.[1] Branches would make nominations from which the Political Committee

---

[1] In 1980, a new leadership school was begun by the new SWP leadership under Jack Barnes; it was called Sandstone University (a reference to Sandstone Prison, where the Trotskyist leaders lived and studied during their 1940s imprisonment under the Smith Act). This was quite different from the old Trotsky School, however, since it contributed to, and seems to have been designed to facilitate, a new leadership layer abandoning the SWP's traditional Trotskyist orientation.

made selections. "The students' political assignment was to study," according to Sell. "They were released from all other political activities as well as from financial responsibility for food, rent, and the small necessities of everyday living. . . . Most of the sessions were conducted seminar-style with guest lecturers supplementing the regular classes." In the 1950s the focus was on an in-depth study of Marx's *Capital* and of U.S. history. The 1960s saw a shift away from *Capital* to the principles of dialectical and historical materialism, with broadened readings from Marx, Engels, Lenin, and Trotsky. "The 1960–61 school was taught by George Novack," Sell notes, "and served to help him organize the materials which were later published in book form by Merit Publishers and Pathfinder Press."[77]

Of course, revolutionary socialists gathered together for more than simply educational purposes. A National Convention—the party's highest decisionmaking institution—generally took place every two years. There would be a three-month period before each convention for oral and written discussion in which each member, as well as organized tendencies, had the opportunity to raise any question for discussion and debate. Several special meetings in each of the branches would be organized for this purpose. A number of special internal discussion bulletins, open to the written contributions of all comrades, would be published—sometimes taking up hundreds or even thousands of pages, most of which would be avidly read by a majority of SWPers. At the conclusion of the preconvention discussion period, branches would elect their delegates to the National Convention. Only delegates had the right to speak and vote at the several-day-long convention, but all members plus invited guests could attend to hear the sometimes heated debates. (In certain periods and areas—especially where there were multiple branches, such as in New York City and California—there might be citywide and statewide party conventions as well.)

The delegates of the National Convention, after discussing and deciding various questions, would elect a National Committee (NC) whose function would be to help implement the decisions made and to oversee the proper functioning of the party between conventions. The NC would meet between two and four times a year (its meetings were called plenums), and it would elect a subcommittee—the Political Committee (PC)—which was to coordinate party work between plenums. Frank

Lovell, who was in a position to observe closely the functioning of these leadership bodies, has offered this account:

> The party leaders who spoke most authoritatively in PC meetings in the transition period in the early 1970s were Dobbs, Kerry, Breitman, Hansen, and Novack. They brought reports of work in the departments of the party apparatus (Pathfinder Press, the weekly newspaper, theoretical journals, fraternal ties with Trotskyists in other countries, the Black liberation movement in the U.S., the shifting political scene, etc.). Most of this was for the information of other PC members and for the record, to be transmitted to National Committee members not resident in New York.
>
> The important decisions were all made in the administrative departments, approved by the administrative secretariat (later called the Political Bureau), and then brought to the Political Committee for approval. The National Committee continued to serve as a rubber stamp for its subcommittee.
>
> In the 1970s this was the accepted practice, a far cry from what was envisioned in 1953 at the conclusion of the faction struggle with the Cochranite minority. At that time Cannon announced for the majority caucus:
>
>> The duty of this faction now is to say: "The task is finished; the faction is no longer needed, and the faction must be dissolved into the party." The leadership of the party belongs henceforth to the cadres as a whole, assembled at this plenum [of the National Committee], All problems, all questions for discussion, should be taken directly into the party branches. [*Speeches to the Party*, pp. 191–192]
>
>> In less than twenty years none of this remained. No one proposed changing the routinism that had become a custom. There was no pressure from the NC members in the branches, an increasingly larger proportion of whom were new and inexperienced. Likewise there was no pressure from branch organizers or the membership. With the influx of YSA members came a new practice of selecting branch organizers by appointment from New York instead of urging branch memberships to elect their local organizers from their own ranks.[78]

Branch organizers had the function of coordinating branch activity, but as part of an executive committee ("exec") whose members were elected by the branch membership at least twice a year. The exec (whose members generally included the organizer, the financial director, and the heads of some of the more important fractions and committees) would generally have lengthy meetings between the weekly branch meetings in order to discuss the various areas of work, deal with problems, develop agendas for branch meetings, and review reports to be given at those meetings. Ideally, this facilitated more focused branch meetings and the possibility of having more adequate discussions in branch meetings. In many areas, branch life had considerable vitality. Often there would be critical-minded discussions by the branch members on how to interpret and apply national party decisions in relation to local realities and specific struggles. And yet the ability of the branches to maintain an essential "rootedness" in these local realities was increasingly undermined by another development identified by Lovell:

> The idea of "footloose rebels" was introduced as a membership norm. During the 1970s the practice of reassigning members to different (often newly established) branches was regularized. The great majority of party members attended the annual gatherings—either national conventions or educational conferences—at Oberlin College in Ohio; there many of them expected to be "moving on," as they said, to another city instead of returning to their SWP branch of the previous year or two. Anyone who remained in a branch for longer than a few years was out of the swim of things, no longer footloose and suspected of not being much of a rebel.[79]

These developments coincided with a decisive shift taking place in the central leadership of the SWP. The shift had been planned well in advance. "By the mid-1960s, coinciding with the student radicalization," writes Lovell, "the central leaders of the SWP, conscious of their age and chronic health problems, began a rather systematic search for 'replacement leaders.'" This became particularly urgent due to losses of some of the most experienced younger cadres, stemming from internal disputes with the Robertson and Wohlforth groups, as well as with Murry and Myra Tanner Weiss. Lovell recounts:

> Jack Barnes was selected as a possible replacement leader by the Dobbs-Kerry leadership team in 1967 because of his outstanding performance as national chairman of the Young Socialist Alliance, his ability to cultivate a pupil/teacher relationship between himself and the top party leaders, and his talent for organizational maneuver among the aspiring youth leaders. Barnes quickly became a favorite of both Dobbs and Kerry. They coached him and promoted his fortunes. . . . He was encouraged

to develop his own leadership team, to which the older comrades were selflessly inclined to defer in order to facilitate a smoother transition.[80]

All the institutions of the SWP, and all the structures into which the party's members were organized, were purportedly based on, designed to advance, and given meaning by the *political program* that has often been labeled "Trotskyism."

It is worth noting that in 1951 the leadership of the SWP proposed that the label of "Trotskyism" be set aside, that instead the party designate itself "in broad public political agitation as 'Socialist' or 'Socialist Workers' or 'Revolutionary Socialist,' alternatively, as the occasion may demand." Cannon explained that a "Trotskyist" self-designation could cause thoughtful workers to view the Socialist Workers Party

> as a sectarian movement, as followers of some individual, and a Russian at that. It is not a suitable characterization for a broad American movement. Our enemies will refer to us as Trotskyists, and we will, of course, not deny it; but we should say: "We are Trotskyists because Trotsky was a true socialist."
>
> What we are presenting against American capitalism and the labor bureaucracy is the principle of the class struggle of modern socialism. . . .
>
> Let our enemies within the movement, that is in the narrow framework of the more political movement, call us Trotskyists. We will not protest. But then we will say we are Trotskyist because he represented genuine socialism and we, like him, are the real Socialists. . . .
>
> We have to think of ourselves more and more as representing the Socialist opposition to the American bourgeoisie. I don't think we should do it under the handicap of what appears to the workers as a sectarian or cultist name. That is what the term "Trotskyist" signifies to them.[81]

George Breitman has commented that "there was a relapse from the wise decision of 1951, starting in 1952 with the fight against the Cochranites and their slogan, 'Junk the Old Trotskyism,'" so that throughout the 1950s, 1960s, and 1970s, the *Trotskyist* label was definitely attached to the SWP. But it is clear that what counted was the political content to which the label alluded.

From Cannon's statement, it is clear that the fundamental class-struggle socialism of the *Communist Manifesto* is at the core of this political content, involving the struggle of the working class for political independence from and final victory over the capitalist class. The notion that a genuine democracy must animate the working-class and revolutionary movements and be at the heart of the socialist goal is also there. There is an understanding that socialism will not automatically issue forth from capitalism, that the working class must fight long and hard if capitalism is to be replaced by socialism. Related to this is the perception that such a process is complex, and that, as Lenin grasped, those who want to see it through to completion—initially a small minority—must organize themselves into a disciplined revolutionary party. This party must not set itself apart from the actual lives and real struggles of the workers and the oppressed, but must be an effective force in the fight for reforms within capitalist society, pushed forward by mobilizations around immediate economic and democratic demands. At the same time, intertwined with these, *transitional demands* must be developed that are rooted in the present-day needs and consciousness of working people, but whose realization would imply the overthrow of capitalism. Since a majority of workers will not be committed to the revolutionary party, it must work to form united fronts with other forces to help ensure an effective struggle, and also to prove itself to increasing numbers of people. There is also the dynamic of "permanent revolution," which posits (1) that democratic struggles, if fought through consistently and to the end, must be carried out under working-class leadership, which ultimately means that the democratic struggle will grow into a struggle for working-class power; (2) that such a victorious struggle will initiate a transition period of social, economic, and cultural transformation through which capitalism is replaced by socialism; and (3) that the global character of capitalism both requires and makes inevitable the international character of the working-class and revolutionary struggles, which also means that socialist revolutions can begin in a single country but are incapable of being won, ultimately, except on a global scale. Thus an organized worldwide movement of revolutionary socialists is absolutely necessary—which is what the Fourth International represents. There is much more than this to "Trotskyism," of course: analyses of and approaches to combatting imperialism, fascism, Stalinism; analyses of a rich accumulation of experience of the labor and socialist movements over more than a century and a half; a substantial body of research-based theoretical studies on economic, historical, and anthropological realities; and so on. And there is a supple, open, yet critical methodological approach (which is dialectical, historical, materialist) for dealing with new, newly under-stood, and always evolving realities.

As an intellectual and political figure, Trotsky represented this kind of revolutionary socialism, or Marxism, particularly against influential reformist, Stalinist, and sectarian distortions. But Trotsky was neither the beginning nor the end of this political program and intellectual tra-dition (nor was he himself inclined to refer to it as "Trotskyist"), so that Cannon's proposal to utilize a different label seemed quite reasonable. On the other hand, there was the sharp challenge to "the old Trotskyism" represented by the SWPers led by Bert Cochran, which seemed to ques-tion important aspects of the traditional revolutionary orientation that had guided the party. Thus "Trotskyism" was unfurled as a banner in the struggle against a revisionist threat.

Yet after the fight against the Cochranite challenge had ended, all was not well for the SWP. There were the harsh realities of decline in the 1950s and the complexities of resurgence in the early 1960s. The Dobbs-Kerry leadership and many members, seeking to ensure the pres-ervation of a theoretical heritage, held on to the Trotskyist label and, in fact, inclined in the direction of institutionalizing something called "Trotskyism" as the covenant preserved within the very core of the party. The 1965 resolution "The Organizational Character of the Socialist Workers Party" offers this summation:

> The Socialist Workers Party, as a revolutionary workers' party, is based on the doctrines of scientific socialism as embodied in the principle works of Marx, Engels, Lenin and Trotsky and incorporated in the basic doc-uments and resolutions of the first four congresses of the Communist International; and as embodied in the Transitional Program, the American Theses and other programmatic documents of the Trotskyist movement. The party's aim is the organization of the working class in the struggle for power and the transformation of the existing social order. All of its activities, its methods and its internal regime are subordinated to this aim and are designed to serve it.[82]

Such statements as these came to reflect what was a sort of "institu-tion" in the SWP—something that bound the membership together—yet not all members were able to understand it in the same way. What is meant by the working class, what is involved in its struggle for power, and how are we to understand the transformation of the existing social order? How are the theory of permanent revolution and the meaning of revolutionary internationalism to be understood? What is the method of Trotsky's *The Revolution Betrayed*? How does one utilize transitional demands in one's own situation? There were some members of the SWP, especially among the older and more experienced—more politically mature—comrades, who had an informed and thoughtful approach to such questions. But for many, the program was an "institutionalized" orthodoxy that was beyond question (and therefore beyond practical utilization), which encouraged superficial self-assurance.

The 1970s

In the late 1960s and 1970s, critics of the Socialist Workers Party as well as some internal dissidents accused it of "sectoralism" and "polyvanguardism"—giving social movements of Blacks, Hispanics, women, students, and youth equal weight with the labor movement, in contradiction of the Marxist dictum that it is the proletariat that must make the revolution. A young SWP leader of that time, Gus Horowitz, explained the importance of the social movements: "Under capitalism, side by side with the exploitation of the working class, there also exist new forms of long-known oppression, the reactionary institutional and ideological remnants of a precapitalist era: the oppression of women and nationalities, religious superstition, the persecution of homosexuals, reactionary social morality, restrictions on civil liberties and human rights are but a few examples." A seasoned veteran in the SWP leadership, George Breitman went beyond this in emphasizing the working-class composition of substantial sectors of these new social movements, commenting that "it is idiotic and insulting to think that the worker responds only to economic issues; he can be radicalized in various ways, over various issues, and he is." Breitman elaborated:

> The radicalization of the worker can begin off the job as well as on. It can begin from the fact that the worker is a woman as well as a man; that the worker is Black or Chicano or a member of some other oppressed minority as well as white; that the worker is a father or mother whose son can be drafted [to fight in Vietnam]; that the worker is young as well as middle-aged or about to retire. If we grasp the fact that the working class is stratified and divided in many ways—the capitalists prefer it that way—then we will be better able to understand how the radicalization will develop among workers and how to intervene more effectively. Those

who haven't already learned important lessons from the radicalization of oppressed minorities, youth and women had better hurry up and learn them, because most of the people involved in these radicalizations are workers or come from working-class families.

Horowitz explained, "We see that movements such as the women's liberation movement, the struggles of oppressed nationalities for self-determination, the gay liberation movement, and the revolution in culture are a part of the general struggle against the outmoded capitalist system," adding that "these new movements are not unimportant or peripheral to the socialist revolution, but at the center of its advance."[83]

On the basis of this orientation, the SWP was able to attract many young activists who sought a Marxist approach that was relevant to their own experience. Writing in 1976, Walter and Miriam Schneir commented that three-fourths of the members of this SWP were thirty years old or under. "Not only were most of them born long after the Great Depression, few are old enough to remember World War II," the Schneirs noted. "Politically, they are children of the cold war, the civil rights struggle, the Cuban Revolution, the Soviet invasion of Czechoslovakia, the new wave of feminism and, most of all, the war in Vietnam."[84]

Similarly, Jim O'Brien observed that "effective leadership in the party was very largely in the hands of younger cadre who had come in through the student movement and had little continuity with the party's working-class roots of the 1930s and '40s." He perceptively added: "Older leaders such as the working-class veterans James P. Cannon and Farrell Dobbs were replaced by younger activists such as Jack Barnes, Peter Camejo, and Barry Sheppard, all of whom had come through the YSA in the '60s. It was not a coup—the older leaders were the ones who had decided to turn toward the campus for recruits—but it did represent a decisive change in composition and tone." The Schneirs added: "Today in semi-retirement, [George] Novack is well-satisfied with the young people who have assumed SWP leadership. They are, he says, following Trotsky's advice to combine Russian Bolshevism with American efficiency. He adds, with obvious pleasure, 'They are the apple of our eye.'"[85]

The new leadership was given plenty of "space" by the semiretiring veterans to make its own decisions, learn from its own mistakes, and develop its own orientation and style. In some of the factional disputes that arose in the 1970s, however, this style could assume a harsh, at times even brutal, tone.

An oppositional tendency in the early years of the decade—organized around the document "For a Proletarian Orientation" and urging, among other things, greater attention to getting members into factories and union jobs instead of such an overwhelming concentration on the campuses—found itself swept aside with a minimum of democracy and a maximum of impatience. A few years later, the acrimoniously critical yet somewhat heterogeneous Internationalist Tendency (IT), representing about 200 people, echoed the Proletarian Orientation Tendency's view that the SWP was simply tailing after petit-bourgeois social movements, was wrong on Black nationalism, and was insufficiently critical of feminism; at the same time, ITers felt that the SWP had been too critical of the broad New Left milieu, and that it had elevated organizational opportunism above theoretical seriousness. The IT fight was also intertwined with international developments. At this time there was, once again, a fierce factional fight inside the Fourth International: the SWP leadership and the substantial Latin American current led by Argentinian Nahuel Moreno headed the somewhat "orthodox" Leninist-Trotskyist Faction in combat against an International Majority Tendency composed of a majority of Europeans and Latin Americans. In the United States, the IT lined up with this international majority, which favored a continental strategy of guerrilla warfare in Latin America and an immersion in the "new mass vanguard" of radicalized youth, left Stalinists, Maoists, Guevarists, and so forth that had arisen in the 1960s. The IT made the mistake of carrying on discussions and activities secretly from the rest of the SWP, which was utilized as a pretext by the SWP leadership to eliminate the opposition through its violation of the party constitution: the tendency's members were suddenly declared to be a separate organization, and through a maneuver dubbed "re-registration," they were—for all practical purposes—instantly expelled without the right to appeal. This precedent did serious damage to the SWP.[86]

At several points during the 1970s, the issue of gay and lesbian rights also was a focal point for disputes. For many years the SWP had (along with most of the organized Left) maintained a backward policy that, for "security" reasons, made homosexual behavior formally incompatible with party membership. In the late 1960s, this policy was ended. Thanks to this positive change, a number of gay and lesbian comrades felt able to "come out" inside the party, and others were recruited. Initially, the Barnes leadership seemed inclined to make gay liberation a significant area of party concern and activity. Then—although a formal position favoring gay and lesbian rights was maintained—there was a visible drawing back from the issue. Some party leaders explained to the members that the gay liberation movement lacked the "social weight" of other social movements and tended to be "peripheral" to the class struggle, and that the party could not take positions on "scientific questions" around whether "gay is good." This generated a series of angry debates in the party. Those who openly challenged the SWP leadership were invariably, predictably, discredited and marginalized in the organization.

The way the leadership handled such disputes in the 1970s was to undermine quite seriously the internal democracy to which the SWP was formally committed. At the same time, it is important to recognize that the bulk of the membership seemed to approve of such treatment of dissident minorities. In large part, this flowed from the intense desire of the party members to reject anything that might divert them from realizing the magnificent opportunities and potential that had opened up for the Trotskyist movement. Yet the 1970s proved to be a more difficult period than expected. Some of this is captured in the "outsider's" observations of Jim O'Brien, written in 1977:

> The Socialist Workers Party, which had thrived in the largely campus-based antiwar movement, carried its same program into the early '70s. It continued to furnish the organizational backbone of such mass demonstrations [of more than 500,000 people] as those in Washington and San Francisco in April 1971 (the largest since November 1969) and it tried hard to step into the organizational vacuum left by the splintering of SDS in mid-1969 by building YSA chapters on more campuses. It tried to carry its formula of precisely-focused mass demonstrations into the area of women's liberation and the formation of the Women's National Abortion Action Coalition in 1971, although WONAAC was never able to build demonstrations larger than about three thousand people. By 1973 the antiwar movement had collapsed with the signing of the Vietnam peace treaty, WONAAC had collapsed with the 1973 Supreme Court decision overcoming state abortion laws, and YSA's main campus focus was to sell newspapers and run candidates in student government elections. . . .
>
> The SWP's major practical successes in recent years have been in exposing federal violations of civil liberties and in organizing around the defense of busing [for school desegregation]. Its suit against government surveillance, filed in 1973 and still in the courts [the SWP finally won

this historic case in 1986], has released thousands of pages of the government's 'Cointelpro' harassment of left and liberal activists. The SWP's suit has been to the benefit of the entire U.S. left. The SWP also initiated the National Student Coalition Against Racism, which helped to build the December 1974 antiracism march and a follow-up in May 1975 called by the Boston NAACP. Its work around busing, which brought a substantial number of Blacks into the YSA and SWP, also served as a bridge into working-class recruitment. The party enunciated a turn toward the working class at its 1975 convention, and began to break up its city-wide branches into separate locals with some being in working-class areas. . . . The party claims to have 59 percent more members than it did two years ago, which probably means that it has somewhere around 1,800 now. At the same time, sales of *The Militant* are only about two-thirds of their peak in 1973.[87]

There were a number of additional issues that the SWP and YSA took up in the 1970s. They were the backbone of the U.S. Committee for Justice to Latin American Political Prisoners (USLA), which played a role in life-saving solidarity efforts after the bloody right-wing 1973 coup in Chile. USLA also defended left-wing political prisoners and the "disappeared" in Argentina during this period, as well as disseminating information on human rights abuses elsewhere in Latin America and seeking to secure freedom for imprisoned activists there. A similar function was served by the Committee for Artistic and Intellectual Freedom in Iran (CAIFI) and by various efforts on behalf of dissidents in the USSR and Eastern Europe.

At various points, militant actions to support the grape and lettuce boycotts organized by the United Farm Workers engaged members' energies. Some SWP and YSA activists in New York City became involved in struggles for community control of the schools, with a focus on multiculturalism and multilingualism. This attracted some Puerto Rican activists. In Texas, California, New Mexico, and Colorado, there was serious involvement in Chicano struggles. The SWP and YSA also played a role in protests against South African apartheid. And there was opposition to Zionism, since the way that Israel had been established—as an exclusively "Jewish state"—inherently involved the oppression of indigenous Palestinians (also creating a situation that Trotsky had warned would be "a death trap for the Jews"); Trotskyists favored a democratic, secular Palestine in which Jews, Arabs, and others could live in peace and dignity—which also implied the need for socialist revolution in the Middle East. The near calamity of a meltdown at the Three Mile Island nuclear power plant in the late 1970s generated a substantial involvement in antinuke struggles. Generally the SWP and YSA were seen as making valuable contributions in such activities, as being consistent, well-organized, and hardworking participants, even by those who had little sympathy for their Trotskyist politics.

Also in the late 1970s, there was a concerted effort on the part of SWP women to build the National Organization for Women (NOW) into an organization that would give greater attention to working-class and low-income women, as well as to the needs and sensibilities of women of color. They believed that NOW should be more inclined to organize mass demonstrations, especially for the Equal Rights Amendment, and should be politically independent of the Democratic and Republican Parties. Although some SWP members and ideas gained credibility in this effort, many NOW leaders and members responded with anger (and sometimes with undemocratic maneuvers) to what they perceived as a hostile move against their organization. In some NOW chapters, there were concerted efforts—in some cases successful—to marginalize or even expel SWP members and supporters. The polarization became so destructive that significant SWP involvement in NOW came to an end, although some meaningful participation continued in some NOW chapters. The SWP also engaged in efforts to help build the Coalition of Labor Union Women (CLUW), although some left-wing rivals accused the party of being far too moderate in this arena.

In the mid-1970s, however, there was a fundamental shift in the party's orientation. According to Walter and Miriam Schneir:

> As party secretary, [Jack] Barnes is responsible for the general direction of SWP. That direction is now undergoing substantial change, based on the central conclusion reached last year [1975] by the party's national convention: "the economic motor forces that produced the relative prosperity of the past decades are becoming more and more exhausted. . . . For the first time since the Great Depression, working people as a whole are feeling the crunch." Barnes reported to his colleagues: "We are at the beginning of the radicalization of the American working class." The party, he said, would be recruiting more workers, blacks, Puerto Ricans, women, and young people.

These goals point up present strengths and weaknesses of the SWP. For while the party has many young people and 40 percent of its members are women, fewer than one member in three is a trade unionist and the number of blacks is barely 6 percent. The reality—which the party is working hard to change—is that the SWP today consists overwhelmingly of young white Americans who were the student protesters of the 1960s.[88]

Among those SWP members doing effective work in the unions, the overwhelming majority were in the dynamic "service sector"—teachers, hospital workers, government employees, and so forth. The old SWP base in the solid industrial unions had yet to be recreated. (The idea that this would become increasingly difficult because U.S. corporations were preparing for a partial but real and substantial "deindustrialization" in the 1980s was simply outside the realm of the thinkable for most of us in the 1970s—and even in the early 1980s.) The reality of the mid-1970s was that the working class was now being hit by an employer offensive that was bound to have a radicalizing impact, although it was not clear what the pace of such radicalization would be.

The party's efforts to adjust to the new realities of the 1970s yielded mixed results. "The SWP has at times tried to apply its mass-demonstrations approach to the problem of social service cutbacks," wrote O'Brien, "but has had little success; for example, a New York demonstration called at the height of that city's fiscal crisis in 1975 drew only 300 people."[89] Similarly, the National Student Coalition against Racism dwindled after its first flush of success, and the decentralized "community branch" orientation failed to yield hoped-for gains. Some of the other activities generated modest successes (such as involvement in the United Farm Workers' boycott campaigns), whereas others involved serious setbacks (such as some of the work in NOW). In contrast, important new ground was broken in the effective work done by the SWP and YSA in support of Ed Sadlowski's "Steel Workers' Fight Back" campaign—which was vigorous, inspiring, yet (when the votes were counted) unsuccessful—to bring "a tough, democratic, socially conscious unionism" to the United Steel Workers of America by defeating incumbent president Lloyd McBride. More gains were made later through building support for the militant nationwide strike of the United Mine Workers. Increasing numbers of party members began to get new experience by joining the industrial workforce and taking their place in a variety of unions.

As American Trotskyism completed its fifth decade, the continuity of the younger and the older generations seemed to be in the process of being reconfirmed in important new ways. Among other things, the factional dispute in the Fourth International between the International Majority Tendency and the Leninist-Trotskyist Faction had finally been brought to an end, with a greater tilt in the direction of Trotskyist "orthodoxy" and broad agreement on the need to "turn to the working class." Having proved itself on the U.S. scene in the 1960s and 1970s, the SWP seemed confident about what the future would bring. The promise of this vital revolutionary Marxist current seemed to be on the verge of realization. George Novack concluded:

> The composition of the party is changing. More of its members are employed in and recruited from basic industry. This is imperative to promote its aim of building a class-struggle left wing in the labor movement. Such a force can give leadership to the millions who want to transform their unions into organizations controlled by the ranks and acting in their interests. . . .
>
> The stress on the importance of the organized labor movement is hardly a new one for the Trotskyists. It is part of the historic proletarian orientation of the Leninist-Trotskyist movement. What is new today is that the thinking and outlook of the U.S. working class as a whole is changing, making possible further strides in applying that orientation within the unions.[90]

Some party members, although agreeing with Novack's comments, were concerned that this new "proletarian orientation" might generate dynamics in the organization that could obliterate the insights and theoretical advances gained during the 1960s and early 1970s. In particular, we have seen that such SWP spokespeople of the early 1970s as George Breitman and Gus Horowitz emphasized the multifaceted nature of the working class, the centrality to the struggle for socialism of the social protest movements arising outside of the unions, and the underlying proletarian nature of these movements. More than this, some SWP members had done important trade union work *outside* of the industrial working class on which Novack's comments were focused. And in fact, as the 1980s opened, there was a growing tendency of the new party leadership to shrug off such gains, to treat them as part of "the long detour" that could now be left behind as the struggles of the industrial working class at long last moved back to "center stage."

A Personal Reminiscence

Here it might be useful to add the observations of a participant in the Trotskyist movement of the 1970s—my own.[91] I became involved in the YSA in 1972 and was a very active member of the SWP from the spring of 1973 until the summer of 1983. Coming out of a six-year experience in the New Left (part of the time in the SDS, part of the time an independent activist, part of the time in a New Left socialist formation called the New American Movement), I approached the American Trotskyist movement as a fairly critical-minded outsider. I joined it only after a considerable amount of study and close observation.

My evaluation of it at the time that I was considering joining is contained in an article entitled "Leaving the New Left," which was published in the SWP's magazine *International Socialist Review* in November 1972. Speaking of the SWP and the YSA, I asserted, "while these organizations are certainly imperfect and in need of growth and improvement on a number of levels, they still represent the most serious attempt to apply, consistently and creatively, revolutionary Marxist theory to the United States." I added: "Certainly the SWP-YSA are far from perfect. A number of serious, valid criticisms could undoubtedly be made. But it seems to me that such criticisms would be on essentially tactical and technical (or even personality) questions. The general political perspective and orientation, on the other hand, are essentially sound." I concluded that "the SWP-YSA have the potential—in the long run—for making the most decisive contributions to the revolutionary process in our country," and that they "clearly have an important role to play in building an effective revolutionary socialist movement in America."[92] My subsequent experience reinforced many of my earlier impressions.

One factor that particularly impressed me was the prominent role of women among the Trotskyists. These included articulate and seemingly self-confident young activists plus seasoned veterans; they combined to make the movement far stronger than would have been the case had it been a predominantly male operation. I was also impressed by what seemed like a serious-minded effort to draw in and develop talented Black and Hispanic cadres. And although I felt in the early 1970s that not enough attention was being given to work in the labor movement, a significant number of the respected older members seemed to have roots and rich experience in the trade unions, and I believed that this would stand us in good stead when the U.S. working class was ready to move in radical directions.

The SWP and YSA were organizationally and politically far more serious than anything I had participated in previously. I received an incomparable and multifaceted education within them. One facet of this was simply practical, resulting from a variety of internal assignments (branch secretary, forum series director, sales director, bookstore director, financial director, education director, branch organizer, as well as executive committee member) that taught me the nuts and bolts of maintaining a very active political organization in which a diverse number of individuals had to work together to accomplish a great deal. As an electoral candidate and as a participant in a number of election campaign committees, I gained valuable experience in explaining socialist ideas to many different kinds of people. And I participated in party fractions that were active in "mass work": opposing the U.S. war in Vietnam; protesting the U.S.-sponsored coup in Chile and working to defend Latin American political prisoners; building support for struggles of the farm workers, teachers, mine workers, and other unions; undertaking civil liberties efforts and opposing the death penalty; participating in student protests against tuition hikes; struggling for abortion rights and the Equal Rights Amendment for women; campaigning against South African apartheid and against racism here at home; and protesting against the dangers of nuclear power.

Such participation helped educate me on a variety of important issues and helped ground me in certain basic movement-building concepts— the need for and techniques of developing nonexclusionary united fronts that were internally democratic and geared toward creating and mobilizing broad support for one or another specific issue. I also learned something else more fully than ever before. Although it was not possible for me personally, at any given moment, to be doing everything that needed to be done, by being part of an organization in which all phases of activity were democratically and collectively evaluated and decided upon, I *could* be involved in far more activity—all of which was interrelated and part of a unified revolutionary, socialist, practical orientation—than would otherwise have been possible.

Not only did this happen on a local and national level, but also on an international level. Through its association with the Fourth International (although strictly limited by reactionary U.S. legislation), the SWP was able to learn from Trotskyist groups throughout the world about the situations in which they were engaged. Often there were sharp differences on how to evaluate the world situation, the situations in particular countries, the value of one or another strategy or tactical orientation, and so on. These debates could greatly broaden one's horizons, give one a vivid sense of the international character of the struggle for socialism, and generate a sharper and more critical understanding of revolutionary politics.

Internal educational activities of the SWP and YSA were taken very seriously, although they were of uneven quality. Sometimes they could be simplistic, superficial, stilted, with participants being spoon-fed the "correct" way to view one or another question. But at their best they would effectively introduce participants to important aspects of Marxist theory and the history of the working-class and revolutionary movements, in a manner that stimulated excitement and critical-minded discussion. Ideas were not treated in an overintellectualized and academic manner, but as being relevant to and of value in real struggles to change the world.

Also important was a sense of revolutionary continuity that came, in part, from having several generations of activists in a single organization. There were time-tested perspectives and norms, a rich pool of knowledge and political experience. Some of the older comrades seemed simply to be glad that they could still be part of a revolutionary movement that was being regenerated by an influx of young activists, whom they embraced with a perhaps too uncritical affection. Others seemed concerned that older revolutionary virtues of their own youth would be lost unless they (sometimes rigidly and imperiously) provided firm guidance, undergirded with long lectures and occasionally punctuated with fierce reprimands. But many of the veteran cadres maintained a balance, relating to the newer forces on a basis of genuine equality—patiently sharing their own knowledge, seeking to learn from new experience, encouraging the full development of the young comrades while frankly putting forward their own thinking on perspectives and directions for the SWP. On the whole, all these older comrades had considerable prestige.

Among the younger members there were many different qualities. There was a tremendous eagerness and vibrancy—sometimes a maddening "eager-beaver" enthusiasm and a youthful "we're-the-greatest" arrogance about the SWP and YSA, which alienated unsympathetic outsiders. Some took to copying the mannerisms of the prestigious elders—talking sagely about "the way we do things" even if they had been members for only twelve months, speaking about the experiences of bygone years (before they had been born) as if they had been participants, hewing sometimes rigidly (unlike many of the older comrades) to imperfectly assimilated orthodoxies. These jostled with the more rebellious spirits who saw no need to cease being outspoken mavericks simply because their rebelliousness had brought them into a revolutionary organization. This by itself guaranteed the flare-up of passionate, animated arguments—sometimes fed by one or another neurosis, and sometimes cohering around genuine political differences. There were also many who were more pragmatically inclined (sometimes interested in discussing ideas, sometimes not) who concentrated their energies more exclusively on working effectively in the mass movements and maintaining party institutions; theories, party history, and critical ideas were judged in more practical terms of how they seemed to advance the party's work in the here and now. The energies of all these young activists contributed to the movement's dynamism in the 1970s.

Much energy was certainly needed for the seemingly endless succession of weekly branch meetings, educationals, fraction and committee meetings, *Militant* sales, forums, activities of the mass movements, and so on that formed a way of life for many of us. This made the SWP an especially demanding environment for normal working people, students serious about their formal education, and those with families.

To many of us, the top leadership layer led by Jack Barnes seemed particularly impressive. As a group, they seemed steeped in the traditions of our movement but alive to new realities; confident in their own ideas but interested in the experiences and opinions of rank-and-file members; bright, patient, determined, open, knowledgeable, down-to-earth. Those within the party who would openly challenge them seemed, almost by definition, to be unserious, off base, destructive. For any critical idea to make sense, it would have to be formulated within a framework that was in harmony with that of our respected leaders; even then, there would be a tendency to question the validity of such an idea unless or until something similar was said by one of the top leaders. Their authority was on an equal plane with, and seemed inseparable from, the authority of the most prestigious older comrades and the authority of the revolutionary program itself. This contributed to a tendency toward conformism among those of us in the majority, a blunting of our inclination to think critically. Many assumed that the leadership would be coming to grips with whatever major questions there were, and some attempted to stay "on the inside track" by figuring out what the leaders thought and then adopting that as their own position. This was inconsistent with the tradition of Lenin, Trotsky, and Cannon, and it was inconsistent as well with the stated policy of the leadership—but the dynamic was strong, nonetheless.

As the 1970s wore on, there were a number of dramatic shifts in SWP activity that may have been too abrupt and extreme, often embarked on with much optimism and enthusiasm, but without sufficient evaluation of previous experience or consideration of complex realities. A standard practice of "drawing up a balance sheet" (i.e., reviewing an earlier projection, analyzing how successfully it was realized and why, and weighing the lessons learned in order to make intelligent future projections) tended to be abandoned. Often an extreme, out-of-balance push around one or another campaign would be justified by referring to a phrase that Lenin once used about "bending the stick too far in one direction in order to straighten it out." Some began to wonder, however, if too much of this might not weaken the stick. In any event, by the end of the decade, a clear tendency was developing that weakened the SWP's ability to evaluate its work (and leadership) critically.

In retrospect, some former members of the SWP have concluded that the late 1970s "turn to industry"—and especially the "turn within the turn" to get a majority of members industrial jobs—was a negative manifestation of this tendency. My own perception was different. The rising peer pressure to make this personal shift did have a negative effect on many party members who were unprepared or unable to "go into industry"; it tended to devalue other important spheres of work and even to create a sense of second-class (non-"proletarian") citizenship among comrades. This was destructive and perhaps avoidable. But for me the shift was helpful. The experience I gained in the shipbuilding and auto industries contributed substantially to my political (and personal) development, and this was also true for others. I believed that the indus-trial turn was essential for the health of the party. Not only would it reintegrate the SWP into the decisive sectors of the proletariat, enabling it to reach workers more effectively with socialist perspectives, but the new context would result in a political maturing—a deepened under-standing of American working-class life and social realities, a greater ability to think critically and to communicate with everyday working people—among the somewhat ingrown cadres. So it seemed to me at the time.

Yet many had expectations that were to prove disorienting. There was a notion that we only needed to "talk socialism to workers" within the context of the general decline of the capitalist economy and then, before too long, our past success in building a massive antiwar movement would be repeated (this time with revolutionary implications) in the industrial workplaces. The working class was rapidly moving to the center of U.S. politics, and the SWP was positioning itself to lead the workers to vic-tory before the end of the twentieth century.

It soon became clear, among those who dared to think, that reality was not conforming to this schema. That brutal fact provides a frame-work for understanding the crisis experienced by the SWP in the 1980s.

Reflections

The devastating crisis of American Trotskyism took a bizarre form. By 1980, the central leaders of the SWP, gathered around Jack Barnes, had concluded that the classic "Trotskyist" outlook could no longer be considered adequate. Instead, the political tendency represented by the Cuban Communist Party under Fidel Castro was seen as representing the revolutionary wave of the future. In part, this was precipitated by the 1979 revolutions in Iran and Nicaragua.

The Nicaraguan revolution, led by Castroist-influenced guerrilla fighters, the Sandinista National Liberation Front, took the SWP by surprise—the Sandinistas' defeat had been confidently predicted in the SWP's *Intercontinental Press* just weeks before their victory. This victory, and that of the New Jewel Movement in the tiny island of Grenada, seemed to fly in the face of the "orthodoxy" of the Leninist-Trotskyist Faction that the SWP leaders had headed in the recently concluded dis-pute in the Fourth International. Meanwhile, on the heels of the over-throw of the shah of Iran through the popular revolutionary upsurge spearheaded by the Islamic fundamentalist Khomeini (whom some SWP members perceived as being similar to Malcolm X), a substantial number of Iranian Trotskyists—after some years of living in the United States and working closely with the SWP—returned to their native land with considerable fanfare. When they attempted to implement the wonderful perspectives they had learned from the SWP, they were quickly destroyed as a political force.

Without discussion, the Barnes leadership rapidly phased out traditional political and theoretical perspectives of the Trotskyist movement (first of all, Trotsky's theory of permanent revolution) and introduced quite different ones associated with the Cuban Communist Party. The Fourth International was denigrated, and a hopeful projection was made about a "new international" that would be led by the Cuban Communist Party. Rather than participating in the work of the world Trotskyist movement, the SWP developed a network of small groups that were in the process of breaking away from sections of the Fourth International in a handful of countries. The party's democratic-centralist norms were also redefined, with a dramatically heightened centralism and a dramatically restricted democracy—all in the name of strengthening the SWP as a genuinely proletarian combat party.

Rather than becoming more activist, however, there was an abstention from a number of actually existing struggles and movements in the United States. Instead, the SWP concentrated on selling the *Militant* and Pathfinder literature, running increasingly narrow election campaigns, and sponsoring tours to Cuba.

In the early 1980s, there were several waves of expulsions of those who objected to these developments. These expulsions included the bulk of the old veterans from the decades preceding 1960, including some who had helped elevate Jack Barnes in order to guarantee the survival of American Trotskyism. Beyond those who were expelled, a majority of party members gradually resigned from the organization in demoralization, leaving perhaps 500 members by 1990. Finally, the *Militant*, in its May 17, 1991, issue, acknowledged some of what had happened:

> From 1979 on . . . accelerating divergences marked the course and character, on the one hand, of the SWP, the Communist League in Canada, and others, and on the other hand, the leadership bodies of the Fourth International.

These differences centered above all on a political assessment of the revolutionary victories in Grenada and Nicaragua, and the character of the workers' and farmers' governments established through those victories; the historical importance and weight of the communist leadership in Cuba and its political trajectory; and the necessity for communist forces the world over to decisively turn toward building parties that are proletarian in composition and leadership as well as program and perspectives.

At the end of the 1980s the Socialist Workers Party and the Communist Leagues of Australia, Britain, Canada, Iceland, New Zealand, and Sweden each decided to terminate their affiliation, whether fraternal or statutory, to the Fourth International.

Through their political work, internationalist collaboration, and place within communist continuity and tradition, these parties had in reality for some time already become communist organizations that no longer considered themselves Trotskyist and were separate from the world Trotskyist movement and its various competing parties and international groupings.

In the wake of the abandonment of American Trotskyism by the party that had been its fountainhead, there was no organized expression of this political tradition except for a few small fragments.

* * * * * * * * * * * * * *

The future turned out, as the future often does, to be more complicated than expected, both for the U.S. class struggle and for the American Trotskyist movement. For those to whom American Trotskyism has been at most peripheral—and also for those who were once inspired by its ideals and vision but have suffered disillusionment—this fifty-year history can be viewed as a sad or even silly story whose bottom line is this: "they failed."

They certainly did fail to become what they had hoped: a powerful working-class socialist movement capable of overthrowing capitalism and establishing a socialist democracy. Given what they were up against—the immense power of the strongest capitalist country in human history, the mighty conservative-reformist undercurrent that this has generated within the workers' movement, the awesome impact of Stalinism, and the terrible calamities of the twentieth century—that they failed is less surprising than that they were able to survive for any length of time. Other left-wing currents became hopelessly compromised and were essentially absorbed by capitalism or were pulled into the Stalinist dead end, or simply disintegrated. American Trotskyism was able to maintain itself, with a high degree of continuity and morale, for half a century, remaining true to its origins while being capable, at times, of relatively effective political activity.

The fortunes of a left-wing organization are intimately related to what is happening in the larger society: economic downturns and prosperity, the ebb and flow of discontent and combativeness among workers and oppressed groups, war and repression, and so on—factors over which such an organization can have little control, at least initially. Yet the manner in which the organization responds to its environment and, no less importantly, the qualities it brings to the activities it engages in, will determine its fortunes as it seeks to survive and grow.

A dispassionate look at the history of American Trotskyism from 1928 to 1978 suggests that it divides into two phases: the period from the beginning of the Great Depression to the post-World War II capitalist recovery (which saw a mighty rise and decline in the class militancy of the U.S. proletariat), and the period from the "new radicalization" of civil rights, antiwar, student, and feminist struggles to the sudden but in many ways muted crisis of the economy (which saw a comparatively modest upsurge in working-class combativeness in the 1970s).

In the first period of American Trotskyism, we see a predominantly working-class current, whose leadership was an organic part of an authentic tradition of U.S. labor radicalism. This leadership had been involved in a process through which some of the most vibrant qualities of that labor-radical tradition were fused with a relatively high quality of Marxist theory and experience emerging from the revolutionary movement of Russia. The result was American Communism. Although cut off, by 1928, from the small but vital and promising American Communist movement, the initial Trotskyist cadres had absorbed its best qualities into the very fiber of their being, and some of these qualities were strengthened by the same circumstances that forced them out of the Communist mainstream.

What were these qualities? There was a deep idealism blended with a determination to put the ideals into action and to struggle against oppression. There was an organizational and strategic sophistication, combined with a practical-minded "horse sense" and flexibility. There was a rootedness in the working class as it actually existed, integrated with a vision of what it could actually become. In addition to this, there was a certain kind of Marxism that provided an analytical framework capable of orienting them in a complex world: a sense of history as a long and contradictory process; a firm grasp of the struggle between classes and of the immense creativity and revolutionary potential of working people; a perspective on the structure and dynamics of capitalism, both as a world system and as an American reality; a practical political orientation in which the immediate struggles of workers and the oppressed are taken seriously in their own right but also related to and combined with the longer-term goal of socialist revolution; an understanding that the working class of any country must attain political independence from its own ruling class but must also make common cause with the workers' struggles of other countries. All this implies a programmatic perspective and, flowing from that, a particular organizational form and mode of operating within such an organization: principles take priority over personalities; comradeship includes critical-minded honesty; fundamental decisions must be made, carried out, evaluated, and—if necessary—altered *collectively*; individual initiative, within the agreed-upon programmatic framework, should be encouraged.

Regardless of complications and mistakes that inevitably crop up in human organizations, these qualities characterized the cadres of American Trotskyism's first period. To the extent that they were able to remain true to these qualities—which was to a far greater extent than the other left-wing currents of the time—the first and second generations of U.S. Trotskyists were able to accumulate substantial moral capital and invaluable experience in the 1930s and 1940s. Then came the "disruption"—the combined prosperity, repression, conformism, and quiescence of the first cold war decade—which deprived the movement, for all practical purposes, of its third generation. "We suffered terrible reverses," Cannon recalled. "We lost a lot of members in the fifties. . . . The persecution, the lack of response, the inactivity of the workers. People began falling away. Our biggest struggle in the whole cold war period was to hold our nucleus together." To a large extent, the aging cadres simply conducted a "holding operation"—holding on to the ideas and passions and visions and lessons, a kind of Marxism and revolutionary socialist orientation infused with the qualities we have mentioned, until they could once again become a force in the practical political struggles. "A revolutionist's spirit and attitude is not determined by the popular mood of the moment," Cannon argued. "We have a historical view and we don't allow the movement to fade away when it runs into changed times, which can happen as we know from experience."[93]

The second period of American Trotskyism was initiated as a fourth generation, emerging from a qualitatively different experience from that of the first and second generations; it flowed into and rejuvenated the movement. To a large extent, the new cadres were able to embrace and benefit from the invaluable resources that the veterans had been saving for them. But there was a difference. "I sometimes wonder," Cannon mused in his last year (1974), "whether our movement today, which is predominantly young, fully realizes where the power lies in this country. The power is in the working class."[94] Cannon was aware, obviously, that the new cadres understood this on a theoretical level, but a "full realization"—one that is part of the very fiber of your being—comes from life, and the life experience of the young Trotskyists had been profoundly dissimilar from that of the Trotskyist veterans. The environment and the struggles of the 1920s, 1930s, and 1940s were also profoundly dissimilar from those of the 1960s and early 1970s.

Even as the young revolutionaries began to flock into the labor movement at the end of Trotskyism's fifth decade, there was an unalterable difference between this and the earlier period, which militated against a reenactment of, for example, the Minneapolis teamsters experience. People like Skoglund and the Dunne brothers had been rooted and immersed in the Minneapolis working class and labor movement for many years, and they also had a considerable authority that cannot be conferred by a resolution or manifesto but only acquired over time. What's more, the leaders of their party in the 1930s included seasoned labor radicals. The situation of the late 1970s was not the same. Even though there seemed to be an unbroken continuity from 1928 through 1978, it remained to be seen how deep that continuity really was. Some chose to believe, as did George Novack, that the determined effort of the older generations of party leaders to ensure such continuity had been successful. But to accept this judgment, one would have to close one's eyes to the actual experience of the following decade.

At the same time, there were important acquisitions of experience and theory in the 1960s and 1970s. World events of the time—in Cuba and Vietnam, for example—facilitated a deeper understanding of the dynamics of imperialism and revolution. The struggles of African Americans, Hispanics, and other oppressed minorities, the youth radicalization and antiwar struggle, and the new wave of feminism not only provided new opportunities for practical work but also compelled revolutionaries to develop a deeper understanding of various aspects of capitalist oppression and of what ultimately would have to be a combining and interpenetration of the class struggle with insurgencies that did not originate from a strictly class basis and were in many cases rooted in racial, national, and sexual oppression. George Breitman in particular was able to grasp and give voice to these insights. There was also an awareness of the changing composition and structure of the working class. "One phenomenon that interests me," Cannon commented, "is the extraordinary development of union action among public workers. It's an entirely new phenomenon. And very widespread, very militant, and continuing."[95] There were, obviously, much-needed contributions that the new generation could provide as it sought to learn from the movement's veterans. It unquestionably made genuine contributions in helping to bring a profound political-cultural change in U.S. society, a new consciousness but also important reforms that altered institutions and policies of the powerful. The question was whether this experience could be integrated into the theoretical-programmatic framework of the SWP's Marxism, and whether the party could at the same time adjust to the shifting realities and challenges of the new decade.

Of course, the 1980s would not only test the revolutionaries of the "1960s generation" and the Trotskyist movement as a whole, but would also provide remarkable new experiences from which additional lessons must be learned. "I don't merely get impatient with Johnny-come-latelies who just arrived from nowhere and announce that they know it all, I get impatient even with old-timers who think they have nothing more to learn," Cannon said in 1966. "The world is changing. New problems arise, new complexities, new complications confront the revolutionary movement at every step. The condition for effective political leadership is that the leaders themselves continue to learn and grow. That means: not to lose their modesty altogether." It could be argued that the party *did*, to a large degree, lose its modesty—and was astonished to find itself floundering in the complex realities of the late 1970s and 1980s. The mix of activist-pragmatism and Trotskyist "orthodoxy" was no longer working, and the new party leadership reacted by curtailing the activism, changing the old Trotskyist "orthodoxy" for a new Castroist "orthodoxy," and instituting an extremely rigid, top-down interpretation of "Leninist" organizational functioning. Cannon felt that the party leadership even in the 1960s was moving in the wrong direction by utilizing tightened organizational norms to ensure political stability. "As far as I can see all the new moves and proposals to monkey with the [SWP] Constitution which has served the party so well in the past, with the aim of 'tightening' centralization, represent a trend in the wrong direction at the present time," he complained. "The party (and the YSA) is too 'tight' already, and if we go much further along this line we can run the risk of strangling the party to death."[96]

The relevance of all this, however, hinges on whether or not the project of the American Trotskyists actually makes sense: organizing for a working-class revolution that will bring socialism to the United States. In his last year, in a discussion with a YSA comrade, Cannon indicated one reason that he thought it still did—that with the existence of nuclear weapons,

> there's a danger that the human race may not continue, it's got to take control of its own social system and reorganize it and plan and eliminate the constant day-to-day danger of annihilation. . . . We're not going to say it's an easy thing to do. It's a lifetime job for each and every one of us. But the thing that inspires one's life and makes it worth living in the face of all this calamitous danger everywhere, uncertainties and insecurity, is to commit yourself to an effort to change it. And not to belittle yourself and think you don't count. You may be the decisive factor.[97]

The desirability of a socialist democracy is not the same as the possibility of actually achieving it. When Cannon asserted, in a 1974 interview about a month before he died, that "capitalism is plunging toward its climactic end," Sidney Lens challenged: "Didn't you say that in the thirties?" Cannon confessed: "I did, yes." Lens pursued, "and in the forties?" "And in the forties." Lens was moved to chide: "I mean, that must sound like something peculiar when you say it every decade." To which Cannon responded: "But when you stop to think, the history of humanity is a very long one, isn't it? And a quarter of a century is only an instant in the history of the human race." Not one to be satisfied with a cosmic view, he added: "I see one crisis piling upon another. I don't think the capitalists have ever been in a jam in this country as they are right now, both politically and economically." In any event, he remained convinced that the necessary transition to socialism "will not take place automatically. It requires the intervention of those who are conscious of the great historical necessity and are capable of explaining it to others, until a sufficient number of workers acquire the same consciousness and act accordingly in a socialist revolution."[98]

The extent to which any of this makes sense will in the first instance be determined by each individual, and in the last instance by the unfolding future. This means that the ultimate meaning of American Trotskyism's history can be found in the future. Of course, the way the future unfolds will be determined through the conclusions drawn and the actions taken by individuals, some of whom may have something of value to learn from the history of American Trotskyism.

Appendix: Membership Figures

Figures given here indicate only formal membership in the Communist League of America (1929–35), the Workers Party of the United States (1935–36), and the Socialist Workers Party (1938–81). Membership requirements included basic agreement with the political program, payment of dues, and agreement to be a politically active and disciplined member of the organization. Thus, these figures generally represent actual cadres rather than "paper members." Not included are sympathizers and supporters—some of whom may have been quite active—in the often substantial periphery of these organizations. Thus, for example, the formal membership of the SWP in 1946 was 1,470, although the size of the Trotskyist movement at this time has been estimated to be twice that. Also not recorded here are those who were members only of youth groups: the Spartacus Youth League and the Young Peoples Socialist League (Fourth International) in the 1930s, or the Young Socialist Alliance in the 1960s and 1970s. The YSA, for example, had 124 members in 1960 and reached a high point of 1,881 in 1975; many were members of the SWP as well and are therefore recorded under that designation, but the size of the movement was still larger than these figures indicate.[99]

YEAR	MEMBERSHIP
1929	100
1932	429
1935	700 (after CLA-AWP fusion)
1936	500–600 (after Oehlerite schism)
1938	1,520 (after expulsion from Socialist Party)
1940	1,095
1942	645 (after Shachtmanite schism)
1944	840
1946	1,470
1948	1,277
1950	825
1952	758
1954	480 (after Cochranite schism)
1957	434
1959	399
1960	518
1963	582
1966	497 (after Wohlforth and Robertson schisms)
1969	520
1972	892
1974	1,140
1976	1,019 (after Internationalist Tendency schism)
1981	1,250

Notes

I have been fortunate, in revising this account of the history of U.S. Trotskyism, to be able to consult with representatives of three generations of that movement—Morris Lewit (Stein), Frank Lovell, and Evelyn Sell. Each of these comrades (who are also valued friends) helped me correct errors and in more ways than one enrich this account. Alan Wald—like me, part of the fourth generation—also gave it a critical reading that was similarly helpful. The responsibility for any inaccuracies that remain, as well as for general interpretation, is mine.

1.   George Novack, "Fifty Years of American Trotskyism," *International Socialist Review*, November 1978, p. 5. The best-known histories of the subject are James P. Cannon, *History of American Trotskyism* (New York: Pathfinder Press,

1972), focusing on internal history and bringing the story to 1938; Tim Wohlforth's factional and highly polemical *The Struggle for Marxism in the United States* (New York: Labor Publications, 1971); and a hostile account, full of errors in scholarship, by Constance Ashton Myers, *The Prophet's Army: The American Trotskyists, 1928–1941* (Westport, CT: Greenwood Press, 1977). Most recent is the more broadly focused study by Robert J. Alexander, *International Trotskyism, 1929–1985, a Documented Analysis of the Movement* (Durham, NC: Duke University Press, 1991), a truly massive volume that contains the equivalent of a book-length history of U.S. Trotskyism. The works by Cannon and Alexander are best.

2. Although much new and valuable scholarship is available on this early period of U.S. labor history, it is still worth consulting some of the standard old accounts: Friedrich Sorge, *Labor Movement in the United States* (Westport, CT: Greenwood Press, 1977); Morris Hillquit, *History of Socialism in the United States* (New York: Dover, 1971); and Philip S. Foner, *History of the Labor Movement in the United States*, 9 vols. (New York: International Publishers, 1947–91). An essential source is Paul Buhle, Mari Jo Buhle, and Dan Georgakas, *Encyclopedia of the American Left* (Urbana: University of Illinois Press, 1992).

3. Christopher Lasch, *Agony of the American Left* (New York: Vintage Books, 1969), p. 35. Among the most useful studies of this movement are Jessie Wallace Hughan, *American Socialism of the Present Day* (New York: John Lane, 1911); John Graham, ed., *"Yours for the Revolution": The Appeal to Reason, 1895–1922* (Lincoln: University of Nebraska Press, 1990); Joyce Kornbluh, ed., *Rebel Voices, an IWW Anthology* (Chicago: Charles H. Kerr, 1988); Stewart Bird, Dan Georgakas, and Deborah Shaffer, eds., *Solidarity Forever, an Oral History of the IWW* (Chicago: Lake View Press, 1985); Ray Ginger, *Eugene V. Debs: A Biography* (New York: Collier Books, 1962); Ira Kipnis, *The American Socialist Movement, 1891–1912* (New York: Monthly Review Press, 1972); James Weinstein, *The Decline of Socialism in America, 1912–1925* (New York: Monthly Review Press, 1967); Nick Salvatore, *Eugene V. Debs, Citizen and Socialist* (Urbana: University of Illinois Press, 1982).

4. Richard Hofstadter, *The American Political Tradition* (New York: Vintage Books, 1974), p. 289; for an excellent analysis of what Franklin D. Roosevelt represented, see pp. 410–59. On the conservative strand in the Progressive era reforms, see James Weinstein, *The Corporate Ideal in the Liberal State, 1900–1918* (Boston: Beacon Press, 1969). Despite certain analytical-theoretical limitations, a helpful overview of U.S. history is provided by Howard Zinn, *A People's History of the United States* (New York: Harper & Row, 1980).

5. Valuable for its understanding of the vitality of 1920s U.S. Communism is Mike Goldfield's essay "Recent Historiography of the Communist Party, U.S.A.," in Mike Davis, Fred Pfeil, Michael Sprinker, eds., *The Year Left, an American Socialist Yearbook* (London: Verso, 1985). This also comes through in Emily Turnbull and James Robertson, eds., *James P. Cannon and the Early Years*

of American Communism (New York: Prometheus Research Library, 1992). Key sources on the origins and early years of U.S. communism are still Theodore Draper's *The Roots of American Communism* (New York: Viking Press, 1957) and *American Communism and Soviet Russia* (New York: Viking Press, 1960), and James P. Cannon, *The First Ten Years of American Communism* (New York: Lyle Stuart, 1962).

6.   On Communist trade union activity, see Philip Foner's *The T.U.E.L. to the End of the Compers Era*, vol. 9 of his series cited in note 2. On communism and radicalism among African Americans, see Theodore G. Vincent, ed., *Voices of a Black Nation: Political Journalism in the Harlem Renaissance* (San Francisco: Ramparts Press, 1973); Harry Haywood, *Black Bolshevik, Autobiography of an Afro-American Communist* (Chicago: Liberator Press, 1978); and Philip S. Foner and James S. Allen, eds., *American Communism and Black Americans, a Documentary History, 1919–1929* (Philadelphia: Temple University Press, 1987).

Some information on women and "the woman question" in the Communist movement of this period can be gleaned from Vera Buch Weisbord, *A Radical Life* (Bloomington: Indiana University Press, 1977), and Peggy Dennis, *The Autobiography of an American Communist, a Personal View of a Political Life, 1925–1975* (Westport, CT: Lawrence Hill, 1977), pp. 22–26, 35–37, 41–42, 56–57; also see Theresa Wolfson, *The Woman Worker and the Trade Unions* (New York: International Publishers, 1926).

On Communist Party intellectual and cultural life in the 1920s, see Joseph Freeman, *An American Testament* (New York: Farrar and Rinehart, 1936), and Daniel Aaron, *Writers on the Left, Episodes in American Literary Communism* (New York: Harcourt, Brace and World, 1961). The quote from Harry Haywood appears in *Black Bolshevik*, p. 120.

7.   Cannon, *History of American Trotskyism*, pp. 13–14.

8.   John Reed's classic *Ten Days that Shook the World* is available in many editions and should be read, among other things, as a primary source for understanding early U.S. Communism. Also relevant in this regard are Granville Hicks, *John Reed, the Making of a Revolutionary* (New York: Macmillan, 1936), pp. 268–402, and Robert A. Rosenstone, *Romantic Revolutionary, a Biography of John Reed* (New York: Alfred A. Knopf, 1975), pp. 278–382. Philip S. Foner, ed., *The Bolshevik Revolution, Its Impact on American Radicals, Liberals, and Labor* (New York: International Publishers, 1967), highlights the centrality of the Russian Revolution for the bulk of the U.S. Left.

On the central importance of the Communist International, and the Comintern of the Russian Communist Party, for U.S. Communists, see the works by Cannon and Draper cited in note 5. On the history of the Communist International, see Helmut Gruber, ed., *International Communism in the Era of Lenin* (Greenwich, CT: Fawcett, 1967), and *Soviet Russia Masters the Comintern: International Communism in the Era of Stalin's Ascendancy* (Garden City, NY: Anchor Books, 1974), plus C. L. R. James, *World Revolution 1917–1936, the Rise and Fall of the Communist International* (Atlantic Highlands, NJ: Humanities Press, 1993). Also important are certain key works by Trotsky: *The History of the Russian Revolution*, 3 vols. in one (New York: Simon & Schuster, 1936); *The First Five Years of the Communist International*, 2 vols. (New York: Monad Press, 1972); *The Third International After Lenin* (New York: Pathfinder Press, 1970).

9. Dennis, *The Autobiography of an American Communist*, pp. 34, 70. The first accurate account in English of the beginnings of Stalinism was by a U.S. sympathizer of Trotsky, Max Eastman, in his classic *Since Lenin Died* (London: Labour Publishing, 1925); also see Eastman's memoir *Love and Revolution* (New York: Random House, 1964).

10. Novack, "Fifty Years of American Trotskyism," p. 5; Dianne Feeley, "Antoinette Konikow: Marxist and Feminist," *International Socialist Review*, January 1972; Cannon, *History of American Trotskyism*, p. 79; Turnbull and Robertson, *James P. Cannon*, pp. 559–60.

11. Alan Wald, *The New York Intellectuals, the Rise and Decline of the Anti-Stalinist Left from the 1930s to the 1980s* (Chapel Hill: University of North Carolina Press, 1987), p. 173. Wald's study contains useful information on both Cannon and Shachtman, plus other matters. A full-scale biography of Shachtman is now available: Peter Drucker, *Max Shachtman and His Left: A Socialist's Odyssey through the "American Century"* (Atlantic Highlands, NJ: Humanities Press, 1993). A study of Cannon's life is being prepared by Bryan Palmer.

12. Julius Jacobson, "The Two Deaths of Max Shachtman," *New Politics* 10 no. 2 (Winter 1973): 96, 97.

13. Les Evans, ed., *James P. Cannon as We Knew Him, by Thirty-Three Comrades, Friends and Relatives* (New York: Pathfinder Press, 1976), p. 108. The material in this volume constitutes an invaluable source.

14. Jacobson, "The Two Deaths," p. 96.

15. George Novack in Evans, *James P. Cannon as We Knew Him*, p. 30; Farrell quoted in Alan Wald, *James T. Farrell: The Revolutionary Socialist Years* (New York: New York University Press, 1978), p. 140; Lewis Coser, "Sects and Sectarians," *Dissent*, Autumn 1954, pp. 363, 365; Dwight Macdonald, "Trotskyism II: Revolution Ltd.," in *Politics Past, Essays in Political Criticism* (New York: Viking Press, n.d.; published as *Memoirs of a Revolutionist* in 1957), pp. 282–83. Cannon's *Letters from Prison* (New York: Merit Publishers, 1968) contains much of interest; his letter on C. Wright Mills and other matters can be found in *Bulletin in Defense of Marxism*, no. 100, November–December 1992.

16. Morris Chertov in Evans, *James P. Cannon as We Knew Him*, pp. 101, 103.

17. Michael Harrington, *Fragments of the Century, a Social Autobiography* (New York: Saturday Review Press/E. P. Dutton, 1973), p. 72.

18. Drucker, *Max Shachtman and His Left*, p. 43.

19. James and Grace Lee Boggs, Freddy and Lyman Paine, *Conversations in Maine, Exploring Our Nation's Future* (Boston: South End Press, 1978), pp. 281–82.

20. Farrell Dobbs in Evans, *James P. Cannon as We Knew Him*, p. 40.

21. Cannon, *History of American Trotskyism*, pp. 65–66, 102.

22. Max Shachtman, "Radicalism in the Thirties: The Trotskyist View," in Rita James Simon, ed., *As We Saw the Thirties* (Urbana: University of Illinois Press, 1967), pp. 22–24. Essential materials on the CLA are Cannon's writings from 1928 through 1934, in *The Left Opposition in the U.S. 1928–31*, ed. Fred Stanton (New York: Monad Press, 1981), and *The Communist League of America 1932–34*, ed. Fred Stanton and Michael Taber (New York: Monad Press, 1985).

23. Much of the material that the Trotskyists published at this time can be found in *Leon Trotsky on China* (New York: Monad Press, 1976), and *The Struggle against Fascism in Germany* (New York: Pathfinder Press, 1971). Another essential work of this period was Trotsky's *The Permanent Revolution* (New York: Pathfinder Press, 1978). Important materials can also be found in Will Reisner, ed., *Documents of the Fourth International, the Formative Years (1933–1940)* (New York: Pathfinder Press, 1973), and Tom Barrett, ed., *The Fourth International: Fifty Years* (New York: Fourth Internationalist Tendency, 1990), especially essays by Max Shachtman, George Breitman, and Ernest Mandel.

24. Novack, "Fifty Years of American Trotskyism," p. 6; Sidney Lens, *Unrepentant Radical, an American Activist's Account of Five Turbulent Decades* (Boston: Beacon Press, 1980), p. 29. Paul Jacobs's autobiography *Is Curly Jewish?* (New York: Random House, 1965), pp. 44–60, includes a view of ethnic-related culture clash within the Trotskyist movement of the early 1930s.

25. David Milton, *The Politics of U.S. Labor* (New York: Monthly Review Press, 1982), p. 52; Thomas R. Brooks, *Toil and Trouble, a History of American Labor* (New York: Dell, 1971), pp. 166, 167; Cannon, *History of American Trotskyism*, pp. 147–48.

26. Milton, *Politics of U.S. Labor*, pp. 62, 144. The most thorough account of the Minneapolis teamsters under Trotskyist leadership is Farrell Dobbs's four-volume work *Teamster Rebellion* (New York: Monad Press, 1972), *Teamster Power* (New York: Monad Press, 1973), *Teamster Politics* (New York: Monad Press, 1975), and *Teamster Bureaucracy* (New York: Monad Press, 1977). Still worth reading is Charles Rumford Walker, *American City, a Rank-and-File History* (New York: Farrar and Rinehart, 1937), providing a historical sketch of Minneapolis and a detailed account of the 1934 strike.

27. Cannon, *History of American Trotskyism*, pp. 141, 154–55. On Muste and the "Musteites," see Nat Hentoff, ed., *The Essays of A. J. Muste* (New York: Simon and Schuster, 1970); Jo Anne Ooiman Robinson, *Abraham Went Out, a Biography of A. J. Muste* (Philadelphia: Temple University Press, 1981); Sam Pollack, "A. J., the Musteites and the Unions," *Liberation*, September/October 1967; Margaret R. Budenz, *Streets* (Huntingdon, IN: Our Sunday Visitor, 1979), pp. 92–156; Sidney Hook, *Out of Step, an Unquiet Life in the 20th Century* (New York: Harper & Row, 1987), pp. 190–207. The substantial efforts of Musteites and Trotskyists in the unemployed movement of the early 1930s—reflected in

Franklin Folsom, *Impatient Armies of the Poor, the Story of Collective Action of the Unemployed 1808–1942* (Niwot, CO: University Press of Colorado, 1991), pp. 340–54, 408–13, 417–20—was also a factor in paving the way for the merger.

28. A. J. Muste, "The Workers Party Is Founded," *New International*, December 1934, p. 129.

29. Novack, "Fifty Years of American Trotskyism," p. 6. Regarding Muste's departure, see Novack's reminiscence, "A. J. and American Trotskyism," *Liberation*, September/October 1967.

30. Among the valuable sources on this period are Victor Serge, *Memoirs of a Revolutionist* (London: Writers and Readers, 1984); two collections of Trotsky's writings, *Leon Trotsky on France* (New York: Monad Press, 1979) and *The Spanish Revolution 1931–39* (New York: Pathfinder Press, 1973); E. H. Carr, *Twilight of the Comintern* (New York: Pantheon Books, 1982); Pierre Broue and Emile Temime, *The Revolution and Civil War in Spain* (Cambridge, MA: MIT Press, 1970).

 For different approaches on the U.S. Communist Party in this period, see: Harvey Klehr, *The Heyday of American Communism: The Depression Decade* (New York: Basic Books, 1984), and Michael E. Brown, Randy Martin, Frank Rosengarten, and George Snedeker, eds., *New Studies in the Politics and Culture of U.S. Communism* (New York: Monthly Review Press, 1993).

31. See Isaac Deutscher, *The Prophet Outcast, Trotsky: 1929–1940* (New York: Vintage Books, 1965), pp. 257–509, and also *The Case of Leon Trotsky* (New York: Merit Publishers, 1968). Trotsky's 1937 classic analysis of the Russian Revolution's bureaucratic degeneration—*The Revolution Betrayed, What Is the Soviet Union and Where Is It Going?* (New York: Pathfinder Press, 1972)—sheds light on these developments as well and had an obvious impact on perspectives of his cothinkers in the United States.

32. Novack, "Fifty Years of American Trotskyism," pp. 6–7. The subsequent evolution of the Socialist Party is discussed in David Shannon, *The Socialist Party of America* (Chicago: Quadrangle Books, 1978), pp. 227–68, and Frank A. Warren, *An Alternative Vision: The Socialist Party in the 1930s* (Bloomington: University of Indiana Press, 1974). Another competing current on the Left that experienced an even more drastic decline was the Communist Party (Opposition), later renamed the Independent Labor League, which dissolved in 1941. Also known as the Lovestoneites (after their leader Jay Lovestone), they were expelled from the American Communist Party in 1929—after they themselves had presided over the expulsion of the Trotskyists—and for a time represented a significant left-wing force. See Robert J. Alexander, *The Right Opposition: The Lovestoneites and the International Communist Opposition of the 1930s* (Westport, CT: Greenwood Press, 1981). The social democratic Socialists and the former Lovestoneites adopted a perspective of moderate labor reformism and by the late 1940s were contributing substantially to the cold war anticommunist crusade, many of them finding employment with

the U.S. Department of State (giving rise to the term "State Department socialists").

33.   The general trade union concentration is mentioned by George Breitman in "Answers to Questions," in George Breitman, ed., *The Founding of the Socialist Workers Party, Minutes and Resolutions 1938–39* (New York: Pathfinder Press, 1982), p. 27; general information of value, plus comments relating to early work in the maritime industry, can be found in Tom Kerry, *Workers, Bosses, and Bureaucrats, a Socialist View of Labor Struggles since the 1930s* (New York: Pathfinder Press, 1980): some factional snapshots relating to trade union work in the auto industry can be found in George Clarke, "The Truth about the Auto Crisis," in James P. Cannon, George Clarke, Leon Trotsky, and Fred Feldman, *Background to "The Struggle for a Proletarian Party"* (New York: Education for Socialists, National Education Department, Socialist Workers Party, 1979), pp. 21–34.

34.   James's discussions with Trotsky, the resolutions he wrote, plus other useful material can be found in George Breitman, ed., *Leon Trotsky on Black Nationalism and Self-Determination* (New York: Merit Publishers, 1967). Also see informative essays about and by James, focusing on this period, in Scott McLemee and Paul Le Blanc, eds., *C. L. R. James and Revolutionary Marxism, Selected Writings 1939–1949* (Atlantic Highlands, NJ: Humanities Press, 1993).

35.   Shachtman, "Radicalism in the Thirties," p. 42. Alan Wald's works *The New York Intellectuals, the Rise and Fall of the Anti-Stalinist Left* and *James T. Farrell: The Revolutionary Socialist Years*—cited in notes 11 and 15—are essential. Also see his fascinating study *The Revolutionary Imagination: The Poetry and Politics of John Wheelwright and Sherry Mangan* (Durham: University of North Carolina Press, 1983) and some of the pieces in his collection *The Responsibility of Intellectuals, Selected Essays on Marxist Traditions in Cultural Commitment* (Atlantic Highlands, NJ: Humanities Press, 1992).

36.   Irving Howe, *A Margin of Hope, an Intellectual Autobiography* (New York: Harcourt Brace Jovanovich, 1982), pp. 53, 57.

37.   Novack, "Fifty Years of American Trotskyism," pp. 7–8.

38.   Ibid., p. 8. Trotsky's *In Defense of Marxism* (New York: Pathfinder Press, 1970) and Cannon's *The Struggle for a Proletarian Party* (New York: Pathfinder Press, 1972) remain classics of the Trotskyist movement and contain, as appendices, major documents giving the Shachtmanites' side of the story. Also see Cannon, Clarke, Trotsky, and Feldman, *Background to "Struggle for a Proletarian Party,"* cited in note 33, and Joseph Hansen, *The Abern Clique* (New York: Education for Socialists, National Education Department, Socialist Workers Party, 1972). Also see Paul Le Blanc, "From Revolutionary Intellectual to Conservative Master-Thinker: The Anti-Democratic Odyssey of James Burnham," *Left History* 3, no 1 (Spring 1995).

On the evolution of the Shachtmanites by one who was a Shachtmanite, see Stan Weir, "Requiem for Max Shachtman," *Radical American* 7, no. 1

(1973), as well as the essay by Jacobson cited in note 12; also see Maurice Isserman, *If I Had a Hammer . . . The Death of the Old Left and the Birth of the New Left* (New York: Basic Books, 1987), pp. 37–75, and Peter Drucker's biography of Shachtman cited in note 11. Valuable information can be found in Paul Buhle, ed., *The Legacy of the Workers Party, 1940–1949: Recollections and Reflections* (New York: New York University Libraries, Tamiment Institute/ Ben Josephson Library, 1985), and Milton Fisk, *Socialism from Below in the United States: The Origins of the International Socialist Organization* (Cleveland, OH: ISO/Hera Press, 1977). Also see Harvey Swados's fictional portrait of the Shachtmanites in *Standing Fast* (Garden City, NY: Doubleday, 1970), and Hal Draper's selected essays in *Socialism from Below*, ed. E. Haberkern (Atlantic Highlands, NJ: Humanities Press, 1993).

39.   James P. Cannon, *Socialism on Trial* (New York: Pathfinder Press, 1973), pp. 51–52.

40.   See Ernest Mandel, *The Meaning of the Second World War* (London: Verso, 1986); William Appleman Williams, *The Tragedy of American Diplomacy* (New York: Dell, 1972); Walter LaFeber, *America, Russia and the Cold War 1945– 1980* (New York: John Wiley & Sons, 1980); Barton J. Bernstein, ed., *Politics and Policies of the Truman Administration* (New York: New Viewpoints, 1974); Bert Cochran, *Harry Truman and the Crisis Presidency* (New York: Funk & Wagnalls, 1973); Noam Chomsky, *American Power and the New Mandarins, Historical and Political Essays* (New York: Vintage Books, 1969).

41.   The trial is the focus of Farrell Dobbs, *Teamster Bureaucracy*, cited in note 26. A transcript of Cannon's trial testimony, plus a critique of SWP trial strategy by Grandizo Munis and a defense by Cannon, can be found in *Socialism on Trial*, cited in note 39. Also see Albert Goldman, *In Defense of Socialism* (New York: Pioneer Publishers, 1944); James T. Farrell, *Who Are the 18 Prisoners in the Minnepolis Labor Case?* (New York: Civil Rights Defense Committee, 1944); and Socialist Workers Party, *Why We Are in Prison: Farewell Speeches of the 18 SWP and 544—CIO Minneapolis Prisoners* (New York: Pioneer Publishers, 1944).

42.   James R. Green, *The World of the Worker, Labor in Twentieth-Century America* (New York: Wang & Hill, 1980), p. 185. A vivid picture of working-class life and struggle in this period is conveyed in Harriet Arnow's novel *The Dollmaker* (New York: Avon Books, 1972), and some of the "rising expectations" are suggested in James Gilbert, *Another Chance, Postwar America 1945–1985* (Chicago: Dorsey Press, 1986), and in a lively contemporary work, sympathetic to the Communist Party, by Elizabeth Hawes, *Hurry Up Please, It's Time* (New York: Reynal & Hitchcock, 1946). Another fine novel giving a sense of post-World War II hopes of the Left, and the bitter disappointments that followed, can be found in K. B. Gilden, *Between the Hills and the Sea* (Ithaca, NY: ILR Press, Cornell University Press, 1989). Also of interest is George Lipsitz, *Rainbow at Midnight: Labor and Culture in the 1940s* (Urbana: University of Illinois Press, 1994).

African American ferment is indicated in Daniel Guerin, *Negroes on the March, a Frenchman's Report on the American Negro Struggle*, trans. and ed. Duncan Ferguson (New York: George L. Weissman, 1956); C. Van Woodward, *The Strange Career of Jim Crow*, 3d ed. (New York: Oxford University Press, 1974), pp. 111–47; Manning Marable, *Race, Reform and Rebellion: The Second Reconstruction in Black America, 1945–1982* (Jackson: University Press of Mississippi, 1984), pp. 12–41; Jervis Anderson, *A. Philip Randolph, a Biographical Portrait* (New York: Harcourt Brace Jovanovich, 1974), pp. 241–95; Martin Bauml Duberman, *Paul Robeson, a Biography* (New York: Ballantine Books, 1989), pp. 296–311; and the materials from 1944 through 1947 in Philip S. Foner, ed., *W. E. B. Du Bois Speaks, Speeches and Addresses 1920–1963* (New York: Pathfinder Press, 1970), pp. 124–227, plus Gerald Horne's *Red and Black, W. E. B. Du Bois and the Afro-American Response to the Cold War, 1944–1963* (Albany: State University of New York Press, 1986), pp. 1–82.

43. Novack, "Fifty Years of American Trotskyism," p. 8. On SWP coverage of African American struggles from 1939 to 1945, see Fred Stanton, ed., *Fighting Racism in World War II* (New York: Monad Press, 1980). Also see Edgar Keemer, *Confessions of a Pro-Life Abortionist* (Detroit: Vinco Press, 1980); material by and about Larry Stewart in Paul Le Blanc, ed., *Revolutionary Principles and Working-Class Democracy* (New York: Fourth Internationalist Tendency, 1992), pp. 298–323; information on Clifton DeBerry in Nelson Blackstock, *COINTELPRO, the FBI's Secret War on Political Freedom* (New York: Vintage Books, 1975), pp. 67–75; Charles Denby, *Indignant Heart, a Black Worker's Journal* (Boston: South End Press, 1978); James Boggs, *The American Revolution, Pages from a Negro Worker's Notebook* (New York: Monthly Review, 1963). Joe Morgan, Milton Richardson, Ernie Dillard, and Louise Simpson are mentioned in Richard Fraser, "A Letter to American Trotskyists: Too Little, Too Late (Memorandum on the Problems of Building a Revolutionary Party)," in *In Memoriam, Richard S. Fraser, an Appreciation and Selection of His Work* (New York: Prometheus Research Library, 1990), pp. 89, 90.

44. The Goldman-Morrow analysis of world realities is capably presented in Peter Jenkins, *Where Trotskyism Got Lost: World War Two and the Prospects for Socialism in Europe* (Nottingham, England: Spokesman, 1977). Goldman's attack on "Cannonism" and his decision to join the Shachtmanites are laid out in Albert Goldman, *The Question of Unity* (Long Island, NY: Workers Party Publishing, 1947). See Alan Wald's *The New York Intellectuals* and *James T. Farrell: The Revolutionary Socialist Years*, cited above in notes 11 and 15, for additional information. Invaluable material on this dispute, and on many other matters, can be found in Cannon's writings from 1940 through 1947, in the following: *The Socialist Workers Party in World War II*, ed. Les Evans (New York: Pathfinder Press, 1975); *Letters from Prison* (New York: Merit Publishers, 1968); and *The Struggle for Socialism in the "American Century,"* ed. Les Evans (New York: Pathfinder Press, 1977).

45. Art Preis, *Labor's Giant Step* (New York: Pathfinder Press, 1972), pp. 282–83. Preis's book remains one of the classics on the U.S. labor movement for the decades of the 1930s, 1940s, and 1950s.

46. Novack, "Fifty Years of American Trotskyism," p. 8; James P. Cannon, *The Struggle for Socialism in the "American Century"*, pp. 265, 271, 281, 304.

47. The best single account of these matters can be found in David Caute, *The Great Fear: The Anti-Communist Purge under Truman and Eisenhower* (New York: Simon & Schuster, 1978). The destruction of the Communist Party's base in the labor movement is analyzed in Bert Cochran, *Labor and Communism, the Conflict that Shaped American Unions* (Princeton, NJ: Princeton University Press, 1977), pp. 248–344. Other aspects of the destruction of the party are treated in Joseph R. Starobin, *American Communism in Crisis, 1943–1957* (Berkeley: University of California Press, 1972), pp. 121–223; George Charney, *A Long Journey* (Chicago: Quadrangle Books, 1968), pp. 135–244; and Ellen Schrecker, "McCarthyism and the Decline of American Communism," in Brown et al., *New Studies in the Politics and Culture of U.S. Communism*, pp. 123–40.

48. A thorough account of this case is provided in James Kutcher, *The Case of the Legless Veteran* (New York: Pathfinder Press, 1973). The Kutcher case is presented in context in Bud Schultz and Ruth Schultz, eds., *It Did Happen Here, Recollections of Political Repression in America* (Berkeley: University of California Press, 1989), pp. 175–81.

49. Novack, "Fifty Years of American Trotskyism," p. 9. Problems in the SWP having to do with racial tensions are touched on in Fraser, "Letter to American Trotskyists," pp. 88–90, and Denby, *Indignant Heart*, pp. 166–74. The French writer Daniel Guerin also makes reference to this, writing: "During World War II . . . the SWP remained faithful to the Negro cause. . . . At a time when every other political organization, the CP above all, tried to subordinate the Negro struggle to the war effort, the SWP filled a real vacuum and stood out conspicuously. . . . If I have certain personal reservations on the position of the SWP in the anti-discrimination struggle inside the Seafarer's International Union, AFL, as well as on the very delicate problem of mixed marriage among party members, and in general on its understanding of the psychology of the Negro, I wish nevertheless to say that these reservations concern only questions of tactics." Guerin, *Negroes on the March*, pp. 131–32. According to Fraser, there were deep tensions around interracial dating and marriage—with some party leaders actively opposing such things, and some members pushing against such pressures as they went ahead to date or marry across racial lines. The National Committee, under Cannon's leadership, took a clear position in 1949 that the SWP was not opposed to interracial marriage, but in Fraser's view, "the damage . . . had already been done. It was just too little and just too late" (p. 90). In contrast, interracial dating and marriage among SWPers were not uncommon in the 1960s and 1970s.

A detailed examination of the Johnson-Forest split and trajectory is provided in my introductory essay to McLemee and Le Blanc, C. L. *R. James and Revolutionary Marxism*. For impressive samples of decades' worth of James's and Dunayevskaya's writings, see Anna Grimshaw, *The C. L. R. James Reader* (Oxford: Blackwell Publishers, 1993), and Raya Dunayevskaya, *Women's Liberation and the Dialectics of Revolution* (Atlantic Highlands, NJ: Humanities Press, 1985).

50.   The summary of what some Cochranites thought is in Al Hansen's introduction to James P. Cannon, *Speeches to the Party* (New York: Pathfinder Press, 1973), p. 14. The quotes from the Cochranite document are from pp. 347, 358, and 367 in the same volume, which reprints the 1953 document.

Conflicting accounts of the split in the Fourth International can be found in Pierre Frank, *The Fourth International* (London: Ink Links, 1979), pp. 80–110; Parti Communiste Internationaliste, *The Lessons of Our History*, English translation of supplement to *La Verite*, no. 548, 1970 (Paris: P.C.I., n.d.), pp. 53–88; Cliff Conner, Les Evans, and Tom Kerry, *Towards a History of the Fourth International: Three Contributions on Postwar Developments* (New York: Education for Socialists, National Education Department, Socialist Workers Party, 1973); and Joseph Hansen, *James P. Cannon, the Internationalist* (New York: Education for Socialists, National Education Department, Socialist Workers Party, 1980).

51.   Two of Cochran's later works are cited in notes 40 and 47. Also worth examining is Bert Cochran, ed., *American Labor in Midpassage* (New York: Monthly Review Press, 1959). In his last book, *Welfare Capitalism and After* (New York: Schocken Books, 1980), Cochran argued that "as a class American workers have no vision of a new society and no will to sovereign power," and therefore "the boundaries within which change can take place" are defined by the rule of wealthy and powerful elites that are compelled to respond to and partially coopt mass pressure: the working class will not make a socialist revolution— instead there will be a socioeconomic crisis that generates a populist upsurge, forcing a great transformation that will come "from above and involves a rearrangement of elites," yielding a hybrid of state capitalism and state socialism that, it is hoped, will have some democratic and libertarian features (pp. 184, vii-xv, 198). One senses here someone who—although not abandoning certain radical inclinations—very much wants to be a hard-nosed realist, someone who "knows the score" and, having learned his lesson the hard way, avoids looking foolishly revolutionary. (Compare this with the "foolish" comments by James P. Cannon to Sidney Lens, cited in the concluding section of this essay.)

Herreshoff's book argues that Marxism has much in common with the Jeffersonian idealism and romantic-based social criticism of such American transcendentalists as Ralph Waldo Emerson; at the same time, while asserting that in the future "it seems likely that there will be new expressions of . . . labor radicalism," he poses a question about whether the outcome would vindicate the views of Thomas Jefferson or of Karl Marx: "Jefferson thought that the class of wage workers created by capitalism would prove politically and morally impotent, but Marx had faith that the victims of modern society would learn to free themselves" (p. 192). See David Herreshoff, *The Origins of American Marxism, from the Transcendentalists to De Leon* (New York: Pathfinder Press, 1973), first published by Wayne State University Press in 1967 as *American Disciples of Marx*.

Harry Braverman's *Labor and Monopoly Capital* (New York: Monthly Review Press, 1974) is the focus of a number of articles by various authors in *Monthly Review*, July–August 1976, in which Braverman himself stressed (p. 124): "I have every confidence in the revolutionary potential of the working classes of the so-called capitalist countries. Capitalism will not, over the long run, leave any choice to these classes, but will force upon them the fulfillment of the task which they alone can perform. This presupposes an enormous intensification of the pressures which have only just begun to bear upon the working class, but I think there is no question that it will happen."

For a valuable interview with Genora Dollinger, see Kathleen O'Nan (interviewer), "The Role of Women, and of Radicals, in the First Sit-Down Strikes," *Bulletin in Defense of Marxism*, no. 123, March 1995, pp. 18–21, 34–35, which covers much more ground than simply what happened in the 1930s.

52. Alice and Staughton Lynd, eds., *We Are the Union: The Story of Ed Mann* (Youngstown, OH: Solidarity USA, n.d. [1990?]), pp. 10–11. Also see Alice and Staughton Lynd, eds., *Rank and File, Personal Histories by Working-Class Organizers* (Boston: Beacon Press, 1973), pp. 254–84.

53. On the rise of the civil rights movement, see Marable, *Race, Reform and Rebellion*, pp. 42–167; August Meier and Elliott Rudwick, *From Plantation to Ghetto* (New York: Hill & Wang, 1976), pp. 232–357; Joanne Grant, ed., *Black Protest* (Greenwich, CT: Fawcett, 1968), pp. 251–505; Harvard Sitkoff, *The Struggle for Black Equality 1954–1980* (New York: Hill & Wang, 1981).

54. The crisis of Stalinism is the focus of many valuable documents and articles in Tariq Ali, ed., *The Stalinist Legacy* (Harmondsworth, England: Penguin Books, 1984), which includes Khrushchev's 1956 speech denouncing Stalin. The Russian invasion of Hungary was the subject of an eyewitness account by London *Daily Worker* reporter Peter Fryer—*Hungarian Tragedy* (London: New Park Publications, 1986), first published in late 1956—giving a sense of the horror the invasion provoked in many Communists.

One account of the consequences for the U.S. Communist Party can be found in Steve Nelson, James Barrett, and Rob Ruck, *Steve Nelson, American Radical* (Pittsburgh: University of Pittsburgh Press, 1981), pp. 380–98, but also see works by Starobin and Charney, cited in note 47, and Isserman, cited in note 38.

55. George Lavan [Weissman], ed., *Che Guevara Speaks* (New York: Grove Press, 1968); Joseph Hansen, *Dynamics of the Cuban Revolution, the Trotskyist View* (New York: Pathfinder Press, 1978). Among more recent works having relevance for these issues are Michael Lowy, *The Marxism of Che Guevara* (New

York: Monthly Review Press, 1973); Michael Lowy, ed., *Marxism in Latin America from 1909 to the Present* (Atlantic Highlands, NJ: Humanities Press, 1993); Michael Lowy, *The Politics of Combined and Uneven Development, the Theory of Permanent Revolution* (London: Verso, 1981). For information on the . Fair Play for Cuba Committee and the SWP's role in it, see Van Gosse, *Where the Boys Are: Cuba, Cold War and the Making of the New Left* (London: Verso, 1993).

56.   See Joseph Hansen, "The Problem of Eastern Europe," in *Class, Party, and the State and the Eastern European Revolution* (New York: Education for Socialists, National Education Department, Socialist Workers Party, 1969), pp. 20–35; Joseph Hansen, *The Workers and Farmers Government* (New York: Education for Socialists, National Education Department, Socialist Workers Party, 1974); Robert Chester, *Workers and Farmers Governments since the Second World War* (New York: Education for Socialists, National Education Department, Socialist Workers Party, 1978).

57.   Novack, "Fifty Years of American Trotskyism," p. 9.

58.   Ibid., pp. 9–10.

59.   Frank Lovell, "The Meaning of the Struggle Inside the Socialist Workers Party," in Sarah Lovell, ed., *The Struggle Inside the Socialist Workers Party 1979–1983* (New York: Fourth Internationalist Tendency, 1992), p. 15. A factional history of the early Young Socialist Alliance is provided by Guy Williams, *The YSA—How It Began* (New York: Labor Publications, 1973), which nonetheless provides some useful documentation. A copy of the October 1960 issue of the newspaper *The Young Socialist* (vol. 4, no. 1), calling itself the "Voice of America's Future" (sold to me outside a Pete Seeger folk music concert when I was thirteen), also contains useful information on YSA activists of the time.

60.   In addition to materials cited in note 50, see *Towards a History of the Fourth International*, vols. 1 and 2 (New York: Pathfinder Press, n.d.), and Joseph Hansen, ed., *Marxism vs. Ultraleftism: The Record of Healy's Break with Trotskyism* (New York: Education for Socialists, National Education Department, Socialist Workers Party, 1974).

61.   A fascinating source for this, and for much else in the history of American Trotskyism from the 1950s through the 1970s, is Tim Wohlforth's memoir *The Prophet's Children, Travels on the American Left* (Atlantic Highlands, NJ: Humanities Press, 1993).

   Two polemical accounts of the Spartacist League are offered in Tim Wohlforth, *What Is Spartacist?* (New York: Labor Publications, 1973), and Bob Pearlman, *Spartacist League: The Making of an American Sect* (New York: Education for Socialists, National Education Department, Socialist Workers Party, 1977). The Spartacists' side of the story is offered in *Marxist Bulletin Series*, nos. 1–9 (New York: Spartacist League, n.d.), and in *Hate Trotskyism, Hate the Spartacist League*, Bulletins nos. 1 and 3 (New York: Spartacist League, 1975); also see *Spartacist*, no. 36–36, Winter 1985–86 ("Healyism Implodes"), and *Spartacist*, no. 38–39, Summer 1986 ("The SWP—A Strangled Party").

Also see *The Organizational Character of the Socialist Workers Party, Resolution Adopted by the 21st National Convention of the Socialist Workers Party, September 1965* (New York: Education for Socialist, National Education Department, Socialist Workers Party, 1970).

62. Carl Feingold, "A Life Worth Living" (memoirs written with assistance of Tod Ensign, manuscript in author's possession), pp. 137–65; Richard Kirk and Clara Kaye, *Crisis and Leadership, Part One: The Crisis* (Seattle: Freedom Socialist Publications, 1969); Socialist Workers Party, *From Trotskyism to Maoism* [materials on the Swabeck case], *SWP Discussion Bulletin* 26, no. 4 (August 1967).

63. Howe, *A Margin of Hope*, pp. 43–45.

64. Sam Gordon in Evans, *James P. Cannon as We Knew Him*, p. 59. Also see "The Lives of Two Revolutionaries: Remarks by Rose Karsner, and remarks by James P. Cannon," in James P. Cannon, *Speeches for Socialism* (New York: Pathfinder Press, 1971), pp. 275–90; Frank Lovell, "Sylvia Bleeker (1901– 1988): Union Organizer, Socialist Agitator, Lifelong Trotskyist," *Bulletin in Defense of Marxism*, no. 59, January 1989, pp. 16–19 (which, the author has alerted me, contains some minor factual errors); Dianne Feeley, "Antoinette Konikow: Marxist and Feminist," *International Socialist Review*, January 1977, pp. 42–46. Additional information on Bleeker comes from a discussion with her lifelong companion Morris Lewit, and information on the Millinery Hand Workers' Union, Local 43 is taken from Foner, *History of the Labor Movement in the United States*, vol. 9, pp. 308–10.

65. Sherna Gluck, ed., *From Parlor to Prison: Five American Suffragists Talk about Their Lives, an Oral History* (New York: Vintage Books, 1976), p. 262.

66. On the 1950s controversy, see Mary-Alice Waters, ed., *Cosmetics, Fashions, and the Exploitation of Women* (New York: Pathfinder Press, 1986), and Myra Tanner Weiss, *Marxism and Feminism: The Bustelo Incident* (New York: Onward Press, 1987). For an extensive account of one impressive, but by no means atypical, woman activist who made valuable contributions to U.S. Trotskyism from the 1930s to the 1990s, see Paul Le Blanc, "Sarah Lovell: Collective Portrait of a Revolutionary," *Bulletin in Defense of Marxism*, no. 118, September 1994, pp. 23–27. Also see material on Lillian Curtiss in *Bulletin in Defense of Marxism*, no. 27, February 1986, pp. 31–32; Dorothea Breitman on "Reba Hansen (1909– 1990)," *Bulletin in Defense of Marxism*, no. 77, September 1990, p. 33; David Weiss on "Ethel Victoria Weiss, 1920–1995," *Bulletin in Defense of Marxism*, no. 124, April 1995, pp. 26–27. There are many others whose stories should be told.

Well worth consulting are the two works that helped launch the new wave of feminism: Betty Friedan, *The Feminine Mystique* (New York: Dell, 1970), and Kate Millett, *Sexual Politics* (New York: Avon, 1971). Also see Robin Morgan, ed., *Sisterhood Is Powerful, an Anthology of Writings from the Women's Liberation Movement* (New York: Vintage Books, 1970); Lois W. Banner, *Women in Modern America, a Brief History* (New York: Harcourt Brace

Jovanovich, 1974); Karen V. Hansen and Ilene J. Philipson, eds., *Women, Class, and the Feminist Imagination, a Socialist-Feminist Reader* (Philadelphia: Temple University Press, 1990).

The SWP contribution to the rise of feminism's new wave is reflected in Evelyn Reed, *Problems of Women's Liberation* (New York: Pathfinder Press, 1970), and Linda Jenness, ed., *Feminism and Socialism* (New York: Pathfinder Press, 1972). Breitman's comment is in his "The Liberating Influence of the Transitional Program," in Paul Le Blanc, ed., *Revolutionary Traditions of American Trotskyism* (New York: Fourth Internationalist Tendency, 1988), p. 48, reprinted in the present volume (see pp. 135–136).

67.   Novack, "Fifty Years of American Trotskyism," p. 10. On 1968 and the new radicalization, see David Caute, *The Year of the Barricades, a Journey through 1968* (New York: Harper & Row, 1988); Ronald Fraser, *1968, a Student Generation in Revolt* (New York: Pantheon Books, 1988); George Katsiaficis, *The Imagination of the New Left, a Global Analysis of 1968* (Boston: South End Press, 1987); Arthur Lothstein, ed., *"All We Are Saying . . . " The Philosophy of the New Left* (New York: G. P. Putnam's Sons, 1970); Tariq Ali, ed., *The New Revolutionaries, a Handbook of the International Radical Left* (New York: William Morrow, 1969); Carl Oglesby, ed., *The New Left Reader* (New York: Grove Press, 1969).

68.   Novack, "Fifty Years of American Trotskyism," p. 10. Among Breitman's key essays are *Marxism and the Negro Struggle* (New York: Merit Publishers, 1968); *How a Minority Can Change Society* (New York: Pathfinder Press, 1971); "Black Nationalism and Socialism," in Ernest Mandel, ed., *Fifty Years of World Revolution* (New York: Pathfinder Press, 1971). Other major contributions include George Breitman, ed., *Malcolm X Speaks* (New York: Grove Press, 1966), and George Breitman, *The Last Year of Malcolm X, the Evolution of a Revolutionary* (New York: Schocken Books, 1968). A number of writings by Black activists in the SWP can be found in Tony Thomas, ed., *Black Liberation and Socialism* (New York: Pathfinder Press, 1974).

The context within which these works were produced is discussed in sources cited in note 53 and in Manning Marable, *How Capitalism Underdeveloped Black America* (Boston: South End Press, 1983); Robert L. Allen, *Black Awakening in Capitalist America, an Analytic History* (Garden City, NY: Anchor Books, 1970); Harold Cruse, *The Crisis of the Negro Intellectual, from Its Origins to the Present* (New York: William Morrow, 1967); John Henrik Clarke, *Notes for an African World Revolution, Africans at the Crossroads* (Trenton, NJ: African World Press, 1991); Dan Georgakas and Marvin Surkin, *Detroit: I Do Mind Dying, a Study in Urban Revolution* (New York: St. Martin's Press, 1975).

On Breitman himself, see Naomi Allen and Sarah Lovell, eds., *A Tribute to George Breitman, Writer, Organizer, Revolutionary* (New York: Fourth Internationalist Tendency, 1987).

69.   Novack, "Fifty Years of American Trotskyism," p. 10. Relevant material can be found in *Revolutionary Strategy in the Fight against the Vietnam War* (New

York: Education for Socialists, National Education Department, Socialist Workers Party, 1975).

70. Fred Halstead, *Out Now! A Participant's Account of the American Movement against the Vietnam War* (New York: Monad Press, 1978). Also see Nancy Zaroulis and Gerald Sullivan, *Who Spoke Up? American Protest against the War in Vietnam, 1963–1975* (New York: Holt, Rinehart and Winston, 1984).

71. Jim O'Brien, *American Leninism in the 1970s* (Somerville, MA: New England Free Press, n.d.; reprint from *Radical America*, November 1977–February 1978), p. 6.

72. Walter and Miriam Schneir, "The Socialist Workers, Square Target of the FBI" (New York: Political Rights Defense Fund, n.d.; reprint from *The Nation*, September 25, 1976), p. 5.

73. Carol Lipman, "Red-baiting in the Women's Movement," *Militant*, January 28, 1972.

74. Sale, *SDS* (New York: Random House, 1973), p. 621.

75. Schneir, "The Socialist Workers," pp. 1–2.

76. O'Brien, *American Leninism*, p. 11; Schneir, "The Socialist Workers," p. 2.

77. Evelyn Sell, *Handbook for Marxist Studies* (New York: Fourth Internationalist Tendency, 1984), pp. B1-B2.

78. Frank Lovell, "The Meaning of the Struggle Inside the Socialist Workers Party," *The Struggle Inside the Socialist Workers Party*, ed. by Sarah Lovell (New York: Fourth Internationalist Tendency, 1992), p. 21.

79. Ibid.

80. Ibid., pp. 18, 37.

81. Excerpt from meeting of SWP Political Committee, April 10, 1951, appended to George Breitman, "Two Proposals," 1965, in author's possession.

82. *The Organizational Character of the Socialist Workers Party* (cited in note 61), pp. 16–17.

83. Gus Horowitz, "Introduction," p. 15, and George Breitman, "The Current Radicalization Compared with Those of the Past," p. 101, both in Jack Barnes, George Breitman, Derrick Morrison, Barry Sheppard, and Mary-Alice Waters, *Towards an American Socialist Revolution, a Strategy for the 1970s* (New York: Pathfinder Press, 1971).

84. Schneir, "The Socialist Workers," p. 1.

85. O'Brien, *American Leninsim*, p. 6; Schneir, "The Socialist Workers," p. 4.

86. Information on the IT and what was done to it can be found in the SWP Internal Information Bulletin of July 1974 entitled *Materials Related to the Split of the Internationalist Tendency from the Socialist Workers Party*. There was also a pro-IMT tendency in the SWP, separate from the IT, with about eight supporters, including Bob Langston, Berta Langston, Alan Wald, Celia Stoddola, and Ralph Levitt.

A valuable source on the dispute in the Fourth International of 1969–75 is Joseph Hansen, *The Leninist Strategy of Party Building* (New York: Pathfinder Press, 1979).

For the impressions of a leading personality in the IMT, see Tariq Ali, *Street Fighting Years* (New York: Citadel Press, 1987); also revealing is Ali's rather salacious lampoon of the world Trotskyist movement in the satirical novel *Redemption* (London: Chatto & Windus, 1990), reflecting the grimly "lighthearted" abandonment of earlier commitments by a layer of the "1968 generation." This stands in dramatic contrast to the political seriousness of another leading personality of the IMT—see Ernest Mandel, *Revolutionary Marxism Today* (London: New Left Books, 1979).

For efforts to move beyond the 1969–75 dispute, see *1979 World Congress of the Fourth International: Major Resolutions and reports* (New York: Intercontinental Press/Inprecor, 1980).

87.   O'Brien, *American Leninism*, pp. 10, 25–26. Substantial information on COINTELPRO can be found in the work by Nelson Blackstock, cited in note 43, and also in Margaret Jayko, ed., *FBI on Trial, the victory in the Socialist Workers Party Suit against Government Spying* (New York: Pathfinder Press, 1988). On the Boston struggle, see Jon Hillson, *The Battle of Boston, Busing and the Struggle for School Desegregation* (New York: Pathfinder Press, 1977).

88.   Schneir, "The Socialist Workers," p. 3.

89.   O'Brien, *American Leninism*, p. 32.

90.   Novack, "Fifty Years of American Trotskyism," p. 10.

91.   For accounts of the experiences and impressions of members from two different generations, see Ben Stone, *Memoirs of a Radical Rank-and-Filer* (New York: Prometheus Press, 1986), and Michael Steven Smith, *Notebook of a Sixties Lawyer* (New York: Smyrna Press, 1992). The memoir by Tim Wohlforth, cited in note 61, contains an account of yet different experiences and impressions.

92.   Paul Le Blanc, "Leaving the New Left," *International Socialist Review*, November 1972, pp. 20, 23–24, 29.

93.   *James P. Cannon, a Political Tribute, Including Five Interviews from the Last Year of His Life* (New York: Pathfinder Press, 1974), pp. 41, 27.

94.   Ibid., p. 34.

95.   Ibid., p. 42.

96.   Le Blanc, ed., *Revolutionary Principles and Working-Class Democracy*, pp. 103, 105. The first point on modesty is from Cannon's talk "Reasons for the Survival of the SWP and for Its Vitality in the 1960s." The points on organizational norms are from Cannon's November 12, 1966, letter to Reba Hansen, Jean Simon [Tussey], and Ed Shaw. Cannon's inclination to keep learning and growing, seeking to enrich his Trotskyist perspective through its interaction with new realities, is indicated in two significant documents of the early 1960s: a 1961 letter to George Novack discussing—among other things—the relation between socialism and democracy, the qualities of radical sociologist C. Wright Mills, and the unfolding of the Cuban Revolution; and a 1964 talk dealing with automation, the civil rights movement, and the nuclear arms race. See James P. Cannon, "Intellectuals and Revolution," *Bulletin in Defense of Marxism*, no. 100, October–November 1992, pp. 59–61, and James P. Cannon,

"The Triple Revolution: Developing a Transitional Program for the Late 20th Century," *Bulletin in Defense of Marxism*, no. 112, January 1994, pp. 18–23, 35.

97.   *James P. Cannon, a Political Tribute*, p. 32.

98.   Ibid., pp. 42, 17.

99.   The source for membership figures from 1929 to 1959 is Alan Wald, *The New York Intellectuals*, pp. 110, 165, 300, citing correspondence from George Breitman of July 17 and July 30, 1985. Information on membership from 1960 to 1976 can be found in *A Fight for Political Rights, What Has Been Won in the Socialist Workers Party Lawsuit against Government Spying and Disruption* (New York: Political Rights Defense Fund, n.d. [1987]), pp. 18–19. The source for 1981 is Lovell, "The Meaning of the Struggle Inside the Socialist Workers Party," p. 22.

2

The Liberating Influence of the Transitional Program: Three Talks

GEORGE BREITMAN

1. The Ludlow Amendment

Many of you know that in our movement there are no official versions of history, whether it's the history of our own movement or anything else. But for the benefit of those who don't know it, I want to mention it at the outset. The only thing you have to accept in order to join our party is its program and the obligation to promote it in accord with its rules and constitution, which of course includes the right to try to persuade the party to change this or that part of its program or constitution. You don't have to agree with every conclusion in Trotsky's *History of the Russian Revolution*, with every formulation in Cannon's books about party building and the development of the Socialist Workers Party (SWP) and its predecessors, with every opinion in the books by Farrell Dobbs and Art Preis on the Teamsters and the CIO, or the writings of George Novack on the philosophy of Marxism, of Mary-Alice Waters on the relations between feminism and the Marxist movement, of Evelyn Reed on anthropology and the matriarchy. We publish and circulate these works because of their value for our Marxist education, because of their general consonance with our revolutionary program, but it would be as silly to demand that all of us must agree with everything they write as it would be to demand that they should write only what we would all agree with 100 percent.

This is my way of saying that my remarks today about certain aspects of the early history of our party, centering around the year 1938, are neither "official" nor "approved." All they represent is my opinion, which is based partly on my memory of that period and partly on recent research, including the reading of documents that I had not seen at that time. I think that the facts I will cite are reliable, and I hope that you will be able to distinguish without difficulty between those facts and my interpretation of them.

In November of this year [1974] it will be forty-six years since James P. Cannon, Max Shachtman, and Martin Abern, expelled from the leadership of the Communist Party, began publishing the *Militant*. But it wasn't until New Year's 1938, in the tenth year of our movement, that the Socialist Workers Party was founded at a national convention in Chicago. Nineteen thirty-eight was also the year when the Fourth International was founded at an international conference in Paris in September, one year before the start of World War II. At this founding conference the delegates adopted as their major programmatic document a resolution written by Trotsky in Mexico, entitled "The Death Agony of Capitalism and the Tasks of the Fourth International," which later came to be referred to as the "Transitional Program."

I am going to talk about some of the problems that arose in the process by which the SWP endorsed the transitional program, and changes resulting from this endorsement that continue to influence the SWP to this day. If I do not speak as much about the transitional program itself as the title of this talk might have led you to expect, it is because of (1) a lack of time, (2) the belief that most of you already know about the transitional program, and (3) the abundance of literature available on the subject in the book *The Transitional Program for Socialist Revolution*. Published last year, that book contains the transitional program resolution itself, a series of discussions by Trotsky with different SWP leaders and members about the program, and at least two useful introductions by Joseph Hansen and George Novack. A second edition of this book has just been published, and that contains a number of additional stenograms of Trotsky's discussions on the transitional program, taken down before the program itself was written, some of which are relevant to my talks.

However, I do want to say a couple of things about the transitional program and the transitional method. Of Trotsky's many valuable contributions to Marxist theory there are two, in my opinion, that stand out above the others. One is his theory of the permanent revolution, conceived when he was twenty-six years old, which challenged the conventional wisdom of the movement of his time about the possibilities and perspectives of revolution in most of the world and, after it was confirmed by the Russian Revolution of 1917, became a keystone in the reorientation of the international Marxist vanguard (although for a number of years after 1917 the term "permanent revolution" was not used by anyone).

The other contribution of which I speak was made by Trotsky in 1938, when he was fifty-eight years old and completing the fortieth year of his revolutionary career. Here, in his full maturity, a few weeks after Stalin's liquidation of Bukharin and Rykov in the third big Moscow trial and two and a half years before his own death, Lenin's collaborator and continuator drew on the experiences of the most eventful four decades in revolutionary history and put them together in a new synthesis that we call the transitional program.

That is usually what new great ideas consist of—a rearrangement of old ones, the sifting out of some, a new emphasis for others, a recasting of priorities and relationships. In and of itself, there was not much that was new in the transitional program; some of the parts dated back, as Trotsky noted, ninety years to the *Communist Manifesto*; other parts were so recent that they had not yet been assimilated or expressed in writing, deriving from the actions of the workers themselves, such as the sitdown strikes in the mid-1930s in France and the United States.

Trotsky's contribution was to take these parts and put them together, to unify them, in a way that even his closest collaborators were at first to find unique, maybe even disturbing. His aim was to write a program that would help the revolutionary vanguard to intervene successfully in the class struggle in a period when conditions were objectively prerevolutionary but the masses were still under the influence of the counterrevolutionary Second and Third Internationals or without any leadership at all. As he put it:

> The strategic task of the next period—a prerevolutionary period of agitation, propaganda, and organization—consists in overcoming the contradiction between the maturity of the objective revolutionary conditions and the immaturity of the proletariat and its vanguard (the confusion and disappointment of the older generation; the inexperience of the younger

generation). It is necessary to help the masses in the process of the daily struggle to find the bridge between present demands and the socialist program of the revolution. This bridge should include a system of *transitional demands*, stemming from today's conditions and from today's consciousness of wide layers of the working class and unalterably leading to one final conclusion: the conquest of power by the proletariat.

The transitional program was written for specific purposes, in the midst of a world depression, on the eve of a world war, for the founding conference of the Fourth International. That has led some people to question or belittle its usefulness for today or tomorrow, when conditions are different. This seems to me the worst kind of formalist thinking, if thinking is the right word. In the first place, it overlooks the fact that the essential conditions are not different—that the contradiction between the maturity of the objective revolutionary conditions and the immaturity of the proletariat and its vanguard is even greater and more pregnant than it was in 1938. If not all the 1938 demands are applicable today (some weren't even applicable yet in 1938), the essential tasks are the same, and the *method* of the transitional program as it was written in 1938 is absolutely applicable today. In fact, the transitional method, in my opinion, is an even greater contribution than the transitional program itself.

In presenting the transitional program, Trotsky emphasized its continuity with the past, rather than what was innovative in it. He said that it "draws the balance of the already accumulated experience of our national sections and on the basis of this experience opens up broader international perspectives." But this was even truer of the transitional method than of the transitional program itself. The transitional method was being used by us before the transitional program was written—after all, the disparity between the maturity of objective conditions and the subjective immaturity of the proletariat and its vanguard did not begin in 1938, and the need for bridges between the vanguard and the masses had existed for a long time.

But before 1938 we weren't conscious of the transitional method that we used on occasion; we certainly were not fully conscious, and we used it haphazardly therefore, or incompletely, or empirically. Trotsky generalized it, concretized it, drew out its implications, showed its logic and necessity, named it, and indelibly imprinted it in our consciousness. For most of us the exposition of the transitional method was quite a revelation, bigger than the one the Molière character had when he learned that he had been speaking prose all his life.

In 1938 the SWP was rather an exceptional organization. That also is an opinion, but there is plenty of objective evidence to back it up. It was the only organization in the United States that fought against the prevailing tidal waves of New Deal reformism and Stalinist opportunism from a revolutionary standpoint, and it was the only organization inside the Movement for the Fourth International that approached the norms of Bolshevism in the quality of its cadres, the solidity of its principles, and the level of its organizational practice. This is not to say that it was free of serious weaknesses, but it is to say that it had serious strengths as well. This was Trotsky's opinion, and it was for this reason in 1938 that he turned to the SWP leaders for discussion before writing the transitional program and that he asked the SWP to adopt and sponsor it at the founding conference of the Fourth International.

A history of our movement in this country from its inception in 1928 to the founding of the SWP in 1938 has been written by Comrade Cannon in the book called *The History of American Trotskyism*. It will have to suffice here to say that the first major turning point in this history came in 1933, after Hitler's victory in Germany, when our movement discontinued its efforts to reform the Communist International and its affiliated parties and set out here in the United States to gather the cadres of a new Marxist party as part of a new, Fourth International.

This meant that we now turned our primary attention away from the Communist Party, and that our main activity, the dissemination of propaganda, began to be combined with intervention and action, where possible, in the class struggle. At the end of 1934, after the Minneapolis strike had shown our competence in intervention and action, our movement merged with a left-centrist current led by A. J. Muste (this became the Workers Party) and then, in the spring of 1936, we entered the Socialist Party in order to merge with young revolutionary elements who had been attracted to that organization. Our forces, considerably augmented, were expelled from the Socialist Party and its youth organization, the Young People's Socialist League (YPSL), in the summer of 1937 (although they represented the majority of the YPSL). The expelled left-wingers then called a national convention to create a new revolutionary party affiliated with the Fourth Internationalist movement and, after an extensive internal discussion, that is how the SWP came to be founded in 1938.

The discussion preceding that convention was very rich, covering a broad number of current international and national problems as well as the fundamental principles to govern and guide the new revolutionary party. From Mexico, Trotsky, who had recently completed his historic work of exposing the Moscow trial frame-ups, participated in this discussion to some extent, but chiefly on the so-called international questions—the Spanish civil war, the Sino-Japanese war, the class character of the Soviet Union, and the nature of democratic centralism in general.

A declaration of principles and a constitution were adopted; a political resolution, resolutions on trade union and unemployed work, resolutions on the Soviet Union and Spain, a resolution on organizational principles and standards, reports on the international movement, the youth movement, the election of a national committee—these were only some of the important things taken up and acted on at the convention. As a young delegate to the convention, I left it not only tired but inspired and certain that we had taken a big step toward the American revolution, and I am sure that that attitude was shared by most of the rank-and-file delegates.

In 1937 Trotsky had been pressing for an international conference to found the Fourth International. He felt that the international conference of July 1936 had made a mistake in not taking that step then, and he kept urging after his arrival in Mexico in 1937 that it be done by the end of that year. But it didn't prove possible, for various reasons, one of them being that the U.S. leadership felt that it had to concentrate first on the founding of the SWP. So after the new party was launched, it was agreed that a delegation of SWP leaders would go to Mexico for talks about the international conference and related matters. And this took place at the end of March 1938, less than three months after the SWP convention.

The SWP delegation consisted of Cannon, Shachtman, V. R. Dunne, and Rose Karsner, and they met with Trotsky and others at Trotsky's home for an entire week. After some initial, introductory discussions, more formal sessions were held on six consecutive days, four of which were devoted entirely or largely to the transitional program and the method it implied. Stenograms were made of these six discussions, which were not corrected or revised by the participants but gave the essence of the exchanges. For security reasons mainly—to protect Trotsky's right of asylum in Mexico—these six stenograms were shown only to the National Committee members of the SWP at a plenum the next month and then were retrieved.

None was ever published in any form, not even an internal bulletin, during Trotsky's life, and until just this year none was ever published anywhere, with one exception—a discussion about the labor party, which was printed in an SWP educational bulletin in 1948. Fortunately, copies of the six stenograms were kept by Trotsky and included by him in the archives sold to Harvard in 1940. Last year Pathfinder Press got access to the stenograms for the first time and permission to print them, and they have just been published as material added in the second edition of *The Transitional Program for Socialist Revolution*. There, in the back of the volume, you can read the material from the four stenograms that dealt with the transitional program (and next year you will be able to read the rest of these stenograms, dealing with other questions, in the second edition of the *Writings 1937–38*). The newly added material should not be confused with the other stenograms about the transitional program in that book, most of them from the period *after* Trotsky wrote the program, which were in the first edition.

No memoirs or reminiscences of the discussions have been published, but it is clear from the stenograms—not just by reading between the lines, but from some passages—that the SWPers must have been startled and even shaken up by some of Trotsky's proposals and arguments and his way of looking at certain things that struck them as new.

On the fourth day of the discussions transcribed, Trotsky began the session by saying, "In the preceding discussions some comrades had the impression that some of my propositions or demands were opportunistic, and others that they were too revolutionary, not corresponding to the objective situation. And this combination is very compromising, and that's why I'll briefly defend this apparent contradiction." Perhaps Trotsky was exaggerating a little here, but he apparently felt that he had not yet fully convinced the other participants in the discussion, because they were not sure about the "orthodoxy" (a word I dislike) or the realism of his positions.

In a number of places the stenograms show them asking Trotsky the same questions, getting him to restate his arguments so that they can grasp them better; in other places, they voice doubts or reservations; in still others, disagreement (Shachtman in particular could not see how slogans on workers' control and workers' militia were applicable in the United States in 1938).

Such a thing is of course quite common, even inevitable, in any free political discussion where new proposals are introduced that require reconsideration of long-established patterns of thought. Besides, this was not an ordinary discussion or an abstract discussion. Some of the positions Trotsky was asking them to reconsider had been passionately reaffirmed less than three months before, in the declaration of principles and the political resolution adopted by the founding SWP convention. So they wanted to be damned sure that they understood what Trotsky was proposing, because even if they were convinced, that wouldn't settle it—they would still have to go home and convince first the Political Committee, then the National Committee, and then the party as a whole. So nobody reading those stenograms today is entitled to cheap feelings of condescension toward those comrades, who bore heavy responsibilities in this situation and acquitted themselves well.

Trotsky himself was aware of the problem facing the SWPers, and his tone throughout was patient, friendly, and pedagogic, for he was talking to close comrades, not opponents. And by the time they left to return to the United States, they had become convinced, if perhaps not fully aware of all the implications, and had agreed that they would ask the SWP to sponsor the transitional program at the coming international conference and to modify certain important points in its national program.

Before continuing the narrative, I am going to turn to two of the questions on which Trotsky wanted the SWP to change its positions. These, I think, are at the heart of the transitional method, and discussing them in some detail will be my substitute for discussing the transitional program and the method as a whole, which I've said has already been done more than adequately by Comrades Hansen and Novack in their introductions to the transitional program book. I should add that I am inclined to do it this way because these two questions were the ones that I personally, as a young SWP activist, found the hardest to figure out. These two questions were the Ludlow amendment and the labor party.

In the 1930s, as the American people began to learn more about World War I, partly through muckraking congressional investigations, and as the threat of World War II began to come closer, a considerable antiwar or pacifist sentiment developed in this country. One of the forms this took was that of so-called isolationism, an expression of a desire not to get involved in foreign wars. Beginning in 1935, the Stalinists attempted to exploit this antiwar sentiment by channeling it behind Roosevelt's foreign policy and the policy of "collective security," according to which war would be prevented through an alliance by the peace-loving countries (the United States, USSR, etc.) against the bad, aggressive, peace-hating countries (Germany, Italy, and Japan).

In 1935 a Democratic congressman from Indiana named Ludlow introduced a bill in the House of amend the U.S. Constitution so that Congress would not have the authority to declare war until such a declaration had been approved by the people voting in a national referendum. Of course the bill had many loopholes, one of which was that this limitation on the war-making power of Congress would not apply if the United States were invaded or attacked; and this wasn't its only weakness. Support began to build for the amendment as fears of war were deepened in this country by the Italian invasion of Ethiopia in 1935, the Spanish civil war in 1936, and the Japanese invasion of China in 1937. The Ludlow amendment was reintroduced in the House in 1937 and in the Senate by La Follette of Wisconsin, and it finally came to a vote in the House in January 1938, nine days after our convention.

The Roosevelt administration was bitterly opposed to the amendment and used all its patronage pressures to bring about its defeat. The Communist Party also opposed it, charging that it was in the interests of the reactionaries and fascists because it would limit the ability of the U.S. government to deter the fascist powers from starting a war. Just before the vote in the House, a Gallup poll showed that 72 percent of the population favored the Ludlow amendment. Most of the new industrial unions supported the bill, along with the National Farmers Union. The pro-Ludlow sentiment in the United Auto Workers (UAW) was so strong that the Stalinist members of its executive board were forced to vote in favor of it. In the House of Representatives the bill was defeated 209–188, a rather close vote, considering all the circumstances.

So far I haven't been able to find any references to the Ludlow amendment in our press before the vote in the House in January 1938, but without any specific articles in our press, I knew at that time what our position on the amendment was, and I approved of it wholeheartedly.

Before explaining what our position was, I shall have to make a correction of what Comrade Hansen said about it in 1971 in a speech included with the introductory matter in the transitional program book. After telling who Ludlow was and what his amendment called for, Comrade Hansen said, "Comrade Trotsky proposed that the Socialist Workers Party should offer critical support to the Indiana Democrat's proposed amendment to the bourgeois constitution of the United States. After a bit of hesitation by some comrades our party adopted this position. Trotsky considered the matter so important that he included a paragraph about it in the transitional program." I am afraid that Comrade Hansen must have relied on his memory here instead of checking the facts—perhaps because he didn't have access to the records when he was making the speech, but in any case, he doesn't have it right.

The fact is that we were opposed to the Ludlow amendment before Trotsky had any opinion about it. If we had had a member in the House on January 10, 1938, he would have voted against the amendment, after making or trying to make a revolutionary speech differentiating the SWP from the nonrevolutionary forces opposing it. And if you had been a sympathizer in 1938, asking me why we were opposed, I would have answered at length along the following lines: "Pacifism is one of the most pernicious elements obstructing the revolutionary struggle against imperialist war. It misleads and disarms the workers, delivering them defenseless at the crucial moment into the hands of the war makers. Lenin and the Bolsheviks taught us that implacable opposition to pacifism and the illusions it creates is obligatory for all revolutionaries. All the documents of the Left Opposition and Fourth International stress the principled character of the struggle against pacifism in all its forms. Our stand on this question demarcates us from all other tendencies. The Ludlow amendment is a pacifist measure, designed to create the illusion that it is possible to prevent war at the ballot box while leaving power in the hands of the capitalists. It misdirects the workers from the real struggle against war, and therefore we cannot support it or assume any responsibility for it. Not to oppose it would be a betrayal of our revolutionary principles."

On the same day that the House voted down the Ludlow amendment, the newly elected Political Committee (PC) of the SWP held its first meeting. The PC minutes of that date show that under one point on the agenda Burnham proposed launching an antiwar campaign, consisting of eight "concrete points." The eighth point read as follows: "For the Ludlow amendment on the general motivation of the opportunities which it, as an issue, provides." All the points were approved, except the eighth, which was defeated by a vote of six to one. A countermotion to that eighth point was made by Shachtman, as follows: "That in our press we criticize the Ludlow amendment and the pacifist agitation connected with it from a principled revolutionary standpoint." This was carried— six for, one against.

In accord with this motion, our paper the *Socialist Appeal* carried a frontpage article by Albert Goldman, introduced with an editorial statement pronouncing it to be "the Marxian view on the amendment." Goldman's article begins by saying that the Ludlow amendment poses an old problem in a new form for Marxists and workers generally. But, he assures the readers, "It is only necessary to apply the accepted principles of revolutionary Marxism to solve the problem correctly." Applying them, he showed all the shortcomings of the Ludlow amendment and the pacifist illusions fostered by its advocates, demonstrated that it would not really prevent war, differentiated our position from that of the Stalinists, and pointed to the destruction of the capitalist system as the only solution to war. I might add that he also said that the Ludlow amendment carried even greater dangers than other pacifist schemes precisely because it added "an element of democratic procedure."

Also in accord with the PC motion were two editorials in the next issue of our magazine. The longer one, which could have been written by Burnham, denounced the pro-imperialist forces that voted down the Ludlow bill and explained why. The shorter editorial, which could have been written by Shachtman, sought to "represent the standpoint of revolutionary Marxism." Among other things, it said:

> Where pacifist nostrums are not outright frauds and deceptions, they are pernicious illusions which drug the masses into pleasant dreams and hallucinations and paralyze their fighting power. To teach the masses that they can "prevent war" by a popular referendum is to foster a disastrous illusion among them. . . . Like the panacea of "disarmament," or "international arbitration courts," the referendum illusion diverts attention from the need of an intransigent class struggle policy against war every day in the year, because it cultivates the idea that when the "real" was danger faces us in the remote future the masses will be able to avert it by the mere casting of a ballot. . . . In sum, to support the Ludlow resolution is to inculcate in the minds of the workers the idea that war can be "prevented" or fought *by some means other than the class struggle,*

that imperialist war can be averted otherwise than by the revolutionary socialist overturn of capitalist rule.

The PC minutes of February 18 have a point called "Ludlow Amendment," followed by this information: "Letter read supporting Burnham's position on the Ludlow Amendment." Not included with the minutes, and not identified as to author, this letter turns out to have been written by Trotsky, although it was signed "Hansen" for security reasons; its text can be found in the second edition of *Writings 37–38*, which should be out next year. The letter was addressed to Cannon, whom Trotsky gave permission to show it to Burnham if he wished. Cannon did, and he also turned it over to the Political Committee as a whole. The letter said that on the Ludlow question Trotsky was with Burnham, not with the majority of the Political Committee. He felt that after the congressional vote the question was settled practically, but he wanted to make some comments on the important question of methodology. The government position against the Ludlow amendment, Trotsky wrote, represented the position of the imperialists and big business, who want their hands free for international maneuvering, including the declaration of war. What is the Ludlow bill? Trotsky wrote:

> It represents the apprehension of the man-in-the-street, of the average citizen, of the middle bourgeois, the petty bourgeois, and even the farmer and the worker . . . looking for a brake upon the bad will of big business. In this case they name the brake the referendum. We know that the brake is not sufficient and even not efficient and we openly proclaim this opinion, but at the same time we are ready to go through his experience against the dictatorial pretensions of big business. The referendum is an illusion? Not more or less an illusion than universal suffrage and other means of democracy. Why can we not use the referendum as we use the presidential elections? . . .
>
> The referendum illusion of the American little man has also its progressive features. Our idea is not to turn away from it, but utilize these progressive features without taking the responsibility for the illusion. If the referendum motion should be adopted, it would give us in case of a war crisis tremendous opportunities for agitation. That is precisely why big business stifled the referendum illusion.

Today's average SWP member will not find Trotsky's thinking on the Ludlow amendment extraordinary or controversial; in fact, it may seem rather commonplace and hardly worth the time I am giving it. This testifies to the political development of our movement since 1938; in certain respects we have come a long way; we live on a higher political plateau now. But what seems simple now to a new member didn't seem at all simple to the politically most astute leaders of our party then, as we can see from what happened after Trotsky's letter was read by the Political Committee.

Trotsky thought that because the referendum had been rejected in the House nothing more could be done about it. The members of the Political Committee knew better, realizing that the amendment would continue to be an important American political question for some time. So they decided, after hearing Trotsky's letter, to formulate their position anew. Goldman introduced a series of four motions, some of which were amended by Shachtman. The first two motions stressed the need to use the interest aroused by the amendment to expose the war preparations and the bourgeois and Stalinist opponents of the bill and to expose all pacifist illusions, by clearly stating at all times that whoever says any kind of referendum will stop war is seriously mistaken. The third motion declared that we cannot assume responsibility for the amendment under any circumstances, and it is impermissible for us or our members in mass movements to organize or participate in or endorse any campaign for the amendment.

Up to this point it's clear and consistent. Goldman's fourth motion, however, says that since the amendment has been adopted by the most progressive forces of the labor movement, since the working class learns through experience, and since we need to be closely connected with those forces, our comrades in the mass movement are instructed to vote in favor of the Ludlow amendment, and to introduce pro-Ludlow clauses in antiwar resolutions, "at all times making clear our position on the amendment."

Shachtman disagreed with Goldman's point four and amended it to instruct our comrades to state our specific position on the Ludlow amendment, either orally or in writing, and to abstain when the vote is cast. Instead of stopping there, however, he added an exception: in those exceptional circumstances where our comrades hold the balance of power between the Stalinists and patriots on one side and pro-Ludlow forces on the other, our comrades are instructed to defeat the Stalinists and patriots by casting their vote for the Ludlow amendment with the qualifications given above.

And this was the position adopted by the SWP on February 10, by five to two (Cannon was absent)—to abstain, except in special circumstances where we should vote in favor in order to defeat the Stalinists and patriots. And although the Political Committee held other discussions on antiwar work during February, this was and remained the SWP's position when its delegation went to talk with Trotsky the following month.

In the back of the second edition of the transitional program book you will find the stenogram of the discussion in Mexico about the Ludlow amendment. There we can see Shachtman especially—who was the chief formulator of the abstentionist position, although of course the Political Committee as a whole was responsible for it—still dragging his heels: "there is great danger that in jumping into a so-called mass movement against war—pacifist in nature—the revolutionary education of the vanguard will be neglected. At the same time, not to enter the movement leaves us mainly in a propaganda position." And at the end, returning to a point he had made in the February magazine article, he asks: "How do you distinguish between our support of the Ludlow amendment and our attitude toward disarmament programs, international arbitration, etc.?"

Trotsky's answer: "They have nothing to do with one another. The Ludlow amendment is only a way for the masses to control their government. If the Ludlow amendment is accepted and made part of the constitution it will absolutely not be analogous to disarmament but to inclusion in the right to vote of those eighteen years old"—that is, a democratic right.

Trotsky's arguments in this discussion were so persuasive that the others were convinced. The Ludlow amendment was not the subject of much debate at the stormy plenum of the SWP National Committee held a month later. It was not taken up until the last hours of the plenum. Then two motions were presented.

Cannon's motion said: "That the Plenum finds that the Political Committee took a correct principled position on the Ludlow amendment but made a tactical error in failing to give critical support to this movement without making any concessions whatever to its pacifist and illusory character."

Motion by Carter: "That the Plenum reverses the position of the Political Committee on the Ludlow Amendment and declares it incorrect; that the PC be instructed to issue a statement in support of a popular referendum on the question of war, with a critical declaration in reference to the pacifist and illusory tendencies in the pro-Ludlow movement."

Seven members spoke during the discussion, and then Cannon made a substitute motion for the whole: "The Plenum finds that the Political Committee was correct in principled opposition to the pacifist illusions contained in the Ludlow amendment—an opposition that was fully justified—the PC nevertheless took a purely negative position which prevented the party from utilizing the entirely progressive sentiment of the masses who supported the idea of submitting the warmongers to the control of a popular referendum before the declaration of war. The Plenum instructs the PC to correct its position accordingly." This substitute motion carried, and the Carter motion was defeated, the vote not given.

A month later, our paper printed a public National Committee (NC) statement reporting the change in the SWP's position on the Ludlow amendment and explaining why. At this point it could be said that the error was corrected and the differences liquidated—so completely that three months later, in August, nobody thought, that it was out of order for the Political Committee to send the National Committee members the copy of a draft written by Goldman for an improved version of the Ludlow amendment, that is, one free of the defects in Ludlow's bill, which we were to try to get some member of Congress to introduce so that we could use it in our antiwar propaganda and agitation.

I have traced the course of this thing, perhaps in too much detail, because I think that a study of mistakes of this kind, frankly recognized and correctly analyzed, can be at least as useful educationally as a study of correct policies or actions. Everybody makes mistakes, even geniuses like Marx, Lenin, and Trotsky. The Russian Revolution of 1917 would have been impossible if the Bolsheviks had not learned many valuable lessons from the defeat of 1905. In politics, mistakes are unavoidable, said Trotsky; what is reprehensible is clinging to mistakes and refusing to correct them. This of course does not apply to the Ludlow dispute. But the Ludlow thing was important methodologically, as Trotsky said in his letter to Cannon. So it deserves further comment.

Reading Trotsky's approach to the Ludlow question now, I am struck by how much more rounded and all-sided it was than the one we had at the time. This enabled him more effectively to select out the major elements of the problem—for example, he began with a concrete class analysis, taking off from the fact that the ruling class was opposed to the Ludlow amendment, whereas that fact was subordinated in our analysis, which tended to center on a secondary factor, the illusions that the Ludlow forces fostered. Of course, what the ruling class wants in a particular case need not always be conclusive (sometimes they make mistakes, too), and sometimes it is not even clear what the ruling class wants (that certainly was the case with the impeachment problem last year). But what the ruling class wanted on the Ludlow amendment was both relevant and clear, and it fructified Trotsky's thinking. For us, the position of the ruling class was something of an embarrassment that we didn't care to dwell on and didn't altogether explain, even poorly, concentrating instead on the question of illusions.

Illusions and the necessity to combat them were a prominent feature not only of the Ludlow discussion but also of other questions facing the SWP at that time. This stems from the abiding obligation we have to help the masses overcome bourgeois ideology in all its forms and variants, including illusions about the nature of bourgeois democracy. Recently, for example, our propaganda and action around Watergate had to take into account, and include material to counteract, the illusions widely generated about Congress, the courts, and the Constitution.

But here, as with everything else in politics, a sense of proportion is needed, and I am afraid that it was sometimes lacking. Sometimes, like today's TV housewife who is driven frantic by the absence of sparkle on a drinking glass or the presence of a ring around her husband's collar, we were a little obsessed by the illusion factor. Perhaps "obsessed" is too strong, perhaps a better word is "overpreoccupied."

But the struggle against illusions is not an end in itself. It is only a means toward an end, and not the central means. Its weight varies from one situation to another, sometimes considerably. And the way in which we struggle against illusions is not uniform and unvarying in all situations; in one case it is best done head-on, in another a more indirect approach proves more effective. And since effectiveness is or should be a paramount factor, a distinction has to be made between merely making the record against illusions, no matter how loudly and vehemently, and setting into motion forces that actually help people to raise their political consciousness.

We tended to throw all illusions into one bag marked "Dangerous, Expose at All Costs." Trotsky was more selective, more discriminating. In a different context, in a 1930 pamphlet that will be in English later this year, he had occasion to refer to the consciousness, mood, and expectations of the revolutionary workers in Russia at the time of the October Revolution, and there he discussed what he called their "creative illusion" in "overestimating hopes for a rapid change in their fate." It was an underestimation of the effort, suffering, and sacrifice they would be required to make before they would attain the kind of just, humane, socialist society they were fighting for. It was an illusion in the sense that between that generation and that kind of society lay civil war, imperialist intervention, famine and cannibalism, the rise of a privileged bureaucracy, totalitarian regimentation and terror, decimation in the Second World War, and much more that they did not foresee; it was an illusion based on an underestimation of the difficulties that would face them after the workers took power in backward Russia, which would have been infinitely smaller if the revolution had succeeded in spreading to the rest of Europe.

And it was creative because the workers' expectations enabled them to deal the first powerful blow against the world capitalist system and open up the era of proletarian revolutions and colonial uprisings. The record shows that the Bolsheviks did not spend much time or energy combating such illusions; they were too busy trying to imbue the masses with the determination to make the revolution.

In any case, Trotsky was able to differentiate among illusions if he could designate some as creative. Even more important, he was able to distinguish different sides or aspects of an illusion, as in the Ludlow discussion. Instead of a single label on the illusion or illusions connected with the Ludlow amendment, he called attention to the fact that certain aspects were progressive at the same time that others were not.

The idea that war can be abolished or prevented without ending the capitalist system that spawns war does not have much to recommend it from a Marxist standpoint. But if the spread of that idea leads masses of people into action to try to prevent the government from going to war, or to set limits on its power to declare war, isn't that a good thing from the standpoint of Marxists? Even if the idea that sets them into motion against the capitalist government is not scientific, and is therefore wrong and illusory, isn't it good, that is, progressive for them to conduct such a struggle? Isn't that precisely the way that they can learn what is wrong and illusory about their ideas on how to end war?

When I read you the second position adopted by the Political Committee on the Ludlow amendment, in February 1938, after Trotsky's letter was read, you may recall that in one place Goldman's motion said, "the working class learns through experience." This was a commonplace in our movement; everyone subscribed to it. But the difference was that Trotsky held that the workers' experience with a struggle for something like the Ludlow amendment was exactly the thing that could help them learn about and go beyond their illusion. The Political Committee, even as it was saying "the working class learns through experience," took the view that we should try to discourage the workers from having such an experience with the amendment and that we should dissociate ourselves from the experience if they went ahead with it anyway.

The PC view was that this is an illusion, therefore we can only expose and denounce it. Trotsky's view was that this is an illusion, but it has a progressive potential. Therefore, without assuming any responsibility for the illusion, and without hiding our belief that it is an illusion—but without making our belief that it is an illusion the major feature of our approach to it—because it has a progressive potential, let us encourage and help the workers to fight against the government on the war question. Let us join this movement and become its best builders, because this is the most effective way of helping them overcome some of their illusions about war and democratic capitalism.

It seems to be the difference between the approach of narrow propagandism and the approach of revolutionary activism. In the first case you write an article explaining "the Marxian principles on war" and hand it out to those who are interested in such matters; you won't affect many people that way, but you have done your duty and presumably can sleep well. In the second case you intervene in the class struggle, helping to set masses into motion against the ruling class or to provide bridges for those in motion from the elementary, one-sided, and illusory conceptions they start out with toward better, more realistic, and more revolutionary concepts about capitalism and war and how to fight them.

I do think that the source of our error was in great part the remnants of the narrow propagandism that prevailed in the first years of the Left Opposition in this country, when we were restricted almost entirely to trying to reach the ranks of the Communist Party with our written and spoken ideas. Subsequently we consciously set out to transcend this phase, with increasing success. But occasionally, especially when new problems were posed, we had a tendency to slip back. The transitional method that Trotsky recommended to us was precisely the thing we needed to enable us to say good-bye forever to such lapses.

If it was not an error of propagandism then it is hard to explain the thing Shachtman said Mexico that I have already cited: "There is great danger that in jumping into a so-called mass movement against war—pacifist in nature—the revolutionary education of the vanguard will be neglected."

At first sight this seems like a non sequitur. Why should jumping into a mass movement, or only entering one with more dignity than jumping provides, present a danger, a *great* danger, that the revolutionary education of the vanguard will be neglected? How does it follow? What is the possible connection? It doesn't make sense unless the reasoning is being done from the standpoint of propagandism, where you feel that the most urgent task you have is to present your entire program without ambiguity or possibility of misrepresentation on all occasions—a necessity that occurs to you because you lack confidence about the revolutionary education, the ideological solidity of the vanguard, that is, of yourselves.

In such a case, if you are not sure of it, the main thing becomes the strengthening of the revolutionary education or ideological condition of the vanguard group, and doing something about that seems more important, much more important, than taking advantage of an opportunity to intervene in the class struggle.

By contrast, let us consider how we would pose the same problem today, after having absorbed the meaning of the transitional method. We would say, "Here is a mass movement that we can enter, where we can win over people to our revolutionary positions and help raise the consciousness of many more. It is a pacifist movement, which means that in order to work effectively there our own members must be well educated about the nature of pacifism, what's wrong with it, and how to counter its influence. Which means, therefore, that before we enter and after we enter we must make sure that our members are immunized politically against pacifism, if that is not already the case. That is, instead of neglecting, we must increase the revolutionary education of the vanguard on this point." Shachtman counterposed mass work and revolutionary education of the vanguard. We, on the other hand, combine them, because not only the masses learn that way, but we, the vanguard, do too.

Methodologically we also seemed to be suffering from a confusion about the relation between principles and tactics. Principles are propositions embodying fundamental conclusions derived from theory and historical experience to govern and guide our struggle for socialism. Relating broadly to our goals, they set a framework within which we operate. Although they are not eternal, they have a long-range character and are not easily or often changed. In fact, we have essentially the same principles today that we had in 1938. The dictatorship of the proletariat, or the struggle for a workers' state, as the form of state transitional between capitalism and socialism—that is a principle with us. Insistence on class-struggle methods against class-collaborationist methods—that is another. Unremitting opposition to pacifism in all its guises, because pacifism is an obstacle to revolutionary struggle—that is a third.

Tactics, on the other hand, are only means to an end. "Only" in this context is not meant to disparage them; without the appropriate tactics, principles cannot be brought to life, so there is clearly an interdependence between principles and tactics. But tactics are subordinate in the same way that means are subordinate to an end. They are good if they enchance and promote the principle, not good if they don't. In addition, tactics are flexible, adjustable, variable. They depend (or their applicability depends) on concrete circumstances. To advance a particular principle, tactic A may be best today; but it may have to be replaced by tactic B tomorrow morning, or tactic C tomorrow night. Meanwhile, the principle remains unchanged.

Principle tells us to oppose pacifism, but it does not tell us whether or not to participate in a certain mass movement; it only tells us that under all circumstances, whether participating or not, we should so function as to counterpose revolutionary ideas and influence to those of the pacifists. There is not a single tactic that follows from any principle; after understanding and grasping the principle, we still have to consider tactics; and tactics, although they are subordinate to principles, have laws, logic, and a domain of their own. Tactics must not, cannot, be in violation of principle (no tactical considerations could even get us to say that we think war can be abolished through a referendum vote), but tactics are not limited to formal reaffirmations of our principles—they are not worth much if that is all they are.

What was the nature of the Ludlow amendment problem? Was it for us a matter of principle or a matter of tactics? If the SWP in 1938 had had any doubts about pacifism, any ambiguity about it, then the matter of principle would properly have been foremost. But if ever there was any party whose members had been trained, indoctrinated, drilled, and virtually bred on a hostility to pacifism, surely it was the SWP. I can testify to that personally; long before I knew some of the most elementary ideas of Marxism, I had been taught about the dangers of pacifism.

Let me try to suggest an analogy: Comrade Smith takes the floor to propose that the branch should participate in a local election campaign by running our own candidates, and explains not only the benefits that would accrue to us from such a campaign but also the facts demostrating that we have the forces and the resources to run such a campaign effectively. But I take the floor to oppose Comrade Smith's proposal on the grounds that the workers have electoral illusions and that these illusions can only be reinforced and perpetuated if we, the revolutionary opponents of bourgeois electoralism, take part in these fraudulent elections. No, I say, our revolutionary principles forbid our participation in bourgeois elections and require that we call on the workers to boycott the elections; any other course would be in violation of our principled opposition to bourgeois parliamentarism.

Such a scene has never occurred at any SWP branch meeting, although it could occur and probably does in some of the Maoist and other sectarian groups in this country. Something not too different occurred in the Fourth International as recently as five years ago, when the French Communist League ran a presidential campaign dominated by the theme that its main task was to combat the electoralist illusions of the French workers.

Such a scene has not occurred at any SWP meetings, but if it did occur, there would not be any lack of comrades, new as well as old, who would point out that Comrade Smith had raised a tactical question and that instead of answering him on the level of tactics I had switched the discussion to the level of principles, leaving aside the question of whether the principles I had invoked were at all relevant to the point at issue.

Nobody in the SWP has ever done this—mix up principles and tactics—in relation to elections and our participation in them. But isn't that precisely what happened in connection with the Ludlow amendment?

From the very beginning of the discussion in January, when Burnham proposed support for the amendment, all that was needed was an answer on the level of tactics, assuming that there were no differences on the level of principle. But Shachtman, instead of giving a tactical answer, replied with a motion to criticize the amendment "from a principled revolutionary standpoint." And even at the end of the discussion, at the plenum in April, Cannon's initial motion, later withdrawn, wanted to affirm that the Political Committee had taken "a correct principled position" on the amendment "but made a tactical error" by not giving the movement critical support. But it was even worse than that, methodologically, in my opinion. When we are confronted with the need for a tactical decision, to be offered instead "a correct principled position" is to be offered at best an irrelevancy, and at worst an evasion, but in all cases not what the situation calls for politically. Pointing in such circumstances to the correctness of the principled position may provide us a measure of psychological consolation—" see, we were only 50 percent wrong"—but how much correctness can a principled position provide in read life if it is given as a substitute for a tactical position?

I think that I have been justified in devoting so much time to the Ludlow dispute for at least three reasons. First, I think that the details were needed, because without them, you would have only some generalizations and would lack the data through which to judge my conclusions.

Second is that the problems posed in that dispute related rather closely to other questions of importance. For example, there was the slogan of the workers' and farmers' government in the transitional program (which more recently we have shortened to the slogan of the workers' government in this country). The stenograms show that the SWPers kept putting questions about this to Trotsky—did he mean by the workers' and farmers' government the same thing that we meant by the dictatorship of the proletariat?—lurking behind which was the implied question: if the workers, and farmers' government means something different from dictatorship of the proletariat, don't we have the obligation to state this very forcibly, to emphasize it, in order to counteract the illusions that the workers may have in anything less than the dictatorship of the proletariat?

In tomorrow's talk I shall show additional evidence of the prominence in the thinking of the SWP leadership of the illusion factor, as well as more about the confusion over tactics and principles. But my point is that clarification of the issues involved in the Ludlow dispute helped the SWP to better understand the transitional program and its method as a whole. And without that clarification, if we had continued to cling to the SWP's first and second positions on the Ludlow amendment, what do you think would have happened decades later when a mass movement against the Vietnam War began to develop in this country? One thing you can be sure of is that we could never have played the role we did in that movement if we had not previously learned the lessons of the Ludlow question through the transitional program discussion. In that case the SWP would be considerably different from what it is today, and I don't mean better.

The other reason I feel justified in giving so much time to the Ludlow dispute is because it helps us to view our party, its cadres, its program, and its method the same way we try to view everything else—historically. Sometimes there is a tendency to think that they suddenly developed out of nowhere, fully formed and finished, with results and acquisitions that can be taken for granted. But it wasn't like that at all. We got where we are ideologically, politically, and organizationally as the result of a good deal of sweat, heart's blood, sleepless nights, trial and error—and struggle.

And that's how it will be as we continue to develop further. We have the advantage over our predecessors of not having to plow up the same ideological and methodological ground that they covered. If we really absorb the lessons they learned and the methods they pioneered, then we should be able to go beyond them and plow up new ground. And we certainly can do that better, the more realistically we understand how they did their work.

Two comrades whose opinions I respect made some suggestions after seeing the first draft of the notes for this talk a couple of weeks ago. I didn't succeed in incorporating most of their suggestions into the talk, mainly because it got so long without them, but I would like to take them up now.

One comrade thought that the emphasis of my talk might be misleading, especially for those who were not familiar with the early years of our movement. After all, he pointed out, we were not on the whole sectarians or abstentionists before 1938; even with our small forces and limited resources, we did some very good work when the opportunity came along. Furthermore, he added, although we didn't have the words "transitional method" or "transitional demands" in our vocabulary then, we did frequently and even effectively use that method and raise such demands in our work, especially after the big turn in 1933. Otherwise, he said, some of our most important work of that period—such as the Minneapolis experience—is inexplicable.

I must say that I agree with his concern, and if I did, or to the extent that I did, derogate or seem to derogate the party or its leadership in the pre-transitional program period of our existence, I certainly want to correct that now. There isn't any trace of muckraking or debunking in my motives for giving these talks. I don't know anyone who has a higher regard than I have for the pre-1938 party and its leadership. I said that it was a remarkable organization, and the more I think about the conditions of that period, the more strongly I hold this opinion. From my own extensive activity in the three years before 1938, I know that the party was not at all sectarian, and it was not abstentionist or dogmatic or doctrinaire, on the whole by at least 95 percent.

If it had been, it could never have accepted the transitional program, it could never have absorbed the transitional method so fast. Certainly no other organization in this country ever understood them at all.

So please understand what I have been speaking about in that context. We were not abstentionists, but sometimes we made abstentionist errors, and the transitional method helped us to overcome them once we understood it and incorporated it into our arsenal. Does telling this story discredit the comrades of that time? Not at all. On the contrary, it seems to me greatly to their credit that they were able to correct their errors and lift the whole movement onto higher ground.

The other comrade's criticism was that in my discussion of principles and tactics, I entirely omitted the question of strategy, which he feels is the area where the transitional program makes its central contribution. I think that he is completely correct on this latter point: the transitional program did provide us with a coherent and viable strategy or set of strategic concepts, perhaps for the first time in this country, and certainly on a scale we had never known before.

(Strategy, I should say parenthetically, was explained by Trotsky as follows in 1928: "Prior to the war [World War I] we spoke only of the tactics of the proletarian party; this conception conformed adequately enough to the then prevailing trade union, parliamentary methods which did not transcend the limits of day-to-day demands and tasks. By the conception of tactics is understood the system of measures that serves a single current task or a single branch of the class struggle. Revolutionary strategy on the contrary embraces a combined system of actions which by their association, consistency, and growth must lead the proletariat to the conquest of power." Tactics are subordinate to strategy, and strategy serves a mediating role between principle and tactics.)

But I did not go into the question of strategy in my talk deliberately: because it was virtually omitted from the 1938 discussion in the SWP; the focus was almost entirely on the principle-tactic relationship. The stimulus given to strategical thinking instead also marked an important step forward, thanks again to the transitional program. My not going into that aspect was not intended to deny that or minimize it. Anyhow, I hope that the comrade who made this criticism will, as I suggested, some day himself speak about the danger of what he calls "tactical think-ing that is not rooted in strategical thinking," and how the transitional program relates to this.

Tomorrow I shall resume the narrative, concluding my account of the chaotic plenum of the National Committee held in April 1938 after the return of the SWP delegation from Mexico, with major attention on the dispute over the labor party question. The following day, I shall make some comparisons between the SWP of then and the SWP of today, based upon a recent reading for the first time of the 1938 minutes of the Political Committee.

2. The Labor Party Question

I can't repeat the ground covered yesterday, but I'll give a brief chronology.

1928—Our movement begins when Cannon, Shachtman, and Abern are expelled for "Trotskyism" from the American Communist Party (CP).

1929—The Communist League of America (CLA) holds its found-ing convention and adopts its platform.

1931—The CLA holds its second convention.

1933—The International Left Opposition, to which the CLA is affiliated, makes the most important shift in its history, giving up its efforts to reform the Comintern and calling for a new International. In this country, the CLA ceases to consider itself a faction of the CP and set out to build a revolutionary Marxist party. This means the begin-ning of a turn away from almost pure propagandism directed at the CP toward intervention in the class struggle, with the aim of linking up with leftward-moving tendencies to construct the cadres of the revolutionary party.

1934—The CLA merges with the American Workers Party (AWP) headed by Muste to form the Workers Party of the United States (WPUS).

Spring of 1936—We dissolve the WPUS and join the Socialist Party (SP) and the YPSL in order to win over to the Fourth International young revolutionaries recently attracted by those organizations.

Summer of 1937—We are expelled from the SP and YPSL, with our forces considerably increased, and begin a discussion in preparation for the founding convention of a new party.

New Year's 1938—The SWP is founded at a convention in Chicago that adopts a declaration of principles and other basic documents to guide the new organization.

End of March 1938—Cannon, Shachtman, Dunne, and Karsner go to Mexico to meet with Trotsky to discuss plans for the founding conference of the Fourth International (FI) to be held later that year.

Trotsky introduces to them the idea of the transitional program, to be written as the basic program of the FI founding conference. They discuss this and related problems for an entire week, and then agree that they will go back to the United States to ask the SWP to approve it and act as its sponsor at the international conference, even though it will require changing certain positions previously adopted by the SWP. One of these is the SWP's position on the Ludlow amendment to the U.S. Constitution for a referendum on war, which I discussed yesterday.

The other is the SWP's position on the labor party, which I shall discuss today. Before doing that, however, I would like to carry the narrative further as regards the disposition of the transitional program as a whole, aside from the labor party question.

Cannon and Shachtman got back to New York in time for a Political Committee meeting in mid-April, nine days before a plenum of the National Committee. The Political Committee adopted an agenda for recommendation to the plenum, which was to be changed a week later on the eve of the plenum; they changed the rules for attendance—previously it was to be open to all members, now it was to be closed except for NC members and a few invited guests—and they received reports from the delegates, the minutes reporting only, "Comrades Cannon and Shachtman give full reports on their journey."

There is no record of the Political Committee deciding to recommend anything regarding these reports; it only designated Cannon, Shachtman, and Dunne reporters to the plenum but did not take a position on anything, which is not how it is usually done. We can assume that the Political Committee wanted time to think over the transitional program and related proposals.

In referring to this plenum yesterday, I called it stormy and chaotic, and I don't think that is an exaggeration, although the minutes contain only motions and a few statements made specifically for the record. In the first place, the plenum was extended from three days to four, an unusual thing; and even so, a considerable part of the agenda was not acted on, and at the end had to be referred to the Political Committee.

The first point on the agenda was a report by Cannon on the matters discussed in Mexico, supplemented by brief remarks on factory committees by Shachtman. The second point was questions from the National Committee members, answered by Cannon, Shachtman, and Dunne. The third point was a five-hour recess to study documents (the first draft of the transitional program had arrived shortly before the plenum), including stenograms of the talks with Trotsky (those that dealt with the transitional program have just been published for the first time in the second edition of the transitional program book).

Then the political discussion began on transitional demands and related questions. But when the political discussion ran out, instead of a vote being taken, voting was deferred to the third day of the plenum; in fact, before the vote was taken, time was consumed with local reports on the branches, labor party sentiment, the antiwar movement, the CP, etc. The members of the plenum were plainly not in a hurry to vote on the key proposals. But the clearest sign of uncertainty or confusion was the nature of the motions presented and finally voted on.

A motion was made by Maurice Spector, supported by Cannon and Abern, that the SWP approve the transitional program, and a motion was made by Shachtman, supported by Burnham, that the SWP approve the transitional program, and the debate over these motions became one of the two focal points of the plenum, leading to roll-call votes duly recorded in the minutes and a division that was sixty to forty. Of course the motions were not exactly the same. But I had to reread them several times before I detected a possible nuance, and three of the twenty-eight who voted—Goldman, Clarke, and Cochran—voted for both motions, with a statement that they considered then essentially the same.

The possible nuance was this. Spector's motion "endorses and adopts" the thesis written by Trotsky, whereas Shachtman's "endorses the general line of the thesis. . . . and adopts it as a draft of an analysis." But this thin line is made thinner yet by the fact that a second part of Spector's motion "subscribes in principle to the conception of the program of transitional demands proposed" in the thesis. So one endorses and accepts while subscribing in principle, and the other endorses the general line and adopts it as a draft of an analysis. The vote was seventeen for Spector's motion, eleven for Shachtman's.

The same thing happened with the second part of these motions, directing the Political Committee to prepare a program of actions based on the transitional program and the conditions and needs of the American working-class struggle. To me, the two motions seem the same, but they led to a thirteen to twelve vote in favor of Spector's. There was agreement only on the third part of the motion, that the program to be prepared by the Political Committee be submitted to the membership for discussion and referendum.

When such a thing happens, when a National Committee is divided thirteen to twelve over motions it is hard to distinguish between, then it is safe to conclude that the situation is not normal, or, to put it another way, that it contains the potential of a crisis. In my interpretation, there were two elements involved. One was what may be called personal. Cannon had been convinced by Trotsky, and he wanted the SWP leadership to endorse the transitional program without equivocation or pussyfooting. Others, including Shachtman, probably still had some reservations, hence wanted to affirm only "the general line." They resented being pushed or pressured; they wanted more time to try to square the new line with what they had said in the past, and they reacted against the motions supported by Cannon as a way of expressing their dislike of him as a "hand-raiser" for Trotsky, as someone who unthinkingly went along with whatever Trotsky proposed, in contrast to themselves as independent thinkers.

This was closely connected with something that had happened the previous year, 1937, when we were still in the SP. Trotsky was the first, in a confidential letter to the leadership, to conclude that the SP experience was coming to an end and that we should prepare to be expelled and set up our own party. Cannon, agreeing, quickly sent a letter from California, endorsing Trotsky's perspective. Shachtman and Burnham, who were in the New York leadership, almost flipped out when they got this letter, because they had settled themselves in for an extended, an indefinitely extended, stay in the SP, and they were bitter about Cannon "the hand-raiser," even after they were compelled to agree with his proposal.

The difference between them was that Cannon was a more astute politician, saw things faster, and did not feel that there was anything shameful about endorsing a good idea just because Trotsky had made it; whereas they, being perhaps less self-confident, had greater psychological difficulty in reaching a decision.

But the other element, a purely political one, played the main role in producing the strange situation of a fight over two similar motions. That was the one I referred to in some detail yesterday. Namely, that the SWP leadership was being asked to sharply change positions on important questions like the labor party, which they had held for several years and which they had reaffirmed just a few months before at the founding convention of the SWP; and that the reasoning Trotsky used in the transitional program seemed in some ways new to them, so new that at first they were jolted by it.

Supporting this part of my interpretation are the facts about what happened after the plenum. A Political Committee subcommittee was set up to draft a national program of action based on the transitional program, which was to consist of two parts, one on transitional demands, the other on the labor party question. In June, Spector and Burnham brought in separate drafts on the transitional program, but as they worked on them, the realization grew that really there were not any significant differences, and what emerged was a joint document. There were differences over various passages, but these were settled by majority vote (except Workers Government or Workers and Farmers Government), and in the end the comrades who had voted against each other at the plenum all accepted the final draft, which was submitted to the membership for the referendum.

So the leadership should be credited with the good sense to reach agreement, once they had a little more time to assimilate the transitional program. They should also be credited with avoiding a factional situation, which was unwarranted and would have done great damage, since there was no political basis for it. Their united presentation of the document did a lot to win the support of the party ranks for both Trotsky's transitional program draft and the American adaptation of it. A full-scale discussion took place in the ranks, and in the referendum that followed, over 90 percent of those voting endorsed the international resolution, and about 95 percent endorsed the American program of action (I'll report on the labor party vote later).

I do not mean to imply that everybody in the party, leadership or ranks, absorbed the full meaning of the transitional method all at once or quickly. Late in the fall, two members of the Political Committee were still trying to get us to replace the slogan of the sliding scale of wages with a "rising scale of wages." There were also some strange things said during the discussion.

One that I remember now with some amusement is a debate that was never settled, echoes of which I still encountered in the 1950s among certain kinds of comrades. That was over the question of whether transitional demands can be realized under capitalism, the implication often being that transitional demands were good or acceptable only if or when they could not be realized under capitalism and could not be supported if they could be realized under capitalism, the further implication being that supporting demands that could be realized under capitalism would lead us into some kind of horrendous trap and make rank opportunists of us all. It sounds more amusing now than it did then.

Anyhow, my point is that we did not grasp the meaning or master the use of the transitional method all at once—it took time, in my own case it was a matter of years, not months. But we did grasp it in part relatively quickly, which testifies to the maturity of both the leadership and the membership, and to the fact that our past had prepared us for this leap forward, for in practice we had been learning basic elements of the transitional approach before 1938, but without ever having generalized it our concretized it or theorized it or worked out the relations between the different parts as Trotsky did for us in 1938.

Now let me get back to the labor party question. Lenin waged a fight in the early years of the Comintern against those sectarian elements who refused to work in or give critical support to the candidates of existing labor parties, and this fight was so successful that hardly any communist thereafter held such a position. The question that concerned our movement in the 1930s was not whether to work in a labor party created by other forces, but whether it was permissible for revolutionaries to advocate the formation of a labor party. In a few moments I will trace the history of our movement on this question, but I will start by referring to my own experience, which began in 1935, when I first joined.

In 1935 the CIO and the new industrial unions were just being born; soon they were to turn their attention to politics—openly capitalist politics, as in their support of Roosevelt in 1936, but also hybrid politics, as in the formation of Labor's Non-Partisan League (LNPL) nationally and the American Labor Party in New York, which had the potential of taking an independent labor party direction. Nineteen thirty-five was also the year when the Stalinists dropped their third-period policies, including opposition to labor parties as social-fascist formations, and began to call for the formation of a national labor party. Labor party resolutions began to be discussed in various unions and other mass movements and often were adopted at union conventions, although that was about as far as it went.

What I learned as a new member was that it was impermissible for us to advocate the formation of a labor party. We could advocate independent labor political action in general, because that encompassed the idea of revolutionary workers' politics, but we could not advocate formation of an independent labor party because a labor party, necessarily reformist, would inevitably betray the workers. I remember that in 1936, when I was writing a pamphlet to be published by the unemployed movement in New Jersey, I felt it necessary, in reporting action taken by this movement, to try to distinguish between its endorsement of independent political action (which we favored) and its endorsement of a farmer-labor party (which we didn't).

In 1936 we joined the SP and YPSL, and our labor party position immediately became, and remained, the clearest point of distinction between our faction, called the Appeal Association or caucus, and the centrist faction, called the Clarity caucus. They advocated a labor party, for reasons that sometimes sounded radical and other times sounded opportunist, and we opposed advocacy. In the year and a half we spent in the SP and YPSL, there must have been thousands of individual discussions and debates around the labor party, no one ever joining our faction without coming to accept our antiadvocacy position. In fact, it was often the crucial point for the revolutionary-minded youth of the SP and YPSL, dominating their decision on whether to join the Appeal or Clarity caucus.

At our founding convention there was no debate on the labor party question. Instead, there was agreement, you could say unanimity, with the statement in the Declaration of Principles that the revolutionary party cannot "properly take the initiative in advocating the formation of Labor or Farmer-Labor Parties," and with the statement in the main political resolution, "Faced with the prospect of the formation of a national Labor party of one kind or another, the [SWP] has no need of altering the fundamental revolutionary Marxian position on the Labor Party question. The revolutionary party cannot take the responsibility for forming or advocating the formation of a reformist, class-collaborationist party, that is, of a petty-bourgeois workers' party."

But having settled accounts with the SP and having turned our eyes to the union movement, it began to be clear to the leaders of the new party that considerable pro-labor sentiment was developing in this country and that the party had better pay attention to it. Burnham took the lead in this respect in the Political Committee, but Cannon also was starting to concern himself with it. Burnham then wrote an article called "The Labor Party: 1938," reviewing the recent developments and urging an active orientation toward them. Even he, however, felt it incumbent to tip his hat to the convention formula: "The revolutionists are not the originators or initiators of any labor or any other kind of reformist party; they not merely give no guarantees or false hopes for such a party but, on the contrary, warn against the illusion that such a party can solve any major problem of the working class. The central task of the period ahead remains the building of the revolutionary party itself."

In the Political Committee, Burnham explained the strategy behind his article: he said that "there is now a labor party movement, and that we have to find ways and means of working in it." With this approach, the question of advocating a labor party could be skipped over; a movement already existed, so we didn't have to advocate it, all we had to do was get in. He asked the Political Committee to endorse his article and recommend its approach to the plenum coming in April. The Political Committee decided merely to refer the whole matter to the plenum, and that is how things stood at the time of the talks in Mexico.

Trotsky also wanted us to work in the labor party movement, but he didn't see any need to be devious about it. Instead, as you can tell from the transitional program book, he argued that we should change our position and begin to advocate the formation of a labor party, and he sought to convince the SWPers that they should do the same.

In the discussion, at the beginning, Cannon said that he thought the prevailing sentiment of the party was "to join the LNPL and become aggressive fighters for the constitution of a labor party as against the policy of endorsing capitalist candidates; if we can do that without compromising our principles, that would be best in the sense of gaining influence." Shachtman too was concerned about the possible compromising of our principles. More than once he reminded Trotsky that we cannot advocate a reformist party and yet he (Trotsky) was advocating something that seemed just that.

Trotsky replied that he was not advocating a reformist labor party. He was trying to find a pedagogical approach to the workers. "We say [to the workers], you cannot impose your [political] will through a reformist party but only through a revolutionary party. The Stalinists and liberals wish to make of this movement a reformist party, but we have our program, we make of this a revolutionary—"

Here Cannon interrupted: "How can you explain a revolutionary labor party? We say: The SWP is the only revolutionary party, has the only revolutionary program. How then can you explain to the workers that also the labor party is a revolutionary party?"

Trotsky: "I will not say that the labor party is a revolutionary party, but that we will do everything to make it possible. At every meeting I will say: I am a representative of the SWP. I consider it the only revolutionary party. But I am not a sectarian. You are trying now to build a big workers' party. I will help you but I propose that you consider a program for this party. I make such and such propositions. I begin with this. Under these conditions it would be a big step forward. Why not say openly what is? Without any camouflage, without any diplomacy."

Cannon: "Up till now the question has always been put abstractly. The question of the program has never been outlined as you outlined it. The Lovestoneites have always been for a labor party; but they have no program, it's combinations from the top. It seems to me that if we have a program and always point to it. . . . "

Shachtman was still not convinced: "Now with the imminence of the outbreak of the war, the labor party can become a trap." He was very much on guard against traps and illusions. "And I still can't understand how the labor party can be different from a reformist, purely parliamentarian party."

Trotsky: "You put the question too abstractly; naturally it can crystallize into a reformist party, and one that will exclude us. But we must be part of the movement . . . we always point to our program. And we propose our program of transitional demands."

It is obvious from reading the stenograms that the SWP leaders were hung up by some of their previous formulas on the labor party question. Trotsky tried to bring new light on the matter, and the way in which he did this, in line with the transitional program as a whole, appeared to them to represent something new: "The question of the program has never been outlined as you outlined it," Cannon said. The problem seemed solved; the only thing that remained was how to explain the change. If the new position was correct, how about the old position? Had the old position been correct in the past but become invalid as the result of new and different conditions? Or had it always been wrong? If so, what was the source of the error?

The voting on the labor party at the April plenum was very much like the voting on the transitional program, except that this time there was a third position, presented by Glen Trimble of California, whose motion would simply reaffirm the position taken at the founding convention, that is, would continue to oppose advocacy. Trimble's motion was defeated seventeen to four. The two major positions were expressed in motions by Cannon and Burnham.

Cannon's was very short: "That we adopt the draft statement distributed to members as the position of the Plenum; and instruct the Political Committee to take this as a basis, concretize it and elaborate it, and submit it to the Party for discussion culminating in a referendum vote." The draft statement he referred to was one written by Trotsky, which appears in the transitional program book under the title "The Problem of the Labor Party."

The motion by Burnham was longer and more detailed, generally along the lines of his recent magazine article, but at no point in real contradiction with the line of Cannon's motion. The vote was closer this time: twelve for Cannon's, ten for Burnham's, two abstentions (weeks later one of the abstentions was changed to a vote for Cannon).

When the time came to draw up the document authorized in the Cannon motion, almost the same thing happened as with the transitional program. That is, virtually everyone who had voted for either the Cannon or the Burnham motion realized that there were no real differences between them on the labor party, and they all voted for a common NC majority resolution and jointly defended it in the referendum discussion against an NC minority resolution introduced by Hal Draper.

But the results in the discussion and the voting were not the same as with the transitional program. Despite the virtual unanimity of the leadership, a large part of the SWP membership (and of the youth) was and remained against the change of position. The new position received only 60 percent in the referendum, as against 90 percent for the transitional program and 95 percent for the American adaptation.

Here I must differ with a statement George Novack made in his introduction to the transitional program book. He notes that the labor party question is not included in the transitional program and says, "This is for good reason. This problem is peculiar to our country, which is the most politically backward of all the advanced capitalist countries," the only one where the workers don't have some party of their own. But obviously this was not true of all countries in 1938 and it is not true today. There are many countries in the world, especially colonial, semicolonial, and neocolonialist countries, where the workers don't have a party of their own class, and where the general labor party approach could be appropriate. And although the Soviet Union was the only workers' state in the world, that didn't stop Trotsky from writing a lot in the transitional program about the problems that were "peculiar" to that country.

But comrade Novack was correct in saying that there was good reason for the labor party not being included in the transitional program. And the reason was that the leaders were aware of the opposition of many members to the new labor party position and were afraid that if the questions weren't separated, so that they could be voted on separately, this might endanger adoption of the transitional program first of all in this country, and secondly, indirectly in the rest of the International. This was good and sound reasoning, in my opinion. In my own case, I could not have voted for the transitional program at that time if it had included a provision in favor of labor party advocacy. At least 40 percent of the party would have been in a dilemma if they had had to vote on the two matters in a single package.

Today, when there isn't anybody in our movement who disagrees on the pro-advocacy position, it may be difficult to appreciate the heat that accompanied that discussion in 1938. The source of the difficulty was that, for several years before 1938, we, the members had been taught that it was unprincipled to advocate the formation of any party but the revolutionary party. And the difficulty was compounded because the leadership, instead of forthrightly stating that this was a mistake that now must be corrected, denied that it had been considered a principled question or tried to sweep it aside as irrelevant. This way of handling the change, which is not typical of Bolshevism or of our movement before or since, complicated the whole situation, distracting the discussion away from the essence of the problem into side issues, and made it more difficult for the members to resolve the question correctly.

"The question of the labor party has never been a question of 'principle' for revolutionary Marxists." That is the opening sentence of Trotsky's draft statement, printed in the back of the transitional program book, which was incorporated with a few changes into the National Committee majority resolution in the referendum. In my opinion, that sentence was wrong. It *had* been a question of principle, and when I say that, I am not concerned with whether it had been formally labeled a principle, but with how the party membership had been educated to view the question.

In the National Committee draft, that sentence was changed from "The question of the labor party has never been a question of 'principle' for revolutionary Marxists" to "The question of the attitude toward an existing labor party has never been a question of principle for revolutionary Marxists." In my opinion, the changed sentence was correct, as it stands, but in the context, it was an evasion of the problem that was troubling and confusing many party members.

I have decided not to try to prove what I have said here—that before 1938 we treated labor party advocacy as a principled question, even if we didn't label it that way. I'll merely repeat what Cannon said in Mexico, that our party would become aggressive fighters for a labor party "if we can do that without compromising our principled position." I'll assume that is sufficient until somebody challenges my statement.

At that time I thought that our principled position had always been against advocating a labor party, and in the course of that discussion, both written and oral, nobody, absolutely nobody, ever said that we had previously had any other position. If they had done so, it would surely have shaken me and the other 40 percent of the membership that voted against the new position and might have persuaded us that we were wrong. But nobody ever mentioned our having had any other position, or even said when we had adopted the one we had up to 1938. You may think that odd, but in those days—before offset printing made possible relatively inexpensive production of the old bound volumes of the *Militant*, and at a time when the resources of our party did not make available the old internal bulletins and documents of our movement— the general membership was not as well informed about the history of our own movement, in the form of accessible documents, as it is today. Anyhow, in the course of that discussion, which I followed closely and anxiously because, for the first time, my confidence in the leadership was shaken, *nobody* ever asked or said when we had adopted our pre-1938 position or if we had had a different position before that.

And so it wasn't until a few weeks ago, in preparing this talk, that I learned that our pre-1938 position had first been adopted in 1931, and that we had indeed had a different position before then—a contradictory one, in fact.

A few months after our expulsion from the CP in 1928, the *Militant* printed a long document by Cannon, Shachtman, and Abern, "The Platform of the Opposition," filling most of the paper's eight tabloid pages. One section was called "The Perspective of a Labor Party." I will read a few passages from it:

> The perspective of coming mass struggles involves the question of developing these struggles in a political direction and unifying them in a centralized form. The movement for a Labor Party is today at low ebb as a result primarily of the passivity of the workers and the decline in movements of struggle in the past period. The coming period of developing economic struggles will very probably be reflected in tendencies toward the revival of the Labor Party movement.
>
> It is not reasonable to expect that the masses of the American workers, who are still tied ideologically and politically to the bourgeois parties, will come over to the Communist Party politically in one step in a period not immediately revolutionary. All past experience, and particularly the recent experiences in the mining, textile and needle trades industries, where the workers who supported Communist leadership in strikes did not vote for the Communist ticket, do not sustain such expectations. The perspective of a Labor Party, as a primary step in the political development of the American workers, adopted by the Party in 1922 after a sharp struggle in the Party and at the Fourth Congress of the Communist

International, holds good today, although the forms and methods of its realization will be somewhat different than those indicated at that time.

It is therefore necessary to keep the perspective of a Labor Party before the eyes of the Party and the working class. We speak here not for the immediate formation of such a Party and surely not for the adventurism and opportunism that has characterized this work in the past, particularly in the organization of fake Labor Parties that had no genuine mass basis. The Labor Party must have a mass basis and must arise out of struggle and be formed in the process of struggle. To this end, the propaganda slogan must be really revived, and as soon as it has found roots in the masses and their experience in the struggle, it must become an agitational, and finally an action, slogan.

The rest of this part of the 1929 platform discusses what a labor party of the kind we would propagandize for cannot be—it cannot be a two-class party, or an enlarged shadow of the CP, and so on, so I won't read those parts.

That was February 1929. We then decided to hold the founding convention of the CLA in May, and the platform containing this position on the labor party was introduced as the leadership's main document for the convention, serving as the basis for discussion first in the branches and then at the convention. There, according to a report on the convention by Cannon in the *Militant*, the labor party question was one of the two sharply debated on the convention floor. After describing minority viewpoints, including some who wanted nothing to do with any labor party even after it was formed, and some who were against advocacy but would work inside a labor party, Cannon wrote:

> It was the opinion of the majority that, although it certainly is not a pressing question of the moment, the labor party question has a great importance for the future when the radicalization of the workers will begin to seek political expression. Therefore it is imperative to have a clear and definite stand on it. A misjudgment of the probable line of development of the American workers or a sectarian doctrine which would prevent us from approaching and influencing new upward movements, might have the most serious consequences later on. The formulation of the Platform on the Perspective of a Labor Party was adopted by a majority after a thorough discussion.

I wish that I had known in 1938 about this stage of our thinking on the labor party nine years earlier. I think it might have helped me avoid a serious error. Because, in my opinion, our 1929 position was substantially correct. It did not make a principle out of what was actually a tactical question. It did not reject taking a clear and definite stand merely because there was no labor party movement of significance in existence. It distinguished between the labor party as a subject for propaganda, and the labor party as a subject for agitation or action. And it had what proved to be a realistic perspective on the relative future growth of the revolutionary party and the mass movement.

That was the position at our first convention, in mid-1929, before the start of the big depression and at a time when all factions of the Communist Party, right, center, and left, were in favor of advocating a labor party, although their motivations and reasoning varied greatly. This position was changed, and even criticized, at our second convention in mid-1931, when the depression was over a year old and when the CP, now deep into its third-period madness, also was opposed to any pro-labor party development.

I don't mean to suggest that the CP's opposition to labor party advocacy was the same as ours. To the CP, anybody who advocated a labor party was a social fascist. We condemned their position, first of all because the whole theory of social fascism was false and suicidal from start to end, and secondly because if that was all their opposition to a labor party rested on, it was insufficient, because it meant that when they ultimately gave up social fascism they might or would return to advocacy of a labor party. (Which, incidentally, they did, in 1935.)

The political resolution adopted at our second convention, in 1931, was a long document, and the section called "Social Reformism and the Perspectives of the Revolutionary Movement" was also long. Contrary to the CP, we warned that the basis for social reformism, far from being "narrowed down," was being extended in the form of a growth of a leftist bureaucracy in the unions and a revival of the social democracy. Most of the section is devoted to a discussion of how to fight the reformists—how the CP should fight them, through the united front correctly understood and applied and so on, in a period when it must not be assumed that the United States was fated to be the last capitalist country to enter the revolutionary crisis.

The labor party question was presented in this context. The resolution saw the AFL bureaucracy, "their socialist assistants and the 'Left wing' progressive toadies of the Muste school" working consciously to erect barriers to the growth of the revolutionary movement in every area. "On the political field most of these elements seek to erect a barrier in the form of a 'Labor' or 'Farmer-Labor' party, that is, a bourgeois workers' party in the image of the British Labor Party."

The 1931 resolution then criticizes the many false formulations of the labor party question held in the American CP from 1923 to 1928, saying that none was based on a Marxian conception of the role of the labor party or of the nature of our epoch. Of course many of these formulations and policies had been adventurist or opportunist, or a combination of both. Now, said the resolution:

> all these conceptions and practices must be thrown overboard because they were originally wrong. . . . The American Communists cannot undertake to organize a petty bourgeois workers' party "standing between" the bourgeoisie and the proletariat.
>
> Abstractly considered, to be sure, were there a mass movement which would organize a labor party, the Communists would have to take up the question of working within it as a revolutionary nucleus. But this is a different matter entirely. Moreover, it is a matter which has less of a timely significance today—even abstractly—than in past years, since there is no substantial movement at all for a labor party in the 1932 elections.
>
> It is the reformists of all shades, the Thomases and the Mustes, who seek to set up this petty bourgeois party as a wall against the workers' progress towards Communism; in this work, they are only fulfilling their mission and role of prolonging as much as possible the "reformist period" in the development of the American working class. It is no accident that the Right wing liquidators of the Lovestone group have as the central point in their program the idea that the Labor Party's formation is an essential and imperative step for the American workers, which the Right wing is ready to initiate, to form and build up. It is this perspective which it recommends to the Communist movement as a whole to adopt. The Left Opposition, at its formative stage, leaned in the direction of this reformist perspective which constituted to a certain extent an uncritical carry-over of the preceding group struggles in the party, prior to the time when the Left wing took shape and was established as a political grouping distinct from all the others in the movement. The firmer establishment of its Marxian position dictates a break with this early standpoint and the adoption of the one outlined here. The adoption of this revised point of view, the result of clarification in its own ranks, marks a step

forward that will enable the Opposition to bring greater clarity on this vital problem into the revolutionary and labor movements as a whole.

That was 1931. A year later, Trotsky had talks in Turkey with Albert, Weisbord, the leader of a small group that was making an approach to the Left Opposition, although it shared many of the ideas of the Right Opposition, including its labor party position. After their discussion, Trotsky wrote a letter to Weisbord and a statement on the labor party, both printed in *Writings 1932*. In the letter he praised the position taken by the CLA at our second convention "because in the theses not only was a correct position taken on the essence of the question but also an open and courageous criticism of its own past was made. Only in this way can a revolutionary tendency seriously assure itself against backsliding."

In the labor party article, he said that he found the CLA convention position on the labor party "excellent in every part, and I subscribe to it with both hands." It is an article very worthwhile, especially for those who may think that we should have been or should be in favor of the formation of a labor party under all circumstances. But I leave all that out to quote two passages:

> 3. A long period of confusion in the Comintern led many people to forget a very simple but absolutely irrevocable principle: that a Marxist, a proletarian revolutionist, cannot present himself before the working class with two banners. He cannot say at a workers' meeting: "I have a ticket for a first-class party and another, cheaper ticket for the backward worker." If I am a Communist, I must fight for the Communist Party.

And a little later, after mentioning how the Comintern's policy toward the Kuomintang and the British Labor Party in the 1920s produced an opportunistic adaptation to the will of the Comintern's allies and, through them, to that of the class enemy, he said:

> We must educate our cadres to believe in the invincibility of the Communist idea and the future of the Communist Party. The parallel struggle for another party inevitably produces in their minds a duality and turns them onto the road of opportunism.

It should be noted that there had been no explicit reference to a principle about the labor party in the 1931 convention's resolution, but Trotsky's use of such a term was not inconsistent with that resolution;

it merely spelled out what was implicit in the whole approach of the resolution.

By now it must be plain that there was a principle involved in the thinking behind the position we held between 1931 and 1938. And it was a most fundamental principle—the principle of the need and primacy of the revolutionary party, whose construction is indispensable for everything else. Those who depart from this principle, or subordinate it, or compromise it, like the social democrats or the Lovestoneites, cannot possibly have the right position on the labor party.

But it does not follow that everybody who advocates a labor party is necessarily subordinating or compromising the principle that the building of the revolutionary party comes foremost for Marxists. It does not follow that advocating a labor party is contradictory to building the revolutionary party; in fact, advocating a labor party is not only consistent with building the revolutionary party in certain conditions but also a means toward building the revolutionary party, if the revolutionaries know what they are doing and how to do it right.

So on the labor party there was a confusion between principle and the tactics that were presumed to flow from the principle, which, as I showed yesterday, is the same thing as happened with the Ludlow amendment. The difference is that the Ludlow amendment mistake was of relatively short duration, a few months, whereas the labor party mistake lasted for seven years and therefore was harder for many of us to correct. The transitional program, or, more exactly, the transitional method that it taught us, enabled us not only to understand this mistake, some of us sooner than others, but also to better grasp the dynamics of unfolding class struggles and how to relate to them in a way that was positive and creative rather than purely propagandist, abstentionist, or dogmatic.

It showed us that advocating a labor party does not necessarily make us responsible for everything that happens in connection with a labor party that is formed under the leadership of other forces, any more than advocating a strike makes us responsible for everything that happens during a strike under the leadership of other forces. The nature of our responsibility depends on the nature of our program and the way we present it. We are responsible only for what we advocate, not for the victory of opponents over what we advocate.

It showed us that advocating a labor party does not necessarily mean that you are advocating the formation of a reformist party. It depends on how you advocate it, on what content you give your advocacy, on what program you advance for the labor party. The posing of the question—can a labor party be revolutionary?—which seemed unreasonable to us before 1938, was very useful educationally. Trotsky did not give the question an absolute or direct yes answer. We will try to make it as revolutionary as we can, he said, and he might have added, just as we do with the unions.

It showed us that advocating a labor party does not inevitably produce in the minds of the revolutionary cadre a duality regarding the primacy of the revolutionary party or turn the cadre onto the road of opportunism. It can do these things, but it need not, if the cadre is firm in principle in the first place and if the leadership is always alert to maintain the cadre's educational-political level and consciousness. Advocating a labor party can result in these retrogressive things, but it does not follow that it must, therefore it does not follow that the mere possibility must compel us to abstain from what can be a fruitful tactic for the building of the revolutionary party.

Of course it is true that a party that is weak on the principle of the revolutionary party will get into trouble with a labor party tactic. But the SWP was not weak on that principle, so that general truth was irrelevant in this case.

In 1931, when we replaced the 1929 position, we said that it had been wrong, for which Trotsky praised us. In 1938, when we replaced the 1931 position, we did not make any such explicit judgment. We said only that the 1931 position was abstract and that conditions had changed sufficiently to make the abstract formulas of the past obsolete. These were valid criticisms, and it is to the credit of the party and its leadership that, with help from Trotsky and the transitional program, we were able to arrive at a correct position, in a relatively short time, without the loss of cadres and without serious damage to morale. Perhaps this was the most that could have been achieved under those conditions.

I did not think so at that time. I resented what I took to be the leadership's refusal to make a judgment about the 1931 position, so much that my resentment prevented me from understanding what was correct and progressive in its 1938 position. In addition, I was basically wrong because I thought that the 1931 position was correct. Later I saw and now I see that the 1931 position was not just abstract but wrong, not just rendered obsolete by new conditions but wrong before the coming of new conditions—not in every word, but on the whole. I think that the public opinion of the party will reach this conclusion too, actually though not officially, when in the not-too-distant future we will make these old documents more available for study by the membership.

The personal lesson that I learned, rather painfully, was the need to be more objective in the analysis of political problems. It was hard for me to admit to myself that we had been mistaken, that I had been mistaken, so hard that I wanted to cling to the error. And I justified clinging to it by the less than perfect arguments used by the leadership to motivate the correction. That's not a good way to reach a decision. A position may be correct even though its proponents do not defend it in the best way possible. We have the obligation to recognize a correct position independently, so to speak, of the arguments of others who find it correct. It took me almost three years after the end of the 1938 discussion before I was able to do that with the labor party question. Fortunately, the party was not so slow.

Although the subject of these talks played a decisive part in my political life, that is not the main reason that I have gone to the trouble of telling you about them.

Building the revolutionary party is a difficult and arduous process. Recently I read the translation of a 1933 article by Trotsky about how hard it is to achieve a healthy society even after the workers have come to power, written for an American bourgeois periodical but not published at that time.

"To achieve harmony in the state," he wrote, "—even on the basis of collective ownership and planned management encompassing all facets of the economy—is only possible as the result of an indefinitely prolonged period of efforts, experiments, errors, crises, reforms and reorganization." That description struck me as appropriate also for the task of building a party capable of leading the revolutionary workers to power— a prolonged "period of efforts, experiments, errors, crises, reforms and reorganization.

We have reason to be proud of the achievements of the SWP. It is qualitatively superior to any of its opponents in this country, and, thanks to the continuity of its leadership, which enabled it to avoid repeating the same errors over and over, it enjoys several advantages over other sympathizing groups or sections of the Fourth International. This did not come about by accident or sheer good luck; it is the result of struggle and consciousness. A correct appraisal of the SWP and its achievements, which is necessary for further progress, is furthered by an awareness of the difficulties it has encountered and the way it overcame them, rather than by an ignoring of those difficulties or a depreciation of their magnitude.

The other reason that I think discussions such as this are justified is that they contribute to party consciousness-raising about the abundance of weapons in our political and theoretical arsenal. The metaphor most commonly used to call our attention to the debt we owe our predecessors is that we are "standing on their shoulders," which explains why we can see some things that they couldn't. I think I prefer a less athletic figure of speech, that of the arsenal. It was built by the pioneers of the Marxist movement and expanded by their successors. It is bigger, and its contents are more varied and useful than anything they had at their disposal. Available to us now are not only the actual weapons—the ideas, theories, programs, principles, strategies, tactics, and so on—but the history of their development, refinement, and improvement, which includes trial and error and experiments that failed as well as those that succeeded. We don't have to start from scratch, with the bow and arrow, and we are not doomed to repeat errors merely because we don't know their history. We can learn from the past, both what to continue and perfect and what to avoid.

No other movement has such a rich arsenal; the others would like to forget the past. The Stalinists, for example, would never dream of reprinting the books they published in the early 1930s, during the period of social fascism; we, on the other hand, are using precious resources to print material from the 1930s by Trotsky and others that we were too poor to print in permanent book form then and that we are determined to add to our arsenal for the benefit of the youth of today and tomorrow.

This arsenal is big, but it's going to have to be bigger before humanity turns it into a museum. You are going to have to build new weapons to hasten that day, but before you can do that you have to master the ones in our present stockpile. These talks are intended as a contribution to that process.

3. The SWP, Then and Now

A by-product of the preparation of these talks, which required that I read the minutes of the Political Committee, the National Committee, and the founding convention of 1938, most of them for the first time this year, was an almost involuntary comparison between the state of the party in 1938 and the state of the party now. I should warn you that these comparisons are drawn from data that is fragmentary at both ends, and that they inevitably reflect the special or subjective concerns I have about certain aspects of party life. And since they have little to do with the overall title of these talks and some of you may feel that you were brought here through false advertising, I hope you will feel free to leave now or whenever you realize you are not interested.

First of all, I should say that I am working comparisons between organizations that are roughly the same size, although I think that the SWP and the Young Socialist Alliance (YSA) together are a little bigger than the SWP and YPSL were between the founding convention in 1938 and the split with the Shachtmanites in 1940.

I have noticed a tendency among some of the younger members, when they look at the older members who have survived from the 1930s, to forget that the older members were once as young, energetic, and inexperienced as they are or were. So I will compare the age levels, since a normal revolutionary party will be a young party. At the 1938 convention, age data about the delegates was not reported, probably not collected. But it was reported the following year, at the 1939 convention, when it could not have been much different from 1938. The average age of the regular delegates was twenty-eight and a half, of the alternates thirty. Comparable figures at our convention last year were not given, but an estimate based on those that were given is between twenty-six and twenty-seven years for the regulars, and between twenty-five and twenty-six for the alternates. So the age levels of the membership are not much different.

The age levels of the central leadership were wider apart, but not as much as you might expect. Cannon was forty-eight in 1938, but he was exceptional. Shachtman was thirty-five, Abern forty, and most of the other PC members were in their thirties, I would guess. Their average age might be between thirty-five and forty, whereas the average age of their successors today might be between thirty and thirty-five. Not a big difference. The central leaders of 1938 had had a longer experience in the movement, which of course is important, but qualitatively this is hard to measure or compare.

There are no statistics about the class composition of the party in 1938. But I think that I should caution you against a tendency to imagine that the differences were greater than they actually were. In those days, when the depression was eight or nine years old, the occupation a person was going to end up with was harder to foresee and more dependent on accident. A college graduate might be working as a busboy and might have jumped at the chance to work on an assembly line; it was only when the war liquidated unemployment that things got sorted out and it turned out that he was going to be a school administrator or a sales executive. This distorts the picture a little so far as comparisons go.

Anyhow, class composition varied considerably from branch to branch. In Newark, where I was city organizer, we had four branches; one of these was made up entirely of workers, most of them unemployed or working on Works Progress Administration (WPA) jobs, and most of them Black; in the other branches, perhaps one-fourth belonged to unions; the great majority were college-age youth who couldn't afford to go to college and were either unemployed or holding low-paid jobs because, at the moment, there was nothing else. This was probably a more proletarian local than some others, including the New York local.

Trotsky, as you may know, was very dissatisfied with the class composition of the SWP, and he felt vindicated two years later when the split of the petit bourgeois opposition headed by Shachtman and Burnham cost us around 40 percent of our membership. He kept pestering the SWP leadership with his solution, which was to reduce to the status of sympathizers all members who failed to recruit a worker in six months. The leaders thought that this was too drastic and preferred to concentrate instead on colonization of members into industry. And in fact, in the next few years, especially when the war began and jobs became available, a considerable proportion of the nonproletarian members who did not leave with the Shachtmanites was successfully colonized.

An artist became a steelworker; a young woman who had studied to be a musician became an electrical worker; a student became a seaman, and so on. But this transformation was the result of politics, of decisions by the party and by the members involved, and it transcended class based on birth or accident. And even if we had useful figures, there's not much to be gleaned from a comparison of the relative class compositions that does not begin with a firm understanding of the primary of politics and concreteness.

An area in which I regret to report no progress is our almost total lack of interest in cultural problems and questions. Reading through the many long resolutions of our 1938 and 1939 national conventions, I noted sadly but without surprise that although the word "cultural" appears three or four times, neither in our resolutions, nor in our press, nor in our political or theoretical work did we display the slightest interest in cultural change or struggle, or any except the most superficial interest. Despite our urban location, we have always had more to say about agriculture than about culture.

This was one of the weaknesses of our movement at that time—its onesidedness, its bias or blindness to everything except the most obviously political or economic aspects of life in the United States. This onesidedness can be explained and, for the beginnings of our movement, to some extent it can even be justified. But I hoped that this defect would be corrected some day, and at the first Socialist Activists and Educational Conference four years ago, when Mary-Alice Waters made some remarks about the so-called cultural and sexual revolutions, I welcomed them and said:

> The sickness of a society that has outlived its usefulness takes many forms, and millions enter the radicalization process at personal and cultural rather than social and political levels. The beginning of the breakup of the authority of American capitalism can be seen in changing attitudes to morals, in revaluations of sexual norms, in the many varieties of escapism we can see around us. To better understand this breakup and its political significance, we ought to pay more attention to the cultural superstructure, beginning with our press. Perhaps the next time we have a conference like this we can have a full session on this question.

This is the fourth conference we've had since then, but there's never been a single talk or class on any aspect of culture. Our press confines itself for the most part to reviews of books and movies, and it often gives the impression that these are printed only when there is a hole to fill.

It took us one-third of a century after his death before we printed one of Trotsky's books on culture, but it is underread and underpromoted in our party, and it would never occur to our educational department to prepare a study guide for it or to recommend its use in party classes.

I had hoped that the present generation of the party, itself very much shaped by the rapid cultural changes since World War II, and sensitive to the problem of workerism, would fill this gap that my generation left in our outlook and analysis. But it hasn't happened yet, and it's difficult to discern any signs of progress.

One of the indisputable disadvantages of our party now as compared to then is that we do not have the benefit of Trotsky's advice and help. The only word to describe their value is enormous. Of course, since he was not in this country, his suggestions were not always practicable, but on the other hand, his physical distance from the problems and pressures sometimes gave him a broader and better view, as in the Ludlow and labor party questions. In addition, he sometimes tended to think that things could be done faster than actually proved possible, which must have been upsetting or exasperating to the comrades involved. But on the whole he was the wisest of teachers and the most loyal of collaborators, and this collaboration was fruitful for both our party and the international.

We haven't had the advantage of direct guidance by Trotsky for a long time. But as partial compensation we have the benefit of a much greater volume of his writings in English, available to all of us, than anybody had in any language in the 1930s. We can still learn much from Trotsky through these writings, if we take the trouble to study them and their method—from Trotsky's writings and from the writings, activities, and example of those who have continued his work during the last third of a century, starting with Comrade Cannon.

Another counterbalancing factor, which constitutes a big plus for us today, is the fact that the SWP leadership is now more homogeneous, more united, than it was in the 1930s. Reading the 1938 minutes convinced me, reconvinced me, that our central leadership at that time included several exceptionally talented and even brilliant people—but people who give the impression of sometimes pulling in different directions. Not all the time, not most of the time, some of the time. The Cannon leadership set out to correct this after Trotsky's death, not in an arbitrary or mechanical way, and the long-range effects have been very positive and noticeable. Our leadership now not only knows how to work as a unit, as a team, but it does it almost automatically, without having to think or strain about it. The consequences can be detected in all areas of party life if you know how to look for them, and they are good in virtually all respects.

Another area of big contrast between then and now is our electoral work, as I've already said in *The Party Builder*. The differences are bigger than between night and day, and they are qualitative as well as quantitative. If I dwell on this too much, it is because I was one of the few ardent advocates of electioneering at that time, long before the central leadership awoke to its opportunities. And since I was usually wrong when I differed with the National Office, I take satisfaction in calling attention to the few times I was right.

Most of the comrades looked down their noses at election work in the 1930s; they weren't opposed in principle, but they didn't see how revolutionaries could take it seriously or devote precious time to it. Most of our few so-called election campaigns consisted by announcing a candidate two or three weeks before election day and printing an article in our paper urging a write-in campaign for Comrade So-and-So (usually Cannon). They never bothered to tell readers how to cast a write-in vote, and even our own members didn't know how. It was the closest you could come to complete abstentionism in electoral activity without renunciation of our principled position.

I had learned better during our sojourn in the Socialist Party, and the other comrades there had the same opportunity to learn better, but most of them shut their eyes to this side of the SP experience, or never opened them. In all of 1938 we had only two places where we even tried to run candidates of the new party—in the mayoral primary in St. Paul at the start of the year, and in congressional and state legislative races in Newark. In the first case we had to settle for a write-in vote, I think, and in the second we actually went out and got petitions, got on the ballot, and got a respectable vote.

(Minnesota, one of the few places where we were interested in elections, was of course the model center of our party for trade union work; and at the founding SWP convention, the New Jersey party's work in the unions and the unemployed movement was cited as being the next best—a circumstance I find worth mentioning, because I think that a branch's attitude to election work is a good index to its political health and sagacity and its real attitude to reaching outward and talking to people other than ourselves.)

Our record was so bad that when the National Committee had a plenum at the end of 1938, it adopted a resolution that was printed in the *Socialist Appeal* under the title "Political Committee Rapped on

Election." This resolution criticized our failure to try to get on the ballot where it was possible, put the responsibility on the Political Committee, and directed it to correct the faults shown in the 1938 elections. But there was little improvement until around the end of World War II.

In 1948 we ran our first presidential campaign, and the change really began to sink in. But it was interrupted by the cold war and deepening isolation in the 1950s, and we did not really get back into stride until our 1968 campaign. Since then the progress has been monumental, in every respect. And all this will be seen as only a tune-up for 1976.

Finances, or rather financial woes and worries, are frequently reflected in the 1938 minutes. Comrade Cannon's *History* told of the poverty under which the movement tried to operate in its earliest years. We were bigger in 1938, and the financial situation was probably better then, but not much better, considering the fact that we were trying to organize a party rather than a faction.

Several times the minutes report that a competent member of the staff has had to be laid off—the national labor secretary, an editor, etc.— because we could not find the $15 a week they and their families needed to live on. A report is made that the party car can be sold for $60, with the money to be allocated for fieldwork in Michigan and Indiana. Sixty dollars was a lot of money then. A report is made in January that we are going to send $30 to the International Secretariat (IS). When Cannon tells Trotsky in March that the sum sent to the IS had by then risen from $30 to $50, Trotsky is overjoyed: "Oh, that's very, very, good."

When it is decided to send two delegates to the founding conference, a big campaign is launched in May to collect $1,000 for their expenses. The money comes in slowly. When half is raised, Cannon sails off, but Shachtman has to wait. In July he is still waiting, and in the end some members have to take out a loan to get him onto a ship. Of course, $1,000 then was a vastly different magnitude.

Trying to make allowances for the inflation and the very different economic situations of the two periods, I have asked myself if it was possible to make a comparison of the levels of financial responsibility to the party between the membership of then and the membership of today. That is, taking the different circumstances into account, was the party membership as ready in those days to make financial sacrifices as it is today? I finally decided, reluctantly, that I could not answer this question with any assurance, but I will tell you my impression, based on memory rather than the minutes: today's membership, which I think performs very well in this area, compares favorably with that earlier generation.

Related to finances and what it says about the membership's morale is the size of the party's staff, or the number of full-time workers. I don't call them professional revolutionaries, for as I understand that term, it applies to a larger part of the membership, including those who are not on the party staff but who make themselves available to the party where and when they are needed, whether on the staff, in a factory, on a campus, or wherever. So I am referring now only to the number on the staff. And I do that because it is a most significant index of the fighting capacity of the party, the best quantitative measure of the party's ability to turn word into deed, to carry out our decisions effectively, to intervene in a serious way in the class and national struggles that will take us beyond radicalization to revolution.

As I've already said, the size of our movement at the end of the 1930s, party and youth combined, was approximately the same as our present size, perhaps a little less then, but approximately the same. Not in the minutes but in an internal bulletin of that period, in a speech by Comrade Cannon after a trip to France in which he compared the SWP with the French party in 1939, I was able to find a figure about the size of our national staff of that time, including full-time workers in the various branches. And the figure was—approximately—one-sixth or one-seventh the size of our full-time staff now.

The membership size is approximately the same; the size of the staff is between six and seven times as large as it was then. Thinking about this ratio may make you more conscious, as it did me, of what a powerhouse, relatively, our still small movement is today—and of what a powerhouse it is, relatively, compared both to our opponents in the radical movement in this country and to the revolutionary movement in other parts of the world.

I think you know that I am not emphasizing this ratio in order to encourage complacency or smugness. I do it in order to heighten consciousness about the uniqueness of certain of our accomplishments, the moral being not only that more is possible now, but also that more is expected of us than of our predecessors.

I did not expect to find much in the 1938 documents about the Black struggle, nor did I find much. There is a short section in the declaration of principles adopted by our founding convention, entitled "Negroes and Other Oppressed Racial Groups." Everything said in this section—about the origins of racial antagonisms, the need to combat chauvinism among white workers, the need for common struggle, and so on—is correct and necessary. But it's not complete. Not complete merely by our present standards, but by the standards our party was to adopt a year later, at our next convention, when we first really began to think about the Black struggle and try to intervene in it. This turn in 1939, one of the crucial ones in our history, was, as is known by readers of the pamphlet *Leon Trotsky on Black Nationalism and Self-Determination*, stimulated and encouraged by the results of another visit to Mexico by a delegation from the United States, this time including C. L. R. James, which went to talk with Trotsky in April 1939 about the Black struggle, among other things.

I didn't know it in 1939, because the records about our history weren't as accessible to the members then as they are now, but that was the second time Trotsky had held discussions with U.S. visitors on the Marxist approach to the Black struggle. The first time was in 1933 when Trotsky, then in Turkey, had told Arne Swabeck that he thought that the Stalinist position on self-determination at that time was more correct than the Communist League of America's position. That was certainly unusual—that the Stalinists were more correct on anything than we!—but I never heard a word about that in the 1939 discussion, or for many years after, until I inherited an old internal discussion bulletin.

I mention this, although it is a little off the track, because I discovered something else that everybody had forgotten only a few weeks ago, when I was delving into the old *Militants* about the evolution of our position on the labor party. That is that the 1939 convention, which I thought was our first to discuss the Black struggle thoroughly, including its aspect as a national struggle, was actually the second where this question was discussed and debated.

The story, briefly, is this: In February 1929, a few months after the CP's expulsion of Cannon, Shachtman, and Abern, they published in the *Militant* a long document entitled "The Platform of the Opposition." This included a section entitled "Work among Negroes," which said in one place:

> The Negro question is also a national question, and the Party must raise the slogan of the right of self-determination for the Negroes. The

effectiveness of this slogan is enhanced by the fact that there are scores of contiguous counties in the South where the Negro population is in the majority, and it is there that they suffer the most violent persecution and discrimination. . . . The Party must at the same time decisively reject the false slogan of a "Negro Soviet Republic in the South" at this time. . . . This theory is still being propagated in the Party press and in official Party literature despite its rejection even at the Sixth Congress of the Comintern.

The Platform of the Opposition, including this section, served as our program until the founding convention of the CLA in Chicago in May 1929, and the platform served as the major document both in the preconvention discussion and at the May convention. Two parts of the platform were the subject of considerable dispute at the convention— the one on the labor party, the other on the slogan of the right of self-determination. Cannon's report on the convention in the *Militant* says:

> Following a discussion of the disputed section of the Platform on the Slogan of the Right of Self-Determination for the Negroes it was decided to defer final action until more exhaustive material on the subject can be assembled and made available for discussion. . . . In view of the profound importance of this question and the manifest insufficiency of informative material and discussion pertaining to it, this decision to defer final action was undoubtedly correct.

Final action was to be deferred ten years, until the 1939 convention, and a deep grasp of the question was not to be reached until the Black radicalization in the early 1960s helped us understand it more concretely and better. Our progress in this field, theoretically and practically, has been tremendous. Its full extent can be measured only by closer acquaintance with where we stood in 1938 and 1939 and, as it now turns out, ten years before then.

A few remarks about the role of women in the party: At the 1938 convention, the credentials committee was occupied mainly with contests in some branches by competing candidates for delegate seats, and it gave little data about the delegates as a whole. But one roll-call vote was taken, over the resolutions on the Soviet Union, and the minutes give the names of all the delegates and how they voted. Out of seventy-seven voting, three were women. The number of alternates and their sex are unknown. It was a little better at the next convention, in July 1939. Out of seventy-eight delegates, six were women; out of thirty-eight alternates, nine. So, at the 1938 convention, around 4 percent of the delegates were women; at the 1939 convention, around 8 percent. The percentage of women in the membership was of course higher than that.

Anybody who has attended recent party conventions and conferences, national or local, knows that the change in this area has been as big as it is progressive. At our convention last year [1973], 39 percent of the delegates and 35 percent of the alternates were women. I don't think that there has been any change in our party in these three and a half decades bigger or more important than this one. And I don't think that the younger members can fully appreciate its magnitude.

There has been as a result literally an explosion of revolutionary energy and talent previously untapped or underutilized throughout the party, from the highest committee to the lowest. Organizers, public representatives, candidates, campaign managers, department heads, teachers of classes, writers, editors, translators, coordinators, fraction heads, delegates abroad, and Janie Higginses—wherever you look, you find the women of the party well represented, making serious contributions to its work. In fact, if they weren't there, it simply wouldn't be recognizable to anybody as the SWP. No section of the radical movement in this country even comes close to us in this respect, and I don't think most of the sections of the Fourth International do either.

This release of revolutionary energy, this liberation of revolutionary energy, has transformed our party and made it a better instrument for its great historic tasks. I am not interested in allocating credit for this change. In great part, of course, it was brought about by the radicalization of the last decade and a half, especially of women, with results that penetrate every nook and cranny of this society. But in part it was also made possible by our responsiveness to this radicalization, our capacity to see what was happening and to meet it constructively, in both our public work and our internal relations and practices. How much credit we deserve for the change is not what interests me here. What I am after is to try, if possible, to make you more conscious of its magnitude.

In this connection I want to say a couple of things about Mary-Alice Waters's pamphlet *Feminism and the Marxist Movement*, based on a talk here two years ago. I consider it an excellent piece of work, a real contribution to the literature of our movement. I fully approved of what I took to be its main aims, which were to refute slanderous and ignorant misrepresentations by anti-Marxists about the record of Marxism in the women's struggles and to prod backward and sluggish elements in the Fourth International who were dragging their feet instead of meeting their revolutionary responsibilities toward the new women's liberation movement.

I happen to disagree with her conclusion that the two traditions of the women's struggle in the Marxist movement coincided generally with the main division in the movement between revolutionaries on one side and reformists on the other. I think that it was more complex than this, and that the evidence shows that there were two traditions among the revolutionaries too, some understanding and championing the women's struggle, and others rejecting it or paying it only lip service. Our line of continuity is with the former, and we have no reason whatever to minimize or ignore the shortcomings of the latter, merely because on other questions they were on the right side.

Comrade Waters's pamphlet has a section called "The Fourth International," but it doesn't have much to say about the Fourth International's theory and practice on the women's movement, and the reason for that is that it didn't do much in this area until recently. Comrade Waters warns us against ahistorical thinking—against "project[ing] backward in time our current level of consciousness or stage of development instead of judging the past by what was known and what was possible then." I endorse that warning wholeheartedly. To it I would add a corollary: avoiding ahistorical thinking does not mean and does not require shutting our eyes to the shortcomings or mistakes of the past, whether by our predecessors or ourselves.

The truth is that in recent years a big leap has been made in the SWP and parts of the Fourth International in both the theory and practice of the women's struggle. The SWP has added something important to our arsenal here. How much and how important this addition is can be measured accurately only by those who have a clear-eyed, historical view of what the situation was before the addition.

So, in summary: There has been much change and considerable progress since the founding of the SWP. Much of this we owe to the pioneers, without whom we couldn't have done half of what we did. But we would have perished if we hadn't gone beyond the pioneers, and we have gone beyond them, learning how to sharpen the ideas and improve the practice that they initiated or developed. And this is good because the time is coming closer when we shall have to storm revolutionary heights that the conditions of their time prevented them from reaching.

The last thing I want to take up is not a comparison, but an estimate of the party in the late 1930s. In a discussion I had with two comrades a couple of weeks ago, after I had related some of the things that happened in the Political Committee and the National Committee in 1938, one asked me about the composition of the Political Committee at that time. It consisted of seven people, I said, making a pedagogic point that in those days a Political Committee of seven was not considered inadequate, and I named the seven, noting that within two years six of the seven had left the SWP.

There were Cannon, Shachtman, Abern, Burnham, McKinney, Widick, and Gould, representing the youth. All but Cannon left the SWP in the 1940 split by the petit bourgeois faction that set up the Workers Party. Burnham quit the Workers Party at its birth and became a reactionary Republican in the course of time. Abern died in the Workers Party. McKinney left it before its members went into the SP, and today he is with the Shankerite A. Philip Randolph Institute. Widick became a professor and commentator on the labor movement, and Gould quit early for refuge in some Jewish organization. "Only one out of seven remained, and that was Cannon himself," said the comrade. "That confirms my feeling that we didn't have a real Trotskyist leadership until the 1940 split."

I've thought about it since this conversation, and I don't agree with his conclusion. To say that we didn't have a real Trotskyist leadership until the 1940 split would be like saying that we didn't have a real Trotskyist organization until then. And that's just not a tenable conclusion. The SWP was superior to all other groups in the International at that time; if it wasn't really Trotskyist, then they weren't either, and neither was the International. Trotskyism then must have been some kind of ideal that did not come into real existence until 1940, or later.

Exactly when, I cannot say. Because if you apply this criterion—of how long the central leadership lasted in the movement—to determine whether it was a real Trotskyist leadership, you would get some baffling results. Take, for example, the Political Committee that was elected October 1, 1939, the first elected Political Committee after the seven-member Political Committee of 1938–39. The war had begun, and so had the faction fight, and the PC was being reorganized to reflect the fact that the National Committee had decisively voted for the majority view on the Soviet Union. The Political Committee was enlarged to eleven, the minority being given three posts (Shachtman, Abern, Burnham), the majority taking eight and, of course, choosing them itself. The eight were Cannon, Morrow, Weber, Clarke, Cochran, Gordon, M. Stein, and Murry Weiss.

This was the Political Committee at the time of the split in 1940, its main additions at that time being Dobbs and Goldman. Well, what happened to these eight? Morrow and Weber succumbed to Stalinophobia during the war and were out soon after. Clarke and Cochran lasted longer, until the Korean War. That is, four of the eight defected in a dozen years. Three of the remainder dropped out individually for various reasons: Gordon, Stein, and Weiss. So out of the PC majority of eight, only one survived to old age in the movement, again Cannon.

The same thing occurs when you examine the International Executive Committee (IEC) elected by the 1938 founding conference of the Fourth International. Out of fifteen, three were murdered: Trotsky and Ta Thu Thau by the Stalinists, Leon Lesoil by the Nazis. Of the remaining twelve, ten defected by the end of the war, leaving only a possible two who still stood with the Fourth International seven years after its foundation. The certain one of this possible two was, again, Cannon.

So it's better to see the SWP and its leadership as development in process, starting in 1928 and continuing through today into the future. When Cannon, Shachtman, and Abern began in 1928, they had less knowledge of some aspects of what is called "Trotskyism" than many people in this room today. But they all made big contributions, including Shachtman and Abern, despite the fact that they defected after a dozen years, and the party was a product of their collective work. The weak and negative sides of Shachtman and Abern came to the fore later, but that shouldn't blind us to their contributions in their best days any more than Plekhanov's ultimate betrayal of the revolution can detract from the progressive role he played in his earlier years in preparing the way for Lenin's party.

Under their collective leadership, or, if you wish, under a bloc of Cannon with Shachtman and Abern, the SWP *never* made the kind of serious mistakes that the Bolsheviks made in March 1917 before Lenin's return to Russia. Under their leadership, the SWP went through some serious tests in the 1930s.

One of these was the French turn, that is, our entry into the SP. That was not an easy thing to carry out without losses or demoralization; it required an organization solidly based in principle and led by people who were tactically very flexible. The French turn was carried out in this country much more effectively than in France, where the Molinier-Pierre Frank split occurred right after the expulsion from the SP and paralyzed the party until World War II; the fact that such crises were averted here says something for the quality of our leadership and movement, and what it says is highly favorable.

Then there was the test of the transitional program, and I've told how that was met. And, soon after, there was the test of World War II, which we also met with success. So it was, on the whole, a pretty good party before 1940, a party developing in the right direction. In my own way, that is what I have been trying to show in these talks, among other things.

Appendix: The Transitional Program—Excerpts from "The Death Agony of Capitalism and the Tasks of the Fourth International" (1938)

Editor's Note: *The transitional program has been one of the core texts of the world Trotskyist movement. Much of it is a conjunctural document—dealing with tactics to use during the Great Depression in the advanced capitalist countries, tactics for the anticolonial struggle, tactics to use in fascist countries, tactics to use in the Soviet Union under Stalin's dictatorship.*

At the same time, as George Breitman comments, it sketches a methodological approach toward the development of socialist strategy: within the context of actual struggles by working people, there should be developed "a system of transitional demands, stemming from today's conditions and today's consciousness of wide layers of the working class," and yet in fundamental conflict with the power of the capitalists, therefore "unalterably leading to one final conclusion: the conquest of power by the proletariat." As Breitman explains, this approach was alien to the dogmatic–sectarian approach that infects many on the revolutionary Left (and that even affects some interpretations of the Transitional Program), instead combining a firm, practical adherence to revolutionary goals with a serious involvement in actual mass movements and struggles for reforms plus an extremely flexible approach to tactics.

The following excerpts (originally selected by George Novack for the anthology he put together with Isaac Deutscher, The Age of Permanent

Revolution: A Trotsky Anthology *[New York: Dell, 1964]) give a sense of that approach and of the way the Fourth International presented itself when it was formally established. It has been widely and frequently published since 1938, although one of the most useful editions is Leon Trotsky, with introductory essays by Joseph Hansen and George Novack,* The Transitional Program for Socialist Revolution, *3d ed. (New York: Pathfinder Press, 1977), which also contains valuable supplementary materials—including relevant transcripts of discussions between Trotsky and leaders of the SWP.*
    —Paul Le Blanc

The Objective Prerequisites for a Socialist Revolution
The world political situation as a whole is chiefly characterized by a historical crisis of the leadership of the proletariat.

The economic prerequisite for the proletarian revolution has already in general achieved the highest point of fruition that can be reached under capitalism. Mankind's productive forces stagnate. Already new inventions and improvements fail to raise the level of material wealth. Conjunctural crises under the conditions of the social crisis of the whole capitalist system afflict ever heavier deprivations and sufferings upon the masses. Growing unemployment, in its turn, deepens the financial crisis of the state and undermines the unstable monetary systems. Democratic regimes, as well as fascist, stagger on from one bankruptcy to another.

The bourgeoisie itself sees no way out. In countries where it has already been forced to stake its last upon the card of fascism, it now toboggans with closed eyes toward an economic and military catastrophe. In the historically privileged countries, i.e., in those where the bourgeoisie can still for a certain period permit itself the luxury of democracy at the expense of national accumulations (Great Britain, France, the United States, etc.), all of capital's traditional parties are in a state of perplexity bordering on paralysis of will. The "New Deal," despite its first period pretentious resoluteness, represents but a special form of political perplexity, possible only in a country where the bourgeoisie succeeded in accumulating incalculable wealth. The present crisis, far from having run its full course, has already succeeded in showing that "New Deal" politics, like Popular Front politics in France, opens no new exit from the economic blind alley.[1]

International relations present no better picture. Under the increasing tension of capitalist disintegration, imperialist antagonisms reach an impasse at the height of which separate clashes and bloody local disturbances (Ethiopia, Spain, the Far East, Central Europe) must inevitably coalesce into a conflagration of world dimensions. The bourgeoisie, of course, is aware of the mortal danger to its domination represented by a new war. But that class is now immeasurably less capable of averting war than on the eve of 1914.

All talk to the effect that historical conditions have not yet "ripened" for socialism is the product of ignorance or conscious deception. The objective prerequisites for the proletarian revolution have not only "ripened"; they have begun to get somewhat rotten. Without a socialist revolution, in the next historical period at that, a catastrophe threatens the whole culture of mankind. The turn is now to the proletariat, i.e., chiefly to its revolutionary vanguard. The historical crisis of mankind is reduced to the crisis of the revolutionary leadership.

The Proletariat and its Leaderships

The economy, the state, the politics of the bourgeoisie and its international relations are completely blighted by a social crisis, characteristic of a prerevolutionary state of society. The chief obstacle in the path of transforming the prerevolutionary into a revolutionary state is the opportunist character of proletarian leadership: its petty-bourgeois cowardice before the big bourgeoisie and its perfidious connection with it even in its death agony.

In all countries the proletariat is wracked by a deep disquiet. The multimillioned masses again and again enter the road of revolution. But each time they are blocked by their own conservative bureaucratic machines.

The Spanish proletariat has made a series of heroic attempts since April 1931 to take power in its hands and guide the fate of society. However, its own parties (Social Democrats, Stalinists, Anarchists, POUMists)—each in its own way—acted as a brake and thus prepared Franco's triumphs.[2]

In France, the great wave of sit-down strikes, particularly during June 1936, revealed the wholehearted readiness of the proletariat to overthrow the capitalist system. However, the leading organizations (Socialists, Stalinists, Syndicalists) under the label of the Popular Front succeeded in canalizing and damming, at least temporarily, the revolutionary stream.[3]

The unprecedented wave of sit-down strikes and the amazingly rapid growth of industrial unionism in the United States (the CIO) is the most indisputable expression of the instinctive striving of the American workers to raise themselves to the level of the tasks imposed on them by history. But here, too, the leading political organizations, including the newly created CIO, do everything possible to keep in check and paralyze the revolutionary pressure of the masses.

"Peoples Fronts" on the one hand—fascism on the other; these are the last political resources of imperialism in the struggle against the proletarian revolution. From the historical point of view, however, both these resources are stopgaps. The decay of capitalism continues under the sign of the Phrygian cap of France as under the sign of the swastika in Germany.[4] Nothing short of the overthrow of the bourgeoisie can open a road out.

The orientation of the masses is determined first by the objective conditions of decaying capitalism, and second, by the treacherous politics of the old workers' organizations. Of these factors, the first of course is the decisive one: the laws of history are stronger than the bureaucratic apparatus. No matter how the methods of the social betrayers differ—from the "social" legislation of Blum to the judicial frame-ups of Stalin—they will never succeed in breaking the revolutionary will of the proletariat. As times goes on, their desperate efforts to hold back the wheel of history will demonstrate more clearly to the masses that the crisis of the proletarian leadership, having become the crisis in mankind's culture, can be resolved only by the Fourth International.

The Minimum Program and the Transitional Program

The strategic task of the next period—a prerevolutionary period of agitation, propaganda, and organization—consists in overcoming the contradiction between the maturity of the objective revolutionary conditions and the immaturity of the proletariat and its vanguard (the confusion and disappointment of the older generation, the inexperience of the younger generation). It is necessary to help the masses in the process of daily struggle to find a bridge between present demands and the socialist program of the revolution. This bridge should include a system of *transitional demands*, stemming from today's conditions and from today's consciousness of wide layers of the working class and unalterably leading to one final conclusion: the conquest of power by the proletariat.

Classical Social Democracy, functioning in an epoch of progressive capitalism, divided its program into two parts independent of each other: the *minimum program*, which limited itself to reforms within the framework of bourgeois society, and the *maximum program*, which promised substitution of socialism for capitalism in the indefinite future. Between the minimum and maximum program no bridge existed, since the word *socialism* is used only for holiday speechifying.[5] The Comintern has set out to follow the path of Social Democracy in an epoch of decaying capitalism: when, in general, there can be no discussion of systematic social reforms and the raising of the masses' living standards; when the bourgeoisie always takes away with the right hand twice what it grants with the left (taxes, tariffs, inflation, "deflation," high prices, unemployment, police supervision of strikes); when every serious demand of the proletariat and even every serious demand of the petty bourgeoisie inevitably reaches beyond the limits of capitalist property relations and of the bourgeois state.

The strategical task of the Fourth International lies not in reforming capitalism but in its overthrow. Its political aim is the conquest of power by the proletariat for the purpose of expropriating the bourgeoisie. However, the achievement of this strategic task is unthinkable without the most considered attention to all, even small and partial questions of tactics. All sections of the proletariat, all its layers, occupations and groups should be drawn into the revolutionary movement. The present epoch is distinguished not for the fact that it frees the revolutionary party from day-to-day work but because it permits this work to be carried on indissolubly with the actual tasks of the revolution.

The Fourth International does not discard the program of the old "minimal" demands to the degree to which these have preserved at least part of their vital forcefulness. Indefatigably, it defends the democratic rights and social conquests of the workers. But it carries on this day-to-day work within the framework of the correct actual, that is, revolutionary perspective. Insofar as the old, partial, "minimal" demands of the masses clash with the destructive and degrading tendencies of decadent capitalism—and this occurs at each step—the Fourth International advances a system of *transitional demands*, the essence of which is contained in the fact that ever more openly and decisively they will be directed against the very bases of the bourgeois regime. The old "minimal program" is superseded by the *transitional program*, the task of which lies in systematic mobilization of the masses for the proletarian revolution.

Editor's Note: *At this point, there is a discussion of possible transitional demands—a sliding scale of wages to keep pace with inflation, and a sliding* scale of hours to eliminate unemployment by reducing the length of the workday to provide jobs for all—which would seem reasonable to most people but which comes into conflict with the continued existence of capitalism, especially during the 1930s. This is followed by a discussion of building a class-struggle left wing in the trade unions, and also the development of democratic shop-floor and factory committees. The program calls for the elimination of "business secrets" used to cheat the workers ("open the books!") and calls for the development of structures to establish workers' control of the workplace. The expropriation of capitalist enterprises and industries, and the nationalization of banks and the credit system, under the control of the working-class majority, are also posed.

The Transitional Program then discusses the tactical escalation of factory seizures (through sit-down strikes) and picket lines, defense guards to protect picket lines and other workers' actions, the development of workers' militias, and the general arming of the working class—all within the context of mass struggles carried on through the radicalizing organized labor movement, which would be subject to attack by thugs in the pay of the capitalists, by fascist gangs, and so forth. A discussion of the need for a workers' and farmers' alliance, and a discussion of the struggle against imperialism and war, are followed by an examination of the formula of the "workers' and farmers' government," defined as a popularization of the concept of working-class political rule (labeled variously by revolutionary Marxists as "dictatorship of the proletariat" or "workers' state" or "workers' democracy"), which should be based on the democratic councils of workplaces and communities that the Russians called soviets.

A substantial section on the struggle against colonialism and imperialism, and the fight for the interests of the workers and peasants, within the economically "backward" countries is followed by substantial sections focusing on struggles in fascist countries and in the USSR. There are critical discussions of left-wing currents that are seen as succumbing to "opportunism and unprincipled revisionism" on the one hand and to "sectarianism" on the other. This is followed by a section entitled "Open the road to the woman worker! Open the road to the youth!" The Transitional Program then concludes with the following section.

Under the Banner of the Fourth International!

Skeptics ask: But has the moment for the creation of the Fourth International yet arrived? It is impossible, they say, to create an

International "artificially"; it can arise only out of great events, etc., etc. All of these objections merely show that skeptics are no good for the building of a new International. They are good for scarcely anything at all.

The Fourth International has already arisen out of great events: the greatest defeats of the proletariat in history. The cause for these defeats is to be found in the degeneration and perfidy of the old leadership. The class struggle does not tolerate an interruption. The Third International, following the Second, is dead for purposes of revolution. Long live the Fourth International![6]

But has the time yet arrived to proclaim its creation? . . . the skeptics are not quieted down. The Fourth International, we answer, has no need of being "proclaimed." It exists and it fights. Is it weak? Yes, its ranks are not numerous because it is still young. They are as yet chiefly cadres. But these cadres are pledges for the future. Outside of these cadres there does not exist a single revolutionary current on this planet really meriting the name. If our International be still weak in numbers, it is strong in doctrine, program, tradition, in the incomparable tempering of its cadres. Who does not perceive this today, let him in the meantime stand aside. Tomorrow it will become more evident.

The Fourth International, already today, is deservedly hated by the Stalinists, Social Democrats, bourgeois liberals, and fascists. There is not and there cannot be a place for it in any of the People's Fronts. It uncompromisingly gives battle to all political groupings tied to the apron-strings of the bourgeoisie. Its task—socialism. Its method—proletarian revolution.

Without inner democracy—no revolutionary education. Without discipline—no revolutionary action. The inner structure of the Fourth International is based on the principles of *democratic centralism:* full freedom in discussion, complete unity in action.

The present crisis in human culture is the crisis in the proletarian leadership. The advanced workers, united in the Fourth International, show their class the way out of the crisis. They offer a program based on international experience in the struggle of the proletariat and of all the oppressed of the world for liberation. They offer a spotless banner.

Workers—men and women—of all countries, place yourselves under the banner of the Fourth International. It is the banner of your approaching victory.

Notes

1.   The New Deal was the policy orientation of the Democratic Party and the U.S. government under President Franklin D. Roosevelt from 1933 until 1939, designed to preserve capitalism by conceding sweeping social reforms and seeking to increase government regulation of the economy during the Great Depression, in the face of ferment and radicalization within the working class and other sectors of the population. It ended when there was a step-up in U.S. preparations for World War II from 1939 to 1941, which is what brought the United States and the world out of the depression. See Howard Zinn's critical-minded anthology *New Deal Thought* (Indianapolis: Bobbs-Merrill, 1966), and Irving Bernstein's glowing yet informative *A Caring Society: The New Deal, the Worker, and the Great Depression* (Boston: Houghton Mifflin, 1985); for a Trotskyist critique, see Art Preis, *Labor's Giant Step* (New York: Pathfinder Press, 1972), pp. 9–18, 44–49, 66–70, 72–81, 113–24.

   The "Popular Front" (also known as the People's Front) was a strategy developed in the mid-1930s by the Communist International. At the Comintern's Seventh World Congress (1935), leading spokesman George Dimitrov argued: "Now the toiling masses in a number of capitalist countries are faced with the necessity of making a definite choice, and of making it today, not between proletarian dictatorship and bourgeois democracy, but between bourgeois democracy and fascism." Georgi Dimitroff, *The United Front, the struggle against Fascism and War* (New York: International Publishers, 1938), p. 110. There was a special concern that the rise of the virulently militaristic and anticommunist dictatorship of Adolf Hitler in Germany—due in part to Communist sectarianism in refusing to work with other left-wing forces to prevent the Nazi rise to power—posed a direct threat to the so-called homeland of socialism, the USSR, as well as to the existence of the workers' movement throughout Europe. Therefore, Dimitrov and others insisted, Communists and social democrats should immediately form a working-class united front, then form a cross-class Popular Front with petit bourgeois and liberal capitalist forces, for the purpose of creating electoral coalitions to elect Popular Front governments. Such governments should preserve capitalism and bourgeois democracy, but also implement substantial social reforms, and—most important—form a foreign policy alliance with the Soviet Union against Nazi Germany. On the development of this orientation, see E. H. Carr, *Twilight of the Comintern, 1930–1935* (New York: Pantheon Books, 1982).

   According to U.S. Communist leader Earl Browder, "Roosevelt's programmatic utterances of 1937, when combined with the legislative program of the C.I.O. (his main labor support), provides a People's Front program of an advanced type." Browder, *The People's Front* (New York: International Publishers, 1938), p. 13.

2.   In Spain there were several major currents on the Left—the largest component made of the Iberian Anarchist Federation (FAI) and the anarcho-syndicalist

labor federation (the CNT), next being the Socialist Party of Spain and its labor federation (the UGT). The Stalinist-led Communist Party was initially fairly small and also participated in the UGT. Split-offs from the CP (including what had once been a sizable Trotskyist-influenced current) formed the Unified Marxist Workers Party, known by the the Spanish acronym POUM.

In 1935 the Socialists and Communists formed an electoral Popular Front with bourgeois liberal forces, narrowly winning national elections and establishing a governmental coalition. When a combined conservative-fascist-military uprising in 1936, led by General Francisco Franco, sought to overturn the democratically elected government, the organizations of the working class effectively mobilized to prevent its victory, and a civil war erupted. The Popular Front government of the Spanish Republic followed relatively conservative social policies so as not to alienate liberal pro-capitalist forces inside and outside of Spain, especially because both social democrats and Stalinists hoped for assistance from the "Western democracies" (such as Britain, France, the United States). Despite this, the more radical anarchists and POUM—while calling for the Spanish revolution to move forward—made far-reaching concessions to the Popular Front government, which in turn (particularly due to Stalinist influence) savagely repressed them. The moderate social policies of the government during the Spanish civil war, however, undermined the effort to mobilize the Spanish masses against the reactionary generals, landowners, and businessmen who led the right-wing insurgents. What's more, the "Western democracies"—eyeing the leftists in the Spanish Republican government—remained neutral, while Hitler's Germany and Mussolini's Italy gave substantial support to Franco's forces, which finally won in 1939. See Pierre Broue and Emile Temime, *Revolution and the Civil War in Spain* (Cambridge, MA: MIT Press, 1970), and Ronald Sanders, *Blood of Spain, An Oral History of the Spanish Civil War* (New York: Pantheon Books, 1979).

3.   In France a right-wing coup attempt in 1934 galvanized the working class, which was organized into the Social-Democratic French Section of the Second International (SFIO), the French Communist Party (PCF), and a divided trade union movement—the antipolitical (syndicalist) CGT, led by one-time anarcho-syndicalist Leon Jouhaux, and the pro-communist CGT-U. A powerful working-class united front, under Socialist-Communist leadership, came into being, and it seemed that the workers might take power. Instead the ferment was channeled into a 1936 electoral coalition that resulted in a Popular Front government—composed of a coalition of the SFIO under Leon Blum, the PCF under Maurice Thorez, and a small liberal-capitalist Radical Party under Edouard Daladier. The government, led by Blum, carried out some social reforms but made numerous compromises to liberal-capitalist elements, dampened popular leftist enthusiasm, and then fell in 1938, giving way to a Radical Party government led by Daladier (which overturned many of the 1936 reforms). See Jacques Danos and Marcel Gibelin, *June '36, Class Struggle and the Popular Front in France* (London: Bookmarks, 1986).

4.   The Phrygian cap refers to the liberty cap of the French Republic; the swastika, of course, refers to the mystical Nordic symbol utilized by the extreme fascistic Nazi (or "National-Socialist") movement led by Adolf Hitler. A classic Trotskyist-influenced analysis of German and Italian fascism is Daniel Guerin's *Fascism and Big Business* (New York: Monad Books/Pathfinder Press, 1973); R. Palme Dutt's *Fascism and Social Revolution* (New York: International Publishers, 1934) presents a documented analysis that is marred by the influence of Stalinism but nonetheless offers much of interest. Also see Franz Neumann's classic *Behemoth: The Structure and Practice of National Socialism, 1933–1944* (New York: Harper & Row, 1966), and Michael N. Dobkowski and Isidor Wallimann, eds., *Radical Perspectives on the Rise of Fascism in Germany, 1919–1945* (New York: Monthly Review Press, 1989). An invaluable memoir by a participant in the German workers' movement in the period leading up to, spanning, and following Nazi rule is Oskar Hippe's *And Red Is the Color of Our Flag* (London: Index Books, 1991), which provides information on German Trotskyism and thoughtful analyses of German realities from World War I to the 1970s.

5.   Two useful studies on this phenomenon are Peter Gay, *The Dilemma of Democratic Socialism, Eduard Bernstein's Challenge to Marx* (New York: Columbia University Press, 1952), and Carl E. Schorske, *German Social Democracy, 1905–1917* (Cambridge, MA: Harvard University Press, 1955).

6.   On the Second International, see Julius Braunthal, *History of the International, 1864–1943*, 2 vols. (New York: Frederick A. Praeger, 1967), and *History of the International, World Socialism, 1943–1968* (Boulder: Westview Press, 1980) for a social democratic account (with some reference to the First and the Third Internationals as well); J. Lenz, *The Rise and Fall of the Second International* (New York: International Publishers, 1932), for a Communist account; James Joll, *The Second International, 1889–1914* (New York: Harper & Row, 1975), for a brief academic account.

      On the Third International, see C. L. R. James, *World Revolution, 1917–1936: The Rise and Fall of the Communist International* (Atlantic Highlands, NJ: Humanities Press, 1993), for a Trotskyist-influenced account; William Z. Foster, *History of the Three Internationals, the World Socialist and Communist Movements from 1848 to the Present* (New York: International Publishers, 1955), for a Stalinist account; Fernando Claudin, *The Communist Movement, from Comintern to Cominform*, 2 vols. (New York: Monthly Review Press, 1975), for a thoughtful and well-documented account by a former Communist.

      On the Fourth International, see Pierre Frank, *The Fourth International: The Long March of the Trotskyists* (London: Ink Links, 1979); Tom Barrett, ed., *Fifty Years of the Fourth International* (New York: Fourth Internationalist Tendency, 1990); Robert J. Alexander, *International Trotskyism, 1929–1985: A Documented Analysis of the Movement* (Durham, NC: Duke University Press, 1992).

3

George Novack, 1905–92: Meaning a Life

ALAN WALD

> In everyday political activity we usually see no further than the public face while the inner life of the person remains hidden.
>
> —George Novack in a letter to
> Alan Wald, May Day, 1983

1

George Edward Novack, who died on the morning of July 30 1992, a week shy of his eighty-seventh birthday, was a unique figure in U.S. Marxist cultural history. Of the many left-wing intellectuals radicalized in the early 1930s, he was among a heroic remnant who remained loyal to the revolutionary socialist convictions of their youth. Throughout World War II, the Cold War, and the New Left era of the 1960s and after, George produced numerous essays and, later, books, defending classical Marxist ideas in history and philosophy.[1] Since his viewpoint was orthodox Trotskyist, and he combined his literary work with almost unbroken activity in a revolutionary political party for nearly fifty years,[2] he is virtually unparalleled among his generation, setting a high standard of commitment for socialist intellectuals who come after.[3]

I first established a friendship with George when he stayed at my apartment in the spring of 1968 to fulfill a speaking engagement at Antioch College in Yellow Springs, Ohio, where I was a student. We stayed up late into the night talking about Marxism and literature. Although his philosophical writing impressed me at the time and later as uneven and sometimes unsophisticated compared with the works of

177

Georg Lukács and Jean-Paul Sartre, in which I was then immersed, I was struck by his breadth of knowledge, even-tempered assessments of literary figures (he had known quite a few personally) and their books, and marked enthusiasm for reading and ideas. When I became a graduate student in the English Department at the University of California at Berkeley a year later, our association intensified due to my decision to conduct original research about U.S. literary intellectuals drawn to Trotskyism.

By the early 1970s, we were in regular contact through correspondence several times a month, in addition to one or two private conferences a year (many of which were tape-recorded) in his apartment in Greenwich Village or else in Oberlin, Ohio, where the Socialist Workers Party (SWP) alternated a convention and educational conference each summer. In addition, George granted me access to his records at Harvard College, where he passed 1922–27 without graduating; to his younger sister, Helen Hirshberg, who would predecease him; and to his former therapist, Robert Litman, a world-famous suicide prevention specialist who treated him in Los Angeles in 1954. With George's encouragement, I also interviewed his first wife, the novelist and biographer Elinor Rice; his college friend, the poet Stanley Kunitz; and several others.[4]

My work thus enabled George to renew some old associations, learn more about his own past and the fate of his friends, and engage in intellectual exchange about historical and theoretical questions that fascinated him and about which he complained that few of his comrades were sufficiently informed to discuss. In addition to all of the above, George reviewed thousands of pages of my manuscripts—not just reading them, but carefully commenting and often making helpful editorial suggestions about them. He never applied pressure to bring me into conformity with his own perspective. Also, unlike so many other intellectuals with whom I have worked, he was neither hypercritical nor defensive in regard to matters pertaining to himself.

Although George knew that my long-term objective was to produce books, he seemed to enjoy the give-and-take simply for itself. Once he learned that Pathfinder and Monad Presses (both associated with the SWP) had no interest in publishing any works by me, he was aggressive in encouraging me in my dealings with university and commercial houses (although the latter were uninterested, too). We never discussed any books or articles of mine as "strategic interventions"; he seemed to favor the appearance of such works simply to add to the general community of knowledge about the intellectual Left, and he seemed to think that their value would be greatest if I went my own way in choice of theme and approach.

The only time our relationship was interrupted was in the winter of 1984, at a time when the SWP was expelling and severing relations with hundreds of members, sympathizers, and one-time collaborators—anyone who openly expressed dismay at the bureaucratic way in which the SWP was transforming itself from an orthodox Trotskyist to a semi-Castroist organization.[5] Prior to that time, George was adamant that our collaboration should proceed uninterrupted and unaffected. This was in spite of the fact that I had never cast a vote in favor of an SWP majority political resolution and had made it known since the early 1970s of my preference for the political views promoted by the Belgian Marxist Ernest Mandel over those of the SWP's major leader, Jack Barnes. George's accepting attitude about my political differences was in marked contrast to the fear and hostility exhibited by vast majority of SWP and Young Socialist Alliance (YSA) members with whom I came in contact, young or old. It wasn't that George ignored the controversial issues or occluded them from discussion, but that we both used restraint in expressing our views.

However, as the SWP entered the climactic stages of its transformation that would lead to its political break with the Fourth International,[6] things became more repressive in the SWP's milieu. Following the meeting of the SWP National Committee after the August 1983 party convention, I sent George a letter, vigorously raising concerns about the organizational and political direction of the SWP, to which he responded: "On the issues currently dividing the party you referred to, we shall simply have to agree to disagree, as we did during the IT episode,[7] and proceed with our collaboration on your project [the early stages of the book that later became *The New York Intellectuals*] on the same basis as before. I anticipate no obstacle to this at the present time."[8] However, in late February 1984, George returned unopened a manuscript that I had sent him in Mexico, where he was living with his new companion;[9] a handwritten note was appended, saying that this action constituted the "suspension" of "our long-standing literary collaboration."[10]

This hiatus lasted about twenty months. Communications after that time were reduced to only a few times a year. Although his notes grew increasingly friendly, most were brief.[11] This may have been due as much to illness and physical enfeeblement as to political differences, since in the same period he also stopped writing for the SWP press.

The last time I visited George was in December 1991, in a senior citizens' residence at 300 Amsterdam Avenue, near Seventy-second Street and Broadway. The previous spring, following an illness and hospitalization, he had moved out of his longtime apartment at 326 West Nineteenth Street. In his room at the shabby residence, he was alone and apparently weak, unable to rise easily from his chair. But he was very friendly, sending through me his "best regards" to mutual friends such as Patrick Quinn and Mike Smith.[12]

On his own, George brought up the subject of the transformation of the SWP, although his language here was less direct and somewhat "Aesopian." He explained to me, as he had done in discussions we had around 1983, that I should understand that, back when he, Joseph Hansen, and Farrell Dobbs had made a decision to transfer leadership of the SWP over to "the Barnes tendency" (this was Novack's phrase), the three of them had made a pledge. They would always give the new people the benefit of the doubt, unless a major "crossing of the class lines" occurred, and not "second-guess" them. (In other words, they would keep any disagreements they had with Barnes's policies or methods secret from the membership of the SWP, and publicly back up Barnes against his critics.) George said that, in fact, he *did* have his own opinions on some of the questions that had come into dispute in the last years. However, since he had not been on top of things, he didn't feel that his views were very important. George emphasized that I would understand his position when I, too, became older and less active.

It seems likely that, based on documentation, one of George's "differences of opinion" was over the decision of "the Barnes tendency" to use the 1979 success of the Nicaraguan revolution to repudiate Trotsky's "Theory of Permanent Revolution."[13] During the heat of this debate, George wrote to me an opinion that I understood to be the same as that of the majority of the Fourth International (and opposed to the views promoted by Barnes): "In their own ways the Sandinistas, Salvadorans, Grenadians and Cubans are implementing in political practice 'the revolution in permanence' heralded by Marx and Engels and espoused by the Fourth International."[14] In person, George had told me in 1983 that he planned to put such opinions in a document. However, the document never appeared. Within a few months, it was clear that any attempt to promote such a view among the SWP membership would bring the likelihood of expulsion—no matter what an individual's previous contributions to the party might have been. It seems to me that if George *had* eventually reversed his opinion on Permanent Revolution so as to repudiate it, he would have mentioned it to me in one of our subsequent exchanges, just to clarify the record.

But I think that it is highly unlikely that George ever considered breaking with "the Barnes tendency" at any time after 1983, even when the relationship with the Fourth International was terminated later in that decade. He was sufficiently a Marxist to know that political principle comes before organizational loyalty, but whether or not the SWP ever incontro-vertibly "crossed class lines" can certainly be disputed. George may well have expressed his opinions privately to Barnes, but publicly he adhered to the pledge not to openly contradict Barnes. Moreover, the splits and mutual recriminations of those in opposition to "the Barnes tendency" in the months following the SWP purge certainly gave George, as well as many others, no reason to believe that an alternative, pro-Fourth International movement in the United States would survive.[15] Direct affiliation with the Fourth International was also out of the question, considering George's training. The SWP attitude toward the Fourth International—from historic party leader James P. Cannon, through the Farrell Dobbs and Tom Kerry years of the 1950s and 1960s, and into the Barnes era—had consistently promoted the view that the United Secretariat leadership wasn't really "orthodox" and "proletarian." SWP members were inculcated with the belief that the *real* political heart and soul of world Trotskyism actually rested in the U.S. cadres assembled and trained by Cannon's disciples. Since Novack never challenged that view after the 1953 split in the Fourth International, he had yet another good reason to stay put.

II

Novack's position in the SWP was generally thought to be that of "intellectual" and "scholar."[16] In my opinion, these labels may result in some confusion that needs to be clarified in order to gain a perspective on the meaning of his life and intellectual contributions. Since Novack had no academic career, he does not fit the more familiar paradigms of his generation of intellectuals drawn to the socialist movement. For example,

the tensions shaping his life and work do not resemble those exemplified
by the young Sidney Hook, who attempted to simultaneously straddle
positions as the foremost Marxist philosophy professor in the United
States and a revolutionary leader.[17] Nor does his pattern resemble the
career of James Burnham, who, in contrast to Hook, threw himself
totally and devotedly into the Trotskyist movement for about five years,
only to suddenly and completely break, finally moving by direct stages to
the far Right. Even the lifelong Trotskyist intellectual John G. Wright
(a pseudonym for Joseph Vanzler) had an earlier career as a freelance
intellectual and colloidal chemist, and then ran a private business manu-
facturing contraceptive jelly.

In distinction, *all* of Novack's successful writing and the vast majority
of his work-life came through his association with the Trotskyist movement. An early career in advertising had been quickly dropped, although
he learned the technical skills of writing and dreamed of producing
a work of philosophy.[18] Only after joining the Communist League of
America and working full time at revolutionary activity (except for
the summers of 1934 and 1935, spent at Yadoo, a writers' and artists'
residence) did he begin producing the historical essays and studies of
intellectuals that constituted the early part of his career. His "bourgeois"
work-life after that was episodic; with the exception of a brief period of
factory work in Detroit during World War II, it was usually in advertising, publicity, and research. Nevertheless, his aura in the SWP was so
much that of "the intellectual" that I have heard YSA members refer to
him as a "professor" or even as an "attorney."[19]

Rather than understanding George's contributions to Marxist culture
in terms of the more familiar tension felt by scholars and intellectuals between a career as a professional (academic or otherwise) and a
party commitment, several other complicating factors ought to be fore-
grounded. One concerns his escape from his family culture as refracted
through the youth rebellion of the 1920s and New York radical Bohemia
in the 1930s. A small part of this was a desire to leave behind the narrow
legacy of the European Jewish ghetto and enter the modern world of science and international culture. George's father changed the family name
from Novograbelsky to Novack, but the son went further and altered his
given names, Yasef Mendel, to the Anglophilic "George Edward." Later
he would use the WASP pseudonyms "John Marshall" and "William F.
Warde." Although he belonged to a liberal Jewish fraternity at Harvard

for reasons of social life, he became a literary disciple of James Joyce and W. B. Yeats and a philosophical admirer of his Harvard teacher Alfred North Whitehead, who was at that time reading draft chapters of *Process and Reality* aloud to George's class. Even after becoming a revolutionary Marxist, elements of Bohemian rebel culture survived, as in his apparently idealized admiration of Jean-Paul Sartre and Simone de Beauvoir's relationship as one based on mutual love and devoid of sexual jealousy.[20]

Equally significant, however, was his desire to escape from and replace his inherited nuclear family. His father, a gambler who ran a Turkish bath, led what George always referred to euphemistically as "a highly irregular life," often leaving his son in the embarrassing situation of not having sufficient funds to pay for his college tuition. George's mother, in response, doted on and sought to entirely control her blond-haired, blue-eyed, slim and handsome son. Years later he recalled to me his humiliation at the memory of himself as a "pampered university brat" who wore "a broad-brimmed black Stetson sombrero, anarchist style, [and] a luxurious raccoon coat with a wide collar, turned up for show." His mother had obtained this "rig" for him from her brother, a furrier in Worcester, and George even wore it when he worked for a while selling flowers for a sidewalk peddler on Tremont Street, opposite Boston Common, in the alley outside his father's Turkish bath beneath the Tremont Theater.[21]

Eventually a major goal of George's life became to escape from his mother, although the vehicles of escape became other women—not only several wives but also, eventually, his sister. Since George never took any pay from the SWP, the financial resources of his companions became important to his functioning as a revolutionary. These women helped take care of him and enabled him to carry out his intellectual pursuits. Although this pattern produced hostile gossip about him, usually exaggerating his financial resources, George accepted and candidly discussed this aspect of his personality.

Such a dynamic of a very human kind of dependency also bears a relation to the most traumatic episode in George's personal life, which came in the 1950s, just prior to the decade of his greatest productivity. Over ten years in our friendship had passed before George felt that he could fully "dredge up memories of a period thirty years back that were fraught with pain and perplexities and are still not easy for me to recall because the *individual-psychological factors are so intertwined with political-organizational considerations*".[22] The political background for the trauma was George's intimate collaborative association with Michel Pablo during the early 1950s while he was on assignment for the SWP in Europe. He returned to the United States in February 1953, committed to healing the growing political differences between the New York-based SWP National Office and the Paris-based International Secretariat of the Fourth International, but he found himself in the midst of a complicated three-way brawl. This was among groupings led by Bert Cochran and George Clarke (who had their own interpretation of Pablo's views), James P. Cannon and Murray Weiss (who, from Los Angeles, had been aggressively sharpening the conflict with Cochran–Clarke) and Farrell Dobbs and Morris Stein (who ran the New York center of the SWP and resented the Cannon-Weiss intervention as arbitrary and unwise). At first, George believed that he had assisted in creating a "truce," preventing a split. But when this proved to be short-lived, a severe personal crisis ensued that nearly destroyed his self-confidence and self-esteem.

George felt that he had personally failed in his mission and that the Fourth International would be severely crippled as a result. He was also torn over where his sympathies lay, just as he had been in 1939, during the earlier stages of the political struggle between Max Shachtman and Cannon. George had great respect for Pablo's leadership capacities, apart from Pablo's pronouncements about the potential longevity of "deformed workers states,"[23] yet he doubted the politico-organizational stability of Pablo's U.S. supporters. On the other hand, he sensed that "the steadfast proletarian core headed by Cannon and Dobbs" would survive and become the basis of a new revolutionary socialist movement once the tide turned.

Complicating the matter, his companion, Evelyn, had a long-standing personal animosity toward Cochran (they had had conflicts while working in the national auto fraction and on the press) and was angry with George for his more nuanced position. As George's psychological condition deteriorated, he agreed to leave Evelyn for Los Angeles to live with his party friend Dr. Harry Fishier, where he could hold discussions more directly with Cannon. Once there, his depression precipitated a suicide attempt. During treatment, he took a leave from the SWP, found a job as an editor of a commercial paper, and was eventually reunited with Evelyn in November 1954. When his emotional equilibrium was regained, he reintegrated himself into the life of the SWP and its leadership.

As a result, George placed a great emphasis ever afterwards on what he called the "Herculean task" of holding together "a revolutionary grouping, especially in the U.S."[24] A crucial part of George's admiration for Cannon was that Cannon had been almost alone in starting a small oppositional grouping and seeing it through to the end of his life. George's acute awareness of the contrasting fates of Albert Weisbord, B. J. Field, Max Shachtman, C. L. R. James, and Bert Cochran was, I believe, a determining factor in the kind of politico-intellectual role Novack came to play.

George was in a difficult position. He had no substantial independent life, friendship circle, family, career, or financial base outside the Trotskyist movement. His scholarship was disgracefully ignored by academics and vilely traduced by political rivals of the SWP on the Left.[25] Like all of us, George needed a worldview to guide his life and provide a framework, enabling meaningful, productive work. Over the decades, and especially after the trauma of 1953–54, this worldview and framework became circumscribed by the Cannon tradition of Trotskyist politics, as it was for so many of the survivors of the 1930s and 1940s Trotskyist movement in the United States.

None of the above is meant to demean George or narrow the meaning of his life; only to provide a perspective. All intellectuals function within the limitations of institutions and worldviews, and George's achievement has vastly surpassed those of most of his critics. Some of these critics were of the 1960s generation who sneered at him for his "orthodoxy." Others were simply mad as hell at George because he didn't join their faction in one dispute or another.

It *is* true that, as a consequence of the conditions under which George produced, he observed a strict "orthodoxy" about writings by Marx, Engels, Lenin, and Trotsky, and his writing was aimed at a different audience than most works of philosophy and history. George once told me that, when he wrote, he always imagined that he was in a meeting hall addressing an "educated worker." On the other hand, it is probably true that a good many college-educated activists on the Left received a basic clarification about dialectics, materialism, historical interpretation, and so forth through reading George's books, which helped them go on to more advanced studies.

It is regrettable how little George's books have been discussed and analyzed. Virtually all the book reviews of his work that appeared in the SWP press were uninspired and uncritical plot summaries. The only enthusiastic and thoughtful response to the appearance of *Pragmatism versus Marxism*, which George regarded as the summa of his life's work, came from Indiana University philosophy professor Milton Fisk.[26] Not a single person has emerged out of the SWP milieu to continue in his field of U.S. history and philosophy.[27] When I asked George, in our last meeting, whether there was some individual currently in the SWP engaged in Marxist theoretical work that might be of importance, he said definitively and sadly, "No."

However, it would be a mistake to assume that political exigency determined all of George's major intellectual pursuits. For example, from the 1930s to his death, he had a special interest in scholarship concerning the U.S. Civil War and especially in the role of the New York antidraft protesters, about which George had conducted original research. To the end, he persisted in defending his own conclusions against the more prominent view on the Left that the uprising had been subjectively and/or objectively reactionary. His opinions on this and other scholarly matters never saw publication; they were communicated in private correspondence, conversation, or manuscripts that had no immediate prospect of coming to print. The situation was similar in regard to his ongoing critical study of the writings of Eugene Genovese on U.S. slavery.

III

These observations about the other side of George—the private person behind the public Marxist scholar and political activist—are not meant as a substitute for the careful, critical reading that his books and articles deserve. Although the corpus is uneven, many items should be reprinted; there are also unpublished letters, manuscripts, and even an autobiography going up to the 1970s (in the possession of the SWP) that should be considered for publication.

Nevertheless, the meaning of George's life cannot be deduced from the public record alone. He knew this well, although, perhaps because of the strong anti-individualist ethos of much orthodox Marxist scholarship, such concerns are not directly reflected in many of his own publications. Nevertheless, he consumed biographies of the personal lives of intellectuals throughout his life, frequently commending various ones to me. When I saw him in December 1991, he told me that, now that he was retired from political activities, such biographies were all that he cared to read, along with the daily *New York Times*.

At the end of that final interview with George, I took his hand between mine and told him how much I appreciated the help he had given me over the years. I believe that there are many others who owe similar, if lesser, debts to George. He was a natural educator and the most responsible person I have ever met in terms of providing conscientious feedback and criticisms of ideas and opinions. It is true that he used his charm, his glow of idealism and self-sacrifice, to raise financial contributions for the SWP from people who later regretted turning over their inheritances and other funds. But, at least through the 1970s, George genuinely believed in the quality of the SWP leadership and its future. Moreover, he also raised money for other worthy causes; for example, in 1983 he was instrumental in securing a $5,000 grant for processing the Max Shachtman collection at the Tamiment Institute section of the New York University library.

Unfortunately, a number of those who owe a great deal to George have found it necessary to obliterate their relation or bitterly traduce him for not following their course—very often toward deradicalization or else immersion in sectarian politics. Some pillory him as the archetypal vulgar Marxist or intellectual factotum of the party regime. The flip side of the caricatures are false idealizations of him as a Marxist "genius" martyred by the bourgeois establishment. None of these exploitations of George's life and work does much to advance and enrich the tradition of Marxist culture we so desperately need if we are going to sustain the struggle for a humanized society.

George was neither a genius (most geniuses can't function as part of a team as well as George did) nor a giant among Marxist theoreticians. But he did have exceptional intellectual skills and gifts. What is important is that he developed these to the best of his ability, making full use of them in behalf of the socialist movement. I don't believe that he withheld anything from the cause, and he was incredibly generous with his time to any worker or student genuinely interested in learning Marxism. Of course, George certainly enjoyed it when his writings got some attention, when his books were translated, or when he was invited to speak at scholarly events beyond those organized by the SWP. Yet his motivation was never fundamentally a desire for fame or prestige, and it certainly wasn't for money. A good deal of it was love of and respect for party leaders and collaborators—especially for Cannon, Joseph Hansen, and Farrell Dobbs, who were unquestionably the new "family" he selected to replace his old one, and to which he became bonded.

George's example is inspiring not because he went to the Left when so many others did in the 1930s, but because he persisted in his work for revolutionary socialism through the hard times. I believe that it was important in the 1960s that George was still on the scene as an active revolutionist. He showed the younger generation that, whether or not one agreed with George's philosophical views or political party, socialism was not a temporary, youthful fad but a lifelong mission. Through his writing, too, George was an authentic culture-bearer from past struggles to the present. And the fact that George survived may well have been instrumental in the survival of other cadres from the 1930s and 1940s into the 1960s, since, under adverse conditions of intense social pressure, every individual who sticks it out alleviates some of the pressure on the · rest of his or her comrades.

The sad fact is that, when the genuine nature of the struggle for socialism becomes clear—that it is not a steady "high" but protracted, complex, and filled with many disappointments—tired radicals can find plenty of reasons to despair, immerse themselves in private lives and careers, or simply switch sides. This was the fate of the preponderance of the 1930s generation; it is perhaps one that will overtake a good number of the 1960s generation as well. But George's life shows that such responses need not be the case, no matter how hard the times and complex the issues facing socialist intellectuals.

In U.S. Trotskyism, George found a movement compatible with his gifts—a movement that needed him and that, in turn, provided the inspiration and support permitting a productive life. Marxist intellectuals and activists of the present generation can learn from George's accomplishments and limitations for the purpose of constructing a new movement that will address the crises of the present difficult moment. Such a movement will enable us to preserve, advance, and communicate socialist culture to the next generation, as George Novack did to ours.

Notes

I borrowed the title of this essay from Mary Oppen's *Meaning a Life* (1978), a stirring memoir of herself and her husband, George, the Objectivist poet and Communist organizer. An earlier version of this essay appeared in *Bulletin in Defense of Marxism*, October–November 1992, pp. 52–57.

1. Among Novack's most significant books and pamphlets are *America's Revolutionary Heritage* (editor; New York: Pathfinder Press, 1976), *An Introduction to the Logic of Marxism* (New York: Pathfinder Press, 1971), *Democracy and Revolution* (New York: Pathfinder Press, 1971), *Empiricism and Its Evolution* (New York: Merit, 1968), *Existentialism versus Marxism* (editor; New York: Delta, 1966), *Humanism and Socialism* (New York: Pathfinder Press, 1973), *Moscow versus Peking* (New York: Pioneer, 1961), *The Origins of Materialism* (New York: Merit Publishers, 1965), *Polemics in Marxist Philosophy* (New York: Monad Press, 1978), *Pragmatism versus Marxism* (New York: Pathfinder Press, 1975), *Understanding History* (New York: Pathfinder, 1972), and *Who Will Change the World?* (Toronto: YSF, 1966).

2. Originally sympathetic to the Socialist Party, he became active in 1932 in the National Committee for the Defense of Political Prisoners, an affiliate of the Communist Party's International Labor Defense. He joined the Communist League of America in the fall of 1933, assisted its fusion with the American Workers Party in 1934 to create the Workers Party of the United States in 1935, and then participated in the entry of the Trotskyists into the Socialist Party in 1936. In 1938 he became a founding member of the Socialist Workers Party, to which he belonged at the time of his death. He served on the National Committee from 1940 to 1973. Among the high points of his political career were his service as secretary of the American Committee for the Defense of Leon Trotsky from 1937 to 1940; national secretary of the Civil Rights Defense Committee from 1941 to 1950; and associate editor of the *International Socialist Review* from 1965 to 1974.

3. I have surveyed Novack's intellectual and political career in two books, *James T. Farrell: The Revolutionary Socialist Years* (New York: New York University Press, 1978) and *The New York Intellectuals, the Rise and Decline of the Anti-Stalinist Left from the 1930s to the 1980s* (Chapel Hill: University of North Carolina Press, 1987), as well in the entry on Novack in Bernard K. Johnpoll and Harvey Klehr, eds., *Biographical Dictionary of the American Left* (New York: Greenwood, 1986).

4. For the most part, George was regarded as likeable, even by those who abhorred his political views, such as the novelist James T. Farrell in his last decades. A few, such as Sidney Hook and Felix Morrow, utterly despised George all out of proportion to reason, and the former subjected me to a tirade of slander—personally and in correspondence with others—when he mistakenly concluded that I was somehow George's political pawn.

5.   The exact nature of this transformation remains under debate. In general, it appears that the SWP today rationalizes positions taken by the Castro leadership by the use of its own interpretation of some of Trotsky's ideas, such as his theory of Soviet Stalinism as the expression of a bureaucratic, parasitic social layer.

6.   Due to the Voorhis Act, neither the SWP nor any other U.S. organization has actually belonged to the Fourth International.

7.   The Internationalist Tendency (IT) was bureaucratically expelled from the SWP in July 1974; I subsequently signed a document drafted by the late Robert Langston warning that the organizational integrity of the SWP was becoming seriously compromised.

8.   Novack to Wald, August 30, 1983.

9.   His second wife, Evelyn Horwit (better known as Evelyn Reed), died in 1979. He frequently referred to his subsequent companion as his "wife," although I have no evidence that they were actually married, and George returned to live in New York mostly by himself in his last years.

10.   Novack to Wald, February 27, 1984.

11.   By 1988 he was again closing his letters with the salutation, "fraternally."

12.   He said that he regretted not being able to attend the book-signing party for Smith's *Notebook of a Sixties Lawyer* (Smyrna Press: New York, 1991), which was the reason I had come to New York.

13.   This was Trotsky's view, annunciated in 1905 and reaffirmed in 1917, that revolutions in economically underdeveloped countries must combine bourgeois-democratic and socialist demands.

14.   Novack to Wald, June 16, 1983.

15.   Within a few months, the expelled oppositionists split into two, and later three (actually four, if one counts the North Star Network led by Peter Camejo), hostile groups.

16.   Ben Stone's *Memoirs of a Radical Rank and Filer* (Prometheus Press: New York, 1986) contains a useful portrait of how George appeared to many ordinary members of the SWP.

17.   Hook wrote the program of the American Workers Party and urged its fusion with the Communist League of America, then surprised many when he did not join the new organization. He next urged Norman Thomas to admit the Trotskyists to the Socialist Party, but again, he held back from joining. In the late 1930s, some aspects of his thought appeared to be identical to that of the Trotskyists, but the advent of World War II brought a decisive switch, although for some time he claimed to be to the left of social democracy, and even at his death he insisted that he was a Marxist.

18.   He began work for a lecture bureau in New York in 1927, then was employed by Doubleday and Company, and finally became advertising Manager tor E. P. Dutton, where he stayed until 1934.

19. The last was probably due to his prominent association with political defense cases such as the Dewey Commission of Inquiry, the Minneapolis Eighteen, the James Kutcher case, and the Political Rights Defense Fund.

20. Recently published letters of de Beauvoir suggest that the relationship was hardly so mutual or idyllic.

21. Novack to Wald, May 1, 1983.

22. Novack to Wald, April 28, 1983, my emphasis.

23. The term refers to social formations undergoing top-down bureaucratic nationalization, especially in conjunction with the extension of the power of the Soviet Union, as in Eastern Europe; Pablo thought that these might survive for centuries.

24. Novack to Wald, July 3, 1983.

25. The most sickening were the campaigns run against George's work and person by the Workers League, inspired by the British sectarian cult leader Gerry Healey.

26. See *Erkenntnis* 2 (1977): 269–73.

27. The only exception might be Peter Camejo, who was much influenced by Novack in *Racism, Revolution, Reaction, 1861–1877* (New York: Monad Press, 1976). However, Camejo has not persisted in such work.

In 1933 Diego Rivera painted this mural at the headquarters of the Communist League of America in New York. Upper row (left to right): unidentified striking mineworker, Rosa Luxemburg, Karl Liebknecht, Frederick Engels, Leon Trotsky, V. I. Lenin, Karl Marx. Lower row (left to right): Ruth Cannon, Sarah Avrin, Edgar Swabeck, Carlo Cowl (son of Sarah Avrin), Arne Swabeck, Max Shachtman, Christian Rakovsky (a leading Left Oppositionist, at that time in a Stalinist prison camp in the USSR), and James P. Cannon.

Martin Abern, one of the Trotskyist movement's most capable organizational minds.

Antoinette Konikow, a physician well known for feminist and birth control efforts, was perhaps the first U.S. Communist expelled for supporting Trotsky.

U.S. Trotskyist leaders James P. Cannon (right) and Max Shachtman (left) in 1934, arrested during the Minneapolis general strike. Photo: Silverman

Morris Lewit and Sylvia Bleeker, who edited *Unser Kampf.*

Pen portrait of A. J. Muste (by Bernard Sanders) in the early 1930s when he headed up Brookwood Labor College, shortly before his brief turn to Trotskyism—after which he became the foremost radical pacifist in the U.S.

C. L. R. James in Britain before coming to the U.S. to become a leader of the Socialist Workers Party.

James Burnham swung from left to right in the 1940s.

Leon Trotsky and his wife, Natalia Sedova, in their Mexican exile, flanked by secretaries Joe Hansen, Jean Van Heijenoort (in hat), and Raya Dunayevskaya in late 1930s.

Teamster militant Farrell Dobbs and his wife, Marvell Scholl Dobbs, visiting with Trotsky and Natalia in Mexico, in early 1940.
© A. H. Buchman, 1939, 1964, 1990

Max Shachtman and Ernest Rice McKinney, not long after
the 1940 split among the U.S. Trotskyists.

Veterans of American Trotskyism (left to right): Arne Swabeck, James
P. Cannon, Rose Karsner, Oscar Coover, and Carl Skoglund in 1949.
Photograph courtesy of Edgar Swabeck

A barefoot Jim Cannon, with Wong, inscribed this photo to friend V. R. Dunne: "Picture of a man and a dog at peace with their own consciences."

Vincent Raymond Dunne, leader of the Minneapolis teamsters strikes, in the late 1940s.

by JAMES P. CANNON

PIONEER PUBLISHERS   10c

Laura Gray's illustration on this 1946 pamphlet by Cannon captured the revolutionary optimism animating the SWP majority during this period.

George Breitman and Dorothea Breitman in 1940, not long before he became editor of the Militant.

Vote for Dobbs and Carlson!
For a Workers & Farmers Government!

Spread the Message of
Socialist Liberation!

•

Support the
Socialist Workers Party
Candidates in the
1948 Election

FARRELL DOBBS
for President

GRACE CARLSON
for Vice-President

Vote for Dobbs and Carlson!

In 1948 the SWP ran its first campaign for U.S. president and vice president, with veteran of the 1934 teamster strike Farrell Dobbs and one of the foremost women leaders of the party Grace Carlson.

Harry Braverman, prominent "Cochranite" who later became closely associated with *Monthly Review* magazine and Monthly Review Press, which published his classic *Labor and Monopoly Capital*.

Bert Cochran, leader of an opposition challenging traditional Trotskyist perspectives in the early 1950s, went on to write a number of books on U.S. labor and politics before his death in 1984 (not long after this photo was taken).
Photo by Jill Krementz

Attending the Trotsky School at Mountain Spring Camp in the early 1950s were (left to right): Tom Kerry, Laura Gray, Carl Skoglund, and Richard (Caterino) Garza.

Murray Weiss, (pictured here with Myra Tanner Weiss) close to James P. Cannon while heading up the Los Angeles branch, was a leader of the SWP during the regroupment period of the late 1950s and early 1960s.

Myra Tanner Weiss, one of the most capable female spokespeople for the SWP, was the party's vice presidential candidate in 1956 and 1960.

Among the mainstays of the dynamic Detroit branch in the 1950s and 1960s were George Breitman (bottom right), Frank Lovell (left), and Sarah Lovell (bottom left). Breitman—perhaps most famous for his work on Malcolm X—later turned Pathfinder Press into a major left-wing publishing outlet. Sarah Lovell, active for many years in labor and socialist politics, edited *Leon Trotsky Speaks*. Frank Lovell became SWP trade union director in the 1970s.

Tom Kerry (1977), the central leader of the SWP in the 1950s and 1960s, with Farrell Dobbs was uncompromising in his defense of Trotskyist orthodoxy. © 1996 by Della Rossa.

Karolyn Kerry (1977), played an essential role in the SWP national office during the 1940s and 1950s. © 1996 by Della Rossa.

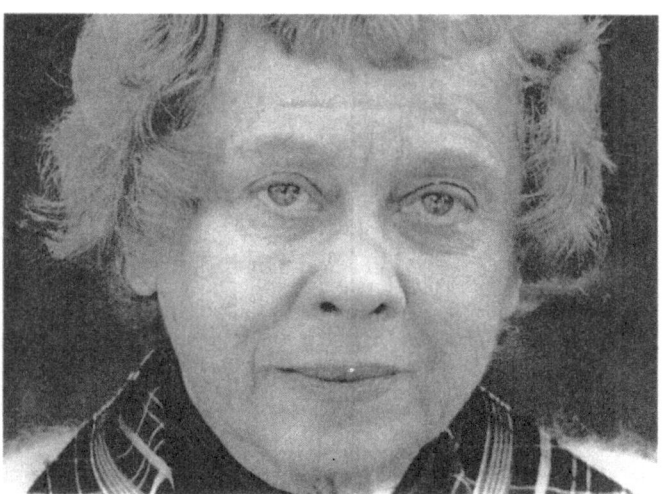

Evelyn Reed, long associated with George Novack, became widely known in feminist circles for her collection of essays *Problems of Women's Liberation*, and for her controversial study *Woman's Evolution*. © 1996 by Della Rossa.

Fred Halstead, a skillful and widely-respected leader in the U. S. Movement against the war in Vietnam, picked up the nick-name "Big Red Fred" among many new left and anti-war activities.
© 1996 by Della Rossa.

Morris Lewit (sometimes known by the party name Morris Stein) in the 1990s.

Joe Hansen and Reba Hansen—pictured here in the late 1970s—began publishing the revolutionary internationalist weekly magazine *Intercontinental Press* in the 1960s.
© 1996 by Della Rossa.

Evelyn Sell at Mountain Spring Camp, 1961.

PART ll

Reconsiderations

4

Leninism in the United States and the Decline of American Trotskyism

PAUL LE BLANC

The collapse of the bureaucratic dictatorships of Eastern Europe in the late 1980s and early 1990s has been hailed by defenders of the capitalist system as the collapse of socialism and definitive proof that the Bolshevik Revolution led by Lenin and Trotsky in 1917 constituted "the road to nowhere." All attempts to establish the rule of the working class over society will lead to chaos and tyranny, we are told by generations of conservatives and neoconservatives. Even many people who sympathize with socialist ideals are presently inclined to question the value of revolutionary Marxism, feeling that the strategic and organizational perspectives of Lenin and the Bolsheviks may indeed be responsible for the subsequent totalitarian nightmare during the reign of Joseph Stalin, followed by the stagnation and ultimate disintegration of bureaucratic "socialism." In the United States, this is certainly heightened by the fact that the so-called Leninist Left—not only the Communist Party but also what used to be its relatively substantial "Trotskyist" competitor the Socialist Workers Party—had been suffering a serious decline even before the recent collapse of so-called communism.

It may be, however, that these years will come to be seen as a renewal period of the socialist movement—involving the clarification of the actual meaning of the revolutionary socialist tradition, as bureaucratic and authoritarian crusts fall away under the impact of critical examination and the especially ruthless criticism of reality itself. Those who identify with the socialist tradition, and especially with the Marxism represented by such twentieth-century revolutionaries as Lenin, Trotsky, and Rosa Luxemburg, have no right to be taken seriously unless they are able to explain and help others learn the lessons of this complex experience. How did something that represented the most radical working-class democracy become so undemocratic and so alien to the actually existing working class—not simply in the Soviet Union, but also in the left wing of the labor and social movements of the United States?

It is certainly not the case that no work has been done on these questions. The decline of the USSR and other such regimes has been the subject of a number of important studies—from Leon Trotsky's *The Revolution Betrayed* to Ernest Mandel's *Beyond Perestroika* and an important anthology edited by Marilyn Vogt-Downey, *Marxism and the USSR*. In the United States, the decline of the U.S. Communist Party has been documented by various participants from James P. Cannon in *The First Ten Years of American Communism* down to Howard Fast in *Being Red*, as well as by such historians as Theodore Draper, Harvey Klehr, Maurice Isserman, Paul Buhle, and others.[1]

The crisis of American Trotskyism, which became manifest in the early 1980s, poses a more complicated problem. After all, the Trotskyists had always denounced the antidemocratic practices of Stalinism as being alien to the very essence of the revolutionary perspectives of the early communist movement that had been led by Lenin and Trotsky. The foremost organizational representative of the Trotskyist tradition in the United States—the Socialist Workers Party (SWP)—came out of the 1960s and early 1970s as a very strong and vital group, with close to 2,000 adherents and an even wider sphere of influence in the radical movement. In less than a decade, however, it took its distance from the perspectives of Trotsky, aligning itself more closely with the perspectives (or a stilted understanding of the perspectives) of Fidel Castro's Cuban Communist Party. In the course of carrying out this change, the new SWP leadership greatly tightened the organizational norms of their party, creating what many would agree was a profoundly undemocratic internal life and forcing hundreds of members out of the organization—especially through a dramatic wave of expulsions in 1983–84. All this was done in the name of implementing "Leninist" norms. The present essay represents part of a larger effort to provide an account and understanding of this development.[2]

This essay is also related to a book I wrote at the request of George Breitman, *Lenin and the Revolutionary Party*. That study attempted to establish the actual historical experience of the original "Leninist party" as it became a powerful force for working-class revolution in Russia, leading up to 1917. In this essay, as a kind of follow-up to that study, I want to suggest some of the lessons of the U.S. "Leninist" experience of the SWP.

I begin with a discussion of essential aspects of the Bolshevik tradition and of its guiding organizational principles, summarized by the term *democratic centralism*. This is followed by an examination of Leninism in the United States, culminating in the emergence of American Trotskyism. This examination includes a critical look at the contributions (and the critics) of James P. Cannon, the SWP's foremost leader from its founding in 1938 through the mid-1950s. A discussion of the changes in the world after the Second World War, and the impact of these changes on the composition and consciousness of the Socialist Workers Party, is followed by a contrast of the Cannon tradition with the new norms established by the later leadership of the SWP. This sheds light on the Leninist and Trotskyist traditions, and on the breakdown of both in the U.S. Left during the late twentieth century.

The Bolshevik Tradition

It is impossible to understand the meaning of historical Bolshevism—the revolutionary wing of the Russian socialist movement—unless it is understood that it was a *working-class* current. This is so easy to say, and to forget, that it is absolutely necessary to give it special stress. The following six memoirs by veteran Bolsheviks will—if read—make this clear (and provide a fascinating inside view of the history of Bolshevism): Semen Ivanovich Kanatchikov, *A Radical Worker in Tsarist Russia*; Cecilia Bobrovskaya, *Twenty Years in Underground Russia*; Osip Piatnitsky, *Memoirs of a Bolshevik*; Aleksei E. Badayev, *The Bolsheviks in the Tsarist Duma*; Alexander Shlyapnikov, *On the Eve of 1917*; Fyodor F. Raskolnikov, *Kronstadt and Petrograd in 1917*.[3]

Eyewitness accounts of the Bolshevik Revolution, such as John Reed's *Ten Days that Shook the World*, have been corroborated by more recent work of social historians—Leopold Haimson, Alexander Rabinowitch,

Victoria Bonnell, Diane Koenker, David Mandel, and many others. The Bolshevik party was deeply rooted in the working class, and it had become the predominant political current in the Russian workers' movement just before World War I and, after a fairly brief interruption, again by the late summer of 1917. The Bolshevik Revolution of October–November 1917 was, in fact, a deeply democratic phenomenon, a proletarian revolution in terms of goals, participants, and popular support.[4]

Lenin sought to explain this reality to foreign revolutionaries at the World Congress of the Communist International in 1921, warning them against the illusion that a left-wing minority could simply seize power in the name of the working class in order to impose its own benevolent rule: "In Europe . . . we must win the majority of the working class, and anyone who fails to understand this is lost to the communist movement. . . . We were victorious in Russia not only because the undisputed majority of the working class was on our side (during the elections in 1917 the overwhelming majority of the workers were with us against the Mensheviks), but also because half the army, immediately after our seizure of power, and nine-tenths of the peasants, in the course of some weeks, came over to our side."[5]

This revolutionary democratic orientation of the Bolsheviks was in harmony with Lenin's explanation of the history and success of Bolshevism, which he offered in *Left-Wing Communism, an Infantile Disorder* (1920). "Only the history of Bolshevism during the *entire* period of its existence can satisfactorily explain why it has been able to build up and maintain, under the most difficult conditions, the iron discipline needed for the victory of the proletariat," Lenin wrote. Many hostile commentators as well as would-be imitators have become fixated on this "iron discipline" as the key to Bolshevik success, but Lenin warned that without certain conditions being met, "all attempts to establish discipline inevitably fall flat and end up in phrase-mongering and clowning."[6]

The prerequisites for such discipline, in Lenin's opinion, were three: (1) the class consciousness and devotion to revolution of significant elements of the working class (whom Lenin termed "the revolutionary vanguard"); (2) the ability of this vanguard layer of the proletariat to link up "and—if you wish—merge, in a certain measure, with the broadest masses of working people," as Lenin put it; and (3) the correctness of the political program and the effectiveness of the leadership of the revolutionary vanguard, and the understanding of this by the broad masses on the basis of their own experience. There is no question that Lenin believed that revolutionary *intellectuals* were also vitally important to the revolutionary vanguard party—but he didn't assume that intellectuals could come only from the "upper classes," and he placed a high priority on assisting in the development of highly developed working-class intellectuals from among the layer of class-conscious workers developing in Russia. In any event, for Lenin, a party of the revolutionary vanguard meant a substantial, "conscious" layer of the working class—not an elite of radical intellectuals who would do the workers' thinking for them.

"Without these conditions," Lenin insisted, "discipline in a revolutionary party really capable of being the party of the advanced class, whose mission is to overthrow the bourgeoisie and transform the whole of society, cannot be achieved." He cautioned: "On the other hand, these conditions cannot emerge at once." Here Lenin's belief in the central importance of Marxism, and his open and creative approach to Marxist theory, becomes evident: "Their creation is facilitated by a correct revolutionary theory, which, in turn, is not a dogma, but assumes final shape only in close connection with the practical activity of a truly mass and truly revolutionary movement."[7]

Sometimes this is referred to as the *program* of the revolutionary party. "It goes without saying that 'every step of real movement is more important than a dozen programs,' as Karl Marx said," Lenin acknowledged in 1899. "But neither Marx nor any other theoretician or practical worker in the socialist movement has ever denied the tremendous importance of a program for the consolidation and consistent activity of a political party."[8] Program involves an analysis of the realities one faces, a conception of what changes are desirable, and a perspective on *how* to change those realities. It involves utilizing *theory* (the accumulation of analyses of history and society, especially accumulated lessons from the class struggle) in order to work out general strategies leading to the socialist goal, and specific tactics that will advance those strategies.

There were three fundamentals at the heart of the program to which Lenin was committed: (1) socialism must become rooted in the struggles and consciousness of the working class in order to be relevant; (2) the working class must win its own freedom through its own efforts; and (3) the working class must become socialist if it is to bring about its own liberation and the forward movement of all society. Other essential aspects of the revolutionary program flow from this:

- The working class must form its own perspectives on all major issues and problems of society.
- The more "privileged" workers (those who are more skilled, better paid, with less exhausting work and more leisure time, more education, and so on) must concern themselves with the interests and needs of the more oppressed workers, not allowing themselves to be seduced into being an "aristocracy of labor" that is satisfied, for example, simply with bread-and-butter trade union gains.
- The working class must concern itself with the plight of all oppressed groups in society—forging alliances and linking their struggles to the general struggle for the triumph of the working class; thus the oppression of women, of subject nationalities, of racial and religious minorities, of dissident intellectuals and students, of impoverished peasants, and so forth should be matters of intense concern to the workers' movement.
- International solidarity of the working class is crucial, and socialism can advance and be won only as a worldwide process. This is especially true given the global (imperialist) character of capitalist production and economic organization.
- *Practical struggles* for democratic and economic *reforms*, to defend the immediate interests of working people and the oppressed, are essential, *but* such struggles must be integrated into a strategic orientation that advances the *political independence* and *hegemony* of the working class.
- If the political independence and hegemony of the working class are achieved on a significant scale, the result can be *socialist revolution*.

The programmatic orientation sketched here will not be realized automatically or spontaneously, but only through a considerable amount of serious work. Under normal circumstances, most people won't do that work. Those who *are* prepared to do the work must organize themselves as effectively as possible—in a democratic, cohesive, coherent political collective: a revolutionary activist organization. Obviously, to the extent that more and more people can be drawn into doing such work, it will become effective. But the creation of a revolutionary socialist majority in society is a *process* that can be advanced only if the present-day revolutionary minority organizes itself to bring this about.

This indicates—if somewhat schematically—the meaning of the revolutionary vanguard party to which Lenin was committed. The internal functioning of such a party has been defined as *democratic centralism*, a term that has been subject to considerable distortion—including in the Socialist Workers Party during the 1970s and 1980s.

Democratic Centralism

The term *democratic centralism* was first introduced into the Russian socialist movement in 1905 by Lenin's factional adversaries, the Mensheviks, but Lenin embraced it and summarized it as "freedom of discussion, unity of action." In Lenin's opinion, the revolutionary party "must be united, but in these united organizations there must be wide and free discussion of Party questions, free comradely criticism and assessment of events in Party life." This would include, he stressed in 1906, "guarantees for the rights of all minorities and for all loyal opposition, . . . recognizing that all Party functionaries must be elected, accountable to the Party and subject to recall."[9]

In this period Lenin argued: "The principle of democratic centralism and autonomy for local Party organizations implies universal and full *freedom to criticize* so long as this does not disturb the unity *of a definite action*; it rules out *all* criticism which disrupts or makes difficult the *unity* of an action decided on by the Party."[10] Some interpreters have asserted that Lenin didn't really mean this, and that he functioned differently, that he *really* sought to subject all discussion and activity in the vanguard party to his own control. Others interpret it as meaning: you can say, write, publish, and do whatever you please, whenever you please, however you please—just so it doesn't disrupt a (narrowly defined) *action*, such as a demonstration, an insurrection, and so forth.

The historical evidence contradicts both interpretations. The Bolshevik party did indeed allow a substantial degree of freedom for its members to express themselves to one another, to the party as a whole, and to those not in the party, even if they held dissident views. Individual activists as well as local organizations also were encouraged to exercise a considerable amount of initiative in carrying out their activities. At the same time, there was an expectation that a significant degree of loyalty to the party, its program, and its organizational statutes would guide these activities. In addition, there was provision that democratically elected leadership bodies would seek to ensure the functioning of the organization in a manner consistent with its democratically established program and organizational principles.

Democratic centralism was seen as involving a dynamic interaction between the individual and the collective and as being a means for generating the maximum amount of participation by the membership in deciding and carrying out the work of the organization. It was also viewed as a means of enabling the organization to be effective in carrying out and evaluating its work. Once a majority came to a decision, a minority that disagreed was to do nothing to undermine the decision. The decision would be tested in practice. The critical perspectives of the loyal minority, far from undermining party unity, would help the organization as a whole to clarify its orientation, learn from its experiences, stay in touch with complex realities, and correct its mistakes.

As if anticipating the danger of bureaucratic-authoritarian degeneration that occurred under the Stalin regime, a resolution on democratic centralism adopted by the 1921 World Congress of the Communist International warned against "formal or mechanical centralization [which] would mean the centralization of 'power' in the hands of the Party bureaucracy, allowing it to *dominate* the other members of the Party or the proletarian masses which are outside the Party." Instead, democratic centralism was to be "a real synthesis, a fusion of centralism and proletarian democracy" that would facilitate "the active participation of working people" in the ongoing class struggle, in an eventual working-class revolution, and in the effort to create a socialist society.[11]

It may be helpful, at this point, to sum up the essential aspects of Lenin's organizational perspectives. We have seen that Lenin, as a Marxist, believed that the revolutionary organization must be a *working-class party*. Beyond this fundamental starting point, Leninist organizational perspectives can be summarized in the following eight points:

1. The workers' party must, first of all, be based on a revolutionary Marxist program and must exist to apply that program to reality in a way that will advance the struggle for socialism.

2. The members of that party must be activists who agree with the basic program, who are committed to collectively developing and implementing the program, and who collectively control the organization as a whole.

3. To the extent that it is possible (given tsarist repression, for example), the party should function openly and democratically, with the elective principle operating from top to bottom.

4. The highest decision-making body of the party is the *party congress* or convention, made up of delegates democratically elected by each party unit. The congress should meet at least every two years and should be preceded by a full discussion throughout the party of all questions that party members deem important.

5. Between congresses, a *central committee*—elected by and answerable to the congress—should ensure the cohesion and coordinate the work of the party on the basis of the party program and the decisions of the congress, (It may set up subordinate, interim bodies to help oversee the daily functioning of the organization.) In addition, the central committee has a responsibility to keep all local units of the party informed of these various units' individual experiences and activities. Under conditions of severe political repression and in the midst of major struggles, the authority of the central party leadership may assume much greater weight than at other times; yet that leadership is always bound by the revolutionary Marxist program of the party, by the decisions of the party congress, and by a responsibility (and accountability) to the membership as a whole.

6. It is assumed that within the general framework of the revolutionary program there will be shades of difference on various programmatic, tactical, and practical questions. These should be openly discussed and debated, particularly (but not necessarily exclusively) before party congresses. Within limits—which vary depending on time, place, and circumstance—such differences can be aired publicly. All members should be encouraged to participate in this discussion process and should have an opportunity to make their views known to the party as a whole. It is assumed that, at times, groupings will form around one or another viewpoint or even around a full-fledged platform that certain members believe the party should adopt. This (as opposed to groupings based on personal likes and dislikes, and ill-defined moods and biases) provides a basis for ongoing political clarity and programmatic development, which are essential to the health and growth of the party.

7. All questions should be decided on the basis of democratic vote (majority rule), after which the minority is expected to function

loyally in the party, and particularly to avoid undermining the specific actions decided on. The organization as a whole learns through the success, partial success, or failure of policies that are adopted and tested in practice.

8. Local units of the party must operate within the framework of the party program and of the decisions of the party as a whole, but within that framework they must operate under the autonomous and democratic control of the local membership.

These eight points describe a revolutionary vanguard organization functioning according to the principle of democratic centralism. They also describe the way in which Lenin thought that an organization should function, and they also describe—more or less—the way that the Bolsheviks functioned from 1903 until the early 1920s.

In the wake of the Bolshevik Revolution of 1917, however, Russia suffered a foreign military intervention and economic blockade, a violent and brutalizing civil war, and the devastating collapse of the economy. Consequently, increasingly authoritarian expedients and bureaucratic distortions began to crop up in the practice of the Bolshevik party, as well as in the Communist International that had been established to assist revolutionaries around the world in working for socialist revolutions in their own countries. These distortions helped lay the basis for the Stalinist degeneration of the Communist movement in the new Soviet Republic and throughout the world. The most clearsighted and dedicated Bolsheviks, including Lenin himself in the last years of his life, struggled against this degeneration—but they were overwhelmed.

Leninism in the United States

The Russian Revolution had a profound impact on the left wing of the U.S. labor movement. As Philip Foner demonstrates in his excellent documentary study *The Bolshevik Revolution: Its Impact on American Radicals, Liberals, and Labor*, the Bolshevik victory was embraced by the overwhelming majority of the substantial Socialist Party, the Industrial Workers of the World, the Socialist Labor Party, and also the International Ladies Garment Workers Union, the Amalgamated Clothing Workers of America, the Chicago Federation of Labor, the Seattle Labor Council, and others.[12]

Eugene V. Debs, the deeply loved and immensely popular spokesman of working-class socialism in the United States, expressed the feelings of many: "Lenin and Trotsky were the men of the hour and under their fearless, incorruptible and uncompromising leadership the Russian proletariat has held the fort against the combined assaults of all the ruling powers of earth. . . . So far as the Russian proletariat is concerned, the day of the people has arrived. . . . They are setting the heroic example of a world-wide emulation. Let us, like them, scorn and repudiate the cowardly compromisers within our own ranks, challenge and defy the robber-class power, and fight it out on that line to victory or death. From the crown of my head to the soles of my feet I am Bolshevik, and proud of it." The leader of the militant Industrial Workers of the World (IWW), "Big Bill" Haywood, responded similarly: "Here is the IWW all feathered out. . . . The Russian Revolution is the greatest event in our lives. . . . It represents all that we have been dreaming of and fighting for all our lives. It is the dawn of freedom and industrial democracy. If we can't trust Lenin, we can't trust anybody."[13]

Yet there was not a clear notion among the would-be American Bolsheviks about what, precisely, Bolshevism meant. One of the first conscious "Leninists" in the United States was the left-wing Socialist Louis Fraina—later known as Lewis Corey—who edited the first English-language anthology of writing by Lenin and Trotsky, under the title of *The Proletarian Revolution in Russia* (1918). In his introductory essays interspersed throughout the collection, he sought to communicate what was distinctive in the Bolshevik-Leninist perspective in this way:

> The epoch of Marx developed the theory of Socialism, the epoch of Lenin is developing its practice: and this is precisely the great fact in Russia— the fact of *Socialism and the revolutionary proletariat in action*. . . . The Bolsheviki constituted the party of the revolutionary proletariat; in the words of Lenin, "the class conscious workers, day laborers, and the poorer classes of the peasantry, who are classed with them (semi-proletariat)." . . . Representing the interests and ideology of the industrial masses, and in continual active contact with them, the Bolsheviki developed that general, creative and dynamic mass action out of which revolutions arise and develop uncompromisingly. . . . The Bolsheviki constituted a practical revolutionary movement, not a group of theoreticians and mongers of dogmas. They worked out a program, a practical program of action in accord with the immediate problems of the Revolution and out of which

would necessarily arise the struggle and power for the larger, ultimate objectives."[14]

All this was fine as far as it went, but it was also rather vague. In the first left-wing accounts by U.S. eyewitnesses, there was almost nothing that went beyond this. "The Mensheviki and the Bolsheviki are branches of the same party, and until 1903 they worked together," wrote Louise Bryant in *Six Months in Red Russia* (1918). "They still have precisely the same program, but they differ as to tactics. . . . The Bolsheviki are in power because they bow to the will of the masses." In the same year, Bessie Beatty's *The Red Heart of Russia* explained: "The Bolshevik believes in the shortest cut to socialism." John Reed's 1919 classic *Ten Days that Shook the World* offered a similar definition: "*Bolsheviki.* Now call themselves the *Communist Party*, in order to emphasize their complete separation from the tradition of 'moderate' or 'parliamentary' Socialism, which dominates the Mensheviki and the so-called Majority Socialists in all countries. The *Bolsheviki* proposed immediate proletarian insurrection, and seizure of the reins of Government, in order to hasten the coming of Socialism by forcibly taking over industry, land, natural resources and financial institutions."[15]

Albert Rhys Williams, in *Lenin, the Man and His Work* (1919), *did* make frequent references to Lenin's "iron discipline" and offered this suggestive passage: "The Russian Social Democratic Labor Party was organized in 1898. At the Second Congress held at Brussels and London in 1903 came the famous breach in the Party. Lenin fought for a centralized party with a central body directing all activities. On this and other points he was bitterly opposed by a determined minority. Agreement was impossible, and the congress split into two factions: the Mensheviki, which means literally 'members of the minority,' and the Bolsheviki, 'members of the majority.'"[16]

During earliest years of the American Communist movement, from 1919 through 1921, such fragments of information as this—plus a sectarian notion by some activists that a *truly* Bolshevik party must function underground, as did the Bolsheviks in tsarist Russia—constituted the essence of "Leninism" in the United States. Made up of substantial yet ragged splits from the Socialist Party, the IWW, and some of the anarchist groups, with numerous egos and factional currents vying for recognition from revolutionary Moscow, the pioneer Communists found it difficult to strike a balance that would allow them to play a significant role in U.S. labor and social struggles. The inclination of many historians has been to portray the Communist Party of the entire 1920s decade—quite inaccurately—as simply a bizarre sect with no connection to American life.

Closer to the truth is the observation of radical scholar Michael Goldfield, in a survey of literature on the history of American Communism, that "the most dynamic activists and leaders of the [Socialist Party] in 1919 left to form the core of the new Communist Party. Within a few years of its formation, the Communist movement, its chaotic and often unrealistic romantic expectations notwithstanding, attracted and absorbed many of the more radical elements of the IWW, the small black socialist milieu, and the bulk of left-wing trade union activists." Paul Buhle, in his uneven but interesting book *Marxism in the United States*, also pointed to important trade union work done by Communists in the 1920s, and especially the base developed within many immigrant working-class communities: "The Party encouraged the uncertain relationship between revolutionary politics and ethnic culture, providing the immigrants with essential services: labor defense, propaganda, English-language spokesmen and organizational contacts. The groups in return gave the bulk of funds for the Party's operation, produced enthusiastic crowds, and formed an authentic radical proletariat. And by the thousands these immigrants proved doggedly loyal, unlike the [native-born] American recruits who had few social settings in which to operate collectively."[17]

Yet this also understates the importance of a layer of native-born U.S. radicals that became an essential component of American Communism. One of these was the midwestern veteran IWW activist James P. Cannon. He was one of the first new leaders of the Communist Party (CP), remembered by another early CP leader, Alexander Bittelman, for "his very skillful championing of the cause of Communist reorientation towards the daily struggles of the masses and to active participation in the trade unions of the American Federation of Labor." In a 1924 talk to a CP conference of coal miners, Cannon commented: "The revolutionary aspirations of our Party comrades generate the enthusiasm and self-sacrifice that give the Party its driving power. Woe to us if we become so 'practical' as to forget this for one moment. All our work must lead toward the proletarian revolution. If we keep this always in mind and measure all our daily work by this standard we will keep on the right road."[18] Yet Cannon's idealism was tempered by a seriousness in regard to practical organizational questions. Bittelman's comments are worth quoting at length:

> As I became better acquainted with Jim, I began to notice and appreci-
> ate his skills in internal party politics. Because of this skill, he was able
> to play a very effective part in helping to bring unity into the warring
> groups of the Jewish Communist and left wing movements. He managed,
> by his political skill as well as charming personality, when he chose to
> be charming, to win the respect and also confidence of our group—the
> Jewish section of the Communist party—as well as of the Olgin-Salutsky
> group—formerly the Jewish part of the Workers' Council [that split from
> the Socialist Party to join the Communists slightly later]. He seemed
> fully aware, not alone of the political differences between the two groups,
> but also of the individual and personal frictions and incompatibilities
> between, say, Salutsky and myself, or between Olgin and Schachno
> Epstein, by way of example.
>
> These skills in intra-party politics, the playing of which he obviously
> enjoyed very much, were unquestionably a source of strength to Jim him-
> self as well as to our party. . . . I remember a certain image of him that I
> acquired after a while. It was the image of a caretaker of a large experi-
> mental institution or laboratory, moving about the various machines,
> tools, gadgets, testing tubes, etc., making sure they operate properly, oil-
> ing, fixing, changing, improving and adjusting. That was Jim's main con-
> tribution to our party; and, for the particular phase in its development, a
> very important contribution. His humor and wit played no small part in
> all of that.[19]

This blend of revolutionary socialist commitment and practical, down-to-earth organizational seriousness—plus a genuine involve-ment in the practical struggles of the multifaceted, multiethnic U.S. working class—represented an extremely promising start for American Leninism. The influence of the Russian Communists, within the frame-work of the Communist International (or Comintern), was quite impor-tant, of course. Cannon later recalled that he and his comrades "learned to do away forever with the idea that a revolutionary socialist move-ment, aiming at power, can be led by people who practice socialism as an avocation. . . . Lenin, Trotsky, Zinoviev, Radek, Bukharin—these were our teachers. We began to be educated in an entirely different spirit from the old lackadaisical Socialist Party—in the spirit of revolutionists who take ideas and program very seriously." Another of the early Communists, Bertram D. Wolfe, noted that before 1925 it was *not* the case that "all important decisions for the American Communist Party were being made in Moscow." Communications from Lenin, Zinoviev, and other Comintern leaders "were intended only as helpful suggestions, often exciting ones, and as successful examples to imitate after adapting them to American conditions, but not as categorical commands."[20]

Indeed, as Paul Buhle comments, in this period there was considerable autonomy for local Communist Party activists: "Decentralization of political initiative, with the inevitable persistence of old habits [from a heterogeneous Debsian-era radicalism], encouraged a wide experimentation at the local level that remained largely invisible to [national] Party leaders—and has so remained for most historians." Writing about his own experiences in California, where the party was remote from the CP national office but "had close linkage with the more progressive section of organized labor," Bertram Wolfe later recalled: "If we agreed with an order from the high command, we tried to carry it out zealously and explain it carefully to our growing body of sympathizers and increasingly friendly progressive trade unions. . . . But if the instructions were unpalatable, poorly justified, or late in reaching us, we simply paid no attention to them and continued working as we had been working." Nor were they ever called to account for it.[21]

As time went on, there was concern among U.S. Communist leaders and activists to develop a more cohesive revolutionary organization, and more attention was given to educating the ranks in Leninist organizational norms. In a 1924 pamphlet for the party youth group, for example, Max Shachtman explained the birth of Bolshevism this way: "It became apparent that a split [among the Russian Marxists] was to take place, Lenin insisting that every comrade must be an active member subject to the discipline of the party, while Martov was ready to leave the door open for vague elements which threatened to liquidate the revolutionary soul of the party." In 1926, a volume of more than 200 pages was published by the CP national office, *Lenin on Organization*, gathering together much of Lenin's writing on this question, along with an authoritative thirty-nine-page essay by an old Bolshevik named Vikenti Mitzkovitch-Kapsukas. This essay, hardly the work of a bureaucratic hack, nonetheless projected an image of "Leninism" that was already marred by authoritarian elements that had developed during the Russian civil war, creating dangerous preconditions for Stalinist degeneration, such as the banning of dissident factions and tendencies in the party. The conception of a monolithic party was advanced in the Comintern under the leadership of Gregory Zinoviev, who influenced Cannon's own formulations in the early 1920s: "It [a Bolshevik party] must be a centralized party prohibiting factions, tendencies, and groups. It must be a monolithic party hewn of one piece." Cannon was attempting to use this conception to combat the unhealthy situation inside the U.S. Communist Party: "At least one-half of the energy of the party has been expended in factional struggles, one after another. We have even grown into the habit of accepting this state of affairs." He was to learn, however, that the prohibition of factions, tendencies, and groups not only runs counter to the historical model of pre-1921 Bolshevism but also it fatally undercuts the possibility of democracy inside the organization.[22]

In fact, a policy of "Bolshevization" was being implemented throughout the Comintern, supervised by the old worker-Bolshevik Osip Piatnitsky, but it was increasingly distorted by the reactionary bureaucracy that was bringing the Russian Communist Party, the Soviet state, and the Communist International under its authoritarian control.[23] A warped version of democratic centralism was established, designed to bring the activity of members under the control of party leaders, and to bring the leaderships of the various national parties under the control of the Moscow bureaucracy headed by Joseph Stalin. Revolutionaries like Cannon, who perceived a growing discrepancy between the triumph of Stalinism and the revolutionary ideals to which they had committed "the whole of their lives," found themselves in opposition, followed by quick expulsion.

Of course, the Stalinized Communist Party continued to project itself as the only truly Leninist organization, and later would-be Leninists—especially those following the special Chinese version of Stalinism, the various Maoist groups arising in the United States—made similar claims. I have touched on these in my study *Lenin and the Revolutionary Party*, indicating that, despite their claims and rhetoric, their practice diverged dramatically from that of Lenin's party. For our purposes here, it makes sense to focus only on those who did not subscribe to the Stalinist mutilation of the Bolshevik tradition.[24]

Cannon and others who were committed to the goal of creating an authentic American Leninism established the Communist League of America in 1929, following the lead of the exiled revolutionary leader Leon Trotsky. Trotsky was a rallying point for those committed to the original goals and methods of the Russian Revolution and the early Communist movement. His U.S. cothinkers were active in union struggles, the unemployed movement, antiracism activities, opposition to war and imperialism, the fight against fascism, and the defense of revolutionary Marxism against the distortions and vicious assaults of Stalinism. Through a series of organizational developments, involving a succession of complex splits and fusions, the Trotskyists in the United States grew from about 100 in 1928 to more than 1,000 in 1938, when they established the Socialist Workers Party.[25]

The SWP was predominantly a working-class party. George Breitman, in a discussion of its founding convention, offered this description in the valuable book he edited, *The Founding of the Socialist Workers Party*:

> Our chief union stronghold was Minneapolis, where our comrades in the Teamsters union led by [Vincent Raymond] Dunne, [Carl] Skoglund, and Farrell Dobbs, were showing the whole country what a union led by revolutionaries could do. It was our aspiration in Newark [where Breitman lived at the time], and I am sure elsewhere, to meet the high standards they were setting. The story of their activity can now be read in Dobbs' books about the Teamsters.
>
> Another gain of that time was the organization of our fraction in the maritime industry, starting on the West Coast. Although he was not at the founding convention, Tom Kerry was elected to the National Committee at this convention, partly in recognition of his work in this fraction, which also served as a model for the party.
>
> Most of our other activity was centered in the new CIO unions that were being born at the time—steel, auto, electrical, and so on. We helped to sign up workers to join the unions, both in the plants and in their homes; we participated in strikes to win recognition and bargaining rights; we joined forces with others to gain, extend, or preserve democracy inside the unions.
>
> The main difference was that the unions then were less bureaucratized and the workers had a greater interest in their unions than they do today [in 1978]. That made it easier for militants to get a hearing from the members in those days.[26]

There were also left-wing intellectuals in the SWP from non-working-class backgrounds, and they were able to make important contributions to the work of the Trotskyist movement. But the working-class roots and commitments of the SWP were unambiguous from the time of its founding until the 1960s (these are touched on in the next section of this essay).

Not only the proletarian composition of the party but also the program and structure unambiguously conformed to the Leninist model that has been described here. "The Socialist Workers Party is a revolutionary Marxian party, based on a definite program, whose aim is the organization of the working class in the struggle for power and the transformation of the existing social order," one of the founding documents of the SWP explained. "All of its activities, its methods, and its internal regime are subordinated to this aim and designed to serve it." The very next sentence of this document is instructive: "Only a self-acting and critical-minded membership is capable of forging and consolidating such a party and of solving its problems by collective thought, discussion, and experience." The document, entitled "The Internal Situation and the Character of the Party," goes on to describe a Leninist party, functioning according to the principle of democratic centralism, as understood by its authors Cannon and Shachtman, the SWP's central leaders. There is sometimes a distinction to be made, of course, between how an organization functions ideally and how people are actually able to live up to the ideal. In 1940, Cannon commented that "our party has not been a homogeneous Bolshevik party, . . . but an organization struggling to attain the standard of Bolshevism, and beset all the time by internal contradictions."[27]

Cannon's own background in the early Communist Party had left its imprint on him, as we have noted, although there were negative as well as positive aspects to this. "I was raised the hard way in politics," he noted. "I was raised in the Communist Party from 1919–28—you know that is nine years of uninterrupted factional struggle. That is, unless you call an interruption a peace to catch your breath and reorganize your forces. Nine years that devoured the energy of the party." Joseph Hansen commented that in this period "the Communist Party was something of a jungle—that is, as far as the internal struggles were concerned. At first, the Communist International under Lenin and Trotsky could play a role in ameliorating the situation and helping the comrades to learn the correct lessons from their mistakes. But later on the Comintern degenerated and itself became a real jungle, in which Jim was one of the best of the jungle fighters. He made errors from which he later learned and never forgot." Hansen added a significant point: "The main difference between Jim and some of the others who also had talents along this line was that Jim operated within the framework of principles, the principles of revolutionary socialism." Comradely pressure and assistance from Trotsky helped Cannon go some distance in allowing mature revolutionary qualities to transcend the factionalist aspect of his political background.[28]

Nonetheless, the supposedly undemocratic "Cannon regime" became a target of dissident currents in the U.S. Trotskyist movement. In the mid-1930s, an ultra-left oppositionist going by the name George Marlen complained: "An unusually subtle, calculating demagogue, Cannon, without the backing of the world-famous figure [Trotsky], would have been an inconspicuous, average political adventurer seeking a field of action in a workers' organization." Adding that "Cannon's record in the Communist Party is as filthy as that of any of the Stalinist careerists," he concluded that "Cannon practices a spurious 'democracy' within the organization, exercising a factual control through his bureaucratic machine."[29]

A minority led by Max Shachtman and James Burnham in the bitter factional fight that wracked the SWP in 1939–40 advanced the same accusation: "For the Cannon faction, Trotsky's politics function precisely as *substitute* for politics of their own. As a bureaucratic-conservative group, they merely utilize Trotsky's politics as they utilize politics in general, as an instrument of their regime. . . . Politics, programs, are more or less routine matters for others to take care of; the business of the 'real Bolshevik' is—to cinch up the majority and retain party control." Even an ostensibly sympathetic (though somewhat factional) account by a later radical asserts: "Cannon was content to take his basic political line as something given to him from abroad, and devoted his energies to building an organization around that political line." Another latter-day commentator—the 1960s radical personality Tariq Ali, reminiscing about the years in which he was attracted to Trotskyism—writes that Cannon's *The Struggle for a Proletarian Party* "shocked my sensibilities" because it documented "the single-minded and relentless pursuit of an oppositional current within the same organization until it was defeated, demoralized, and expelled." Ali doesn't know what he's talking about here: although Max Shachtman, James Burnham, Martin Abern, and the others Cannon argued against *were* defeated, none of them was expelled—they split and set up their own rival party, taking many of the resources of the SWP with them. Giving as good as they got in this tough factional fight, they were hardly the tender idealists and persecuted victims Ali seems to imagine: Shachtman and Abern were experienced political infighters from the early days of the Communist Party; the well-to-do Burnham quickly split from the new group and soon found a comfortable new role in the Central Intelligence Agency and on the editorial board of the right-wing weekly magazine *National Review*.[30]

The denigration of Cannon's own abilities as a political thinker is belied by the impressive quality of his many writings and speeches. Although his special talent lay in the extremely important area of effectively popularizing Marxist, Leninist, and Trotskyist ideas, he also demonstrated a genuine ability for developing down-to-earth, insightful, sophisticated political analyses on a variety of international, national, internal organizational, historical, and more abstractly theoretical questions. While making no pretense about being an original theoretician, he produced a body of work that holds up far better than that of many seemingly more intellectual left-wing leaders of his time. More than this, a strong case can be made for the proposition that his contributions to building a revolutionary organization were of extremely high quality, involving considerable internal democracy, despite the complaints of his factional adversaries. It is worth noting the judgment of C. L. R. James—the prominent Black Marxist theorist who had been part of the Shachtman faction—that "the existing documents of both the Majority and the Minority in 1940 prove that there was not the slightest basis for the charge being made today [in 1947] that the Minority of 1940 had been bureaucratically mishandled by the Cannon-led majority."[31]

It is necessary to go beyond the personality of Cannon, however, to take an accurate measure of the SWP that survived the 1940 split. The Shachtmanites listed those they considered the most prominent members of the Cannon faction in 1940: Morris Lewit, Sam Gordon, V. R. Dunne, Carl Skoglund, Jack Weber, Larry Trainor, George Clarke, Bert Cochran, Felix Morrow, John G. Wright, Murry Weiss.[32] Other "Cannonites" of the 1940s could be listed: Sylvia Bleeker, Harry Braverman, Dorothea Breitman, George Breitman, Arthur Burch, Kay Burch, Grace Carlson, Anne Chester, Bob Chester, Charles Curtiss, Lillian Curtiss, Farrell Dobbs, Duncan Ferguson, Albert Goldman,

Laura Gray, Joseph Hansen, Reba Hansen, Rose Karsner, Karolyn Kerry, Tom Kerry, Antoinette Konikow, Frank Lovell, Sarah Lovell, George Novack, Ruth Querio, Evelyn Reed, Ray Sparrow, Arne Swabeck, Augusta Trainor, David Weiss, Myra Tanner Weiss, Connie Weissman, George Weissman, and more. (For example, Milt Alvin [Genecin], who had originally lined up with Shachtman, soon returned to the SWP and became a firm "Cannonite.") It would be necessary to produce a collective portrait of this cluster of revolutionaries to get a living sense of the reality that was the Socialist Workers Party in the 1940s. Even this would not be adequate: one would have to trace the connections between their individual lives and the lives of the other comrades, the internal life of the various branches of the party, the cultural and occupational contexts of the membership, the involvement in trade union and community struggles, the SWP's theoretical and educational work, the interpenetration of the party and the larger social and political environment. Much could be learned from such a study.

Naturally, not all the "Cannonites" continued to agree with Cannon in the face of the complex realities arising with World War II and afterward (some of which are touched on in the next section of this essay). In 1945–46, a small grouping around Albert Goldman and Felix Morrow—deeply concerned about the postwar resiliency of Stalinism and affected by the "democratic capitalist" stabilization in Western Europe and the United States—developed sharp political differences with the SWP majority, and they articulated a critique of "Stalinist germs in the SWP" that should be critically examined.

Goldman, explaining his defection from the SWP to Shachtman's rival Workers Party (WP), wrote that "the leadership of the SWP was turning away from a Leninist-Trotskyist conception of a revolutionary party and toward a Zinovievist conception." We have noted that in the early 1920s Cannon, along with other pioneers of American Communism, was influenced by supercentralist organizational conceptions propagated in the Comintern under Gregory Zinoviev. "It was Zinoviev who introduced the idea of a monolithic party," Goldman wrote. "Stalin developed that idea. In the days when Cannon was a member of the Communist Party, Cannon was an ardent defender of the monolithic party. He is far more careful now; he does not say that he wants a monolithic party as in his early days, but actually he is working to create just such a party. Some of his followers substitute the word 'homogeneous' for that of 'monolithic.'" Yet Goldman's own description of the actions of his own faction suggest that it was playing fast and loose with the democratic centralist norms of the SWP: "Four members of the SWP were censured for organizing a discussion on the Russian question with some members of the WP. . . . The Minority openly declared its intention to fraternize politically with the WP. It organized socials and classes, inviting members of the WP to participate. I spoke at meetings of the WP members. . . . Under the circumstances, the Minority decided to continue political fraternization with the WP regardless of the policy of the Majority." In defense of such behavior, Goldman offered this theoretical rationale: "Our party must be a disciplined party but its discipline is not based on rules and regulations. It is the discipline of comrades devoted to a great cause and conscious of the fact that without discipline in action they can achieve nothing. It is a discipline based primarily on the correctness of the leadership and not on the ability of the leaders to order people."[33]

There are elements of truth in Goldman's argument. We have seen that Lenin insisted on a form of discipline "in action" that is based on comrades being devoted to a common cause, not on arbitrary orders from leaders or formalistic rules and regulations. On the other hand, Lenin didn't *counterpose* such self-discipline to organizational rules and regulations—in fact, he took rules and regulations quite seriously. Nor did Lenin ever argue that the decisions of an elected leadership should simply be ignored or flouted if an individual comrade or a minority in the party believed such decisions to be incorrect. Whenever such things developed between the Bolsheviks and Mensheviks, or within the Bolshevik party, they constituted *not* any kind of normal democratic functioning but instead an impending organizational split. The political decisions, and the organizational rules and regulations, democratically established by the party membership, provided the framework within which disciplined comrades were expected to function. The approach of Cannon reflected something more akin to the Leninist tradition:

> Our conception of the functioning of the party is the Leninist conception, that not only do members have rights of free discussion in the party, but they have duties. And one duty is this: that all their political activity has to be carried on under the supervision and control of the party. Does that mean that they cannot talk to members of other parties, as has been alleged against us; that they cannot fraternize with them; that they cannot collaborate with them? Not at all. Our comrades in the trade unions

are talking, fraternizing, and collaborating every day. Work could not be carried on without it. It is not the prohibition of talking, fraternizing, collaborating that has ever been at issue in our ranks. It is that the collaboration with other political elements—either Shachtmanites, or Socialists, or progressives, or labor partyites—that the collaboration, which is absolutely indispensable for the development of our work in many instances, has to be done as a party task.[34]

The Goldman-Morrow group was not able to win, according to Goldman, because the SWP majority were "Cannonite cliquists to whom prestige is more important than political ideas." Yet Cannon and his cothinkers developed an innovative application of Bolshevik perspectives to the mid-twentieth century United States, the "Theses on the American Revolution," whose ideas are eloquently articulated in Cannon's "The Coming American Revolution." A clear analysis of key developments in twentieth-century capitalism and a bold vision of the possibilities of revolutionary working-class struggles in the United States, the American Theses sought to underline the relevance of Leninist-Trotskyist conceptions in the most powerful capitalist country. Cannon insisted upon the central importance for the entire world of a socialist revolution in the United States, the nature of the U.S. working class and its capacity to make such a revolution, and the vital role of the Socialist Workers Party in this process. "At the bottom of all our conceptions was the basic idea that the proletarian revolution is a realistic proposition in this country, and not merely a far-off 'ultimate goal,' to be referred to on ceremonial occasions," Cannon explained. "Our part is to build up this party which believes in the unlimited power and resources of the American workers, and believes no less in its own capacity to organize and lead them to storm and victory."[35]

Unfortunately, the SWP failed to realize this promise. Various shortcomings of individuals, party perspectives, policies, and practices can be listed as contributing to this failure. Allegedly fatal flaws of "Cannonism" have sometimes been given the dubious credit for the subsequent development of new factional tensions in the SWP and the party's partial fragmentation during the fifteen years following World War II: the split of the Goldman-Morrow group in 1946, the split of the Johnson-Forest group (led by C. L. R. James and Raya Dunayevskaya) in 1951, the split of the Cochran group in 1953. But this is a superficial view, giving both too much and too little credit to Cannon and those around him. Although there can be debates about the imperfections of Cannon, there is no controversy over the fact that he had imperfections. Yet none of these was of a nature that would wreck the effort to build a working-class revolutionary vanguard party. In fact, Cannon's great strengths were ideally suited to facilitate the development of such an organization. Great as his strengths were, however, and great as were the strengths of his comrades, the SWP found itself up against a larger reality that would necessarily overwhelm the labors of the most dedicated, farsighted, flexible, and effective revolutionaries that one might imagine.

We have noted that the existence of a class-conscious layer of the working class is an essential precondition for the kind of party that Lenin insisted was necessary for a socialist revolution. The Marxist concept of workers' class consciousness involves *not* simply whatever notions happen to be in the minds of various members of the working class at any particular point in time. It involves an understanding of the insight that was contained in the preamble of the American Federation of Labor from 1886 to 1955: "A struggle is going on in all the nations of the civilized world, between the oppressors and the oppressed of all countries, a struggle between the capitalist and the laborer, which grows in intensity from year to year, and will work disastrous results to the toiling millions, if they are not combined for mutual protection and benefit." Not all workers have absorbed this insight into their consciousness, but those who have done so can be said to possess at least an elementary form of class consciousness.[36]

Class consciousness, from the standpoint of revolutionary Marxists, embraces a range of perceptions and commitments, including an understanding that there is a distinct working class that one is part of, whose interests are counterposed to the capitalist class; a sense of solidarity with other members of one's class; a belief in the need for and the possibility of successful struggles—political as well as economic—to advance the interests of one's class; a conviction that the working-class majority can and should become the dominant political force in society ("winning the battle of democracy," as Marx and Engels put it), reconstructing the economy so that it is collectively owned by all, democratically controlled by all, and operated in the interests of all—making possible the dignity and free development of each person in society.[37]

Such consciousness does not exist automatically in one's brain simply because one sells one's labor power for wages or a salary. But from the period spanning the end of the Civil War in 1865 through the depression decade of the 1930s, a vibrant working-class subculture had developed throughout much of the United States. Often this "subculture" was more like a network of subcultures having very distinctive ethnic attributes, but these different ethnic currents were at various times connected by left-wing political structures (such as the old Knights of Labor, Socialist Party, IWW, Communist Party, and so on) and also, to an extent, by trade union frameworks. Within this context flourished the class consciousness that is essential to the success of Leninism. Cannon and many of his comrades were a product of this radical workers' subculture. And they sought to make their own revolutionary contributions to it, and to help it become a revolutionary socialist force capable of transforming society.[38]

The "patriotic" hysteria and repression accompanying U.S. entry into the First World War, followed by the economic and cultural changes of the 1920s, represented a serious assault on this subculture—the effects of which were felt as many children of the radicals sought to assimilate into the seemingly more attractive "modern" culture of the American mainstream.[39] Nonetheless, the shock of the Great Depression gave new life to working-class radicalism. With the Second World War and its aftermath, however, the distinctive realities that had sustained a proletarian class consciousness within a sizable minority of the American working class eroded dramatically and seemed to pass out of existence.

The realities generating this dilemma posed an almost insoluble problem for the American Trotskyists. This brings us, first of all, to a question that has so far been given too little attention here but is, in fact, central to any serious discussion of Leninism—revolutionary internationalism. More than this, we must touch on the interplay between world events and unfolding realities inside the United States, and the impact of this on the consciousness of the American working class and on the membership base of the SWP.

The Changing World

The development of American capitalism has always been intimately bound up with *international* developments: from the first European explorers representing the tentative probe of a rising merchant-capitalism, to the establishment in the Americas of the European great powers' rival colonial-mercantile empires, to the development of the slave trade that was a key element, as well, in the triumph of the Industrial Revolution (slave-based cotton plantations supplying the English textile industry's "dark Satanic mills"). Both the American Revolution of 1775–83 and the American Civil War of 1861–65 were part of the global sweep of "bourgeois-democratic" revolutions. Industrialization and trade connected and transformed increasing numbers of peoples and cultures on all inhabited continents. The American working class was composed, and periodically recomposed, of immigrant waves generated by the "push-and-pull" dynamics of the world capitalist economy. Capitalist developments and class struggles in the British Isles, France, Germany, and elsewhere had an impact on and found reflection in what was happening in the United States. And the United States, as it grew into the foremost industrial and imperial power, itself had a profound impact on international developments.

The understanding of such international dynamics resulted in the creation of the first three working-class internationals—the International Workingmen's Association (1864–76) led by Karl Marx, the Socialist International (1889–1914), and the Communist International (1919–43). In each case, momentous developments of international importance provoked crises that resulted in decline but also created the basis for new advances. The revolutionary Paris Commune of 1871, and the brutal repression generated by this heroic but ill-fated workers' government, frightened away trade union moderates and led to a furious split between anarchists and socialists in the First International. On the other hand, a self-consciously socialist Second International, representing mass parties and left-wing trade unions, soon took shape. The weaknesses and divisions within this increasingly reformist-dominated Second International became evident when the eruption of the First World War literally tore it apart. But revolutionary Marxists and working-class militants, in the wake of the devastating world war, and deeply inspired by the creation of a Soviet Republic in Russia, built the Third International.[40]

These three internationals—and also the world historic events with which they were connected—had a profound impact on the development of the left wing of the workers' movement, and on the development of class consciousness, in the United States. The degeneration and collapse of the Third International as a revolutionary force, and the realities with which this was connected, had no less of an effect. The accumulation of working-class defeats in Europe (Italy, Hungary,

Germany, Austria, Spain) and in China, coupled with the rise of fascism and Nazism, combined with the murderous, totalitarian corruption of Stalinism in the USSR and the world Communist movement, and the approach of a new, more massive round of imperialist slaughter that was the Second World War—all this necessarily undermined the strength of the U.S. working-class left, just as surely as revolutionary victories of the Chinese, German, or Spanish workers' movements would have generated soaring morale and renewed self-confidence.[41]

The seeming collapse of capitalism in the 1930s did not result in the working class coming to power in any country of the world, but the Great Depression did generate working-class upsurges in many countries—in some cases forcing through important social reforms that were beneficial to working people (such as the right to form unions, the winning of higher wages and other employment benefits, as well as unemployment insurance and social security). It also helped the more powerful capitalists to eliminate less efficient practices and competitors—resulting in a strengthened capitalism. More than this, it encouraged the competing capitalist classes to expand their overseas operations, compelling them to harmonize their different interests—or, when this proved impossible, to turn to militarism and war. The Stalinist and social democratic leaderships of the labor movements in the "democratic capitalist" countries of Western Europe and North America led the workers' organizations into a far-reaching alliance with their countries' capitalist classes during World War II.[42]

Small groups of workers and intellectuals throughout the world sought to preserve perspectives that had infused the revolutionary wing of the young Second International and the original founders of the Third International. They joined with Trotsky to form the Fourth International, which was formally proclaimed in 1938. Four years earlier, Trotsky had expressed his hopes and fears regarding the future Fourth International: "It may be constituted in the process of the struggle against fascism and the victory gained over it. But it may also be formed considerably later, in a number of years, in the midst of the ruins and the accumulation of debris following upon the victory of fascism and war." After the founding of this "world party of socialist revolution," Trotsky optimistically predicted that the coming Second World War would generate an even greater wave of militant working-class insurgency than had been the case with the First World War. Working-class revolutions would sweep away

Stalinism in the USSR and would also break the power of the capitalists in the advanced industrial countries. "The new generation of workers whom the war will impel onto the road of revolution will take their place under our banner," he asserted on the eve of his death in 1940.[43]

The devastation of World War II did generate revolutionary upsurges throughout the colonial and semicolonial countries of Asia, Africa, and Latin America. But Stalinism took a renewed hold on life in the post-war period. It seemed as solid as ever in the USSR, given the immense authority gained through "the Great Patriotic War," which drove back and destroyed the Nazi aggressor. Stalinism also took advantage of radical ferment in Eastern Europe to establish its hold on this area, setting up Communist Party dictatorships that were loyal to the USSR to form a buffer zone between the USSR and its erstwhile wartime allies of the capitalist West. In the capitalist countries of Western Europe, which had been devastated by war, masses of workers flocked to the already existing Communist, Social Democratic, and Labor Parties.

To prevent the "loss" of these lands, the unquestioned new world power—the United States of America—established the Marshall Plan to rebuild the economies of Europe on a firm capitalist basis; the North Atlantic Treaty Organization was fashioned to prevent the Soviet Red Army from expanding further westward, but also—and no less important—to prevent indigenous revolutionaries from replacing weakened bourgeois regimes with new workers' republics. The reformist Social Democratic and Labor Parties, still loyal to a reconstituted Second International, decided to forge a firm alliance with what was left of their own capitalist classes, and with U.S. imperialism, as the cold war set in. The world seemed divided between capitalist versus "communist" superpowers: the "Free World" bloc (which included many right-wing dictatorships) led by the United States versus the "Iron Curtain" countries (with Stalinist dictatorships but postcapitalist economies) led by the USSR.

Anti-imperialist and anticolonial ferment in the "third world" countries of Asia, Africa, and Latin America created an equivocal and more or less left-nationalist "neutralist" bloc. The revolutionary stirrings in the third world and the renewed power of Social Democratic and Labor Parties in Western Europe (not to mention massive Communist Parties in Italy and France) gave many hope that positive possibilities existed to move beyond capitalism. But this was largely overshadowed by the fact that world politics appeared to be locked into a grim "superpower" confrontation that threatened to spiral into a new world war—an especially devastating prospect, since both sides had developed nuclear weapons.[44]

This complex situation—combined with the obvious incorrectness of Trotsky's prediction regarding postwar realities—generated a sharp controversy inside the Fourth International. Some of its European leaders (the central one being Michel Pablo) predicted a third world war, with the Stalinist-led labor movement and bureaucratized workers' states on one side and U.S. imperialism on the other. In such a situation, they believed, the Fourth International must critically support the Stalinists. Trotskyists should recognize, they asserted, that the path to socialism would probably lie through an extended period of Stalinist-led "deformed workers' states," which would eventually become democratized partly through the work, on the "inside," of the Trotskyists. They argued that Trotskyists should not maintain an independent, "sectarian" small-group existence, but instead should carry out a "deep entry" into the mass workers' movements led by either the Stalinists or the Social Democrats. Seeking to impose a fairly rigid conception of "international democratic centralism," some of these leaders attempted to bring all the parties of the Fourth International into line with this general outlook.

The world Trotskyist movement was split by this issue. A minority in the SWP—in part agreeing with Pablo's perspectives, but in part feeling deeply demoralized by the disappointment of earlier revolutionary expectations—initiated a factional struggle in the United States that resulted in a large section of the party's trade unionists and other valuable cadres leaving the organization. The SWP majority, led by Cannon, helped spearhead a struggle inside the Fourth International against what they saw as Pablo's adaptation to Stalinism and tendency to liquidate the program and organization of the world Trotskyist movement. This crisis and the 1953 fissure in the Fourth Internationalist forces—both in the United States and worldwide—greatly weakened the morale and capacity for effective political action by U.S. Trotskyists. Even after the reunification of the Fourth International in 1963, scars and partly unhealed wounds remained from the 1953 split.[45]

There were additional problems that undermined the ability of the U.S. Trotskyists to realize much of the potential for American Leninism that had been evident in the 1930s and 1940s. One obvious reflection of the cold war was the development of a far-reaching campaign of domestic anticommunism. During the Second World War, social democratic and Stalinist currents in the United States, both of which enjoyed substantial influence in the American Federation of Labor (AFL) and the Congress of Industrial Organizations (CIO), had helped rally militant and socially conscious working people to a broad patriotic, class-collaborationist war effort against an expansionist "foreign menace" of German fascism and Japanese imperialism; this was facilitated by the earlier support that both social democrats and Stalinists had given to the Democratic Party's New Deal coalition for social reform headed by Franklin D. Roosevelt. Any notion that U.S. capitalism was also imperialist and expansionistic, fostering a foreign policy counterposed to the interests of the workers, was not consistently voiced by any organized force in the workers' movement except for the small number of Trotskyists.

The mind-set fostered during the New Deal and the Second World War facilitated the enlistment of the bulk of organized labor into a "bipartisan" crusade against a new "foreign menace"—the USSR and the world communist "conspiracy." The moderates and social democrats inside the labor movement took the lead in advancing this perspective, and the trade unionists of the Communist Party—which for more than a decade had failed to build a working-class socialist base that was politically independent from the (now fiercely anticommunist) Democratic Party liberals—suddenly found themselves isolated. Anticommunist hysteria and purges swept the labor movement, workplaces, educational institutions, and cultural life throughout American society, wrecking the organizations and obliterating the influence not only of the Communist Party but also of other left-wing currents, including the Trotskyists. Working people were intimidated, in many different ways, from giving serious consideration to any and all left-wing perspectives.[46]

This dovetailed with a double erosion of the radical working-class base that was also taking place. One aspect of the erosion was the fading out of immigrant radicalism and of the vibrant working-class ethnic subcultures, which had been so important to labor's left wing since the mid-nineteenth century. The closing off of immigration in the 1920s combined with powerful cultural-assimilationist dynamics. This, in turn, combined with another significant change—the fact that the working-class struggles that had been led by radicals had helped make capitalist society a better place to live for many workers, so they came to have much more to lose than simply the "chains" of capitalist oppression.

Steve Nelson, a Communist Party organizer with significant experience among foreign-born workers, described the realities he found in the late 1940s in a way that merits substantial quotation:

We asked ourselves what was happening to the foreign-born in this country. Were they becoming integrated into American society? . . . It was a fact of life—the older generation was not pulling the younger into the [communist] movement. Increasingly, first and second generations not only spoke different languages but also opted for different lifestyles. . . . World War II was a watershed. Sons who went to high school and then served in the armed forces thought in far different terms than their fathers. Daughters who worked in the shipyards and electrical plants were a world away from their mothers' experiences with domestic service and boarders. Industrial workers after the war were no longer just pick and shovel men. Machine tenders who enjoyed the security provided by unions with established channels for collective bargaining could not appreciate the chronic insecurity of the pre-CIO era. Life was changing, and we had to urge the old ones to understand and accept it.

But despite our recognition of these changing cultural patterns, we were limited in what we could offer, for we were still trying to present a socialist vision based on the model of the Soviet Union. The sons and daughters of immigrants, often far better-educated than their parents, couldn't accept our claim that the Soviet [i.e., Stalinist] model represented a better life. . . .

Although I experienced the changes in working-class values and culture primarily in terms of the foreign-born community and their children, I can see now that the entire American working class was undergoing a transformation during and after the war. I was to learn this with a vengeance during the [anti-communist hysteria of the] fifties. The Party, which had historically been rooted in a heavily immigrant working-class culture characterized by economic insecurity and political alienation, was unable to adjust to these changes. We could not evaluate the significance of the changing composition of the work force and its new patterns of community life and consumption. In a sense the activities of the Left were undercutting the role of the [left-wing] fraternal groups in the ethnic community. Gains such as unemployment compensation and social security as well as the greatly enhanced sense of security brought by the CIO unions made the fraternal organization less necessary in meeting the needs of working people. At the same time, participation in the labor movement and especially the war effort . . . eased the process of acceptance [into the "mainstream" of U.S. culture] of the foreign-born and their children.[47]

Although Nelson's focus here centers on how the Communist Party was affected, there is obvious significance beyond that. "Life is not determined by consciousness, but consciousness by life," Marx and Engels had argued.[48] The description above traces the erosion of the material basis of class consciousness for an important sector of the American working class. It is also described in the following 1953 discussion by James P. Cannon of developments within the once left-wing United Auto Workers union, led by exsocialist Walter Reuther:

> It is now sixteen years since the sit-down strikes made the new CIO unions secure by the seniority clause. These sixteen years of union security, and thirteen years of uninterrupted war and postwar prosperity, have wrought a great transformation in the unprivileged workers who made the CIO. . . .
>
> The pioneer militants of the CIO unions are sixteen years older than they were in 1937. They are better off than the ragged and hungry sit-down strikers of 1937; and many of them are sixteen times softer and more conservative. This privileged section of the unions, formerly the backbone of the left wing, is today the main social base of the conservative Reuther bureaucracy. They are convinced far less by Reuther's clever demagogy than by the fact that he really articulates their own conservatized moods and patterns of thought. . . .
>
> Some of the best militants, the best stalwarts of the party in the old times, have been affected by their new environment. They see the old militants in the unions, who formerly cooperated with them, growing slower, more satisfied, more conservative. They still mix with these exmilitants socially, and are infected by them. They develop a pessimistic outlook from the reactions they get on every side from these old-timers, and unknown to themselves, acquire an element of that same conservatism.[49]

"A new middle class arose which included a large number of young people of working-class background," wrote radical sociologist John C. Leggett a few years later, noting that many prospering working people had moved out of traditional working-class communities to become home owners in the suburbs. "The class struggle abated with the end of the post-World War II strikes, although repeated flare-ups between management and workers occurred during and after the Korean War," he added in his description of the same auto workers discussed by Cannon.

"At the same time, another trend pointed up this harmony. Governmental boards and labor unions often helped minimize class conflict as unions grew more friendly toward companies which were willing to bargain with, and make major concessions to, labor organizations. Prosperity reached almost everyone. Even working-class minority groups [e.g., some African Americans] improved their standard of living and sent sons and daughters into the middle class." A Black auto worker named James Boggs, who had passed through the Trotskyist movement in earlier years, asserted in 1963: "Today the working class is so dispersed and transformed by the very nature of the changes in production that it is almost impossible to select out any single bloc of workers as working class in the old sense." By this "old sense" he meant class-conscious workers: "The working class is growing, as Marx predicted, but it is not the old working class which the radicals persist in believing will create the revolution and establish control over production. That old working class is the vanishing herd."[50]

Similar developments were taking place in all the "capitalist democracies," of course. "Fear of revolution and a desire for social appeasement stimulated the governments of Western Europe," explained French scholar Maurice Crouzet in 1970, to "set themselves the aim of creating prosperity and expanding a prosperity which would benefit all classes" in the post-World War II period, through policies providing "higher wages, shorter working hours, paid holidays, full employment and the virtual disappearance of unemployment, construction of wholesome and cheap housing, social security protection against sickness, loss of work, and old age." The dramatic development of the welfare state after 1945—in large measure won through the pressure of labor movements led by Social Democratic and Labor Parties—did not fully live up to this idealized picture, let alone reform all capitalist oppression out of existence. The same writer offers some clues as to its limitations: "Generally speaking, the standard of living has risen in all European countries. Working conditions have improved—first, through the growing importance of mechanization which requires, on the whole, less muscular effort (though it increases nervous tension); and then through the reduction of working hours and through paid vacations." The mechanization of labor under capitalism, it should be stressed, involves the degradation of labor—introducing greater employer control over the labor process and not only increasing nervous tension among those keeping up with assembly lines but also eroding their skills and power in their daily work. More than this, there are some sectors of the working class—especially foreigners and nonwhites—for whom more traditional forms of working-class oppression were maintained: "use [of] foreign labor . . . has become so important that the expansion of certain industries is closely dependent on it. Immigrant workers provoke grave problems, even in Great Britain where a liberal attitude towards foreigners and the absence of racialism have been traditional. . . . These immigrants constitute a proletariat, often leading a wretched type of life."[51]

In the United States, too, there developed an increasingly severe stratification within the workforce, with African Americans, Hispanics, and many Asian Americans being pushed into substandard living conditions, more strenuous and lower-paying occupations, higher rates of unemployment, and so on. This institutionalized racism was reinforced by cultural and psychological biases on the most personal level. (This had obvious implications for the rise of civil rights and Black nationalist struggles, but that brought to the fore a consciousness of race far more than of class.)[52]

And for white workers as well as Black, technological developments imposed by employers created increasing on-the-job alienation, undermining working-class power at the point of production. With little difficulty, astute social critics such as Harvey Swados were able to puncture the "myth of the happy worker" and the "myth of the powerful worker." The myth that the working class was simply evaporating altogether, being absorbed into a nebulous middle class, was also effectively refuted with ample facts and figures by more than one critical-minded writer. There was also abundant evidence that the American working class had a sense of being different from other classes—even though many working people referred to themselves as "middle class" (certainly not "*lower* class"!). Distinctive patterns of culture and consciousness continued to distinguish the working class in the larger society.[53]

On the other hand, there is something to the assertion of Stanley Aronowitz that there has been a tendency "toward the replacement of all the traditional forms of proletarian culture and everyday life—which gave working-class communities their coherence and provided the underpinnings for the traditional forms of proletarian class consciousness—with a new, manipulated consumer culture which for convenience's sake we can call mass culture." Regardless of precisely what one wants to make of this, the fact remains that there was flattening and fragmentation of much that had sustained the old radical working-class consciousness. This hardly meant that workers' minds simply turned to mush, or that they simply accepted whatever their bosses or televisions told them. The distinctive philosophy of many disaffected workers, one observer commented, was not any of the traditional left-wing ideologies but *cynicism:* "Cynicism is a variant of anarchism—anarchism without ideals or ultimate illusions, apathetic, easy-going instead of strenuous, non-sectarian, hence more broadly appealing and far more suitable to the conditions and mentality of contemporary workers than the older tradition of militant idealism and self-sacrifice." The *class-conscious layers* of the American working class—the key to understanding the Socialist Party of Debs and the IWW, the early Communist Party, and the pioneer Trotskyists—had, certainly by the end of the 1950s, ceased to exist as a distinctive social force. "The surest way to lose one's fighting faith is to succumb to one's immediate environment; to see things only as they are and not as they are changing and must change; to see only what is before one's eyes and imagine that it is permanent." This had been Cannon's appeal to his comrades, and many were able to accept that—but this was only a tiny fragment of the U.S. working class.[54]

The social basis for the kind of revolutionary party that Lenin himself discussed in *Left-Wing Communism, an Infantile Disorder* had ceased to exist. All that remained for the stalwart veterans of the SWP in the 1950s was to maintain enough of an organization to keep alive the ideals and general theoretical perspectives of revolutionary Marxism, the understanding of history and the revolutionary tradition. If this could be accomplished, if the SWP could survive until the next radical upsurge that capitalism would inevitably generate, then American Trotskyism would have something to contribute to it, the Leninist-Trotskyist project would be renewed and revitalized, and a Leninist party could finally be built in the United States that would be capable of leading a working-class revolution.

The generation that came to young adulthood in the late 1940s and early 1950s generated a few recruits for the SWP; Fred Halstead, Evelyn Sell, Nat Weinstein, Catarino (Dick) Garza, Al Hansen, Beatrice Hansen, Ed Shaw, Rita Shaw, and a handful of others. But for the most part, this was the "lost generation" in regard to left-wing activity. It was supplemented by a few recruits in the "regroupment" period of the late

1950s, largely from a dissident left wing of the Shachtmanites' Young Socialist League and also from the Stalinist milieu—but this hardly made up for the losses of major trade union cadres that the party had suffered several years earlier. The hopes for the party lay in the future, although it turned out not to be from the "classconscious proletariat," which was central to the traditional conceptions of U.S. Marxists.

The Problem of Consciousness in the SWP

The 1960s and 1970s saw a new layer of radicalized youth come into the Socialist Workers Party. An interesting description of this phenomenon is given in Ben Stone's memoir of returning from the San Francisco to the New York branch of the party:

> I had resumed my activity in the New York branch of the SWP and in the Painters Union, rejoining my old Local 442. The year was 1960 and I was 48 years old; getting up there, all right. One noticeable difference from the time I had left New York was the age level of the Party members. I remembered when I had come into the Party in 1945, at the age of 33. Most of the comrades were of my generation, most a little younger and some a little older. Now the rank-and-file member was much younger, a generation removed, most of whom I hardly knew. For the first time I began to feel like an old man in the Party, almost a stranger in my own house.
>
> As the next years went by, the Party attracted even younger members, kids in their teens and early twenties. This was due to the fact that its youth organization, the Young Socialist Alliance (YSA) had been established a short while before. The 60s was a time of radical ferment on the college campuses and the Party attracted some of these youth, certainly in greater numbers than ever before. Within a few years, the YSA began to numerically equal the Party. As these YSA members got older and more politically experienced, most "graduated" into the Party. So it was not very long before almost all of them looked like my son or daughter (or even an earlier [i.e., younger] generation).[55]

This reflects a complex development, and both strengths and weaknesses can legitimately be associated with this younger layer that became predominant in the SWP membership. Rather than attempting a full and final assessment here, I concentrate on two interrelated questions: the social composition and consciousness of the new membership, and the relationship of this to the manner in which Leninist organizational norms came to be understood and practiced.

When I joined the Trotskyist movement in 1972, I addressed the question of the class composition of the SWP and the YSA. What I wrote then was only the beginning of an analysis:

> The working class is defined, in Marxist terms, not simply as all manual laborers, but as those who, not owning the means of production, sell their labor power in order to make a living. The capitalist class, on the other hand, is that class which makes its living through the ownership of businesses. The "middle class" has been defined as an intermediate strata of small businessmen, small shopkeepers, independent craftsmen and artisans, and the small layer of professionals and white collar employees (doctors, lawyers, journalists, teachers, social workers, government workers, clerical workers, service workers, etc.)—all of whom are sometimes swayed by the workers' struggles, sometimes swayed by the pressures and influence of the capitalists. But this small layer of professionals and white collar employees has, in advanced capitalist society, grown to immense proportions. In the United States it represents over 40 percent of the labor force. The needs and dynamics of capitalism have resulted in a dramatic expansion and proletarianization of many white collar occupations, making them an important new section of the working class. (Most students are being trained to assume roles in this new section of the working class.) While many white collar workers have little sense of class consciousness (the same being true, by the way, for many blue collar workers), the material conditions for a change in consciousness now exist, and the growth of white collar unionism indicates that a change is taking place. In short, the Trotskyists have a base in an important new sector of the American working class.[56]

All this was true. But additional points need to be made in order to make sense of what happened to the SWP.

First of all, this was the layer of the SWP that I was part of. To a large degree, although most of us were or had been students, my impression is that a majority of us came from working-class backgrounds. That is, our parents were neither big capitalists nor small-time businesspeople (petit bourgeois), but instead sold their labor power to make a living, working for wages and salaries in either blue-collar or white-collar occupations.

On the other hand, this shouldn't be overstated. One highly questionable—in fact, slanderous—study of several top SWP leaders of the 1960s generation (all of whom came to the movement as student activists) does have the merit of offering occupational information on their parents: a commercial tire salesman, the president of a small private college, a physician-surgeon, a professor of biochemistry, a Congregationalist minister, two lawyers, two dentists, a pharmacist.[57] Of course, by itself this means little. Marx's father was a lawyer, Engels's was a manufacturer, Lenin's was a school inspector, Luxemburg's managed the family timber business, Trotsky's was a commercial farmer—yet each of these revolutionaries became intimately and fruitfully involved with the class-conscious workers' movement.

Here is the rub, however. Even those of us who came from more strictly "working-class" backgrounds, and who sometimes had to get jobs to support ourselves (which generally involved selling our own labor power to one or another employer)—even we were unable to be part of a classconscious workers' movement, because this didn't exist in the sense that it had existed for those from Marx through Trotsky. In terms of our objective *class location*, it could be said that many of us were indeed part of a broadly defined proletariat. But there are three complications, all relating to the complex question of *class consciousness*.

First, many of us came from working-class layers that saw themselves as being different, better than other layers of the working class, and as providing an upward mobility for their own kids that would provide permanent positions in well-paying and higher-status "professions" far removed from blue-collar drudgery. Such desired social positions had more in common with what we call the "petit bourgeoisie" than with the proletariat. Most of us who rejected any such careerism still had no real desire (as opposed to romantic impulses) to turn away from our interesting intellectual and cultural pursuits in order to "waste time" (except for brief excursions) in the more mundane working-class reality of our parents or grandparents. The fact that much of this was permeated with illusion and "false consciousness" is less important than the fact that it affected how many of us viewed our world, our own possible futures, and our personal realities.

Second, in this period (i.e., the period in which we were growing up and joining the Trotskyist movement), the working class as a whole—including most of the organized labor movement—did not have a very highly developed sense of class consciousness. It was a time of genuine affluence and opportunity for many working people, and there was a general sense that "the working class" was fading away, that we were all becoming "middle class" now. George Meany, head of the AFL-CIO, was expressing a common perception among his members when he said precisely that in 1972: "Our members are basically Americans. They basically believe in the American system, and maybe they have a greater stake in the system now than they had fifteen or twenty years ago, because under the system and under our trade union policy, they have become 'middle class.' They have a greater stake."[58]

Even in the early 1990s, a period of declining opportunities and diminishing illusions, many American working people still referred to themselves as "middle class" rather than "working class." What's more, from the early 1950s through the late 1980s, the bulk of the labor movement was embracing a narrow bread-and-butter unionism combined with an openly class-collaborationist "partners in progress" social vision. "I believe in free, democratic, competitive capitalism," the president of the International Ladies Garment Workers Union, Sol Chaikin, explained in 1979, concluding that "managers should manage and then workers should sit down with them to collectively bargain for their share of the results of management efficiency and worker productivity."[59] It would not be stretching things too far to call this "petit bourgeois ideology," since it quite explicitly sees organized labor as a junior partner of the capitalist. The fact that "middle class" consciousness and ideology, as opposed to a clear sense of proletarian class consciousness, were predominant in the actually existing labor movement also affected the thinking and practice of many young radicals.

Third, many of us were, for all practical purposes, déclassé. We went through an extended period in which we were supported by our parents or by scholarships and financial loans as we went to college. Those of us who dropped out of college to do political work may have supported ourselves through various jobs, but in many cases these jobs (often economically marginal) were peripheral to our "real" lives. Our "real" lives were immersed in a peculiar political subculture of the YSA and SWP that, being composed of "students, petty-bourgeois radicals, a few older workers facing retirement, and functionaries," as Frank Lovell puts it, had little in common with the actual daily lives of U.S. working people. To the extent that we stepped out of that peculiar subculture, we tended to be involved in the broader student-and-youth-centered radical movement of the time, which was not distinguished by any highly developed sense of class consciousness.

In fact, a pernicious form of elitism developed among many radicals of the 1960s and 1970s in the absence of a powerful, vibrantly class-conscious, self-activated working-class movement. Looking to third world revolutions (especially Cuba), where "a *small minority* of activists did learn to mobilize *broad masses*," some of the new student radicals constituted what two perceptive analysts of a similar phenomenon in France described as a "frustrated intellectual elite, the representatives of a modernist petty bourgeoisie whose increasing importance in demographic, economic and cultural terms was in contradiction to its marginalization at the political level." The vision that they could somehow become Castros and Guevaras of a U.S. revolution—a vision of "Leninism" projecting them as "a small group to lead a potential revolt and harness the energy of the masses"—resulted in a heady combination of idealism and self-interest: "As suffering humanity liberated itself, a minority which was intellectual, dissatisfied and sometimes humiliated would find its own road to success."[60]

There was a cynical attitude toward people that could be fostered by such an outlook. I was told by a young SWP national staff person that, in 1972, many of the new leaders in the party's national headquarters were fascinated by Francis Ford Coppola's classic *The Godfather*, a film about the brutal, far-ranging, Machiavellian strategies patiently developed by tight-knit Mafia organizations to outwit, humble, and eliminate their rivals and achieve—by the end of the film—the ultimate victory. There was clearly a note of admiration in the way some of them jokingly repeated the key phrase of the film: "I want to make you an offer that you can't refuse." A central figure in the party's new leadership—who was viewed by some as an "American Lenin"—commented to another young party member: "In case you feel bad, just remember what shit Lenin made the Russian Revolution with."[61]

It is hardly a fair generalization that the new layer of Trotskyists admiringly fantasized over the warped operations of murderous gangsters, or that they viewed Lenin's comrades (and their own) as "shit." That such attitudes existed, and that they could not have been as much in evidence in an organization infused with a genuine proletarian class consciousness, also seems a fair statement. Such consciousness implies a deep commitment to the struggle against all forms of oppression and to the egalitarian ideals that would permeate the socialist future, a devotion to doing all that is necessary to advance the self-emancipation of the working class, an elementary respect for and honesty among one's comrades—what Trotsky called "the revolutionary morality of the Bolsheviks."[62]

The notion of *revolutionary morality* might have seemed "corny" or "unmarxist" to some young YSAers and SWPers, but Trotsky believed in the importance among professional revolutionaries of relations that were devoid of "a single reprehensible, contemptible act, a single deception or lie," an atmosphere that Lenin referred to as "a close and compact body of comrades in which complete, mutual confidence prevails." Nor had such feelings been alien to those close to Cannon. "The true art of being a socialist consists not merely in recognizing the trend of social evolution from capitalism to socialism, and striving to help it along and hasten on the day," Cannon had argued. "The true art of being a socialist consists in anticipating the socialist future; in not waiting for its actual realization, but in striving, here and now, insofar as the circumstances of class society permit, to live like a socialist; to live under capitalism according to the higher standards of the socialist future."[63]

The limitations of the consciousness within the new layers of Trotskyist cadre do not minimize the importance of the objective class location (proletarian or near-proletarian) of a majority of SWP and YSA membership in the 1960s and 1970s, but that location has to be balanced with the essentially petit bourgeois consciousness that was no less a defining characteristic of the membership. In referring to consciousness, I mean not just *ideas*; our ideas, in fact, tended to be strongly influenced by the highly proletarian class consciousness that is intimately associated with Marxism. But these vital ideas coexisted uneasily with assumptions, habits, ways of seeing things and understanding ourselves that could be appropriately referred to with the shorthand term "petit bourgeois." It should be added that this was not the case only with the SWP and YSA. It was generally true throughout the New Left and the younger layers of all the existing left-wing groups. It inevitably affected the manner in which "Leninism" was interpreted and applied—leading to no end of what Lenin had warned against in *Left-Wing Communism, an Infantile Disorder*: "phrase-mongering and clowning."

Elements of the older generation, in various ways, formed a powerful counterinfluence in the SWP to the misinterpretation and misapplication of Leninist norms, and some of these seasoned veterans finally sought—again, in various ways—to organize a resistance, with the support of a minority of the younger comrades, to the increasingly severe distortions of democratic centralism that were becoming an integral part of party life (and that were also intimately associated with the covert programmatic revision being carried out by the new leadership of the SWP). The fact that they found it necessary to carry on that fight, and that they lost, is related to the great weakening of American Trotskyism that took place under the impact of the developments examined above. At the same time, certain serious organizational mistakes in which some of us who later became oppositionists had acquiesced, or that we had failed to challenge, also contributed to our own later defeat.

The Erosion of the Cannon Tradition

The meaning of the Cannon tradition is reflected in the comments of Harry Braverman, author of the latter-day Marxist classic *Labor and Monopoly Capital*, many years after Braverman had broken from the SWP during the Cochran split of 1953:

> He spoke to us in the accents of the Russian revolution and of the Leninism which had gone forth from the Soviet Union in the twenties and the thirties. But there was in his voice something more which attracted us. And that was the echoes of the radicalism of the pre—World War I years, the popular radicalism of Debs, Haywood, and John Reed. And he spoke with great force and passion. . . .
>
> Cannon invested the full force of a not inconsiderable personality in his convictions, as if to say that one could not hope to convince others of ideas which inspired in oneself only lukewarm feelings. This, I think, is useful to remember at a time when the ideas of socialism and the critique of capitalism are too often treated as mere mathematical exercises, the outcome of formulas, or the comparison of alternative models. It seems to me that the ruling force of Cannon's political life, insofar as I know it, was the passion for the political principles spread by the Russian revolution in its early years. He lived by these principles and by these alone, and he became expert at separating every other impulse that plays a role in socialist politics from the thing that mattered most to him—adherence to these principles. Now, I would not pretend that this kind of dedication to principles, taken by itself, and without reference to all other requirements, theoretical and practical, is a sufficient basis for sound socialist politics. It can also be the basis for sectarianism, and usually is. But

without it the politics of even the best-meaning people can become a swamp and a tangle.

Cannon's adherence to the principles that inspired him in his youth was a manifest thing that shaped his whole life and life's activity. The emphasis that he gave to what he called principled politics was clear in every speech and every article. He tried to have his every political act and association reflect his principles and reflect them clearly and unambiguously.[64]

Cannon's political principles involve an understanding of socialism that is indistinguishable from a revolutionary approach to the question of democracy. He expressed it in this way in 1957, at a time when Stalinism was wracked with crises:

> We will not put the socialist movement of this country on the right track and restore its rightful appeal to the best sentiments of the working class of this country and above all to the young, until we begin to call socialism by its right name as the great teachers did. Until we make it clear that we stand for an ever-expanding workers' democracy as the only road to socialism. Until we root out every vestige of Stalinist perversion and corruption of the meaning of socialism and democracy, and restate the thoughts and formulations of the authentic Marxist teachers. . . .
>
> Socialists should not argue with the American worker when he says he wants democracy and doesn't want to be ruled by a dictatorship. Rather, we should recognize his demand for human rights and democratic guarantees, now and in the future, is in itself progressive. The socialist task is not to deny democracy, but to expand it and make it more complete. That is the true socialist tradition. The Marxists, throughout the century-long history of our movement, have always valued and defended bourgeois democratic rights, restricted as they were; and have utilized them for the education and organization of the workers in the struggle to establish full democracy by abolishing the capitalist rule altogether. . . .
>
> In the United States, the struggle for workers' democracy is preeminently a struggle of the rank and file to gain democratic control of their own organization. That is the necessary condition to abolish capitalism and "establish democracy" in the country as a whole. . . . So the fight for workers' democracy is inseparable from the fight for socialism, and is the condition for its victory. Workers' democracy is the only road to socialism, here in the United States and everywhere else, all the way from Moscow to Los Angeles, and from here to Budapest.[65]

These principles come through in Cannon's orientation toward party building and internal democracy. In one of his letters from the mid-1960s, he notes: "Probably the hardest lesson I had to learn from Trotsky, after ten years of bad schooling through the Communist Party, was to let organizational questions wait until the political questions at issue were fully clarified, not only in the National Committee but also in the ranks of the party." He added, "our party owes its very existence today to the fact that some of us learned this hard lesson and learned also how to apply it in practice." This meant discussing differences inside the party—even when a dissident minority might impatiently act in an undisciplined manner—"in an atmosphere free from poisonous personal recriminations and venomous threats of organization discipline." The maintenance of a democratic atmosphere when there were sharply disputed questions was essential, Cannon felt, for the party to educate its cadres in rich lessons of the past as well as in complex new realities. This was especially important as the party sought to renew itself through recruiting new members, and through training these new members in the method of principled politics and democratic centralism. "Our young comrades need above all to *learn*; and this is the best, in fact the only way, for them to learn what they need to know about the new disputes," he wrote. "The fact that some of them probably think they already know everything, only makes it more advisable to turn the plenum sessions [of the National Committee] into a school with questions and answers freely and patiently passed back and forth."[66]

The entire spirit of this letter, as well as the specifics, stands in stark contrast to what we see in the long, grim exposition by Jack Barnes, "The Organizational Norms of a Proletarian Party," delivered in 1982. Barnes described the reason that "the organization question" was coming to the fore in the early 1980s. First of all, there was *the turn to industry*: "our determination to lead the large majority of our leadership and membership in building fractions of the party in industry . . . [and] in the industrial unions." Second, there was *the primacy of Cuban revolutionary leadership*: "our turn to industry was only a year before the victories in Grenada and Nicaragua. That is, only a year away from the extension—after almost two decades—of the Cuban socialist revolution, which had opened the socialist revolution in our hemisphere and brought to power the first genuinely revolutionary leadership . . . since the Bolshevik

Party in the time of Lenin." It was now necessary to strengthen the "proletarian organizational norms" of the SWP:

> Regardless of what any member thinks of the political positions and other decisions of elected leadership bodies of the party, those *are* the decisions that have full force and effect. *All* decisions they make are binding on all members unless and until they are changed by that body or overturned by a higher one. . . .
>
> We have . . . had [a] series of challenges to our organizational norms [involving whether] an individual party member can unilaterally decide to organize the party's internal life [by circulating] private polemical discussion articles [among friends in the party] when no discussion has been opened by the [National Committee]. . . .
>
> This now comes to a halt. Totally. . . .
>
> We are a political organization with elected bodies, and we function through those elected bodies, not as individuals and not as groupings of friends and like-minded people. . . .
>
> We don't need norms for disloyal members. . . . The party just catches them and throws them out. We have organizational norms *for the cadre of the party*, because that's the only way we can build a workers' party. . . .
>
> There is no absolute right, at any time and under any circumstances, to organize tendencies in our party or in the YSA. A higher right than the rights of tendencies exists: the right of the party, through its elected leadership bodies, to regulate its internal affairs. . . .
>
> [A revolutionary centralist party] . . . means a party that does not tolerate private discussions and decisions by self-selected groupings, open to some and closed to others, defined by friendship, past relationships, or other subjective and arbitrary criteria.

At the same time, another new SWP leader, Mary-Alice Waters, misquoted Cannon's comrade Tom Kerry, making it sound like the revolutionary party was a religious fetish: "Without the party we are nothing; with the party we are all." Garbling party history and distorting Kerry's and Cannon's ideas, she spoke of the way that Kerry had allegedly helped lead the SWP, beginning in the late 1950s, to "more disciplined, centralized functioning," away from functioning "as a discussion circle . . . to return to the norms of a politically homogeneous Leninist party." Waters's obvious implication was that Kerry (who shortly before his death had, in fact, declared war on the Barnes leadership) was an initiator of the "Bolshevization" process that was now being continued and stepped up by the Barnes leadership.[67]

"The worst and most reprehensible single thing about the article, in my opinion, is the myth it concocts about some golden age in SWP history (during the 1940s evidently) when the party functioned through the norms of a politically homogeneous Leninist party, that is, with strong proletarian organizational norms that enabled it to be disciplined and centralized." This was the irritated reaction of party veteran George Breitman at the time. His criticism of Waters's historiography intertwined with his anger over what he saw as the authoritarian and bullying policies of the new top SWP leaders in pushing through the "turn to industry" and programmatic revisions:

> But there never has been a time in SWP history when our norms were like the ones now being introduced. Not in the 1940s, not in the 1930s, not at any time. We built industrial fractions in the 40s and 30s but we did it through political persuasion and education, not through administrative directives, pressure, castigation of comrades who were slow to go into industry or did not want to go into it at all; nobody was made to feel like a pariah or encouraged to drop out of the party for being unable or refusing to go into industry.
>
> We sold our press at plant gates, in greater numbers than today, but we did it by convincing the members that it was politically necessary, not by administrative rules that make sales mandatory for members. We were a centralized party but not an overcentralized one that is afraid to leave initiative to the branches and fractions or to let them learn through their own experiences. We were a disciplined party, carrying out the decisions of conventions and plenums, but we never had rules that prohibited a loyal member from showing other members of the party an article he had written for our press merely because the officials of the party didn't like it.[68]

There have been some suggestions that the tradition of Cannon included undemocratic practices against, for example, an opposition led by Hugo Oehler in 1934–35 and another opposition led by Bert Cochran in 1952–53, similar to the undemocratic practices of the Barnes leadership against the oppositionists of 1983–84. A careful examination by Breitman in early 1984 indicates that there are only the most superficial grounds for such assertions. It is worth giving some attention to these two historical incidents, since they were first alluded to in a 1984 document by one of the most serious historians of American Trotskyism, Alan Wald. The well-reasoned conclusions presented by Breitman highlight a vital norm in the Trotskyist movement: democracy requires that disciplinary organizational measures not be permitted to short-circuit a full educational discussion and political clarification among the membership; even when a minority is perceived as violating democratic centralist norms, it is essential to place the highest value on having it fully express its views, in order to have a thorough and serious discussion of those views. "You can't learn much from expulsions, [or] from personal fights, except that one person is good, another bad, etc.," Cannon once noted. "That creates demoralization and discouragement. But from the discussion of great political issues . . . the whole new generation of party members can learn great lessons."[69]

Wald himself suggested that "anti-Cannonism is a disease in the anti-Stalinist left that has disoriented, among others, all the Shachtmanite and state capitalist groupings, and that it is often a mask for what is really a resistance of some rather large egos to organizational discipline." He maintained that "Cannon's record on the organizational question balances out on the positive side, and I see no evidence for the charge that, under his leadership, the SWP was monolithic (at least in the sense that the term 'monolithic' is ordinarily used)." This is clear, Wald argued, in light of some of the factional struggles inside the SWP: "In the case of the 1940 split, it seems to me that he made the Shachtmanites fair and reasonable organizational offers, and in the Goldman-Morrow dispute there was a good deal of latitude on the organizational side of things (with minority documents appearing in the theoretical magazine and repeated warnings to the minority about their open collaboration with a rival party)."[70]

Breitman's views were even stronger, reflecting the lived experience of a seasoned revolutionary cadre. "My idea is not that we're going to go back to the beginning of the Marxist movement and try to find out what is wrong with Marxism in order to discover what Barnes did," he concluded. "And it's not my idea that we should go back to Lenin and to Leninism in order to find out what's wrong with Barnesism. I am very satisfied with Marxism and Leninism and with the American version of that, which came to get the name of 'Cannonism' in our movement. . . . We have to say that Barnesism is a negation of 'Cannonism,' not its continuation."[71]

A former SWP member who had been one of the most prominent female leaders, Myra Tanner Weiss, recalled that the American Trotskyist movement of the 1930s practiced a "real socialist freedom" in which "no one could, or to my knowledge would even try to repress discussion or confine it to a particular time or place. We discussed with anyone at any time whatever differences we discerned. Differences were welcome. There was creative excitement, and comradeship, in controversy."[72]

There were some tensions and problems around the role of women in the SWP, she noted, but male prejudices were actively challenged. Weiss recalls one controversy that she believes demonstrated a conflict between the rights of women comrades and the inclinations of some members of the party's substantial maritime fraction, a controversy in which Weiss intervened and drew sharp criticism from certain male comrades. She writes, "Jim Cannon, at that time the 'head' of the Party, defended me and did so by flatly accusing the men of male chauvinism. 'Seamen are notoriously chauvinists,' he charged and the matter was dropped. But I often wondered if anyone had learned anything from the incident. Discussion of it simply went underground."[73]

This relates to another problem that Weiss perceived as developing in the late 1940s: "When Cannon spoke the discussion tended to come to an end. Was everyone convinced? Or were differences just being dropped, suppressed? At the very least there was evident a lack of security, a lack of confidence that differences could be batted around freely without any adverse consequences. As a result, not everything that should be said got said. The discussion was constricted." The period to which she refers was that preceding the 1952–53 fight and split inside the Fourth International, which included a struggle between a Cannon-led majority (of which the Weisses were an integral part) and a minority faction led by Bert Cochran and George Clarke. There was a strong inclination by many, including the new SWP national chairman Farrell Dobbs, to avoid this conflict. It was largely through Cannon's pressure that the political differences were brought into the open and debated. Many of the cadre "came to fear splits that resulted from differences," as Weiss puts it—but the Cochran fight and split were probably unavoidable. During the 1950s and early 1960s, Murry and Myra Tanner Weiss themselves became the center of a current that was increasingly at odds with the Dobbs leadership, although the peacemaking efforts of the partially retired Cannon helped overcome some of the tensions for a time. The Weisses initially enjoyed considerable popularity and played a major role in the SWP's "regroupment" efforts in the U.S. Left in the late 1950s, orienting especially toward elements that were breaking (or partially breaking) from Stalinism in that period. They became somewhat marginalized as a growing number of party cadres concluded that too great an adaptation was being made to Stalinism; even Cannon pointedly complained about making too great a virtue of "political togetherness." This culminated in the Weisses' open opposition to the Dobbs leadership around various political and organizational questions.[74]

Whatever problems and differences existed, well after her angry mid-1960s departure from the SWP, Myra Tanner Weiss stressed that the functioning of the SWP of the 1950s was similar to its functioning in the 1930s and 1940s in regard to a fairly high degree of democracy. She describes the inner life of American Trotskyism over those three decades as being marked by substantial openness, diversity, and a capacity for learning and growing. Different SWP branches maintained distinctive norms on how branch executive committees functioned, how restrictively internal bulletins were (or were not) circulated, and how flexibly majority positions were carried out (and in some cases how minority positions were allowed to be tested in practice alongside majority positions).[75]

On the other hand, the objective realities inevitably warped these democratic traditions in various ways. The SWP suffered a serious deterioration in the 1950s, due to the anticommunist repression and the cold war mentality that became prevalent in the popular consciousness, plus the prosperity-induced consumer culture and deradicalization of the working class. An entire generation of the 1950s was lost to recruitment, and veteran party members either fell away in discouragement or dug in to maintain what they could of American Trotskyism. Tim Wohlforth, who had been involved as a young activist first in Max Shachtman's Independent Socialist League and then the SWP during the late 1950s, later recalled:

> Dues were paid and the *Militant* was always sold. The party was run in a modest, but smooth and professional manner. The problem was that the party was comprised of a generation of workers and intellectuals—those recruited in the 1930s and during World War II—which was getting old and tired. Cannon did a better job than Shachtman in holding on to his aging cadres and, on the whole, he and his followers kept the revolutionary faith. But as will and energy departed, faith was about all they had

left. Cannon could not defy the general trends affecting the working class in the 1950s.[76]

As we have seen, Cannon sought to turn over the leadership of the SWP to a cadre younger than himself—Farrell Dobbs and Tom Kerry. The Political Committee included these two plus Arthur Burch, Joe Hansen, Morris Lewit (Stein), Dan Roberts, Murry Weiss, and Myra Tanner Weiss. Wohlforth, as the leader of the Young Socialist Alliance (in the process of formation in the late 1950s, reflecting the ferment and vitality of the early youth radicalization), was added to this body and offers this recollection:

> The Political Committee functioned reasonably well in those days; its regular, brief meetings reflected the overall organizational efficiency of the Dobbs-Kerry regime. . . . It concerned itself with organizational matters and dealt with these matters largely in a routine fashion. World events were rarely discussed; one wonders if they were even thought about. Unlike the YSA, the Socialist Workers Party in general in the late 1950s was a rather dull place and Dobbs' PC was no different. A typical PC meeting was a two-hour battle to keep awake. I had arrived at the very top of the most revolutionary party in the United States and had trouble not falling asleep![77]

From the West Coast, Cannon sought to maintain some critical perspectives and generate discussions (among National Committee members in California and also—through letters and personal contacts—at the party center in New York) that would help keep the political juices flowing. In the center itself, some top leaders such as Joseph Hansen continued to make outstanding contributions to the intellectual life of the movement, especially in his analysis of the Cuban Revolution and in preparing the reunification of the Fourth International. George Novack also played a role in the development and dissemination of Marxist ideas. In other areas, leading party activists worked to help the organization grow. Between 1954 and 1967, to take one case, George Breitman not only made pathbreaking theoretical contributions to the party's understanding of the Black liberation struggle but also made immensely creative and innovative party-building contributions through his work to rebuild and lead the Detroit branch of the SWP—for example, through the institution of the Friday Night Socialist Forum, a politically and sometimes culturally exciting weekly series, which was successfully adapted in other cities as well. In a 1958 letter he explained his approach, which was also that of a substantial number of the older comrades:

> Those who sent me to Detroit didn't intend that I should stay there; they thought in terms of a year or two, an improvement in the internal situation, etc. I told them I was going for good. . . . I had set my heart on . . . helping the younger comrades, so far as I could, to develop all their powers, to realize their potential. I think I made a beginning at it. I know I helped some a little, some substantially, some not at all. I know that I helped to create a healthier climate in the branch, in which development could be encouraged in the right direction.[78]

Not all innovations in every branch were particularly positive. A phenomenon of "branch-factions," under the distinctive political leadership of one or another strong personality, developed in some cities. In Milwaukee, a cult developed around James Boulton; in Seattle, Dick Fraser and Clara Kaye developed the branch into what would soon split off to become the Freedom Socialist Party; and in Buffalo, Sam Marcy built the branch into a centerpiece for what would become the Workers World Party.

In addition, in the repressive (and therefore, for leftists, ingrown) political atmosphere of the 1950s, there were powerful undercurrents of intense personality conflicts and rivalries that assumed political proportions and took organizational form. Perhaps related to deep resentment against the "dual center" that Cannon had created in California, Farrell Dobbs and those close to him came into sustained conflict with a grouping in New York around Murry Weiss. There were also particular personality traits that had an impact. Tom Kerry, a tough-minded political thinker and an organizational tower of strength, "approached a political dispute with the subtlety of a barroom brawler," as Tim Wohlforth put it. "For Tom there was the party, with which he completely identified, and the opposition, which he viewed as riff-raff to be summarily dealt with."[79]

Although this trait sets a tone inconsistent with the best elements of the Cannon tradition, Wohlforth's complaint is related to the fact that he was on the receiving end of Kerry's wrath. This was because in 1961–64, Wohlforth helped lead a bitter and somewhat irresponsible factional conflict, culminating in a ten-year political adventure as the founder and leader of a sectarian split-off called the Workers League (with fellow youth leader and SWP cofactionalist James Robertson founding the Spartacist League). This selfelimination of a top layer of new youthful recruits to the SWP poignantly raised a fundamental question for the SWP leadership: how can the party leadership be renewed in a manner that will ensure the continuation and relevance of the SWP's revolutionary traditions? The problem was especially pressing with the blossoming youth radicalization of the 1960s.

The most serious errors by the SWP "old guard" were made after Cannon's retirement from the central leadership. These were associated, in part, with the selection and grooming of Jack Barnes as the new central leader of the SWP. He was allowed to assemble his own leadership team, and the kind of authority that Cannon, Dobbs, and Kerry had enjoyed was conferred upon him. It may have seemed reasonable that this talented young militant, with a sharp mind and powerful personality, should be raised into the upper echelons of the party. But Barnes did not rise through the ranks to a position of central leadership by virtue of his abilities in mass struggles, in party building, and in applying and developing Marxist theory. He was not elevated over time by his peers on the basis of what he actually accomplished. He was elevated by his elders, by the Dobbs-Kerry leadership, on the basis of what they believed he represented and on the basis of what they believed he would be able to accomplish.

Barnes wrapped himself in the mantle of "Cannonism," modestly claiming the role of someone maintaining the continuity of American Trotskyism, and doing this in a manner that was alive to new realities. In a 1968 introduction to Cannon's *Letters from Prison*, he seemed to strike just the right balance:

> *Letters from Prison* does not challenge each of us to be a Marx, a Lenin, or a Trotsky. We are simply challenged to be ourselves, to study what went on before, and to apply the discoveries of our predecessors to the problems of our time. By standing on the shoulders of the earlier working-class fighters, American Marxists, as a *team* of revolutionists, can accomplish the tasks before them. . . .
>
> The current struggles in Latin America, Vietnam, and America's Black communities testify to the contradictions and continuing decline of imperialism. These struggles bear witness anew to the combativity and courage of the working masses. The central question remains the same as when Cannon was viewing the United States and the world from prison

in 1944: How are revolutionists going to build a party equal to the task of leading the working masses to the conquest of power?[80]

This approach reassured his elders and exercised a strong attraction to those of his own generation. The role he played in helping, behind the scenes, to lead the SWP's immensely successful antiwar work during the Vietnam War seemed to vindicate those who had placed such high hopes in him, as did the intensity with which he approached organizational questions. Barnes also demonstrated an impressive ability to articulate, clearly and forcefully, substantial political analyses at party gatherings. There was a great personal charm—a directness and unpretentiousness—that he was able to employ in dealing with comrades, yet also an underlying toughness, even a ruthlessness, that sometimes came to the surface. This latter quality was seen by some as an essential "hardness" for a revolutionary leader prepared to go all the way.

The impact of Barnes in the SWP is a reflection not of Leninist principles or the tradition of Cannon, but of basic human psychological dynamics. The functioning of some SWP members, responding to the powerful personality and tremendous authority that Barnes assumed, brings to mind Freud's insights on group psychology: "the individual gives up his ego-ideal [i.e., *individual* sense of right and wrong, duty, and guilt] and substitutes for it the group-ideal as embodied in the leader." The authority of the leader (in the minds of at least many members) becomes essential for the cohesion of the group, and the approval of the leader, or a sense of oneness with the leader, becomes a deep-felt need that is bound up with one's own sense of self-worth. The member of the group enjoys "a feeling of triumph" when his or her thinking coincides with this leader's judgments, and is vulnerable to "delusions of inferiority and self-depreciation" whenever inner doubts arise about the leader's authority. Indeed, "opposition" is perceived to be "as good as separation" from the group and is "therefore anxiously avoided." The compelling "group ideal" that Barnes symbolized for such members involved a powerful mix of strongly held values, accumulated theoretical wisdom, and hopes for the future triumph of socialism. His authority flowed from the continuity that he seemed to represent with previous revolutionary generations.[81]

The continuity turned out to be quite illusory. Cannon and Barnes were the products of quite different experiences. The nature of "the working masses" to which Barnes referred in his commentary on Cannon was, in fact, quite different in 1938 and 1968, and the relationships of these two men to these working masses were qualitatively different. Their understanding of Leninism, and their capacity for applying this understanding to their own particular contexts, also proved to be worlds apart. The erosion of the Cannon tradition was not reversed but completed as Barnes took control. Moving into a position of central leadership in the late 1960s and early 1970s, Barnes helped shape new norms that further undermined the party democracy that is essential to Leninism.

Anti-Leninist Precedents and Organizational Degeneration

The phenomenon of "Barnesism" in the SWP, I have argued here, can be understood adequately only as arising from a broad constellation of social, economic, political, and cultural developments. It cannot be attributed to fatal flaws in one or another organizational precedent of American Trotskyism. From the late 1960s to the late 1970s, however, as Barnes was assuming leadership of the SWP, organizational norms evolved that undermined the party's traditional Leninist principles. Some of these are suggested in the critical letters offered by Cannon, and it is clear that Jack Barnes was not responsible for all of them. Yet they did contribute to the degeneration of the SWP, in certain cases being utilized and further developed by the Barnes leadership to transform the organization. Something can be learned from such organizational mistakes, as we seek to build a revolutionary socialist movement. Five of these mistakes are examined here.

1. Problems in the 1965 Organizational Resolution

In the struggle against the Wohlforth and Robertson factions in the early 1960s (which were expelled from the SWP and went on to become the Workers League and the Spartacist League), there were certain positions taken by the majority of the SWP leadership. These positions were later codified in a resolution adopted at the 1965 national convention of the SWP entitled "The Organizational Character of the Socialist Workers Party." Much of this resolution simply restates the long-standing organizational norms of the SWP—in some sections repeating word-for-word the 1938 resolution "The Internal Situation and Character of the Party." There are also significant additions, however. One of the innovations involves prohibition against something called "double-recruitment." Another innovation established a stricture limiting members' right to advocate dissident views inside the party. Related to this is a third innovation regarding private discussions between comrades.

Double-recruitment was defined as recruiting new members "first to their tight faction, then formally to the party, on the basis of the faction's own program and methods; indoctrination of contacts against the party program, convention decisions, and organizational principles before they applied for party membership."[82] As defined, this certainly involves an extremely unhealthy form of factionalism, and it came to be prohibited behavior for party members after the adoption of the 1965 resolution. This prohibition against double-recruitment developed into a cure that was worse than the disease. It came to be interpreted as a prohibition against telling nonmembers what you really thought (even in a manner not designed to subvert the party's program, decisions, and organizational principles), especially if you were trying to recruit those nonmembers, if you happened to disagree with one or another party policy or position. It became an undemocratic device for marginalizing, intimidating, and driving out dissidents.

"Some opponents of the disciplinary action [against the Robertsonites] have argued . . . that in principle anyone can advocate anything he pleases within the party," the 1965 resolution noted. It responded:

> As a voluntary and revolutionary organization the SWP has the right to define the basis for its existence. The party exercises that prerogative by putting distinct limits on the right of advocacy within its ranks, as determined by majority decision through the official bodies, acting in compliance with the party's program, principles and convention decisions. Disloyal people not only cannot advocate anything they please within the party; they cannot be allowed to carry on their advocacy behind the back of the party. Those who don't want to comply with the party's democratically-decided definition of the basis for its existence have the right to withdraw from the organization and form one of their own.[83]

This raises serious questions. How is the term "disloyal people" to be defined? Is it disloyal to believe that a particular convention decision undermines the party's program and is contrary to its principles? Should someone who believes that the party program is in need of revision, in the light of new realities, be considered "disloyal" to that program, and should that person be expected to withdraw from the organization and form one of his or her own? Who decides whether a member is disloyal? It may be necessary to bar from membership any member who wants to advocate racist or sexist doctrines inside the organization, but the vague and open-ended language of the 1965 organizational resolution could be (and was) misused to intimidate and eliminate dissenters in a manner that greatly damaged party democracy.

Another innovation relates to the issue of "factionalism and party unity." It is expressed in a manner that starts off well but ends up with a dubious formulation:

> A properly conducted discussion of internal political differences contributes to the good and welfare of the party. It facilitates the hammering out of a correct political line and it helps to educate the membership. These benefits derive from the discussion provided that every comrade hears all points of view and the whole party is drawn into the thinking about the questions in dispute. In that way the membership as a whole can intervene in disputes, settle them in an orderly way by majority decision and get on with the party work. This method has been followed by American Trotskyism throughout its history and has resulted in an effective clarification of all controversial issues.
>
> Concentration on private discussions of disputed issues, on the other hand, tends to give the comrades involved a one-sided view and warps their capacity for objective political judgment. Inexperienced comrades especially are made the target of such lopsided discussion methods. The aim is to line them up quickly in a closed caucus, and prejudice their thinking before they have heard an open party debate. When dissident views are introduced into the party in that manner groupings tend to form and harden, and the dissenting views tend to assert themselves in disruptive fashion, before the party as a whole has had a chance to face and act on the issues in dispute.[84]

The importance of a full discussion of internal differences, explained in the first paragraph, has already been stressed. Yet the second paragraph appears to counterpose such full, partywide discussion of differences to private discussions about such differences that might take place between two or more comrades. Of course, there are different ways to read this. *Concentration* on private discussions (not any or all private discussions) *tends* to give (not inevitably gives) comrades a one-sided view. A reasonable way to read this passage could be as a warning about a danger, not as any kind of prohibition. But there is a real ambiguity in the passage, which soon fed into an authoritarian trend. The Barnes leadership took this even further, eventually prohibiting private discussion, whose dangers were hypocritically inveighed against, while at the same time preventing the partywide discussion through which critical perspectives could be communicated.

2. Factional Organizational Maneuvering Against a Minority Tendency in 1971

In the period leading up to the 1971 national convention of the SWP, a minority tendency developed that called itself the Proletarian Orientation Tendency (POT), with about 100 supporters. (The SWP had close to 1,000 members at this time.) The POT claimed to stand closer to an "orthodox" Trotskyist position, questioning some SWP policies regarding the antiwar, feminist, Black nationalist, and student movements and centering its struggle "against the SWP's abandonment of a proletarian orientation . . . [and] its abandonment of viewing the working class as the revolutionary force in history," in the polemical words of one POT supporter. According to former adherent Alan Wald, it "only argued for an augmentation of the campus orientation with the establishment of a viable trade union fraction and the voluntary colonization [into industrial jobs] of non-campus comrades, plus increased work on Third World and working-class community college campuses and among GIs."[85]

The POT's loyalty to the party was questioned in the ensuing internal debate, although committed party veterans such as Larry Trainor had been associated with it. On the basis of an allegation that it was an "unprincipled combination," the tendency was denied representation on the SWP National Committee, although minority representation on leadership bodies had been a tradition in the Trotskyist movement. In fact, National Committee members who had been associated with the POT (including 1968 vice presidential candidate and Black activist Paul Boutelle) were not reelected to that body. Far more serious was the treatment accorded members of the chapter of the Young Socialist Alliance in Oakland-Berkeley. One SWP majority supporter described the situation in this way in the summer of 1971:

> About a year ago a number of the comrades in the present sectarian tendency [the POT] became the majority in the Berkeley YSA, though they

remained a minority in the party branch. They were hard workers, some of them quite talented, and did good work. . . .

This was not a healthy situation, but we managed to do our work fairly well because the national leadership and this branch—leadership and membership—followed a good organizational policy. We tried to involve all the comrades in the work, regardless of their opinions or personal characteristics. We tried to build a collective leadership for the branch, with comrades from both sides on the executive committee and in the fractions. Everyone was given a fair shake and the opportunity to put their abilities to work. There were difficulties in this, of course, but we managed.[86]

Unfortunately, this exemplary manner of functioning broke down after the national convention. Major credit for the breakdown would seem to be due to the national organization secretary at the time, Jack Barnes. Eleven additional majority supporters had been transferred into the Oakland-Berkeley area to become part of the YSA before the convention. After the convention, however, forty-nine more majority supporters were transferred in. Two POT members' bitter memory was that these new arrivals "came laughing and giggling into the [Oakland-Berkeley party] headquarters, at a rate of five or six a day, acting as if they had arrived at summer camp. They gave smart alecky responses to questions asked about their presence by the indigenous branch members, and they rapidly moved to shut P.O. members not only out of the political life but the social life of the branch as well." The consequences were destructive:

The record shows that—despite intentions or beliefs of various individuals involved in the operation—the purpose was precisely to drive supporters of the minority view out of activity, and out of the party itself. Prior to this swamping operation the leaders and members of the P.O. had carried out major assignments in all areas of party work: Comrade Graumann as YSA Organizer, Comrade Levitt as SWP Education Director, Comrade Wald as SWP candidate, Comrade Stodola as full-time NPAC [National Peace Action Coalition] staff, Comrade L. Charous as Berkeley campus fraction leader, etc. Although differences arose from time to time on specific points, the P.O. supporters did not come under criticisms for incompetence or irresponsibility. But by the time Barnes' swamping operation was over, a number of P.O. supporters had resigned from the party, and those remaining had been stripped of all responsible assignments.[87]

Regardless of any mistakes or malfunctioning that might be attributed to the POT, this episode stands as a model of how a responsible, politically mature party leadership should *not* function. Instead, it became a model for how other minorities would be dealt with in the future.

3. Prohibition on Comrades' Democratic Right to Communicate With One Another Without Leadership Permission

A party member named David Keil wrote an article on working-class organizing and trade union activity in Europe (with implications for the party debate on "a proletarian orientation"), which he showed in manuscript to various comrades. One of the people he showed it to was his branch organizer. In a letter to the Political Committee of the SWP dated February 25, 1971, Keil described what happened next: "He told me that, since it is not preconvention discussion period, it might be best for me not to show the article to comrades, since the other side had no chance to answer." He asked the Political Committee, "do I have the right or permission to show this article to comrades before the preconvention discussion starts? In any case, I would not distribute it to any and all comrades, just those I think might agree with it or to better show my position to comrades with whom I get into a discussion." He also asked whether—as someone had told him—comrades living in different cities did not have the right to coauthor a document, for reasons similar to that given him by his branch organizer. A March 22, 1971, response from National Organization Secretary Jack Barnes did not give a direct answer to his questions but simply referred him to the 1965 organizational resolution, "especially to the section of 'Factionalism and Party Unity' which deals with the problem of selective discussions prior to our regular pre-convention discussion period."[88]

In a letter dated July 11, 1971, Keil wrote to the Political Committee indicating that he was circulating among some party members, "in order to obtain suggestions and sponsors," a draft of an amendment to the leadership's draft political resolution. He asked whether the amendment would be considered friendly or as representing a counterline. Barnes wrote back to him that his question represented "asking the Political Committee to make a private political commitment to you behind the back of the party." This and the private circulation of the amendment were "entirely out of line," Barnes asserted, quoting the two paragraphs on "Factionalism and Party Unity" from the 1965 resolution examined earlier. He concluded: "In keeping with the discussion norms set forth in the above quotation, any amendments you may wish to offer concerning the National Committee draft resolutions should be submitted directly and openly to the party as a whole through the internal bulletin."[89]

In a letter dated February 13, 1979, Keil informed the Political Committee that he had sent copies of a document disagreeing with the party's position on Cuba to several members of the SWP as well as to several members of sections or sympathizing groups of the Fourth International in other countries. He received a letter signed by Larry Seigle, for the Political Committee, telling him: "The party's organizational principles prohibit the private circulation of discussion articles and other forms of political activity outside normal channels." Quoting the two familiar paragraphs from the 1965 resolution, "The Organizational Character of the SWP," Seigle went on to explain that "circulation of 'drafts' to arbitrarily selected individuals has nothing in common with the normal process of leadership collaboration and discussion that is the responsibility of the *elected* leadership of the bodies of the party to carry out." He concluded: "Until such time as the 1965 organizational resolution is amended or superseded, all comrades are bound to abide by it as a condition of membership. This means you must cease any private circulation of documents. The place for such discussion is in the [internal preconvention] discussion bulletin."[90]

This increasing restriction of the right of SWP members to communicate with one another was alien to the actual ideas of Lenin and the practice of the Bolshevik party, nor did it have anything to do with the manner in which James P. Cannon functioned or expected his comrades to function. Many SWP members did not believe that this was how the 1965 organizational resolution should be understood, and—in many cases unaware of the correspondence with Keil—they were not inclined to curtail their communications with one another. But a growing number of the members *did* come to understand this prohibition, and to function accordingly. By the early 1980s' there was no longer any room for misunderstanding.

4. Expulsion of the Internationalist Tendency
In 1974, a sizable dissident faction, the Internationalist Tendency (IT), was expelled from the SWP in a manner that severely undermined

party democracy. The fact that so damaging an act was endorsed by the overwhelming majority of the SWP leadership and membership—including "old guard" veterans who should have known better, and independent-minded activists who would later become oppositionists—can be understood only if we briefly examine the nature of the IT itself. As was the case with the POT, in the course of this factional fight, some very unhealthy organizational practices were employed against the IT. And some members of this oppositional current were not above employing a provocative factionalism themselves.

The IT consisted of a somewhat heterogeneous collection of oppositionists, some of whom were former members (now somewhat embittered) of the POT. The IT as a whole identified with positions of the International Majority Tendency (IMT) in a factional dispute that had arisen inside the Fourth International. The SWP majority, including the overwhelming majority of the party's "old guard" plus the emergent leadership layer around Barnes, helped organize the Leninist-Trotskyist Faction (LTF) in this international dispute. The IMT represented a current·that was adapting to "far-left" trends arising out of the worldwide youth radicalization of the 1960s, influenced by the Vietnamese revolution, Maoism, and the guerrilla warfare strategy articulated by Che Guevara and Regis Debray. The LTF represented a current that fought to maintain traditional Trotskyist perspectives, a refusal to adapt to what it viewed as dangerous ultra-leftism, and an insistence on maintaining what it termed "the Leninist strategy of party building." In addition to endorsing IMT positions in the international dispute, the IT advanced an extremely sharp critique of SWP perspectives in the United States—denouncing the party's student orientation, its approach to building a broad-based (and thus insufficiently "revolutionary") antiwar coalition against the Vietnam War, its support of Black nationalism, and its alleged capitulation to "bourgeois feminism." The IT represented about 150 people in the combined membership of 2,000 that made up the SWP and YSA.[91]

The IT mistakenly believed that the factional fight between the IMT and LTF would culminate in a new split in the Fourth International. It almost enthusiastically favored this split, and it expected to become the U.S. representative of the IMT-led Fourth International. Its critique of the SWP was quite fundamental. It argued that "the Barnes leadership's grotesque mutations" were rooted in "negative features of the Cannon tradition," including "an over-emphasis on the administrative side of politics and the apparatus side of the party," at the expense of real experience in struggles and the development of program; an organizational sectarianism in union work; an irrational, obsessive fear of Stalinism; and a dogmatic approach to theory. The Barnes-dominated leadership amplified these weaknesses, according to the IT. Abandoning "the specific historic role of the party, that of injecting revolutionary class consciousness into the working class," the SWP had reduced itself to chasing after nonproletarian mass movements that it sought "to control administratively and liquidate politically," according to IT leader Bill Massey. This focus, combined with a concentration on selling SWP literature (and treating other radical groups in a sectarian manner) became a substitute for building a revolutionary proletarian party. Characterizing the entire SWP leadership as "a monolithic social club" composed of "a handraising chorus of political eunuchs," the IT concluded that "the party has programmatically divorced itself so completely from the proletariat that there is little hope for any . . . regeneration." A retrospective look by some of the less vitriolic IT supporters asserted: "In sum, the SWP, in spite of its Trotskyist veneer, must be characterized as *centrist* [midway between revolutionary socialism and reformism] politically, *monolithic* and *bureaucratic* organizationally, *sectarian* and *dishonest* in its methods and style of work."[92]

It is hardly surprising that SWP members holding such opinions would have difficulty functioning in anything like a disciplined manner in the party, or even discussing disputed issues in a comradely fashion. Among the great majority of SWPers, considerable ill will was generated against the IT members as a result of the attitude many of them displayed in the debate and their manner of functioning in SWP branches and YSA chapters. Given the increasingly tightened organizational norms referred to earlier, the IT faction felt compelled to organize itself in partial secrecy: a covert IT national conference was held, complete with IT internal discussion bulletins, to discuss its perspectives in the SWP fight and beyond. All this was discovered by the SWP leadership—which had little difficulty persuading many serious party members that the oppositionists were utterly disloyal to the SWP.

A case can be made for the expulsion of the IT. This is mitigated by the substantial contribution of the Barnes leadership in creating, maintaining, and intensifying a highly factionalized atmosphere. There is also the important question of the extent to which extreme administrative measures would cut across the necessary process of political clarification within the party, thus creating an internal atmosphere that was far less tolerant of the consideration of *any* dissident views. The fact is, however, that the IT was not formally expelled. To expel the ITers would, according to the SWP constitution, make it necessary to allow them to appeal their expulsion—a lengthy and potentially complicated (and, given the relationship of the IT to the majority current in the Fourth International, politically delicate) piece of business.

Instead, the SWP Political Committee announced, on July 4, 1974, "that the Internationalist Tendency's status as a separate, rival party [would] be recognized and that the members of the Internationalist Tendency party [would] be informed that this status places them outside the constitutional provisions of membership in the Socialist Workers Party." It also decided "to instruct each branch to re-register its membership by removing from its rolls as of this date all of the 69 known members of the Internationalist Tendency party."[93] This "reregistration out of the party," as opposed to expulsion, denied IT members any right to appeal. It made unnecessary any discussion whatsoever. This maneuver was based on a fiction: the IT was certainly a hardened faction on a split trajectory, but it had not decided to split, and it was by no means a "rival party." The Political Committee was also playing fast and loose with the SWP's traditional organizational norms and formal constitutional provisions. The reregistration nonetheless seemed to many to be a clever move that would avoid a debilitating factional discussion inside the party.

The entire manner in which this expulsion was carried out, and the manner in which the factional dispute with the IT was handled by the party leadership, helped further codify supercentralist norms and strengthen uncritical attitudes toward the Barnes leadership. Little effort was made to reach out to some of the more reasonable ITers, to give any sense that IT comrades or their concerns should be taken seriously, or to defuse the situation in any way. Instead, throughout the entire factional struggle, the opposition was treated in a manner that would encourage unhealthy attitudes of suspicion or intolerance among many members toward any criticisms or dissent arising within the SWP.

5. The Development of "Leadership Body Discipline"

A norm exists in the American Trotskyist tradition regarding a "higher body"—such as a branch executive committee, the party Political Committee, and, at least to some extent, the broader National Committee—tending to keep its deliberations (that is, comments and disagreements of committee members) to itself. The logic of this, in part, is to allow each member to speak with complete candor and to develop certain thoughts tentatively, without these remarks in any way being used against him or her in an intimidating manner; it facilitates free discussion and collective give-and-take within leadership bodies. Another aspect of this norm's logic is that it is best not to try to "line up" members behind (or against) one or another position expressed in such a leadership body; that such "lining up" can best take place in the course of a full discussion in the party, with all comrades having the opportunity to express—or in some cases to revise—their positions in their own words, as opposed to being quoted or misquoted by another member of the leadership body.

Another norm that evolved in the SWP is the inclination of comrades, especially those in leadership bodies, to consult with one another informally if some problem or disagreement arises, as opposed to openly expressing differences. Sometimes a misunderstanding can be eliminated or a disagreement narrowed in this manner. This was seen as an especially useful procedure in regard to possible differences with a central party leader. After all, it is far better to quietly help strengthen the leadership than it is to undermine its authority unnecessarily. If significant differences continue to exist, then they should be openly confronted and presented—but a premature confrontation in the party can cut across the clarification of real differences.

As the Barnes leadership consolidated its position in the SWP during the 1970s, these norms became warped into new and restrictive rules that undermined party democracy. This became a means by which even a significant number of leading Barnes supporters were marginalized and finally pushed out of the party. One example involves Peter Camejo, the SWP's candidate for president in the 1976 elections. "I noticed over time that whenever I attempted to raise questions that differed from the leadership's opinion, it resulted in a heated organizational atmosphere," he wrote in 1982. "Only if I limited myself to informing Jack Barnes or some other officer of the Party in private could hostilities and organizational conflicts be avoided, or at least minimized." While stressing the value of such informal discussions about political differences, Camejo added: "Looking back, however, I can see that I would often use such a discussion as a substitute for what I should have said at a formal meeting." His elaboration on this deserves attention:

> For instance, when I privately met with Jack Barnes to inform him that I thought it was wrong to project that the YSA should be permanently student-oriented, I should have so stated in the Political Committee and voted accordingly. I didn't. But the prevailing mode of operation in the SWP leadership is to consider such private meetings as an act of loyalty, of "teamwork." In my case, it wasn't working out too well because I would periodically raise differences in the PC or in local executive committees and even, though rarely, vote against the majority or make my own proposals, if only on minor matters.
>
> As relations began to deteriorate, I had various meetings with Jack Barnes and Mary-Alice Waters, at my request, to try and reverse the drift I sensed toward a policy of non-collaboration with me [after 1979]. I made various efforts to try to maintain comradely and collaborative relations, but they did not work.
>
> I continue to feel, as many other comrades do, that once you begin to voice differences, real collaboration stops. This makes comrades hesitate to function in a correct Leninist manner.
>
> Any party functioning under full Leninist norms would have differences and conflicting votes over at least some questions once in a while. To believe otherwise is non-materialist. Yet the SWP leadership has gone for years upon years with the central leadership voting on every question in unison even when the votes meant a sharp reversal of what they had voted for only a short period before. . . .
>
> Every leader, almost without exception, who has voted against a majority proposal at a PC or NC meeting in recent times has ended up having strong difficulties being able to function on a normal collaborative basis with the present core of leaders. This is true, in my opinion, whether they are experienced proletarian leaders coming out of the 1930s and 40s, such as George Breitman, Frank Lovell and Nat Weinstein, or NCers recruited in more recent decades, such as Les Evans, Ray Markey, Lynn Henderson, myself and many others.[94]

Among those who were part of the Barnes "leadership team" in this period were Barry Sheppard and Malik Miah, each of whom had held—at one point or another—various top positions, including that of

SWP national chairperson (subordinate, however, to national secretary Barnes). Within a few years they too found themselves marginalized and stumbling over increasingly restricted interpretations of organizational discipline. In 1987, after he had been pushed out of the central leadership, Sheppard raised a difference with a position adopted by the National Committee about a report that was to be given at a membership conference; a motion was then adopted stating that all members of the National Committee had to support this report at the membership conference. By 1988, profoundly demoralized, Sheppard resigned from the party. Miah was expelled in 1989 for expressing his disagreement with the party leadership at a national trade union fraction meeting. "I must put forward the views of the PC in the fraction even if I disagree with them. That's correct," Miah commented. "But I also have the right to say I don't agree with that line and will raise my views in the proper manner. That's been our tradition when differences have arisen in the past." Citing the 1965 organizational resolution, the Political Committee responded that "no minority in the National Committee has the right to decide when to open a discussion in the party membership, nor do they have the right to organize around a counterline. It is up to the party, through its democratically elected bodies—not individual members who place themselves above party democracy—to decide when and under what circumstances discussion on party line is in order."[95]

The retrospective comment by Sheppard and Miah, although still formulated in a too restricted manner, is to the point: "The National Committee has every right to determine how its positions will be reported to the party. But it is a violation of all past practice of the SWP to interpret this right to mean that NC members who happen to be members of a body lower than the National Committee cannot speak freely about their opinions on whatever subject is on the agenda of a meeting of that lower body. Such 'committee discipline' obviously violates the democratic rights of the entire membership to be fully informed of the opinions of the other members of whatever body is in session."[96] In fact, in the party of Lenin, and also in the era of "real socialist freedom" in the American Trotskyist movement under Cannon, party members had a right to speak freely about their opinions not only in meetings under the appropriate agenda point but also in communication with one another outside of meetings.

From 1965 to 1990, we can see a process in the SWP in which *organizational norms* that seemed reasonable, if understood broadly and interpreted flexibly as suggested modes of behavior, came to be interpreted with increasing restrictiveness and transformed into *strict rules* whose violation would result in expulsion. More than this, the notion of a "leadership team" came to involve a conception of *leadership body discipline*, which had the effect of transforming the "team" into a permanent and undeclared faction organized around the person of Jack Barnes. Any openly expressed (let alone organized) disagreement with this Barnes leadership became exceedingly difficult to harmonize with continued party membership.

It sounds reasonable to say that "the party as a whole" has the right to regulate its internal discussions. It sounds quite democratic to add that this should be done "through its elected leadership bodies." But the interpretation of the 1965 organizational resolution developed by the Political Committee under Barnes meant that the phrase "the party through its elected leadership bodies" became equivalent, for all practical purposes, to investing decision-making power in the hands of the SWP national secretary.

Such functioning is alien to the tradition of Lenin, Trotsky, and Cannon. Despite the Barnes leadership's repeated stress on "proletarian organizational norms," it is alien to the traditions of working-class democracy and labor radicalism, out of which the revolutionary socialist movement arose. It has, instead, gone in the direction of creating a small, secure, totalitarian universe buoyed up with grand illusions. With no authority in a genuinely class-conscious working-class movement, artificial attempts to elaborate and enforce rules to establish "the iron discipline needed by the revolutionary proletariat," as Lenin put it, "inevitably fall flat and end up in phrase-mongering and clowning."

"Great energy has been expended by the leadership," Miah and Sheppard observe, "in working through intricate reasoning on exactly what the true proletarian norms are in matters such as members holding baby showers, proper times and places for breast feeding, when children can be present at political events, and other such 'critical questions' of world revolution."[97] Unfortunately, this is not a caricature. Such "proletarian norms" have nothing to do with working-class life, or with Marxist theory, or with what it will take to make a working-class socialist revolution. They reflect a tragic degeneration of an organization that once represented a high point in world Trotskyism and in the history of American radicalism.

These negative lessons of the SWP experience must be learned by serious revolutionary socialists who seek to become a relevant force not in some mythical working class that embodies Barnes's "proletarian norms" but within the working class as it actually is. Only by taking root in this real working class can Leninism take on life and can the proud tradition of American Trotskyism be renewed. There are indications that objective conditions in the actual experience of the U.S. working class may be creating the basis for such a development as the twentieth century nears its end.[98]

Leadership, Membership, Revolutionary Democracy

There are also positive lessons to be learned. The Socialist Workers Party, even as it was beset by the growing problems indicated in the previous section of this essay, had tremendous strengths. In the 1960s and 1970s—in part through the earlier theoretical and programmatic acquisitions of revolutionary Marxism and American Trotskyism, in part through the richness of experience encompassed in the lives of the older comrades, and in part through the idealism, energy, and creativity of new young members—the SWP made important contributions. Some of these are indicated in materials gathered in this book.

It is important to recognize that "Barnesism" finds its antidote from resources *within* the tradition of American Trotskyism. This should be clear from an examination of materials by James P. Cannon already discussed, and also from an examination of Trotsky's own advice on essential aspects of building a revolutionary party. Consider the conception of *party leadership* that shines through in Trotsky's discussion of party democracy:

> What is party democracy?
>
> a. The strictest observance of the party statutes by the leading bodies (regular conventions, necessary period of discussion, right of the minority to express its opinions in the party meetings and in the press).
>
> b. A patient, friendly, to a certain point pedagogical attitude on the part of the central committee and its members toward the rank and file, including the objectors and the discontented because it is not a great merit to be satisfied "with anybody who is satisfied with me." When Lenin asked for the expulsion of Ordzhonikidze from the party (1923),

he said very correctly that the discontented party member has the right to be turbulent, but not a member of the central committee. Methods of psychological "terrorism," including a haughty or sarcastic manner of answering or treating every objection, criticism, or doubt—it is, namely, this journalistic or "intellectualistic" manner which is insufferable to workers and condemns them to silence.

c. The solely formal object of the democratic rules as indicated under (a) and the solely negative measures—not to terrorize, not to ridicule—under (b) are not sufficient. The central committee as well as every local committee must be in permanent, active, and informal contact with the rank and file, especially when a new slogan or a new campaign is in preparation or when it is necessary to verify the results of an accomplished campaign. Not every member of the central committee is capable of such an informal contact, and not every member has the time for this or the occasion, which depends not only upon goodwill and a particular psychology but also upon the profession and the corresponding milieu. In the composition of the central committee it is necessary to have not only good organizers and good speakers, writers, administrators, but also people closely connected with the rank and file, organically representative of them.[99]

Trotsky also had much to say on the responsibility of the party *membership* in guaranteeing the effectiveness of party democracy:

A Bolshevik is not merely a disciplined person; he is a person who in each case and on each question forges a firm opinion of his own and defends it courageously and independently, not only against his enemies, but inside his own party. Today, perhaps, he will be in the minority in his organization. He will submit [to the majority decision], because it is his party. But this does not always signify that he is in the wrong. Perhaps he saw or understood before the others did a new task or the necessity of a turn. He will persistently raise the question a second, a third, a tenth time, if need be. Thereby he will render his party a service, helping it to meet the new task fully armed or to carry out the necessary turn without organic upheavals, without factional convulsions. . . .

What . . . a fighting mass organization needs is not sycophantic functionaries but people who are strongly tempered morally, permeated with a feeling of personal responsibility, who on every important question will make it their duty to work out conscientiously their personal opinion and will defend it courageously by every means that does not violate rationally (that is, not bureaucratically) understood discipline and unity of action.

... That is why bureaucratic obsequiousness, spurious docility, and all other manners of empty well-wishers who know which side their bread is buttered on, cannot be tolerated. What is needed is criticism, checking of facts, independence of thought, the personal elaboration of the present and the future, independence of character, the feeling of responsibility, truth toward oneself and toward one's work.[100]

Trotsky's description of the revolutionary party stands as an eloquent rebuttal of authoritarian organizational norms propagated by the Barnes leadership. It is this revolutionary democratic spirit, forging a bond between the traditions of Bolshevik-Leninism and American radicalism, that permeates the struggle of the many U.S. Trotskyists reflected in this volume. If a substantial sympathizing section of the Fourth International is recomposed in the United States, and to the extent that class consciousness and a revolutionary socialist movement take root in the U.S. working class, this spirit and tradition will be an invaluable resource.

Notes

I would like to acknowledge here the direct influence on this essay of the following people: Tom Bias, Steve Bloom, Frank Lovell, Sarah Lovell, Carol McAllister, Dave Riehle, Dan Rosenshine, Evelyn Sell, and Alan Wald. Some contributed more, some contributed less, and responsibility for what I have done in this essay is mine alone—but I want to thank each of them for information and/or insights shared.

1.   Leon Trotsky, *The Revolution Betrayed* (New York: Doubleday, Doran, 1937); Ernest Mandel, *Beyond Perestroika* (London: Verso, 1989); Marilyn Vogt-Downey, ed., *Marxist Perspectives on the USSR* (Atlantic Highlands, NJ: Humanities Press, 1993).

Memoirs on the Communist Party of interest include James P. Cannon, *The First Ten Years of American Communism* (New York: Lyle Stuart, 1962); Howard Fast, *Being Red* (Boston: Houghton Mifflin, 1990), and his earlier *The Naked God* (New York: Frederick A. Praeger, 1957); Peggy Dennis, *The Autobiography of an American Communist, a Personal View of a Political Life, 1925–1975* (Westport, CT: Lawrence Hill, 1977); Steve Nelson (with James R. Barrett and Rob Ruck), *Steve Nelson, American Radical* (Pittsburgh: University of Pittsburgh Press, 1981).

Histories of U.S. Communism include Theodore Draper, *The Roots of American Communism* (New York: Viking Press, 1957), and *American Communism and Soviet Russia* (New York: Viking Press, 1960); Harvey Klehr,

The Heyday of American Communism, the Depression Decade (New York: Basic Books, 1984); Maurice Isserman, *Which Side Were You On? The American Communist Party during the Second World War* (Middleton, CT: Wesleyan University Press, 1982), and *If I Had a Hammer . . . The Death of the Old Left and the Birth of the New Left* (New York: Basic Books, 1987). Two surveys of Marxist-influenced movements in the United States that have substantial sections on the Communist Party are Daniel Bell, *Marxian Socialism in the United States* (Princeton, NJ: Princeton University Press, 1967), and Paul Buhle, *Marxism in the United States*, rev. ed. (London: Verso, 1991).

2.　The "larger effort" includes, especially, a three-volume work (including a mass of documentation and analysis adding up to more than 800 pages) published under the title "In Defense of American Trotskyism." The chronology of the subject matter would place the volumes in this order: Sarah Lovell, ed., *The Struggle Inside the Socialist Workers Party, 1979–1983* (New York: Fourth Internationalist Tendency, 1992); Paul Le Blanc, ed., *Revolutionary Principles and Working-Class Democracy* (New York: Fourth Internationalist Tendency, 1992); Paul Le Blanc, ed., *Rebuilding the Revolutionary Party* (New York: Fourth Internationalist Tendency, 1990). It is from the second volume listed here that the present essay is adapted.

3.　Reginald Zelnik, ed., *A Radical Worker in Tsarist Russia, the Autobiography oj Semen Ivanovich Kanatchikov* (Stanford CA: Stanford University Press, 1986); Cecilia Bobrovskaya, *Twenty Years in Underground Russia, Memoirs of a Rank-and-File Bolshevik* (Chicago: Proletarian Publishers, 1976); O. Piatnitsky, *Memoirs of a Bolshevik* (New York: International Publishers, n.d. [1930?]); A. Badayev, *The Bolsheviks in the Tsarist Duma* (London: Bookmarks, 1989); Alexander Shlyapnikov, *On the Eve of 1917, Reminiscences from the Revolutionary Underground* (London: Allison Busby, 1982); F. F. Raskolnikov, *Kronstadt and Petrograd in 1917* (London: New Park Publications, 1982). Also see Georges Haupt and Jean-Jacques Marie, eds., *Makers of the Russian Revolution, Biographies of Bolshevik Leaders* (Ithaca, NY: Cornell University Press, 1969).

4.　The classic accounts of the Russian Revolution include John Reed, *Ten Days that Shook the World* (New York: International Publishers, 1926); Victor Serge, *Year One of the Russian Revolution* (New York: Henry Holt, 1972); Leon Trotsky, *History of the Russian Revolution*, 3 vols. in one (New York: Simon & Schuster, 1936); William Henry Chamberlin, *The Russian Revolution, 1917–1921*, 2 vols. (New York: Grossett & Dunlap, 1963).

　　The important new scholarship includes Alexander Rabinowitch, *The Bolsheviks Come to Power* (New York: W. W. Norton, 1976); Victoria E. Bonnell, *Roots of Rebellion: Workers' Politics and Organizations in St. Petersburg and Moscow, 1900–1914* (Berkeley: University of California Press, 1983); Diane Koenker, *Moscow Workers and the 1917 Revolution* (Princeton, NJ: Princeton University Press, 1981); David Mandel, *The Petrograd Workers and the Fall of the Old Regime* and *The Petrograd Workers and the Soviet Seizure of Power*

(New York: St. Martin's Press, 1984). Also see two good collections: Daniel H. Kaiser, ed., *The Workers' Revolution in Russia, 1917: The View from Below* (Cambridge: Cambridge University Press, 1987); Ronald Suny and Arthur Adams, eds., *The Russian Revolution and Bolshevik Victory*, 3d ed. (Lexington, MA: D. C. Heath, 1990).

5. Lenin, "Speech in Defense of the Tactics of the Communist International," *Collected Works*, vol. 32 (Moscow: Progress Publishers, 1973), pp. 470, 474–75.

6. Lenin, "Left-Wing Communism—An Infantile Disorder," *Collected Works*, vol. 31 (Moscow: Progress Publishers, 1974), pp. 24–25.

7. Ibid., p. 25.

8. Lenin, "A Draft Program of Our Party," *Collected Works*, vol. 4 (Moscow: Progress Publishers, 1972), p. 229.

9. Lenin, "Report on the Unity Congress of the R.S.D.L.P.," *Collected Works*, vol. 10 (Moscow: Progress Publishers, 1972), p. 380, and "Social Democrats and the Duma Elections," *Collected Works*, vol. 11 (Moscow: Progress Publishers, 1962), p. 434.

10. Lenin, "Freedom to Criticize and Unity of Action," *Collected Works*, vol. 10, pp. 442–43.

11. Alix Holt and Barbara Holland, eds., *Theses, Resolutions and Manifestos of the First Four Congresses of the Third International* (London: Ink Links, 1980), p. 235.

12. Philip S. Foner, ed., *The Bolshevik Revolution: Its Impact on American Radicals, Liberals, and Labor* (New York: International Publishers, 1967).

13. Ibid., pp. 162–63; Joseph R. Conlin, *Big Bill Haywood and the Radical Union Movement* (Syracuse, NY: Syracuse University Press, 1969), p. 195.

14. N. Lenin and Leon Trotsky, *The Proletarian Revolution in Russia*, ed. Louis C. Fraina (New York: Communist Press, 1918), pp. xviii, 14.

15. Louise Bryant, *Six Months in Red Russia* (London: Journeyman Press, 1982), p. 54; Bessie Beatty, *The Red Heart of Russia* (New York: Century Co., 1918), p. 135; Reed, *Ten Days that Shook the World*, p. xv.

16. Albert Rhys Williams, *Lenin, the Man and His Work* (New York: Scott and Seltzer, 1919), p. 34.

17. Michael Goldfield, "Recent Historiography of the Communist Party USA," in Mike Davis, Fred Pfeil, and Michael Sprinker, eds., *The Year Left, an American Socialist Yearbook, 1985* (London: Verso, 1985), p. 322; Buhle, *Marxism in the United States*, p. 129.

18. James P. Cannon, "Our Aims and Tactics in the Trade Unions," *Daily Worker*, August 2, 1924; reprinted in *James P. Cannon and the Early Years of American Communism, Selected Writings and Speeches, 1920–1928*, ed. Emily Turnbull and James Robertson (New York: Prometheus Research Library, 1992), p. 214.

19. Excerpts from Alexander Bittelman's memoirs, chapter 12, in Tamiment Library collection, New York University Bobst Library, quoted in the introduction to *James P. Cannon and the Early Years of American Communism*, p. 28.

20. James P. Cannon, *The History of American Trotskyism* (New York: Pathfinder Press, 1972), pp. 14–15; Bertram D. Wolfe, *A Life in Two Centuries* (New York: Stein and Day, 1981), p. 229.

21. Buhle, *Marxism in the United States*, p. 128; Wolfe, *A Life in Two Centuries*, p. 257.

22. Max Shachtman, *Lenin, Liebknecht, Luxemburg* (Chicago: Young Workers [Communist] League, n.d. [1924?]), p. 27; *Lenin on Organization* (New York: Workers Library Publishers, 1926); Cannon's remarks, in a speech to the New York Workers' School, were printed as "The Bolshevization of the Party," in *Workers Monthly*, November 1924, and are quoted in a later factional pamphlet, Albert Goldman, *The Question of Unity* (Long Island, NY: Workers Party Publications, 1947), p. 27; also see *James P. Cannon and the Early Years of American Communism*, p. 237.

23. "Bolshevization" is discussed in Draper, *American Communism and Soviet Russia*, pp. 153–85. A report on the progress of "bolshevization" can be found in O. Piatnitsky, *The Organisation of a World Party* (London: Communist Party of Great Britain, 1928), but in ways a more illuminating discussion can be found in the account of Karl Volk and Jules Humbert-Droz, writing under the pseudonym Ypsilon, in *Pattern for World Revolution* (Chicago: Ziff-Davis, 1947), pp. 73, 102–3, 108–11, 112, 116–18, 300–301. Cannon also made interesting (and not totally negative) reference to this years later, in a 1941 political report at an SWP convention, contained in James P. Cannon, *The Socialist Workers Party in World War II* (New York: Pathfinder Press, 1975), p. 176.

24. The autobiography of the Stalinized Communist Party can be found in William Z. Foster, *History of the Communist Party of the United States* (New York: International Publishers, 1952), and Philip Bart et al., eds., *Highlights of a Fighting History, 60 Years of the Communist Party USA* (New York: International Publishers, 1976). A brief historical survey of various U.S. groups calling themselves Leninist, including the Maoists, is worth consulting: Jim O'Brien, *American Leninism in the 1970s* (Somerville, MA: New England Free Press, n.d.), reprinted from *Radical America*, November 1977–February 1978.

25. The broad outlines of this period are covered in Cannon's own *History of American Trotskyism*, as well as in Robert J. Alexander, *International Trotskyism, 1929–1985: A Documented Analysis of the Movement* (Durham, NC: Duke University Press, 1991), pp. 761–90.

26. George Breitman, ed., *The Founding of the Socialist Workers Party, Minutes and Resolutions 1938–39* (New York: Monad Press, 1982), p. 27.

27. "The Internal Situation and the Character of the Party," in ibid., pp. 160–63; James P. Cannon, *The Struggle for a Proletarian Party* (New York: Pathfinder Press, 1972), p. 53.

28. Cannon, *The Socialist Workers Party in World War II*, pp. 371–72; Hansen in Les Evans, ed., *James P. Cannon as We Knew Him* (New York: Pathfinder Press, 1976), p. 14. The comradely pressure from Trotsky is reflected, for example, in his intervention in the 1932–33 factional situation in the Communist League

of America, involving currents led by Cannon and Shachtman, respectively; he wrote: "It also seemed to me that the majority, as the leading faction in the central committee, showed a certain impatience and applied or attempted to apply organizational measures which, without giving permanent results, could not help but sharpen the conflict." See James P. Cannon, *The Communist League of America, 1932–34* (New York: Monad Press, 1985), p. 392, where this April 17, 1933, letter from Trotsky is reprinted. Also see Dianne Feeley, Paul Le Blanc, and Tom Twiss, *Leon Trotsky and the Organizational Principles of the Revolutionary Party* (New York: Fourth Internationalist Tendency, 1984), pp. 52–58.

29.   George Marlen, *Earl Browder, Communist or Tool of Wall Street; Stalin, Trotsky or Lenin* (New York: Author, 1937), pp. 156, 157. Yet another attack on Cannon's allegedly undemocratic functioning—cited, however, as standard Leninist practice in a piece of cold war scholarship by a one-time SWP dissident—can be found in Philip Selznick, *The Organizational Weapon, a Study of Bolshevik Strategy and Tactics* (Glencoe, Ill.: Free Press of Glencoe, 1960), pp. 167–68.

30.   Max Shachtman et al., "The War and Bureaucratic Conservatism," in Cannon, *Struggle for a Proletarian Party*, pp. 275, 277; Tim Wohlforth, *The Struggle for Marxism in the United States, a History of American Trotskyism* (New York: Labor Publications, 1971), p. 42; Tariq Ali, *Street Fighting Years, an Autobiography of the Sixties* (New York: Citadel Press, 1991), p. 246. Also see Paul Le Blanc, "From Revolutionary Intellectual to Conservative Master-Thinker: The Anti-Democratic Odyssey of James Burnham," *Left History* 3, no. 1 (Spring 1995).

31.   J. R. Johnson [C. L. R. James], F. Forest [Raya Dunayevskaya], Martin Harvey [Martin Glaberman], *Trotskyism in the United States, 1940–47: Balance Sheet* (Johnson-Forest Tendency, August 1947), p. 16; this positive judgment of Cannon's commitment to genuine inner-party democracy is essentially reiterated by veterans of the Johnson-Forest tendency writing many years later: James and Grace Lee Boggs, Freddy and Lyman Paine, *Conversations in Maine, Exploring Our Nation's Future* (Boston: South End Press, 1978), pp. 281–87.

32.   Cannon, *Struggle for a Proletarian Party*, p. 281.

33.   Goldman, *The Question of Unity*, pp. 27, 28, 29, 38.

34.   James P. Cannon, *The Struggle for Socialism in the "American Century"* (New York: Pathfinder Press, 1977), pp. 246–47.

35.   Ibid., pp. 291, 304.

36.   Albert Fried, ed., *Except to Walk Free: Documents and Notes in the History of American Labor* (Garden City, NY: Anchor Books, 1974), p. 153.

37.   Class consciousness is discussed in my own *Lenin and the Revolutionary Party* (Atlantic Highlands, NJ: Humanities Press, 1990), for example pp. 24–29, 43–46, 51–52. More complex discussions can be found in Eric Hobsbawm, "Notes on Class Consciousness," in *Workers: Worlds of Labor* (New York: Pantheon Books, 1984), pp. 15–32, and István Mészáros, "Contingent and Necessary Class Consciousness," in *Philosophy, Ideology and Social Science* (New

York: St. Martin's Press, 1986), pp. 57–104—both commentaries on Georg Lukács' classic *History and Class Consciousness* (Cambridge, MA: MIT Press, 1968). Also of interest is George Rudé, "Ideology and Class Consciousness," in *Ideology and Popular Protest* (New York: Pantheon Books, 1980), pp. 15–26, which draws from Antonio Gramsci's important discussions on the role of revolutionary organizations in the development of class consciousness and of "organic intellectuals" rising within the working class, contained in *Selections from the Prison Notebooks* (New York: International Publishers, 1971). The work of E. P. Thompson, in *The Making of the English Working Class* (New York: Vintage Books, 1966), on the complex relationships between culture and consciousness in the formation of a politically cohesive working class, has also influenced me.

38. Much of this is traced in the work of Herbert Gutman and David Montgomery. See Gutman's *Work, Culture and Society in Industrializing America* (New York: Vintage Books, 1977) and *Power and Culture: Essays on the American Working Class* (New York: Pantheon Books, 1987), and Montgomery's *Beyond Equality, Labor and the Radical Republicans, 1862–1872* (New York: Alfred A. Knopf, 1967), *Workers' Control in America* (Cambridge: Cambridge University Press, 1979), and *The Fall of the House of Labor: The Workplace, the State, and American Labor Activism, 1865–1925* (Cambridge: Cambridge University Press, 1987). Also see Philip S. Foner, *History of the Labor Movement in the United States*, 9 vols. (New York: International Publishers, 1947–91).

Some superficially knowledgeable people contest the very existence of the class consciousness and radical subculture within the U.S. working class that is discussed here, but there is too much evidence for its existence to shrug it off. Additional works documenting this phenomenon include Mari Jo Buhle, Paul Buhle, Dan Georgakas, eds., *Encyclopedia of the American Left* (Urbana: University of Illinois Press, 1992); Paul Buhle and Alan Dawley, *Working for Democracy, American Workers from the Revolution to the Present* (Urbana: University of Illinois Press, 1985); Leon Fink, *Workingmen's Democracy, the Knights of Labor and American Politics* (Urbana: University of Illinois Press, 1983); Hartmut Keil and John Jentz, eds., *German Workers in Industrial Chicago, 1850–1910* (De Kalb: Northern Illinois University Press, 1983); Dave Roediger and Franklin Rosemont, eds., *Haymarket Scrapbook* (Chicago: Charles H. Kerr, 1986); Bruce C. Nelson, *Beyond the Martyrs, a Social History of Chicago's Anarchists, 1870–1900* (New Brunswick, NJ: Rutgers University Press, 1988); John Laslett, *Labor and the Left, a Study of Socialist and Radical Influences in the American Labor Movement, 1881–1924* (New York: Basic Books, 1970); Ray Ginger, *Eugene V. Debs: A Biography* (New York: Collier Books, 1962); Joyce L. Kornbluh, ed., *Rebel Voices, an IWW Anthology* (Chicago: Charles H. Kerr, 1988); Staughton Lynd, ed., *American Labor Radicalism, Testimonies and Interpretations* (New York: John Wiley & Sons, 1973); Alice and Staughton Lynd, eds., *Rank and File, Personal Histories by Working-Class Organizers* (Boston: Beacon Press, 1973).

39.   Issues of antiradical repression are dealt with in Robert K. Murray, *Red Scare, a Study in National Hysteria 1919–1920* (New York: McGraw-Hill, 1964), and more generally in Robert Justin Goldstein, *Political Repression in Modern America, 1870 to the Present* (Cambridge, MA: Schenkman, 1978). Also useful on the impact of the 1920s on labor are J. B. S. Hardman, "Postscript to Ten Years of Labor Movement," Lewis Corey, "The New Capitalism," and James Rorty, "The Post-War Social Mind," all in J. B. S. Hardman, ed., *American Labor Dynamics in the Light of Post-War Developments* (New York: Harcourt, Brace, 1928), pp. 5–36, 43–72, 73–92. Two poignant snapshots of the toll such things took on the left wing of the labor movement are David Karsner, "The Passing of the Socialist Party," *Current History*, June 1924, reprinted in H. Wayne Morgan, ed., *American Socialism 1900–1960* (Englewood Cliffs, NJ: Prentice-Hall, 1964), pp. 98–102; and Samuel Yellen, "A Socialist Boyhood," *American Mercury*, October 1930.

40.   A useful, if flawed, three-volume study on the first three internationals—written from a social democratic perspective—is Julius Braunthal, *History of the International, 1864–1943*, 2 vols. (New York: Frederick A. Praeger, 1967), and *History of the International, 1943–1968* (Boulder, CO: Westview Press, 1980). Somewhat further to the left, and briefer, is Wolfgang Abendroth, *A Short History of the European Working Class* (New York: Monthly Review Press, 1972).

41.   These realities are movingly captured by the revolutionary novelist Victor Serge in *The Midnight of the Century* (London: Writers and Readers, 1982), *The Case of Comrade Tulayev* (Garden City, NY: Doubleday, 1950), and *The Long Dusk* (New York: Dial Press, 1946)—read in this order, moving from 1934 to 1940.

It is also worth examining the 1941 analysis of a former Trotskyist leader, the wealthy intellectual James Burnham, who captured this dilemma in his own particular way in *The Managerial Revolution* (Bloomington: Indiana University Press, 1962), pp. 53, 54:

The important social groups having as their professed aim the transition to socialism are the various Marxist political parties. Practical *success* for such parties does not at all guarantee the victory of socialism as the Russian experience shows: in general, there is no necessary correspondence between the professed aims of a political party and what happens when it takes power. But practical *failure* of these parties is additional, and strong, evidence against the prediction that socialism will come, since it removes one of the chief social forces which have been pointed to as motivation for the prediction. And the fact is that during the past two decades [1921–41] Marxist parties have collapsed on a world scale. Their fate can be pretty well summed up as follows: they have all either failed socialism or abandoned it, in most cases both.

These parties, it should be recalled, comprised in their ranks and sympathizing circles, tens of millions of persons throughout the world. During the past twenty years, they have simply disappeared from existence in nation after nation. Wherever fascism has risen . . . the Marxist parties have gone under, usually without even a fight for survival. The greatest of all Marxist movements, that of Germany, bowed to Hitler [in 1933] without raising a hand. [The massive German Communist and Social Democratic Parties failed to form a united front that would obviously have stopped Hitler's rise to power, and they were not prepared for the fact that he would rapidly destroy them once he took control of Germany's state apparatus in 1933.—P. L.]

But the physical elimination of many Marxist parties is not the only form of their collapse. . . . In Russia a Marxist party took power. Within a short time it abandoned socialism, if not in words at any rate in the effect of its actions. In most European nations there were, since the last months of the first world war and the years immediately thereafter, social crises which left a wide-open door for the Marxist parties: without exception they proved unable to take and hold power. In a large number of countries—Germany, Denmark, Norway, Sweden, Austria, England, Australia, New Zealand, Spain, France— the reformist Marxist parties [of the Second International] have administered the governments, and have uniformly failed to introduce socialism or make any genuine step toward socialism; in fact, have acted in a manner scarcely distinguishable from ordinary liberal capitalist parties administering the government. The Trotskyist and other dissident opposition wings of Marxism have remained minute and ineffectual sects without any influence upon general political developments. The last distorted partial upsurge of the Marxist parties, in connection with the Popular Front movement (which was, in origin, simply a device of the Communist International for implementing one side of the Kremlin's foreign policy of the moment), shows a record of utter incompetence and weakness (France) and disastrous, no matter how heroic, defeat (Spain); and ended with a whimper at Munich.

This stark appraisal would be done differently by a revolutionary Marxist— for example, see the writings of Trotsky in *The Struggle against Fascism in Germany*, ed. George Breitman and Merry Maisel (New York: Pathfinder Press, 1971); *Leon Trotsky on France*, ed. David Salner (New York: Monad Press, 1979); *The Crisis of the French Section (1935–36)*, ed. Naomi Allen and George Breitman (New York: Pathfinder Press, 1977); and *The Spanish Revolution (1931–39)*, ed. Naomi Allen and George Breitman (New York: Pathfinder Press, 1973).

Nonetheless, the factual thrust of Burnham's account is quite accurate, and the impact of these realities wore down the revolutionary morale not only of many left-wing intellectuals but also of some left-wing proletarians.

42. The gains won in this period through struggles by U.S. workers are indicated in the left-wing classic by Art Preis, *Labor's Giant Step, Twenty Years of the CIO* (New York: Pathfinder Press, 1972). Covering some of the same ground from a reformist-liberal standpoint, but with much additional information, is Irving Bernstein's trilogy: *The Lean Years, a History of the American Worker 1920–1933* (Boston: Houghton Mifflin, 1960), *Turbulent Years 1933–1941*

(Boston: Houghton Mifflin, 1969), and *A Caring Society: The New Deal, the Worker, and the Great Depression* (Boston: Houghton Mifflin, 1985). A scholarly demonstration—in contradiction to arguments of sophisticated academics—that radical-led working-class action in the 1930s was decisive in bringing about the New Deal reforms is Michael Goldfield, "Worker Insurgency, Radical Organization, and New Deal Labor Legislation," *American Political Science Review* 83, no. 4 (December 1989): 1257–82.

The class-collaborationist policies of Stalinists and social democrats during the "People's Front" period (1935–39) are discussed in Trotsky's works on France and Spain cited in note 41, but also see Martin S. Alexander and Helen Graham, eds., *The French and Spanish Popular Fronts, Comparative Perspectives* (Cambridge: Cambridge University Press, 1989)—in particular, essays by Tom Kemp, "Trotskyist and Left-Wing Critics of the Popular Front" (pp. 104–15), and Paul Heywood, "The Development of Marxist Theory in Spain and the Frente Popular" (pp. 116–30).

On World War II, see Ernest Mandel, *The Meaning of the Second World War* (London: Verso Books, 1986). On the reformist left-labor alliance with the bourgeoisie during the war, in addition to the work by Art Preis, see Nelson Lichtenstein, *Labor's War at Home, the CIO in World War II* (Cambridge: Cambridge University Press, 1987). We can see the ultimately self-destructive evolution of Communist Party trade union policy from the 1930s to the early 1950s in Bert Cochran, *Labor and Communism, the Conflict that Shaped American Unions* (Princeton, NJ: Princeton University Press, 1977).

The Trotskyist approach during the years of the Great Depression and World War II is clearly documented in Farrell Dobbs's fine four-volume account: *Teamster Rebellion* (New York: Pathfinder Press, 1972), *Teamster Power* (New York: Monad Press, 1973), *Teamster Politics* (New York: Monad Press, 1975), and *Teamster Bureaucracy* (New York: Monad Press, 1977).

43.   Leon Trotsky, "The Way Out," in *The Writings of Leon Trotsky, 1934–35*, ed. George Breitman and Bev Scott (New York: Pathfinder Press, 1974), p. 85; "Imperialist War and World Revolution," in Will Reisner, ed., *Documents of the Fourth International, the Formative Years: 1933–40* (New York: Pathfinder Press, 1973), p. 344. On the Fourth International's origins, see Max Shachtman, "Ten Years—History and Principles of the Left Opposition," George Breitman, "The Rocky Road to the Fourth International, 1933–38," and Ernest Mandel, "The Reasons for Founding the Fourth International and Why They Remain Valid Today," all in Tom Barrett, ed., *Fifty Years of the Fourth International* (New York: Fourth Internationalist Tendency, 1990), pp. 7–111.

44.   A useful survey of the development of Stalinism during this period is included in Fernando Claudin, *The Communist Movement, from Comintern to Cominform*, 2 vols. (New York: Monthly Review Press, 1975). Important surveys of the development of U.S. imperialism can be found in William Appleman Williams, *The Tragedy of American Diplomacy*, 2d rev. and enl. ed. (New York: Dell, 1982), and Harry Magdoff, *Imperialism: From the Colonial*

Age to the Present (New York: Monthly Review Press, 1978). C. Wright Mills, in his incisive (and sometimes wrong) polemic *The Causes of World War Three* (New York: Ballantine Books, 1960), brilliantly describes the confrontation of the "superpowers" at the height of the cold war. Important left-wing scholarly analyses are provided in Thomas J. McCormick, *America's Half-Century, United States Foreign Policy in the Cold War* (Baltimore: Johns Hopkins University Press, 1989), and Gabriel Kolko, *Confronting the Third World, United States Foreign Policy 1945–1980* (New York: Pantheon Books, 1988).

45. Pierre Frank, in *The Fourth International, the Long March of the Trotskyists* (London: Ink Links, 1979), lightly covers some of this ground, though more information can be found in Cliff Conner, Les Evans, and Tom Kerry, *Towards a History of the Fourth International, Part 1: Three Contributions on Postwar Developments* (New York: Education for Socialists, National Education Department, Socialist Workers Party, 1973), and in Fred Feldman, ed., *Towards a History of the Fourth International, Part 4: Struggle in the Fourth International, International Secretariat Documents 1951–1954*, 4 vols. (New York: Education for Socialists, Pathfinder Press, 1974). A brief summary is included in Paul Le Blanc, "James P. Cannon and the Fourth International," in Paul Le Blanc, ed., *Revolutionary Traditions of American Trotskyism* (New York: Fourth Internationalist Tendency, 1988), pp. 12–15.

46. See works by Preis, Lichtenstein, and Cochran cited in note 42, showing how the Stalinists made essential contributions to their own defeat and to that of labor's left wing. The major work on the post—World War II anti-Red campaign in the United States is David Caute, *The Great Fear, the Anti-Communist Purge under Truman and Eisenhower* (New York: Simon & Schuster, 1978). The SWP perspective in this period was defined by James P. Cannon's "American Stalinism and Anti—Stalinism," in the collection of his works of 1945–47, *The Struggle for Socialism in the "American Century"* (New York: Pathfinder Press, 1977), and in the account of a Trotskyist stalwart's struggle against government purge and blacklisting, James Kutcher's *The Case of the Legless Veteran* (New York: Monad Press, 1973).

47. Nelson et al., *Steve Nelson, American Radical*, pp. 284–85.

48. Marx and Engels, *The German Ideology*, excerpted in Howard Selsam and Harry Martel, eds., *Reader in Marxist Philosophy, from the Writings of Marx, Engels, and Lenin* (New York: International Publishers, 1963), p. 190.

49. James P. Cannon, "Trade Unionists and Revolutionists," *Speeches to the Party* (New York: Pathfinder Press, 1973), pp. 57, 58, 59.

50. John C. Leggett, *Class, Race, and Labor: Working-Class Consciousness in Detroit* (London: Oxford University Press, 1968), pp. 52, 53; James Boggs, "The American Revolution, Pages from a Negro Worker's Notebook," *Monthly Review*, July–August 1963, pp. 15, 16.

51. Maurice Crouzet, *The European Renaissance since 1945* (London: Harcourt, Brace, Jovanovich, 1970), pp. 89, 90, 93, 92.

52. On the African American reality, see Julius Jacobson, ed., *The Negro and the American Labor Movement* (Garden City, NY: Anchor Books, 1968); James Boggs, *Racism and the Class Struggle, Further Pages from a Black Worker's Notebook* (New York: Monthly Review Press, 1970); Dan Georgakas and Marvin Surkin, *Detroit: I Do Mind Dying* (New York: St. Martin's Press, 1975); Manning Marable, *How Capitalism Underdeveloped Black America* (Boston: South End Press, 1983). Of special importance are the works of George Breitman, such as his pamphlets *Marxism and the Negro Struggle* (New York: Merit Publishers, 1968) and *How a Minority Can Change Society* (New York: Pathfinder Press, 1971), and his classic study *The Last Year of Malcolm X, the Evolution of a Revolutionary* (New York: Schocken Books, 1968).

53. The "persistence" of the working class in the period under examination is conclusively documented in Andrew Levison, *The Working Class Majority* (New York: Coward, McCann & Geoghegan, 1974). Harvey Swados's demolition of the myths of the happy and powerful worker were reprinted in his collection *A Radical's America* (Boston: Little, Brown, 1962), whose themes were also explored and developed in Patricia Cayo Sexton and Brendan Sexton, *Blue Collars and Hard Hats, the Working Class and the Future of American Politics* (New York: Vintage Books, 1971); William Serrin, *The Company and the Union, the "Civilized Relationship" of the General Motors Corporation and the United Automobile Workers* (New York: Vintage Books, 1974); and Charles Spencer, *Blue Collar, an Internal Examination of the Workplace* (Chicago: Lakeside Charter Books, 1977). The distinctive discontents and consciousness of the white working class in the 1950s to 1970s is the focus of Louise Kapp Howe, ed., *The White Majority, between Poverty and Affluence* (New York: Vintage Books, 1970), and William Kornblum, *Blue Collar Community* (Chicago: University of Chicago Press, 1974). The classic work on degradation of labor through capitalist mechanization is Harry Braverman, *Labor and Monopoly Capital, the Degradation of Work in the Twentieth Century* (New York: Monthly Review Press, 1974).

54. Stanley Aronowitz, *False Promises, the Shaping of American Working Class Consciousness* (New York: McGraw-Hill, 1973), p. 95; Donald Clark Hodges, "Cynicism in the Labor Movement," in Maurice Zeitlin, ed., *American Society, Inc.* (Chicago: Markham, 1970), p. 446; Cannon, *Speeches to the Party*, p. 61.

55. Ben Stone, *Memoirs of a Radical Rank & Filer* (New York: Prometheus Press, 1986), pp. 86–87. A fine history that provides a rich account of one of the SWP's (and the younger layer's) greatest contributions in this period is Fred Halstead's *Out Now! A Participant's Account of the American Movement against the Vietnam War* (New York: Monad Press, 1978). Some sense of continuity between the older and younger generations in the party, and their contrast with others on the left, comes through in Duncan Williams, ed., *The Lesser Evil? The Left Debates the Democratic Party and Social Change* (New York: Pathfinder Press, 1977), in which George Breitman debates Carl Haessler, Jack Barnes debates Stanley Aronowitz, and Peter Camejo debates Michael Harrington.

56. Paul Le Blanc, "Leaving the New Left," *International Socialist Review*, November 1972. This approach to class analysis coincides with that suggested in Frederick Engels's 1888 footnote to the *Communist Manifesto* ("by proletariat [is meant] the class of modern wage-laborers who, having no means of production of their own, are reduced to selling their labor power in order to live"), elaborated in such works as Braverman's *Labor and Monopoly Capital*, cited in note 53, as well as, for example, Louis B. Boudin, *The Theoretical System of Karl Marx* (Chicago: Charles H. Kerr, 1907), pp. 205–7, and essays in Ernest Mandel and George Novack, *The Revolutionary Potential of the Working Class* (New York: Pathfinder Press, 1974).

57. Workers League, *The Carleton Twelve* (New York: Labor Publications, 1981), pp. 15, 18, 20, 22, 24, 25, 26, 28, 29, 30. This publication was part of a vicious international smear campaign, orchestrated by a factional adversary of the SWP, the British Workers Revolutionary Party under the leadership of Gerry Healy, claiming that the SWP leadership had been in the employment of the FBI, CIA, GPU, and so on. These charges are effectively refuted in a substantial collection issued by the Socialist Workers Party, *Healy's Big Lie, the slander campaign against Joseph Hansen, George Novack, and the Fourth International* (New York: Education for Socialists, National Education Department, Socialist Workers Party, 1976). Healy's own organization expelled him in 1985 (see Doug Jenness, "The Shattering of a British Sect," *Intercontinental Press*, December 2, 1985, pp. 725–30), and the organization went on to expose the spurious nature of the slander campaign (see Doug Jenness, "Giant Blow to Agent-Baiting Campaign: 'Workers Press' Repudiates Healy's Big Lie," and related materials, *Intercontinental Press*, March 10, 1986, pp. 147–54). Only the Workers League in the United States, a tiny and pathological sect, continued to maintain these charges into the 1990s. From the standpoint of Marxism, the evolution of the SWP cannot be understood by reference to bizarre conspiracy theories, but only by reference to the workings of much larger social forces. The class background of new SWP leaders, however, does have some (though by itself minimal) relevance.

58. Archie Robinson, *George Meany and His Times, a Biography* (New York: Simon & Schuster, 1981), p. 294.

59. Sol Chick Chaikin, *A Labor Viewpoint: Another Opinion* (Monroe, NY: Library Research Associates, 1980), p. 220.

60. Jean-Pierre Garnier and Roland Lew, "From the Wretched of the Earth to the Defence of the West: An Essay on Left Disenchantment in France," in Ralph Miliband, John Saville, and Marcel Liebman, eds., *Socialist Register 1984* (London: Merlin Press, 1984), pp. 304, 312, 314. The quote from Frank Lovell in the previous paragraph is from Frank Lovell, "The Meaning of the Struggle Inside the Socialist Workers Party," *The Struggle Inside the Socialist Workers Party*, ed. by Sarah Lovell (New York: Fourth Internationalist Tendency, 1992), p. 36.

61.   Notes from discussion between Jack Barnes and Dan Rosenshine, January 1973, in Dan Rosenshine, "Major Document I, May 1972–January 1974," p. 53, manuscript in author's possession.

62.   Leon Trotsky, *Their Morals and Ours* (New York: Merit Publishers, 1969), pp. 34, 38–39, 25.

63.   Leon Trotsky, *Stalin: An Appraisal of the Man and His Influence* (New York: Stein and Day, 1967), p. 58; Lenin, "What Is to Be Done?" in *Collected Works*, vol. 5 (Moscow: Progress Publishers, 1973), p. 477; James P. Cannon, "Happy Birthday, Arne Swabeck," *Bulletin in Defense of Marxism*, no. 31, June 1986, p. 33.

64.   Braverman in Evans, *James P. Cannon as We Knew Him*, pp. 203–4.

65.   James P. Cannon, "Socialism and Democracy," in *Speeches for Socialism* (New York: Pathfinder Press, 1971), pp. 354, 356, 361.

66.   James P. Cannon, letter of February 8, 1966, reprinted in James P. Cannon, *Don't Strangle the Party* (New York: Fourth Internationalist Tendency, 1985), pp. 9–10; reprinted in Le Blanc, *Revolutionary Principles and Working-Class Democracy*, pp. 95–96.

67.   Jack Barnes, "The Organizational Norms of a Proletarian Party" (March 1982), reprinted in Le Blanc, *Revolutionary Principles and Working-Class Democracy*, pp. 369–70; Mary-Alice Waters, "Tom Kerry: Proletarian Fighter," *The Militant*, January 28, 1983, p. 13.

68.   Undated memo from George Breitman [February 1982], photocopy in author's possession.

69.   Cannon, *The Struggle for Socialism in the "American Century,"* p. 249. The historical debate on the Oehlerites and the Cochranites is presented in Alan Wald, "Fatalism versus Critical Consciousness," *Socialist Action Internal Discussion Bulletin*, no. 1 (1984), and in an audiocassette discussion by George Breitman, February 4–5, 1984, in author's possession. Breitman's views are supported by an independent historian with no taint of Leninism or "Cannonism": Robert J. Alexander, *International Trotskyism*, pp. 780–81, 835–42.

70.   Wald, "Fatalism versus Critical Consciousness," pp. 30–31.

71.   Breitman, audiocassette discussion, February 4–5, 1984.

72.   Myra Tanner Weiss, "Open Letter to SWP Comrades" [October 3, 1983], in *Workers Power Discussion Bulletin*, November 1983, p. 53.

73.   Myra Tanner Weiss, *The Bustelo Incident, Marxism and Feminism* (New York: Onward Press, 1987), pp. 56–57. It is not clear that Weiss remembers the particular controversy with complete accuracy. Her reference is to the role of women in the special maritime branch in New York City's Chelsea area. See George Clarke, "The New York Local—Report and Tasks," *Internal Bulletin* no. 1, March 7, 1947 (issued by Socialist Workers Party, Local New York), pp. 9–10.

74.   Weiss, "Open Letter," p. 56, 55; Weiss, *Bustelo Incident*, p. 58; Alexander, *International Trotskyism*, pp. 834–48; Wohlforth, *The Struggle for Marxism in the United States*, pp. 141–42, 151. A recollection somewhat different from that

of Weiss is given by Frank Lovell, who also adds information on the Weiss current in the SWP (letter to author, January 27, 1992).

75. Weiss, "Open Letter," pp. 55–59.

76. Tim Wohlforth, *The Prophet's Children Travels on the American Left* (Atlantic Highlands, NJ: Humanities Press, 1994), p. 91.

77. Ibid., p. 83.

78. Naomi Allen and Sarah Lovell, eds., *A Tribute to George Breitman, Writer, Organizer, Revolutionary* (New York: Fourth Internationalist Tendency, 1987), pp. 21, 22. In the same volume (p. 22), Evelyn Sell recalls that Breitman's exemplary approach in the SWP "was not the norm in the 1950s."

79. Wohlforth, *The Prophet's Children*, p. 79. Frank Lovell indicates that from 1955 to 1975, the Dobbs-Kerry leadership was following "the guiding line" suggested by Cannon himself. In a June 5, 1955, letter to Dobbs, Cannon wrote of "the political trend of both classes toward maintaining the status quo and avoiding any showdown struggles," adding: "This does not improve the prospects for the expansion of our revolutionary party in the next period. But that's the way it is, as it looks from here. The lull in the class struggle gives us more time to prepare for the stormy future. That is the important thing to remember—and make the most of." Quoted in Frank Lovell, letter to author, January 27, 1992.

80. Jack Barnes, introduction to James P. Cannon, *Letters from Prison* (New York: Merit Publishers, 1968), p. xix.

81. Sigmund Freud, *Group Psychology and the Analysis of the Ego* (New York: W. W. Norton, 1975), pp. 61, 62, 63, 64, 50. (I am indebted to the late Daniel Rosenshine for this reference.) The "ego ideal" was later called by Freud the *superego*; useful discussion can also be found in Otto Fenichel, *The Psychoanalytic Theory of Neurosis* (New York: W. W. Norton, 1945), pp. 105–7, 109–10.

A succinct summary of "group psychology" and its place in the larger context of Freud's thought can be found in Peter Gay, *Freud, a Life for Our Time* (New York: Anchor Books, 1989), pp. 403–7. Although Gay indicates that the words "mass" or "crowd" would have been a more accurate translation than the milder term "group" from the German title *Massenpsychologie und Ich-Analyse*, for our purposes here the word "group" is quite appropriate. The developing mental structure of people, according to Freud, involves incorporating the values, strictures, and expectations of outside authority figures—beginning with parents—in order to secure affection, acceptance, and approval; this is the basis of our "conscience," which begins to develop in our earliest years within the family, but other authority figures can later assume the function of parents in larger social contexts, especially in tight-knit political groups.

Freudian and Marxist analytical tools each yield insights that are essential for understanding the kind of realities discussed in the present essay. Trotsky suggested as much in "Culture and Socialism" (1926), reprinted in Leon Trotsky, *Problems of Everyday Life and Other Writings on Culture and Science* (New York: Monad Press, 1973), pp. 233–34, though the question is discussed more substantially by others, for example, in Erich Fromm's 1932 essay "The Method and Function of an Analytic Social Psychology, Notes on Psychoanalysis and Historical Materialism," *The Essential Frankfurt School Reader*, ed. Andrew Arato and Eike Gebherdt (New York: Continuum, 1988), pp. 477–96.

It is interesting that Fromm attempts an explanation of the way that *revolutionary character* differs from the kind of *authoritarian personality* (whether leader or follower) suggested here. "The most fundamental characteristic of the 'revolutionary character' is that he [or she] is *independent*—that he [or she] is *free*," in the sense that "the individual thinks, feels and decides for himself [or herself]." More than this, "the revolutionary character is one who is identified with humanity and therefore transcends the narrow limits of his [or her] own society, and who is able, because of this, to criticize this or any society from the standpoint of reason and humanity." In addition, "the revolutionary character thinks and feels in what one might call a 'critical mood'—in a critical key, to use a term from music. . . . He will be particularly critical when he hears the judgment of the majority, which is that of the market place, of those who have power." This critical-minded humanism is then translated into *action*, the life-activity of the revolutionary within the personal sphere as well as in the larger society—but also within the revolutionary group. Related to this, although not "underestimating the role and functions of power," the true revolutionary is in no way "*morally* impressed by power." One must instead be true to one's self, to one's own critical mind and humanist commitments, to an elemental honesty and dignity in regard to one's self and others. See the essay "The Revolutionary Character," in Erich Fromm, *The Dogma of Christ and Other Essays on Religion, Psychology, and Culture* (Garden City, NY: Anchor Books, 1966), pp. 151–71.

This coincides with Trotsky's own views on "revolutionary morality," cited above, and his description of how revolutionaries should function, quoted at the end of this essay. Readers of this volume will see that it also corresponds to the views of Cannon; similarly, to those of Lenin, as shown in Ronald W. Clark, *Lenin, a Biography* (New York: Harper & Row, 1988) and my own *Lenin and the Revolutionary Party*. On yet another example, see Paul Frölich, *Rosa Luxemburg: Her Life and Work* (New York: Monthly Review Press, 1972), and Hannah Arendt, "Rosa Luxemburg, 1871–1919," in *Men in Dark Times* (New York: Harcourt, Brace & World, 1968), pp. 33–56.

82.   *The Organizational Character of the Socialist Workers Party* (New York: Education for Socialists, Education Department, Socialist Workers Party, 1970), p. 9.

83.   Ibid., pp. 11–12.

84.   Ibid., p. 12.

85.   Alexander, *International Trotskyism*, p. 875; Alan Wald, letter to Asher Harer, February 7, 1983, copy in author's possession.

86.   Allin Taplin, *SWP Discussion Bulletin* 29, no. 20 (July 1971): 30.

87. Alan Wald and Celia Stodola, Memorandum to International Control Commission, November 13, 1974 (typed manuscript; copy in author's possession), pp. 11, 4–5.

88. Socialist Workers Party, *Defending the Organizational Principles of a Proletarian Party*, Internal Information Bulletin, September 1982, pp. 108–9.

89. Ibid., pp. 109–10.

90. Ibid., pp. 107–8.

91. For much of the SWP majority's position in the struggle inside the Fourth International, see Joseph Hansen's still valuable collection of articles and polemics, *The Leninist Strategy of Party Building, the Debate on Guerrilla Warfare in Latin America* (New York: Pathfinder Press, 1979).

92. Hank Williams [Bill Massey], "Our Tendency and Its Tasks," reprinted in Socialist Workers Party, *Materials Related to the Split of the Internationalist Tendency from the Socialist Workers Party*, Internal Information Bulletin, July 1974, pp. 77–84; former members of the IT, "Crisis in the Internationalist Tendency," *Workers Power Discussion Bulletin*, November 1983, p. 44.

93. *Materials Related to the Split of the Internationalist Tendency from the Socialist Workers Party*, p. 15.

94. "A Reply and Clarification by Pedro Camejo, with Attachments," in *Defending the Organizational Principles of a Proletarian Party*, pp. 127–28.

95. Socialist Workers Party, *Leadership Lessons from 1988–90: Defending the Turn and the Party*, Information Bulletin, August 1990, pp. 7–8, 11; Malik Miah and Barry Sheppard, *Where Is the Socialist Workers Party Going?* (Information Bulletin no. 1, published by Milwaukee Revolutionary Socialist Group, n.d.; originally published as a series in *Socialist Action*, June, July, August and October 1990), p. 3.

96. Miah and Sheppard, *Where Is the Socialist Workers Party Going?*, pp. 3–4.

97. Ibid., p. 3.

98. Such possibilities are explored in Paul Le Blanc, "The Current Political Situation in the United States" and Jerry Gordon, "Changes Brewing in the Labor Movement," both in *Bulletin in Defense of Marxism*, December 1991. Also see Fourth Internationalist Tendency, *Revolutionary Internationalism and the Struggle for Socialism in the United States* (New York: FIT, 1991); Kevin Phillips, *The Politics of Rich and Poor, Wealth and the American Electorate in the Reagan Aftermath* (New York: HarperCollins, 1991); and Alan Wolfe, ed., *America at Century's End* (Berkeley: University of California Press, 1991).

99. "More Thoughts on the Party Regime," *Writings of Leon Trotsky, 1936–37*, ed. Naomi Allen and George Breitman (New York: Pathfinder Press, 1978), pp. 476–77.

100. Leon Trotsky, "The New Course," in *The Challenge of the Left Opposition, 1923–25*, ed. Naomi Allen (New York: Pathfinder Press, 1975), pp. 127, 134–35.

5

From the Old Left to the New Left and Beyond: The Legacy and Prospects for Socialism in the United States

ALAN WALD

Crisis of Socialism or of Socialist Movements?

The Left in the United States in the 1990s faces the possibility of near extinction unless it generates fresh perspectives for the construction of an organized socialist movement. The two largest organizations after the social democractic Democratic Socialists of America (DSA)—the Socialist Workers Party (SWP) and Communist Party (CP-USA)— have undergone debilitating splits; the most significant one-time Maoist groups, such as the League of Revolutionary Struggle, Line of March, and Communist Party/Marxist-Leninist (formerly the October League), have formally dissolved. These developments suggest the usefulness of examining the weak and fragmented U.S. revolutionary socialist movement of the post-USSR and post—Gulf War era in relation to its more successful predecessors.

One major predecessor, usually called the "Old Left," became a major political force in the 1930s. This Old Left enjoyed a brief revival immediately after World War II, only to be shattered by external and internal crises during the next decade. The other predecessor is popularly referred to as the "New Left," and it was largely a product of the struggles of the

1960s. Quite heterogeneous, this movement declined in the 1970s following the end of the war in Vietnam.

A debate by contemporary socialist activists over what might be called the "continuity question," entailing the relationship among the Old, New, and Future Lefts, is rendered necessary by the current political situation, nationally and internationally. This discussion of continuity, however, does *not* exist because it is primarily linked to reconsiderations of the definition of socialism itself. Fortunately, the definition of socialism is *not* a matter of debate for those engaged in this discussion who come out of a revolutionary socialist, non-Stalinist, and critical Leninist tradition. Rather, the impetus for such an exchange of views comes mainly from the splintering, practical impotence, inability to consolidate substantial regroupment, and demoralization that attend the Left in all but a handful of countries around the world. In choosing to make this particular distinction, I am arguing that the Left faces less a "crisis" of Marxist and socialist *theory*, and more a "crisis" of Marxist and socialist *movements*. Of course, theory and movements have close relationships.

My approach might be apprehended as a critical extension of the Trotskyist proclamation of the late 1930s, which, regrettably, has by now degenerated into a tired cliché mouthed by most Trotskyist organizations: "The world political situation as a whole is chiefly characterized by a historical crisis of the leadership of the proletariat."[1] For Trotsky and his supporters in 1938, "leadership" *primarily* meant adherence to a political program—the Trotskyist program codified in the "Transitional Program," which remains today a fascinating, relevant, and provocative document.[2]

For revolutionary socialists in the 1990s, however, a "correct program" is a far less simple and less central part of the equation for establishing socialist presence and power in the United States than it apparently was for their predecessors. One has now witnessed five decades in which struggle over a "correct program" has failed to significantly shift the relationship of class forces in the United States. This includes not only the decades of the 1930s and 1940s, when Communists and Trotskyists fought for their programs on very unequal footings. It also covers the post-1956 era, when Trotskyists and other non—Communist Party currents were given a second chance, with a far more equal relationship of forces, to prove that their programs could build a more effective socialist movement. That second era has now ended, and no organization has very much about which to brag in terms of success.

Equally disconcerting, as a focus of internal debate and intraorganizational conflict, the fixation on a correct program has probably been more divisive than productive. Groups that seem to have the same "main enemy"—the bourgeoisie—devoted reams of paper and their most vitriolic language to excoriating each other's programmatic deviations and alleged class betrayals.

One can always, of course, blame all failures of the socialist movement on the *absence* of a correct program and leadership. That takes little imagination, which may be why it has been the routine complaint of a wide range of self-proclaimed vanguard sects. It is certainly difficult for anyone to argue against having *better* programs and *better* leaderships, when one is told that that is what one needs. It is also virtually impossible to deny that any "really existing" leaderships and programs of "really existing" mass parties and revolutionary conquests are exempt from significant criticisms.

However, if program itself really were the alpha and omega of revolutionary politics, we would also see a reasonable number of contemporary successes that are attributable primarily to a revolutionary (specifically Trotskyist) program. Yet the defining events of our epoch—the defeat of fascism in World War II, the wrenching free from U.S. imperial domination of Cuba in 1959 and Vietnam in 1975, the collapse of Stalinism in 1989—cannot be said to have been guided by adherence to a conscious revolutionary program, least of all a Trotskyist one.

The very best that one can say is that such changes "unconsciously" approximated a revolutionary policy, due to the pragmatism of leaders or the press of objective forces, or that such changes would have gone more smoothly and to a better conclusion if the leaders had possessed "the correct program." Regarding the United States, one can at best claim that the independent movements against the Vietnam War, for women's rights, for union democracy, and for self-determination only got as far as they did because of the presence of those fighting for the "correct program."[3]

Although these types of arguments have an important measure of truth—who can deny the importance of learning lessons from the infamous disasters in Indonesia in 1965, in France in 1968, and in Chile in 1973?—they can also promote certain dogmas. Many are ultimately premised on a "we could do better if we were in charge" metaphysic, which easily becomes a direct transit to vanguardism. Still, one should underscore that to decenter the fixation on the search for "the" correct revolutionary program is not at all to obviate the crucial importance of a set of coherent policies. Program is necessary but insufficient.

The corollary that a program must be *realized* through resourceful, experienced, and committed human beings who are effectively organized, and who really have their fingers on the pulse of contemporary political realities, today looms far greater than was allowed by previous theorizations. It is certainly a far more complex matter than simply declaring the need for "correct leadership," defined by adherence to Leninist precedent. It is also more complex than abstract invocations to "follow the rank and file," or to "take one's cue from the masses," or to "institute democracy and more democracy," with which no one can disagree. This is because there is no formula for determining who actually speaks for such heterogeneous entities as "the rank and file" and "the masses." Beyond certain obvious norms, there is no clear measurement for determining what forms are or aren't more "democratic"—unless one equates a "democratic decision" with the victory of one's own viewpoint, which is too frequently the case.

In the 1990s, those who are embracing and extending the revolutionary socialist tradition are talking about fostering an entire *organizational culture* in which the membership (especially those members most silenced in the dominant culture of a society) is fully informed and has the freedom and motivation to shape through democratic structures a policy truly linked to emergent social movements in a way that assists and respects the autonomy of those movements. As the January 1992 Fourth International Executive Committee resolution, "Building the Fourth International Today," explains, unity on the Left is facilitated or blocked not just by formal programmatic positions but by "internal or external practice . . . sectarianism, a rejection of internal democracy, bureaucratic functioning, a rejection of feminism, manipulative practices within the mass movement, the idea of an International sect, etc. For us, all of these points are absolutely decisive."[4]

It is surprising how few of the useful commentaries on program in general, and on the Transitional Program in particular, deal with the nitty-gritty human side of leadership and organizational functioning. Such writings rarely treat, for example, the kind of issues Michael Dover raises in his 1991 *Crossroads* article on "The Roots of Discord on the Left," where he mentions competition for staff positions in the "radical labor market" and lack of turnover among Left political elites.[5]

There is also very little written about the pressures most individuals face when they join a radical group that opposes the dominant culture and the values of most of its citizens. In 1972, Paul Le Blanc published a valuable testament called "Leaving the New Left," in which he describes how he moved from anti-Trotskyism to Trotskyism solely on the basis of studying program and observing practice.[6] Without denying that such things happened, there is evidence that, for a large number of the New Left and the Old Left, the movement recruitment experience was much more like the one described by Todd Gitlin in his book *The Sixties*. He recalls his attendance at the Students for a Democratic Society (SDS) convention at Port Huron as follows: "I was drawn into a circle of energy . . . whose bonds were intellectual and moral, political and sexual at once."[7] People recruit people as much as programs recruit people.

Beyond this, there's virtually nothing in Left historiography that confronts the real problems of ego, arrogance, and self-righteousness involved in radical movements, where outcasts and rebels against the dominant racist, heterosexist, and patriarchal culture seek to establish an alternative way of life. In spite of all our talk about "objectivity" and "science," it is often the case that the more such self-effacing virtues are invoked and egotism is denied, the more egotism may actually be present. Egotism, the will to power, and the simple human need to be recognized, to get attention, and to be valued can also be problems for those claiming to speak on behalf of the oppressed, the disenfranchised, and the silenced—whether in society at large or within Left movements.

It's worth noting how many "interventions" in organizational discussions, and contributions in bulletins, implicitly or explicitly involve a defense of oneself and one's own practice. I don't mean to exempt myself from any of these critical observations, or to suggest that there is a mechanism for purging the will to self-affirmation that so often hides behind the mask of self-abnegating altruism. But I do insist that, as we study the fate of radical as well as most other movements, these all too human traits are a reality that create more havoc by denying them than by acknowledging that they exist.

Perhaps the most insightful material about the realities of building radical movements in the United States consists of the recent studies of the history of American Communism that focus on local practice, such as Robin Kelley's remarkable *Hammer and Hoe* (1990) and a number of the more candid autobiographies of U.S. Communists, such as Al Richmond's *A Long View from the Left* (1972). One can only hope that veterans of Trotskyism and other Left movements will produce similar studies and rich autobiographies. Even today, James P. Cannon's letters and portions of his *History of American Trotskyism* (1944) are still the best personal reflections we have illuminating that tradition.[8]

Several novels about Communist personalities and building Communist movements are also among the richest sources for understanding the human factors involved in movement building—especially Nadine Gordimer's *Burger's Daughter* (1979), with its link between heroic self-sacrifice and emotional toughness; K. B. Gilden's *Between the Hills and the Sea* (1971), whose complex personalities are drawn from different classes and ethnic groups in the radical movement; and Dorothy Doyle's *Journey through Jess* (1990), with its depictions of racial and sexual tensions within a Left party. The Gay Communist Left has recently been explored in Harry Hay's *The Trouble with Harry Hay* (1990), Eric Gordon's *Mark the Music* (1989), and Harold Norse's *Bastard Angel* (1987).

Human dynamics notwithstanding, theoretical considerations, although not all-determining, are clearly of central importance, and the most advanced debates today about organization building are fully cognizant of the problematic nature of "program" itself. Indeed, it is dubious whether there can be a program for global transformation to socialism in a unified, holistic sense, possessed by a group dedicated to its propagation and with the perspective of guiding its implementation. Those in the United States who formed the socialist organization Solidarity (which sponsors the journal *Against the Current*) in 1986 opted for the view that, at the least, what is desired is a *range* of "programs" on many issues (although, clearly, not on all). These must be bound in a restrained, tensive interaction by comrades who recognize that the domination of one program would probably be a Pyrrhic victory—just as a completely heterogeneous mishmash of all political programs, from reformist to ultra-left, would paralyze and ultimately explode us as it did the Socialist Party after World War I or SDS in 1968. A Solidarity leader, David Finkel, put it this way in his article "Solidarity after Six Years": "We propose our method of constructing a revolutionary organization around a set of principles rather than a full 'program' as the best bet for the left today."[9] This is regarded as an important component of what has enabled Solidarity to survive so far, and a key feature to retain if it is to have a future. I'm inclined to agree with Finkel that, although certain aspects of Trotskyism remain vital theoretical conquests, anyone seeking to convert a socialist organization like Solidarity to "a correct revolutionary program" so that it can "win the leadership" of the socialist movement is dragging Solidarity backward to failed strategies, not forward to fresh ones.

The view that I am suggesting here clearly rejects the traditional "Marxist-Leninist" perspective that the problem with the *New* Left is that it was a *departure* from the *Old* Left. This is partly because I think that the debate on the issue of whether the New Left was authentic in its own right, or merely an interlude or a temporary precursor to a return of the earlier forms of radicalism, has already been decided by history. The New Left *was* authentic. One has to realize that, in the post-New Left period, instead of going "back" to what was regarded as a more classic model of radicalization such as that of the 1930s, the radical movement already appears to be moving into a genuine new stage of socialist advance, although, admittedly, at this time it more resembles a "socialist survival" than a new beginning.

The full shape of this new stage is by no means clear, but there are enough distinctive objective conditions to sketch its parameters:

- The collapse of the USSR;
- The high-tech Gulf War slaughter;
- The new political situation in Latin America with the electoral defeat of the Nicaraguan FSLN, the peace accords signed by the El Salvadoran FMLF, the isolation of Cuba, and the development of the Brazilian PT;
- The Los Angeles rebellion;
- The current Supreme Court threat to abortion rights; and
- The impact of the Perot campaign.

Thus we must now, more than ever, incorporate and augment the cluster of theoretical, organizational, and practical experiences that can, for the sake of this overview, be grouped into Old Left and New Left "moments." There are, of course, other ways of categorizing and classifying experiences, and neither the moment of the Old Left nor that of the

New was homogeneous or existed in pristine isolation. Just as political currents descended from Old Left movements (primarily Communist, Trotskyist, and social democratic) continued to be present in the 1960s, so features now considered part of the New Left (especially radical feminism, national identity of oppressed minorities, and an emphasis on community and culture) were somewhat anticipated in earlier decades. Such overlappings and hybrids are further evidence that we are looking at a broad radical tradition from which we must assimilate the most useful components, with necessary augmentations. The usefulness of the terms "Old Left" and "New Left" does not flow from a fundamental identification of all trends influential in the 1930s as opposed to all trends influential in the 1960s. It is preposterous to politically amalgamate Stalinism and Trotskyism. But the Old Left traditions have in common the same referent to the objective conditions in which they came to fruition in a formative way in the 1930s. Something similar can be said for the heterogeneous movements of the 1960s.

Thus, any argument that we are now on the verge of a new stage of radicalism beyond the Old Left and New Left must also start with the conditions that are creating the context for new kinds of radicalisms. That is why we are not hunting for the "true Red revolutionary thread," to which we must then attach ourselves as its latest incarnation, tracing back our lineage to the pure strain at every juncture when "we" allegedly took the "correct position." To accomplish a fresher, broader, and less tedious reconstitution and advance, one needs the freest possible comradely debate, with all shibboleths subject to review. At the same time, one must proceed with a respectful awareness of what our predecessors actually wrote, said, and did, and how others have tried to draw the links. To the extent that one allows oneself to caricature, oversimplify, and wax demagogic, one fails to carry out one's task and dooms oneself to the likely repetition of mistakes.

Moreover, it should be recognized that U.S. radicalism has always had a rather self-conscious and self-critical strand within it, even though it is more known for its blind spots and dogmatisms. There are hundreds of books, articles, and documents, by left-wing scholars as well as militants, that deal precisely with the "continuity problem."[10] Although the quality of such material is uneven, there is nevertheless wisdom to be gleaned if one takes the time to examine it.

A major motivation for this essay is my dismay about the character of a large amount of the recent "rethinking" of the Left. This "rethinking" has mainly been generated in the past few years by the dismantling of the Soviet Union, the Sandinistas' loss in the Nicaraguan elections, the persistence of right-wing ideological and organizational growth in the United States, and the inability of the Left to halt the high-tech massacre of Iraqi civilians in the Gulf War. But much of this so-called rethinking has proceeded as if the present generation was practically the first to confront problems of reform and revolution, democracy and social change, racism within the Left, bureaucratization of the Left, party and state, party and class, the persistence of the national question, the inability of the socialist Left to achieve a national presence, and multiparty versus single-party systems.

Indeed, many of those on the U.S. Left look with hope and support to the recent split from the CP-USA that formed the Committees of Correspondence, regarding their members as talented and devoted comrades with whom they hope to collaborate. Yet it is rather disconcerting that these comrades could generate thousands of pages of discussion bulletins and dozens of articles in *Crossroads*, the *Guardian*, and the *Corresponder* with so little reference back to the crisis of global Communism in 1956. The enormous outpouring of criticism following the Khrushchev revelations produced a wide range of rich material with direct relevance to organizational and political issues under dispute today.

Such an absence of historical awareness is hardly limited to our friends in the Committees, which represent a segment of the traditional Old Left generated by the experience of the Russian Revolution and decisively formed in the 1930s. An analogous lack of historical appreciation is mirrored in the vestiges of the New Left and its Latin American component, evidenced by the May 1992 issue of NACLA's *Report on the Americas*[11]—an entire issue of a journal produced by committed, intelligent, and informed activists, in which the crisis of the socialist movement is surveyed almost exclusively from the vantage of our generation being "the first" to confront these myriad problems.

It is true, of course, that some aspects of the present situation *are* new:

- Socialists do not have a long track record in dealing with issues such as ecology and gay, lesbian, and bisexual rights.

- We are just now beginning to come to grips with Eurocentrism, patriarchy, and many complex aspects of multiculturalism.
- No political tendency came close to predicting the manner in which the Soviet bloc crumbled, and few have come up with adequate responses to the debilitating interethnic nationalism unleashed in the process.
- The current political terrains in El Salvador and South Africa are also in many ways unprecedented.

However, as I have indicated above, many features of the contemporary crisis are quite familiar and were the subject of intense debate by our predecessors. The inability to reconcile new and old, mainly by leaving out the old, is a sign of significant political weakness and causes me to worry about where the current rethinking may actually lead.

To be sure, one is quickly put to sleep by those sectarians who merely pronounce that it has all happened before, and that holy books by Lenin, Trotsky, and Mao have most of the answers. But the unique contribution that revolutionary socialists might make to this debate is to participate in the discussion in the following ways.

First, one should proceed as activists on the front lines of the anti-racist, pro—working class, pro-feminist, anti-homophobic, pro-environmental, antiimperialist, and democratic struggles occurring today. Radicalizing young people of the 1990s seem to take one's "position"— meaning social location—far more seriously than ever before, and the revolutionary socialist "position," regardless of gender, color, or class background, must be on the inside of today's social movements and at one with Third World resistance struggles.

Second, one should proceed as critically informed students of the history of the United States and the world Left, reading with a respectful and unprejudiced eye the writings, and studying the actions, of previous generations of socialists of all colors, genders, sexual orientations, and political tendencies. The method of discrediting a theorist or activist with a simplistic label—such as social democrat, Stalinist, liberal, Maoist, nationalist—to prevent a dispassionate hearing of his or her views is unacceptable. A self-proclaimed "liberal" such as I. F. Stone made a longer-term and more substantial contribution to Left politics than many of his reddest Marxist-Leninist critics of the 1960s and 1970s. In surveying various radical political currents, one must recognize, for example, that there were many Maoisms, just as there were many Trotskyisms. One should not blind oneself to the fact that some Maoist groups carried out certain areas of work more successfully than ourselves, and that their veterans have many things to pass on to us.

Third, one should proceed as a person of the future who accepts the possibility that previous theorizations of social change, social formations, and the idea of progress itself might prove to be profoundly inaccurate. One must be ready to accept the consequences of such eventualities without thereby losing one's bearings and spinning precipitously into despair, cynicism, and apostasy—a characteristic fate of so many of our predecessors.

To the extent that these three postures can be kept in balance—that of the front-line activist, the rigorous and fair-minded student of the past, and the nondoctrinaire visionary of new world realities—revolutionary socialists can move forward into a useful place in the coming socialist struggles of the twenty-first century.

Critical Legacies

What then of our legacies and their critical extensions into the twenty-first century? One should regard the Old and New Lefts not as binary oppositions but in a dialectical synthesis that may help lead to a resolution in the form of a New Socialist Left of the 1990s. As Marxists, one must begin, of course, with the conditions that brought the Old and New Lefts into being; then proceed to lines of continuity and overlap; and finally move to at least a preliminary survey of what is new and what is continuous in the contemporary "moment" of anticapitalist struggle.

The traditional studies of U.S. radicalism accurately present the Old Left as galvanized into action by a combination of national and international political crises—most notably, the stock market collapse of 1929 and the ensuing Great Depression, which occurred while fascism was spreading throughout Europe. The U.S. working class, from the urban centers to rural agricultural areas, was largely unorganized. The university campuses were still mostly (with the exception of those in New York City) elite enclaves. The Russian Revolution and the USSR had gained worldwide authority as the representation of a viable socialist alternative. Thus the Left of the 1930s was a product of its time—centered on the organization of the working class nationally, and focused on the role of both the Soviet Union and the fascist powers internationally.

This scenario does not exclude the existence of significant carryovers to the 1930s from earlier radical traditions. Indeed, all the leaders of the main Left movements in the 1930s were products of radicalizations prior to or at the time of World War I, and the prominent intellectual spokespersons for the Left had been heavily influenced by the Bohemias and expatriatism of the 1920s. The Old Left was therefore a blend of earlier traditions with new objective conditions.

This combination proved adequate to become a significant factor in the 1930s and 1940s, because the major Old Left organization, the Communist Party with its close ties to the USSR, was not yet seen as significantly tarnished, except by the Right wing, which, of course, had been slandering the Bolsheviks since the revolution. It also seemed plausible to many that the crisis conditions of the 1930s were a verification and vindication of the Communists' predictions. The power of that mix of factors simply overwhelmed all political rivals, even though the Trotskyists had gained genuine authority by leading the Minneapolis teamsters strikes in 1934 and had made a distinct mark on New York cultural life through the greater sophistication of the intellectual and cultural critique generated by some of its leaders and supporters.

There were also student movements as well as some autonomous struggles on the part of women and people of color. But the zeal, confidence, vision, and international connections of the Communist movement surpassed and dwarfed all alternatives. Despite twists, turns, contradictions, and scandals such as the Hitler-Stalin Pact, the power of the Communist Party was sufficiently great to reemerge intact after World War II. However, it was not strong enough to do much more than fight a defensive war against the postwar McCarthyite witch-hunt. Whether the power of a strengthened capitalism was too great against the Communists, or whether the party's own mistakes (such as capitulation to Western imperialism during World War II and its cover-ups of Soviet atrocities) are mainly to blame for its weaknesses, is a topic still under debate.

In contrast, the New Left was the product of very different factors. If one traces its political origins to the civil rights, peace, and student movements of the late 1950s and early 1960s, one sees these set in objective conditions of a U.S. economy that was not in crisis (although the "Other America" of millions of poor was indeed a reality) and a world situation characterized not by the rise of reactionary fascism but by progressive anticolonial struggles in Africa, Latin America, and Asia. Moreover, the U.S. working class in the 1960s was now considerably better organized than it had been in the 1930s, although weighted down by a bureaucratized leadership. Significantly, the student population was by now transformed into a much larger and less elite body by the postwar baby boom and capitalism's need for a more educated workforce.

These are some of the key factors determining the social and political character of the New Left. However, also important was the New Left's relation to earlier radical traditions, which was very different from that of the 1930s Old Left to its predecessors. In the early 1960s, the Old Left, although retaining some authority because of its past battles and some status as martyrs during the witch-hunt, was usually regarded as a negative example. The expression "Don't trust anyone over thirty," according to Todd Gitlin's book, The Sixties, was originally coined to warn Free Speech activists on the University of California—Berkeley campus against the influence of the Old Left Communist Party.[12] The Old Left was widely seen as having a dogmatic ideology, authoritarian political structures, a fixation on the USSR, and an insensitivity to individual needs. The working-class base to which it remained oriented was no longer radical, and new sources of rebellion—ghetto Blacks and students—were largely outside its influence.

Moreover, as the African-American struggle escalated to center stage with its angry militancy, autonomy, and pride, its style became infectious and helped shape in important ways the character of other unfolding struggles. These were struggles not only of people of color (Latinos, Asian Americans, and Native Americans) but also of women and, after Stonewall, gays and lesbians.[13] But if the New Left began by defining itself against the Old Left, the relationship became increasingly dialectically intertwined. Certain Old Left traditions and practices began to be regarded with greater interest because of the inability of the New Left to construct a viable organization of its own and to sustain a convincing theory of social transformation.[14]

Organizational impotence and ideological incoherence contributed without doubt to the greatest failures of the New Left. What happened to the New Left as a result constitutes compelling arguments in favor of devoting oneself to groups such as Solidarity and the Fourth International. Although these oppose the self-proclaimed vanguardism of the Old Left, they are far more serious about organization and theory than was the New Left.

As Todd Gitlin notes, the elitism of the Leninist party was replaced in the New Left with de facto elites of other kinds, kinds that didn't even have the staying power of the Leninist party. Even in the case of the totally "self-abnegating style of participatory democracy" promoted by SNCC (Student Nonviolent Coordinating Committee) leader Bob Moses, leadership was not eliminated but "disguised": "The de facto leaders were still influential; followers were swayed willy-nilly. Diffident leaders in disguise couldn't be held accountable, and ended up more manipulative than when they stood up tall, made their authority explicit, presented solid targets."[15]

Moreover, the development of opposition to the Vietnam War as the central protest theme of the 1960s (something the New Left was initially reluctant to recognize) forced the young radicals to think more about relating to broader sectors of the U.S. population, including the working class. The war also raised the question of socialism. After all, the heroic fighters against U.S. domination throughout the colonial world, and not just in Vietnam, tended to be socialists and Marxists of one sort or another. Moreover, many in the militant wing of the Black movement in the United States., from Malcolm X to the Black Panthers, began to call themselves socialist. And almost all attempts by New Leftists to "name the system" ended up in agreement that it was some form of capitalism, to which some form of socialism stood as the main alternative.

Beyond this, the New Left soon found itself competing with vestiges of the Old Left. Although neither the Communists nor the Trotskyists were significant enough to be in on the ground floor of the creation of the New Left nationally, they were present in certain cities, especially Berkeley, where forty-four-year-old Trotskyist Hal Draper significantly influenced the Free Speech movement, and on the East Coast, where middle-aged SWP members played a key role in launching the Fair Play for Cuba Committee.

All Old Left groups were initially marginalized by the spectacular growth of the student movement, and they contributed little to its formation. But by the late 1960s, several tendencies—especially the Communist Party/Young Workers Liberation League, the Socialist Workers Party/Young Socialist Alliance, and the Progressive Labor

Party/Worker Student Alliance—had grown to be formidable alternatives because they had ideological coherence, staying power, and organizational stability.

Due to its heterogeneity and decentralization, the New Left (mainly SDS, which claimed 100,000 members) simply could not compete. Faced with an attempt by the then Maoist Progressive Labor Party to take over the leadership of SDS, some currents of the New Left attempted to mimic international exemplars such as urban guerrillas (by forming Venceremos and Weatherman) or Maoism (by forming the Revolutionary Union and October League). Others drifted eventually to social democracy; most notably, a majority of the New American Movement (NAM) fused with Michael Harrington's Democratic Socialist Organizing Committee (DSOC) to create Democratic Socialists of America (DSA). Although nationalist movements of people of color and the women's movement had their own dynamics, they met a more or less similar fate—breaking up on the shoals of ultra-leftism or gravitating toward reformism.

Yet there was one surprise development almost defying Marxist theory. In a kind of extreme "superstructural lag," the impact of New Left *thought* on U.S. political life seemed to *grow stronger* as the organizations declined. In particular:

- The Vietnam syndrome lasted until the Gulf War of 1990–91.
- The "second wave of feminism" is still a major cultural force.
- Although the leading militant organizations of people of color are gone, ideas of African American pride, Latino/Latina pride, and so on remain strong.
- Despite Reaganism and the reactionary Bush presidency, there have been remarkable shifts in U.S. culture that have enabled, for example, radical and feminist African American writers such as Toni Morrison and Alice Walker to be accepted among the major cultural figures of our time.[16]
- It is also important to note that in some ways the culture of universities is much more radical today than in the 1960s, in that radicals are allowed to teach and present egalitarian perspectives in their classes that were unheard of twenty-five years ago.
- The sensational 1992 exposé of sexual harassment in the U.S. Navy, which was surely just as bad twenty years ago, is another reflection

of the growth of trends unleashed by the New Left upheaval of the 1960s.

- Despite the homophobia unleashed by the Right in reaction to the AIDS epidemic, the gay, lesbian, and bisexual liberation movements are by far more open, proud, and aggressive than they were at the height of the New Left.

Toward a New Socialist Left

What, then, might one speculate about the new stage of radicalism that we now seem to be entering? The political landscape today certainly has its enigmatic features, requiring one to draw more than ever on past lessons and experiences to fathom the route to socialist survival and success. As is so often the case, past expectations and predictions have become realized in unexpected ways. A few examples:

- The Soviet-type societies proved unviable, just as Trotskyists always said they would, and they are now discredited. But this did not, as we also had insisted, come through the struggle of mass working-class movements from below seeking to democratize a nationalized economy.
- Capitalism has failed miserably to abolish racism. Indeed, its failure is of such a magnitude in urban centers, where a huge percentage of African American and Latino youth is being propelled into gangs and prisons and strife between oppressed minorities is intensified, that the antiracist forces seem to have insurmountable obstacles to overcome.
- Most of the Left has now come to understand the crucial importance of socialist pluralism. Yet the first major international effort in that direction resulted in an electoral defeat for the Sandinistas.

All these examples of the "irony" or "cunning" of history (one can select one's term of choice from Deutscher or Hegel) mean that a new socialist Left of the 1990s and the twenty-first century will have to be acutely aware of both the objective conditions that are bringing it into being and its relation to the prior traditions of Old and New Left, if it is to cope with these conundrums. Clearly the economic situation, although not resembling that of 1929, is far more fragile and problematic than in the 1960s. It is hard to disagree with the recent Fourth

International resolution that begins, the "world balance of forces has deteriorated for the working masses."[17]

- The United States is in a terrible economic malaise;
- The working class is less organized than it was thirty years ago;
- The former Soviet bloc societies and the Third World are stagnating it not on the verge of economic catastrophe;
- There is a dangerous resurgence of international competition among capitalist powers—a new kind of economic division of the world seems to be under way among the U.S. "free trade" zone, Europe (led by united Germany), and Japan;[18]
- Openly racist, anti-Semitic, and fascist movements are on the rise in Europe, the former USSR, and the United States; and
- High-tech slaughter has acquired a new legitimacy.

In U.S. civil society, the Los Angeles rebellion graphically illustrates the legitimate anger of the most oppressed sectors of the U.S. population. Yet there seems at the moment to be no way out, except the syndrome of violent rebellion and police repression.

In the realm of the political state, the Perot campaign showed that anger over the bankruptcy of the two-party system is greater than ever, yet the Perot campaign revealed no progressive features, ideologically or organizationally. This suggests that the socialist left is more marginalized than ever in the electoral arena, even as there is greater openness to the idea of candidates outside the twin-party system.[19]

What is hopeful, however, is that much of the national debate objectively concerns precisely the arenas in which U.S. revolutionary socialists are poised to intervene: racism, war, inequality, independent political action, defense of workers' living conditions, defense of women's rights, and preservation of the environment. Moreover, the traditional socialist modes of struggle—independent mass action, the creation of democratically controlled unions and autonomous organizations—remain the best routes to social progress. This situation contrasts dramatically with the greatest failure of socialist theory in the present era: the disrepute into which Marxist ideas have fallen regarding the mechanisms of transferring power in Third World national liberation struggles and surviving the high- and low-intensity hostilities unleashed by class enemies.

There is a vacuum for an organized socialist movement that is the bearer of the best from the socialist legacy, yet structured to be open to what is unique to the struggles of the 1990s. Solidarity is among the few groups that have already contributed to filling that vacuum, and there is a lot more that it can do if it can strengthen itself as an organization. But here one must introduce the complex issue of the "generation gap," hostile tensions between different age groups, which may well become a serious issue as a new radicalization unfolds.

It is true, as the late Trotskyist theoretician George Breitman emphasized in his notable essay "The Current Radicalization Compared to the Past," that "there is always a generation gap. . . . By and large, in every revolutionary upheaval, it's youth and radicals on one side and old people and conservatives on the other."[20] Clearly this generation gap has implications for radicals of one generation: 1960s radicals now in their forties or older, who are entering a period of activity generated by women and men in their teens and twenties who are often on or fresh from the university campus.[21]

The patterns revealed by our past experiences with generation gaps are not conclusive. By and large, the generation gap that confronted the 1930s and 1940s Old Left radicals was not a major source of division; older leaders blended with the young, who more or less respected their elders as veterans. It is significant, however, that many of these older leaders of the 1930s stayed on and on and on, leading their movements into the 1940s and even into the 1950s—for example, William Z. Foster (b. 1881), James P. Cannon (b. 1890), and Norman Thomas (b. 1884).[22] This superlongevity of key leaders reflects a weakness of U.S. radicalism. The most generous interpretation is that the more experienced were forced to stay on longer than they had anticipated, due to a lack of qualified replacements. A more skeptical view would suggest that this phenomenon may also show the corrupting power of leadership, which one becomes reluctant to relinquish once one has it in one's grip.

In contrast, hostility between wings of the generation gap definitely *was* the name of the game in the New Left. The young mostly followed the young. Many New Left leaders were at best just a few years older than the ranks, and not that many stuck it out very long, especially once they were voted out of top posts or staff positions. Moreover, there were features of a generalized youth rebellion that shaped the 1960s generation as one that was more sexually, culturally, and intellectually liberated than their elders. As longtime Communist Gil Green observes in his book *The New Radicalism*, "The youth consciousness produced by the upsurge of the Thirties was not counterposed to the growing class consciousness of the time, but tended to merge with it. Today's [1971] brand of youth consciousness is different. It tends to think of youth as a separate class, even an oppressed class."[23]

Historic Communist, Trotskyist, and Socialist Party leaders did not appear in the streets in their suits with their briefcases to lead any 1960s movements. Farrell Dobbs (b. 1907) and Gus Hall (b. 1910) were not known outside of their respective Old Left milieux. The Old Left party figures who *were* known among the New Left are few: Fred Halstead (b. 1927) was in his thirties when he started playing an important role in the New York City antiwar movement; Angela Davis (b. 1944) was in her early twenties when she became a prominent Black member of the Communist Party on the West Coast in 1968. A few nonaffiliated Old Left activists played significant roles in the antiwar movement: David Dellinger (b. 1915), a pacifist and World War II draft resister; Sidney Lens (b. 1912), a Chicago-based labor organizer and former Trotskyist; and A. J. Muste (b. 1885), a pacifist clergyman who had also passed through the Trotskyist movement.

What is more important is the undeniable role that *children* of the Old Left played in creating the New Left. This is now commonly acknowledged in scholarship and memoirs, although, due to the residual depths of anticommunism in our culture, it is difficult to "name names." These "Red Diaper Babies" of Communist and fellow-traveling families had mostly grown up in the Left culture of the McCarthy era. As Todd Gitlin points out, it wasn't necessary that they become the major organizers and theoreticians of the movements; only that a large number of activists knew such people, were drawn to them, and were influenced by them. Thus the children of the Old Left became the central transmission belt for radical continuity in the formation of and throughout much of the early history of the New Left.

Still, their presence and role did *not* necessarily mean friendlier organizational links to the Old Left, and especially to the Communist Party. Most children of Communists and others active in the New Left were inoculated against orientations toward the CP-USA, although some evolved into Trotskyists. Basically, the Old Left organizations recruited from the New Left by working alongside and demonstrating in practice certain qualities that the New Left lacked: organizational stability, an alternative perspective, staying power, and the ability to create radical institutions where whites and people of color could collaborate in the same organization. The Old Left organizations were not part of, nor did they serve as leadership of, the New Left, although there were some unusual instances in which a very young Angela Davis or a strategically situated Hal Draper or a warm and articulate Fred Halstead had a real impact.[24]

Will there be a generation gap in the new stage of radicalism, and, if so, what will be its form? At the moment, it does not appear that those of us who are over forty-something and sustaining important parts of the organized socialist movement in this difficult interregnum will enter the new era with tremendous authority. We have not built powerful organizations, nor do we have many material achievements. We *have* kept alive an attractive vision and perspective of bottom-up egalitarian, antiracist socialism in the labor movement, on the campuses, in the women's movement, and in academic and intellectual circles. But we have not done much more than that. There is simply no comparison between the legacy of the 1960s generation as it survives today and the legacy of the Communist Party after World War II. Moreover, our credentials are perhaps not even as strong as those of the Trotskyists, both the SWP and the Independent Socialist League (ISL), in the 1950s. They had fought the bloody battles in the 1930s to build the CIO; they had struggled against the imperialist Second World War; they went hammer and tongs against Stalinism when it was a *real* force on the Left; they saw their leaders imprisoned under the Smith Act; and they organized the "Troops Home Now" movement at the close of World War II. Even the intellectual apostates from Trotskyism managed to dominate New York cultural life in the 1950s; and trade union apostates from Trotskyism rose to important positions in the AFL-CIO.

However, our comparatively paltry achievements do not mean that we are a bad lot. Our lesser glories are partly because of the nature of our generation and our times. For all its accomplishments in expanding socialist theory (especially in the areas of race, gender, and culture), our generation of revolutionary Marxists failed miserably at building socialist organizations. We did not lead struggles comparable to building the CIO, although the civil rights, antiwar, and abortion rights movements did have far-reaching consequences. And we did not show an internationalist commitment approaching that of the Abraham Lincoln

Brigade, when close to 3,000 young people volunteered to leave the United States illegally to fight fascism in Spain.[25]

Some of these comparative weaknesses of the 1960s generation may have been due to the class character of 1960s movements; after all, middle-class students had an "out" to live a more individualist life as professionals, or even as "slackers" (from the recent movie by that name), compared with the 1930s generation before the postwar era of relative prosperity.

Part of the explanation may also be the lack of a high degree of fervent belief that allows one to sacrifice one's life; for example, the belief of Communists in the 1930s and 1940s that the Soviet Union was *living proof* of viable socialism. Another cause of the failure, however, was probably the result of objective conditions that did not favor the development of organizations or forms of commitment that parallel the 1930s calibre.

In any event, this outcome of the New Left era, and the decades that followed, puts us in a special bind. Lessons of the past can be more easily lost because their bearers are smaller, weaker, less authoritative; yet, precisely because of the existence of these limitations, lessons of the past are more crucial than ever. Without a collective memory of those lessons, the danger of repetition of errors, and the inability to rectify weaknesses, is very great.

This, of course, suggests that we must find ways to transmit experience that will receive attention. Such a goal must be part of the strengthening of our socialist counterinstitutions, our regroupment and consolidation of far Left activist forces, and our placing a greater priority on reaching young activists and figuring out ways to relate to them.

Clearly, we can expect that many young activists will regard 1960s veterans as "out of it," with comfortable lifestyles, living in a nostalgic world of tall tales about the good old days. On the other hand, veterans of the 1960s who are still on the front lines will no doubt view some novitiates with suspicion, as potential flashes in the pan who won't make a long-term commitment and still be around when their own middle age starts to loom on the horizon.

There is some truth in these mirror images. A survey of existing socialist organizations in the 1990s would probably reveal that young blood is not flowing into positions of responsibility in these organizations. Old "forty-something" blood, despite talk to the contrary, is increasingly tired and doing less in regard to contemporary struggles relating to the young. One also suspects that many 1960s veterans are partially blind to or even snide about crucial features of contemporary youth culture to which they can't relate.

However, in looking to past experiences, as I have tried to do throughout this essay, we can note several factors that may assuage the potential generation gap conflict. One is that organization is necessary; even if new movements start locally or regionally, and with no interest in those who came before, the logic of the situation demands that at some point the existing organized socialists *will* be checked out. Even if we are rebuffed at first, and we may very well be, the best elements will eventually come knocking at our office doors, if only to pick up some of our literature. In this situation, the generation gap issue will be a greater or lesser problem to the extent that we stand apart, or aloof, from the concerns and interests of the young. When the Old Left organizations began to grow in the 1960s, it was not *just* because New Leftists changed and wanted to make a more serious commitment; it was also because some Old Leftist organizations *made considerable changes* in their style, practices, and policies, too. This can be documented by looking at the publications of the Old Left youth groups in the mid and late 1960s.

A second observation is that a cultural divide between the current generations may not necessarily become as wide, and such a site of bitter warfare, as it was in the 1960s. By and large, the tremendous liberalization of the 1960s in personal dress, sexual behavior, and so forth is shared by both generations, despite some relatively minor differences in matters such as musical taste.

A third observation is that there are ways in which the surviving radicals of the 1960s and the more recent recruits to socialism could mesh nicely in what they have to offer each other politically. For example, the 1960s generation was shaped by the Vietnam War, which was initially prosecuted by a Democratic Party administration. As a result, there was more of a recognition of the deceptive nature of the two-party system. In contrast, many radicals of the 1980s were shaped by the experience of Nicaraguan and El Salvadoran revolutionists under seige from a Republican administration. As a result, many of these have yet to cast off their illusions about the Democrats. The 1960s radicals were often disoriented by the Stalinist features of the Vietnamese leadership, whereas the 1980s generation had the benefit of learning more democratic and less sectarian revolutionary practices from some sectors of the Latin American left and, of course, from the collapse of the Soviet model.

A final observation is that it is simply not possible to tell in advance who among the young generation is serious and will remain for the long haul, and who is just passing through. In terms of activist longevity and political reliability, veterans of the 1930s as well as the 1960s have experienced many surprises in the trajectories of their comrades. For this and many other reasons, activists of the 1960s generation must give the benefit of the doubt to the young to the point of enthusiastic support for autonomous youth publications, conferences, and a separate organization when the appropriate time comes. The radicals in this post-New Left stage may not always look like the older radicals, talk like them, or share their tastes in music or food. It has been suggested that the younger activists read less and watch videos more. They may not know about Kronstadt, the workers and farmers government debate, or the falling rate of profit. Indeed, as a recent Fourth International document put it, "We . . . have to grasp the new form of political thinking in the young activist generations . . . where ideological references and above all experiences will have to be largely changed from the past."[26]

Nevertheless, if these young people are in the steets; if they show an internationalist spirit; if they hate racism, sexism, and heterosexism; if they want to build a better world with working people; and if they are willing to "fight the power"—then they should be taken seriously and our doors should be opened wide to them. Neither the experiences of the 1930s nor those of the 1960s show that any established political currents were destroyed or even damaged simply because they overadapted to the young. On the contrary, those who failed or delayed in reaching out to the new generation did so at their own peril. The U.S. Left must listen now, and listen carefully, to the young voices astir in the ghettos and the barrios, on the shop floors, in the communities, in the high schools, and on the university campuses. Nothing less is at stake than the redemption of the revolutionary socialist tradition itself.

Notes

An earlier version of this article was presented as a talk at the August 4–7, 1992, Socialist Summer School sponsored by Solidarity, a U.S. revolutionary socialist organization, in St. Louis, Missouri. I am grateful to participants in the discussion that followed for many insights, and particularly to Patrick Quinn for making a number of editorial and other suggestions on the manuscript. This essay is dedicated to the memory of Celia Stodola Wald (1946–92), my comrade and lover during twenty-five years of activity to build the U.S. socialist movement. An earlier version of this essay was published in *International Marxist Review* 14 (Winter 1992): 85–108.

1. Leon Trotsky, *The Death Agony of Capitalism and the Tasks of the Fourth International* (New York: Pioneer, 1964), p. 5.

2. Some useful discussions of the origin, nature, and relevance of the Transitional Program can be found in Leon Trotsky, *The Transitional Program for Socialist Revolution, with Introductory Essays by Joseph Hansen and George Novack* (New York: Pathfinder, 1973); George Novack, *The Role of the Transitional Program in the Revolutionary Process* (New York: Education for Socialists, 1972); Leon Trotsky, *Discussions with Leon Trotsky on the Transitional Program* (New York: Education for Socialists, 1969); and George Breitman, *The Liberating Influence of the Transitional Program* (New York: Education for Socialists Bulletin, 1974).

3. There is no question that the slogan "Out Now!" played a positive role in unifying the U.S. anti—Vietnam War movement. However, a single united front slogan is hardly the same thing as a political program around which parties unify.

4. "Building the Fourth International Today," *Report on the January 1992 IEC Meeting* (Detroit: Solidarity, 1992), p. 27.

5. Michael A. Dover, "The Roots of Discord on the Left," *Crossroads*, no. 13, September 1991, pp. 23–28.

6. Paul Le Blanc, "Leaving the New Left," *International Socialist Review* 33, no. 10 (November 1972): 18–29.

7. Todd Gitlin, *The Sixties: Years of Hope, Days of Rage* (New York: Bantam, 1987), p. 109.

8. The few scholarly studies to date continue to be weighted heavily toward the "correct position" approach, as in Christopher Z. Hobson and Ronald Tabor's *Trotskyism and the Dilemma of Socialism* (Westport, CT: Greenwood Press, 1988) and A. Belden Fields' *Trotskyism and Maoism: Theory and Practice in France and the United States* (New York: Praeger, 1988). Ben Stone's *Memoirs of a Radical Rank and Filer* (New York: Prometheus Press, 1986) is a good popular history of the Socialist Workers Party. Michael Smith's *Notebook of a Sixties*

Lawyer (New York: Smyrna Press, 1991) contains useful information about the SWP's activities in the 1960s and 1970s.

9.   David Finkel, "Solidarity after Six Years," *Solidarity Discussion Bulletin*, no. 5, July 1992, p. 2.

10. Some of these writings are be referred to in passing in the notes of this essay.

11. "The Latin American Left: A Painful Rebirth, "*Report on the Americas* 25, no. 5 (1992).

12. Gitlin, *The Sixties*, p. 161.

13. In June 1969, New York City police raided the Stonewall Inn, a gay bar, precipitating several nights of rebellion and the formation of the Gay Liberation Front.

14. One of the most compelling critiques of New Left strategy, which describes what might have been done differently, is Tim Wohlforth's "Reflections on the Sixties," *New Left Review* 178 (November–December 1989): 105–23. Another valuable survey of recent studies of the New Left is Maurice Isserman, "The Not-So-Dark and Bloody Ground: New Works on the 1960s," *American Historical Review* (October 1989): 99–110. Several of the many other useful sources putting the New Left in historical perspective are Paul Buhle, *Marxism in the United States* (London: Verso, 1987); Ileana Rodríguez and William L. Rowe, eds., *Marxism and New Left Ideology* (Minneapolis: Marxist Educational Press, 1977); and James Weinstein, *Ambiguous Legacy: The Left in American Politics* (New York: New Viewpoints, 1975). A collection of essays that analyzes the New Left from a social democratic perspective is Irving Howe, ed., *Beyond the New Left* (New York: Horizon Press, 1970). A fresh interpretation appears in the chapter "Reconstructing the Experiment: Political Culture and the American New Left," in Stephen Eric Bronner, *Moments of Decision: Political History and the Crises of Radicalism* (London: Verso, 1992). An impressive collection of scholarly essays is Barbara Tischler, ed., *Sites on the Sixties* (New Brunswick, NJ: Rutgers University Press, 1992).

15. Gitlin, *The Sixties*, p. 149.

16. Of course, it is true that some of the influence of these radical, antiracist, feminist ideas is commercialized and trivialized by the consumerism of our society. But if we live in a consumer society, it is better to have the population consume the lush fruit of Morrison's *Beloved* than the junk food of John Updike's *Couples*.

17. "Building the Fourth International Today," p. 25.

18. See Robert Brenner, "Nature of the Period" and "The New World Disorder: What Is Imperialism Today?" in *Solidarity Discussion Bulletin #1 (April 1992), Pre-Convention Series* (Detroit: Solidarity, 1992), pp. 1–25.

19. See the analysis of the Perot campaign by Steve Ashby in *Against the Current* 40 (September–October 1992).

20. George Breitman, "The Current Radicalization Compared to the Past," in Jack Barnes et al., *Towards an American Socialist Revolution* (New York: Pathfinder, 1971), p. 93.

21.   Of course, we are talking here about relations to major radical upheavals, which is not necessarily determined by chronological age. There are some activitists in their sixties who are just now entering Left politics for the first time, and there is a sizable number in their early thirties who were radicalized in the 1980s and who have been militant for over a decade. Some in this latter group might feel closer to the 1960s movements (especially if they have relatives who were active), and others might feel more a part of the radical movements of the post-1989 period.

22.   Max Shachtman (b. 1904) was significantly younger in the 1930s but still led his tendency up to his death in 1972.

23.   Gil Green, *The New Radicalism: Anarchist or Marxist* (New York: International, 1971), p. 9.

24.   This should probably be qualified in the case of Maoism in the United States, which did have features of Third Period Stalinism even though most Maoist cadres (with the exception of some of the founders of the Progressive Labor Party) did not come from the Old Left. Part of the appeal of Maoism was its association with a Third World country, blending effectively with the intense antiracism of U.S. radicals, and also its association with the Chinese cultural revolution, which was in some cases artificially identifed with the U.S. youth radicalization. Also, Maoism was possibly enhanced by China's geographical proximity to the Vietnamese revolution.

25.   Two thousand of these were killed. The civil rights martyrs Chaney, Schwerner, and Goodman, along with Benjamin Linder, are our closest equivalents to the Lincoln Brigade volunteers, although they were victims of armed violence, not military combatants.

26.   "Building the Fourth International Today," p. 26.

6

The End of "American Trotskyism"? Problems in History and Theory

ALAN WALD

Why should revolutionary socialist political activists in the 1990s be concerned with the history and theory of U.S. Trotskyism? Radical anticapitalist activists today are feminists, opponents of imperialism and Eurocentrism, militant supporters of gay and lesbian rights, committed to ecological transformation, and, in light of the "bad example" set by so many self-proclaimed "Leninist" organizations, skeptical of self-proclaimed vanguards. Why should they give signal attention to the ideas and experiences of those who identified with Trotskyism in the United States? Why not just put Trotskyism on the shelf next to Debsian socialism, anarchism, Black nationalism, Communism, and a variety of other left-wing experiences from which activists can draw upon as it suits their particular needs?

After all, it has been sixty-seven years since James P. Cannon, Max Shachtman, Antoinette Konikow, and other expelled members of the Communist Party of the United States (CP-USA) established the Trotskyist movement in the United States with one hundred people in 1928. Only those who live within a highly circumscribed reality can fail to see that, in a society where winning the support of the majority means the ability to influence millions, the balance sheet of the political accomplishments of Trotskyism after nearly seven decades tends toward the negative. Thus it is fair to raise the question, "Are we now at the *end* of 'American Trotskyism?'"[1] And one should not be astounded if many young activists reply, "Yes, we are."

The Test of Two Eras

For starters, one has the discouraging evidence of the net gains for Trotskyism after having passed through two major eras of political radicalization, the 1930s and the 1960s. In these periods, the Trotskyist movement (a broad term that I'll use for the moment to include all its components), although it grew and made noteworthy contributions, never achieved anything remotely like a sustained organizational or political breakthrough. If one takes an overview or if one assesses the situation from the perspective of long-term gains, Trotskyism never clearly outdistanced rival currents on the political left, particularly those associated with the Communist and social democratic traditions.

Those forces calling themselves Trotskyist in the mid-1990s are not quantitatively stronger in political influence than groups that have shifted away from Trotskyism, such as the Socialist Workers Party (SWP) and Workers World Party (WWP); nor are they stronger than those from the Communist tradition, such as the CP-USA and the Committees of Correspondence (C of C). It is harder to judge the political weight of groups calling themselves Trotskyist in comparison with the Democratic Socialists of America (DSA), especially since the existing Trotskyist groups rarely collaborate and generally consider all the other Trotskyists either hopelessly sectarian or irredeemably opportunist. The combined weight of all such Trotskyist groups, even if one could imagine them working together for a moment or two, is probably no greater than the disparate forces that come out of the Maoist tradition (Line of March, Marxist-Leninist Party, Communist Labor Party, Communist Workers Party, Progressive Labor Party, Revolutionary Communist Party, and so forth).

Only in very limited frameworks of "moments" when a campaign or strike was victorious, or a political strategy appeared to win out, as in the 1934 Minneapolis teamster strikes or the 1960s U.S. anti-Vietnam War movement, can one talk of "Trotskyism's achievements" in the United States as major, although certainly, in addition to these two, there are a few other memorable ones. Yet, at the end of each of these two major radical eras, Trotskyism was not only smaller and less influential than it had been at their height (late 1930s and late 1960s), but it had also produced a new round of bitter splits and intra-Trotskyist recriminations that only further divided and confused the political landscape.

Even more distressing, the first era, the 1930s, may well have produced greater Trotskyist accomplishments than the more recent era, the 1960s; a decrease in achievements also occurred in the pro-Soviet Union Communist movement, the CP-USA. At the very least, we should recognize that, in terms of membership numbers and political authority, forces calling themselves "Trotskyist" in the United States were not significantly stronger at the end of the 1960s-1970s radicalization than they had been decades earlier, at the end of the 1930s-1940s radicalization.[2] If one tries to identify leading figures in this history of U.S. Trotskyism, almost all belong to the generation of the 1930s or earlier, such as James P. Cannon, Max Shachtman, Antoinette Konikow, C. L. R. James, Farrell Dobbs, Hal Draper, George Novack, George Breitman, and Joseph Hansen. How many well-known figures in the trade union movement, the women's movement, the African American or Latino movement, or any other social movement were won to Trotskyism in the 1960s? At best, there are a handful of left-wing unionists and labor educators who came out of the International Socialists (heir to the left-wing Shachtman tradition). Fred Halstead, the only really prominent Trotskyist in the antiwar movement, was won to Trotskyism in the 1940s and was the son of Trotskyists. Although a number of 1960s activists went on to become impressive scholars and professionals, none have at this date achieved the intellectual stature of Sidney Hook, Meyer Schapiro, Irving Howe, Leslie Fiedler, the *Partisan Review* editors, and so forth.[3]

In fact, one might conclude that Trotskyist forces are in greater disarray in the 1990s than they were during the post-World War II labor upsurge of the late 1940s, just prior to the onslaught of the antiradical witch-hunt. At that time, the two major groups, the Socialist Workers Party and the Workers Party, numbered about 2,000 and were leading citywide struggles in major urban centers. The most likely moment comparable to U.S. Trotskyism's present situation might be in the mid to late 1950s, following numerous political crises that depleted the cadre of Trotskyists in the Socialist Workers Party, leaving it with less than 400 members after conflicts about Stalinism, the labor movement,

Hungary, China, Cuba, and the early civil rights movement. At that time, Trotskyism experienced, as it did during the new and perplexing political period of the 1980s, a hemorrhage of splits and expulsions that created the Workers World Party, the Spartacist League, the Workers League, and the Freedom Socialist Party, among others. The Trotskyists in the Independent Socialist League, led by Shachtman, were fractured by Shachtman's turn to the right wing of the Socialist Party. The supporters of the journal *American Socialist*, a former Trotskyist grouping led by Bert Cochran and Harry Braverman, dissolved in 1959. The state capitalist currents led by C. L. R. James and Raya Dunayevskaya were irreconcilably ruptured into rival groupuscules, with *News and Letters* separating from *Correspondence* in 1955.

Of course, one might speculate that the Left is on the verge of yet another 1930s or 1960s type of upheaval and fantasize that the political crises of the last decades have cleared the way for the "true revolutionaries" with the "correct program" and "Leninist" organizational policies to make big gains in the coming epoch. All that would be needed are aggressive "party-building" tactics and promotion of "the historic Trotskyist program," together with some "principled regroupment" with other self-proclaimed Trotskyist organizations to demonstrate "nonsectarianism."

After all, it is certainly true that current economic, political, and cultural trends tend to confirm many of the classic Marxist criticisms of capitalism, portending new social crises. Moreover, the evidence shows that socialism will never be advanced and defended unless its partisans take the step of constructing collaborative organizations to participate in struggles and advance theory. However, several overriding new features must be taken into account before one moves from point A, the coming crises and need for organization, to point B, a revival of Trotskyism that will lead to a breakthrough. Many of these new features of the 1990s have to do with the near disappearance of what Trotskyists have called "Stalinism," that is, bureaucratized postcapitalist or noncapitalist societies. "Stalinism" was a model of socialism for millions, but for Trotskyists, it was a counter-model representing socialism's betrayal.[4]

The historical appeal of Trotskyism in the United States was largely based on its claim to combine what was liberating in the experience of the October Russian Revolution and subsequent similar social transformations with a rejection of what was negative. True, the need for such a distinguishing trait is rather important. Many small groups can accomplish effective political work on a local level, through the talents of devoted activists, even if their worldview is misguided. If one is simply an effective activist in one's community, one can play a positive role and a few people will join one's group—which is why many intelligent and committed activists will continue to join various small leftist organizations whose individual members work alongside and make a favorable impression on them. But to survive and expand in numbers and influence over various politically diverse periods of time, to obtain a national coherency and a kind of "moral authority" extending far beyond one's actual members, a group must fill some plausible space on the political terrain. To some extent, this was historically the case with U.S. Trotskyism, inasmuch as it stood to the left of the reformism of social democracy and was unencumbered by the embarrassing albatross of the Stalinist societies.

So it was a "dual assessment" of the October legacy that distinguished Trotskyist analysis, highlighting the progressive and the reactionary aspects of the process of the Russian Revolution. However, different trends within Trotskyism theorized that dual assessment in different ways when addressing the dynamics of noncapitalist societies. These trends produced analyses that characterized these societies as degenerated workers states, state capitalist states, bureaucratic collectivist states, and so forth, all of which had various interpretations and applications too labyrinthine to adequately recapitulate here.[5]

But now we are faced with the fact that the collapse of Stalinist societies in the Soviet Union and Eastern Europe, coming when it did and in the way that it did, vastly undermines for most people the notion that there is anything positive to be recouped from that experience at all. There are very few signs of nostalgia for the traditions of the October Revolution among those outside of the formerly privileged groups in post-Soviet societies, even though there have been social losses—in areas such as women's rights, job security, and the disappearance of aid, albeit token, to anti-imperialist struggles—that might be regarded by progressive-minded people as unfortunate.[6] That enigmatic Soviet dissident Yevgeny Yevtuskenko summed up the feelings that now exist among many former Soviet citizens for the tradition of October in the poem "Goodbye, Our Red Flag," which he read to an overflow crowd on July 23, 1993, the occasion of his sixtieth birthday:

Goodbye our Red Flag,
You were our brother and our enemy.
You were a soldier's comrade in trenches,
you were the hope of all captive Europe,
But like a Red curtain you concealed behind you
the Gulag
stuffed with frozen dead bodies.
Why did you do it,
our red Flag?[7]

What may be most important is that the collapse of the USSR and Eastern European society did not occur due to the resurgence of progressive forces from within: there were no mass insurgencies based on a positive assessment of the legacy of the Russian Revolution, whether that positive assessment referred to social gains of bottom-up and democratically controlled nationalizations or simply to a memory of working-class power. Instead, masses of people associated the 1917 Revolution with the stultifying bureaucracy that disgusted them. This rejection of the Russian Revolution was the case, even though there were stages in the collapse when the potential for a resurgence of a revolutionary socialist perspective appeared to be about to surface; for example, the manifestations of a drive for workers' power evidenced in the very early days of Polish Solidarnosc, and in the ideas of a few genuine socialist currents extant when the USSR finally collapsed.[8]

The Soviet collapse occurred under the ambiguous rubric of "democracy against authoritarianism." At the same time, there was the Chinese Stalinist regime staving off its own demise through the massacre of dissident students and others. There were also general crises of a different nature in various left-wing movements around the world, as in Nicaragua, El Salvador, and South Africa. But *nowhere* was there anything suggesting a substantial turn in the direction of that Trotskyist "dual assessment." Indeed, Trotsky's name came up only in the USSR, not in China, Central America, or South Africa. Usually this was in the context of a refusal of the Soviet reformers to rehabilitate him; Trotsky's legacy was rejected in favor the lesser figure of Bukharin. No significant current within the USSR or anywhere else took up Trotskyism as a viable alternative, or even as a starting point for a socialist renaissance.

The assessment given by Alex Callinicos, a leading theoretician of the British Socialist Workers Party, at the beginning of his short book

Trotskyism strikes me as quite accurate. According to Callinicos, Trotsky, the person and the historic actor, remains of considerable interest to some scholars and activists because of his stature as a thinker and writer, and because he had the "good fortune to have his life recorded by Isaac Deutscher in what is without doubt one of the outstanding biographies of our time." On the other hand, Trotskyism itself is largely dismissed "as a welter of squabbling sects united as much by their complete irrelevance to the realities of political life as by their endless competition for the mantle of orthodoxy inherited from the prophet."[9]

Beyond this, the vision of socialist transformation represented by the paradigm of the October Revolution clearly has less credibility than was the case for earlier generations of radicals. At the moment, it is unclear what alternative experiences will form the foundation for a new paradigm of socialist revolutions.[10] We may still see in this decade transformative upheavals in semiindustrialized or industrialized countries, which, from the point of view of Marxist abstractions, could have more promise than October 1917. After all, the prospects for anticapitalist revolution in countries such as Brazil are enhanced by the existence of organizations professing to have learned lessons from failures of the past, and of a mass industrial base that was not present in tsarist Russia or, for that matter, in China, Cuba, or Nicaragua. Yet, even if such upheavals occur, one cannot be blindly optimistic. Rather than the achievement of socialism, the consequences could alternatively be the emergence of neocolonialism or an "Allende-like" catastrophe.

Even more disturbing, specifically in regard to the United States, one must now acknowledge that the main explanation for the failure of Trotskyist traditions to make a "breakthrough" back in the 1930s is not applicable to Trotskyism's failures in the 1960s and after. During the 1930s and 1940s, Trotskyism could make no real headway because of the overwhelming political weight of the CP-USA and the unquestioned authority of the Soviet Union as a bulwark against fascism during World War II (the eighteen-month period of the Hitler-Stalin Pact notwithstanding).

The radicalization of the 1960s, however, occurred in a qualitatively new situation. The Trotskyists began that decade with a core of trained militants numbering in the hundreds; the Communist Party had a somewhat demoralized residue of a few thousand. Within a short time, the relationship of forces was roughly equal, with the CP having a stronger apparatus but the Trotskyists (especially the SWP and the International Socialists) seeming to be more youthful in composition. Trotskyist accomplishments in the all-important anti-Vietnam War movement were probably more significant than those of the CP, and, as a result of sending members into industry in the 1960s, Trotskyist cadres were clearly more important than the CP in at least one union, the Teamsters. Still, all Trotskyist groups ended that period with exploding splits instead of a great leap forward—enjoying the same fate as the Communists and Maoists.

Moreover, regarding the crucial role of racism in the United States, the Maoists had a much greater influence on Third World radical currents of the 1960s in the United States than any Trotskyists. Trotskyists operated on a perspective of Black workers constituting the vanguard, and the most effective Trotskyists (the SWP and the International Socialists) held a subtle theory supporting nationalist struggles of the oppressed. But even though the SWP had an early and sophisticated appreciation of Malcolm X, not to mention a friendly relationship with him, it and other Trotskyist groups accomplished far less in recruitment, influence, and leadership of African Americans than even the CP, which was anti-Malcolm X and anti—Black nationalist.[11]

For me, the experience of the 1960s, regarded with the hindsight of over a quarter of a century, closes the discussion on earlier paradigms of Trotskyism as models for leading sustained and national-level emancipatory social struggles in the United States under its own banner. If I'm wrong about this, then one should see the growth in influence and authority of at least *one* of the dozen or so contending organizations that are attempting recreate that older model in various ways, such as Socialist Action, which is based on a Trotskyist strategy that was successful in the 1960s and 1970s (particularly in building the antiwar movement), and the Spartacist League, purporting to reproduce Trotskyist strategy of the 1930s and 1940s (particularly that used to critique Popular Frontism).[12] However, I anticipate that neither can surpass the figure of a thousand members (and I'm probably being generous here) without suffering splits or else undergoing major political and organizational rethinking and restructuring, which would mean possibly falling into the hands of a new and very different kind of leadership. In my view, it is much more likely that activists emerging from Trotskyist experiences can play a more productive role as a well-integrated current (not tendency or faction) within a broader organization of the far left.

In sum, after the experience of the radical era beginning in the 1960s, one can no longer blame Trotskyism's failure as an autonomous tendency simply on the greater material resources of Stalinism. One can, of course, always find other "objective conditions" to blame; for example, one can say that, although Soviet-type Stalinism in the 1960s was not the overwhelming force it once was, the U.S. working class in the 1960s was not the major player it had been in the 1930s or even late 1940s due to postwar prosperity, the bureaucratic stranglehold of the union bureaucracy, and illusions in the Democratic Party. One can declaim that if the working class had been freed of these and therefore at center stage, *then* Trotskyism would have had its day.

Or one can start blaming the leading groups of the time; for example, arguing that if the SWP had not committed this or that "sin" (if it had not built a single-issue antiwar movement, "tail-ended petit bourgeois nationalism and feminism," abandoned the theory of Permanent Revolution—one can fill in one's political "crime of choice" here), then today there would be a "mass Trotskyist party." However, sixty-five years of blaming objective conditions and more successful rival groups for such meager results[13] is an explanation that should be pretty hard for rational individuals to swallow. Naturally, "objective conditions" must be assessed, and there is no question that the *entire* Left is organizationally, if not also politically, in crisis, so we are not talking about a defect unique to Trotskyism.[14] But the canonical means that Trotskyism has historically employed to overcome difficult objective conditions now appear to have exhausted themselves. So, for me, the discussion now shifts to what elements within the Trotskyist tradition may be retained as components of the contemporary struggle. Which ones need to be revamped? Which ones need to be rejected? How important are any of these in relation to the legacy of other radical traditions, or to the newest lessons to be drawn from emancipatory struggles of the present?

Trotskyism in Perspective

In my view, there are many important elements that warrant retention, but the overriding issue is how to theorize them. For example, the 1930s experiences of Minneapolis and the 1960s experience of the antiwar movement are the most memorable. But there are also other recuperable episodes, such as James P. Cannon's World War II political strategy,[15] the Workers Party's fight against the No Strike Pledge, the theoretical work of C. L. R. James and George Breitman on Black nationalism, Hal Draper's "socialism from below" concept, and perhaps the Independent Socialist League's economic analysis of the Permanent War Economy. Although these achievements are insufficient as a foundation, condemning any movement to continuing isolation if made its centerpiece, they can be powerful contributions to some larger project. For the latter to happen, one must do the necessary housecleaning; one must think seriously about the problematical features of the legacy, not simply repeat mythologies created to justify different Trotskyist traditions from one generation to the next.

Unfortunately, no clear answers to any of the most difficult questions about this legacy are available. This is because, for all the internal debating and document writing within U. S. Trotskyist organizations on conjunctural issues, surprisingly little serious research or even creative thought has been applied to the broader concerns. For example, despite the fact that the one arena in which Trotskyists might hope to have a claim to future radical activities is the labor movement, very little detailed and circumspectual information exists in readily available form about the past experience:

- There is Art Preis's *Labor's Giant Step* (1964), which had some influence among New Left writers in the 1960s, and Farrell Dobbs's four volumes—*Teamster Rebellion* (1972), *Teamster Power* (1973), *Teamster Politics* (1975), and *Teamster Bureaucracy* (1977)—which have been ignored by recent scholars.[16]
- There is one quarter century-old dissertation on the Minneapolis strikes, "The Labor Movement in Minneapolis in the 1930s" (University of Minnesota, 1970) by George Tselos, which was never published and is rarely cited.
- There is some brief mention of Trotskyists in Martin Glaberman's *War-Time Strikes* (1980), David Milton's *Politics of U.S. Labor* (1982), and Nelson Lichtenstein's *Labor's War at Home* (1982).
- There are a number of essays and books that provide Trotskyist and semi-Trotskyist perspectives on episodes in U.S. labor history, but for the most part, there are no detailed descriptions of what real female and male Trotskyists actually did in specific situations.[17] Among such authors, who vary considerably in the degree and kind of "Trotskyism" that shapes their outlooks (and who may

well have adopted dramatically different political perspectives by now), one might include Steve Briar, Paul Buhle, Charles Capper, Bert Cochran, Mike Davis, Michael Goldfield, Tom Kerry, Dan LaBotz, Bruce Levine, George Lipsitz, Frank Lovell, Staughton Lynd, Kim Moody, George Rawick, David Roediger, Stan Weir, and Seth Wigderson, among others.

Yet the area of labor scholarship, which is characterized mainly by evidencing the impact of Trotskyist analysis and a minimal representation of Trotskyist practice, is probably the high point of research on U.S. Trotskyism. For example, although there has been a major advance with Peter Drucker's fine political biography of Max Shachtman, *Max Shachtman and His Left: A Socialist Odyssey through the "American Century"* (1994), the general histories of U.S. Trotskyism are almost universally marred by a corrupting kind of partisanship. Obviously a clear point of view is necessary for such a project, but too often the political hobbyhorse of the author drives out two crucial elements.[18] One such element is the need for rich and multifaceted primary research, since a political movement is not just words on paper but lived experiences in meetings, on shop floors, and in personal life. Another is an elementary good-faith effort to reproduce fairly other points of view before smashing them on behalf of views reflecting one's own partisan allegiances. Refuting a caricature is, to say the least, a Pyrrhic victory, useful mainly for bolstering the morale of one's own small circle.

Obviously, extreme partisanship and a priority on proving one's own faction's "correctness" may be expected, and perhaps even desired, in works published by party presses and authored by party leaders, such as James P. Cannon's *History of American Trotskyism* (1944) and Tim Wohlforth's *The Struggle for Marxism in the United States* (1971), or even in the memoirs of rank-and-file activists loyal to one group or another, such as Ben Stone's very useful *Memoirs of a Radical Rank and Filer* (1986). But works of a scholarly, historical, or theoretical character aimed at a broader audience should be held to a higher standard. Alex Callinicos's book *Trotskyism*, focusing mainly on the United States and England, gets off to a promising start, worthy of the considerable abilities and admirable political commitment of its author. Within a short time, however, a large number of important issues are treated through the prism of British Socialist Workers Party leader Tony Cliff's version of state capitalism. Most of the important rivals to Cliff are depicted as near idiots (or, at best, like Max Shachtman and Ernest Mandel, praised as slick debaters), whereas Cliff, an important figure to be sure, is portrayed as never having made a political blunder in his life.[19] Christopher Z. Hobson and Ronald Tabor state in the introduction to their massive *Trotskyism and the Dilemma of Socialism* that the work was intended to be a history of the Trotskyist movement with only a "relatively brief discussion of the Trotskyist movement's mistaken position on Russia." In the end, however, the authors discovered that they had devoted "nearly half the book" to castigating all other Trotskyists for their failure to understand the authors' view of state capitalism![20]

In my opinion, the tendency to study Trotskyism mainly by filtering everything through a "line" (usually on "the Russian question") to which one had a previous loyalty is partly due to the previously discussed problem of so much of Trotskyism's validity depending on its relation to the model of the Russian Revolution. But narrow "line evaluation" is also the mode of thought predominating for another reason: it is easier to resort to ideological hair-splitting based on documents, polemics, and periodicals (often spiced at crucial points with unverifiable personal "horror stories") than to confront in a fair and sympathetic manner the ambiguities of lived experience. Thus, when Hobson and Tabor mention in passing issues that might be rich with lessons for subsequent generations of radicals—for example, the 1939 "auto crisis" in the Trotskyist movement, which reveals early on the difficulty of navigating between anti-Stalinism and reaction; or race relations in the SWP during the 1940s, when hundreds of Black proletarians joined the organization—they present one-sided smears of the Socialist Workers Party.

It is also unfortunate that the biographical component of Trotskyist historiography is so weak. No biography of Cannon has been written,[21] and the sustained essays that exist, such as the recent one by the Spartacist League's Prometheus Research Library that introduces *James P. Cannon and the Early Years of American Communism: Selected Writings and Speeches, 1920–1928* (1992), tend to omit references to aspects that complicate their one-dimensional portrait.[22] It is also regrettable that, at this late date, there is no serious study of Trotskyist women in the United States—even though, until recently, several rather crucial figures, such as Raya Dunayevskaya and Grace Carlson, were living and available to assist, and other leaders such as Myra Tanner, Dorothy Schultz, and Genora Dollinger are alive yet.[23] The work on African American Trotskyists is only slightly better, thanks to the efforts of George Breitman and the international fame of C. L. R. James. Still, there is very little on Ernest Rice McKinney, other than Dianne Feeley's mostly unpublished research on the unemployed movement, or on Edgar Keemer, other than his own autobiography; and there is almost nothing on other important African American Trotskyist women and men.[24]

Although I have devoted efforts to literary Trotskyists, the cultural field offers many other possibilities—such as the composers George Perl and Noah Greenberg and the artists Laura Slobe (Laura Gray) and Jesse Cohen (Carlo). The 1993 obituary for Vincent Copeland in the *New York Times* may have surprised many with its discussion of Copeland's acting career.[25] Local studies of Trotskyist political activities—in Chicago (where there were several major antiracist campaigns), San Francisco, Los Angeles, Detroit, and elsewhere—are virtually nil, although, fortunately, historian Bruce Nelson (who comes from a different political tradition rather than from Trotskyism) is now writing about Trotskyist steelworkers in Youngstown.[26]

There are no studies of gay and lesbian Trotskyists. The gay, one-time Trotskyist leader Tom Stamm was interviewed only by Robert Alexander, and exclusively on the French Turn dispute. The discussions some of us held with Phil Clark, a gay rank-and-filer and occasional branch organizer of the SWP in the 1940s, before his death were never tape-recorded or properly authenticated, and the participants now disagree about what he said.[27] Hence, the information available remains highly contradictory, although it is still possible for more detailed research to be pursued. In 1985 I corresponded with George Breitman in regard to homosexuality in the SWP. Breitman insisted that he never heard any deliberations about any aspects of sexual orientation among the leadership on the National Committee or in the National Office until the 1960s, although it is possible that he was simply ignorant of such discussions. Moreover, he recalled that during the time he served as branch organizer in Newark during the 1930s and 1940s, no one ever suggested to him that homosexuals should be prohibited from joining, and he is certain that homosexuals were active in the membership and leadership of the branch. In his recollection, the argument that homosexuals might be blackmailed by the FBI during the witch-hunt was never raised until the 1960s. Although he had heard, after he joined, that Tom Stamm was gay and had taken a leave of absence for a while, he was skeptical of Clark's memory that Novack, on behalf of the Political Committee, had urged Clark to leave the SWP until he had been "cured" by a Freudian therapist.[28] On the other hand, Frank Fried, a onetime Chicago activist in the SWP, is certain that a number of female party members working in the packinghouses were forced out in the post—World War II period, around 1947, for lesbianism.[29]

With the signal exception of Tim Wohlforth's warm and lively *The Prophet's Children: Travels on the American Left* (1994), Trotskyist autobiographies are both thin and sparse compared with those of former Communists.[30] Neither Cannon's written nor Shachtman's oral histories are particularly searching, and they are certainly not very self-critical in light of the major problems of the movement.[31] Albert Glotzer's *Trotsky: Memoir and Critique* (1989) too rapidly abandons the memoir component in order to reiterate the familiar argument that Leninism led to Stalinism.[32] Irving Howe's autobiography, *A Margin of Hope*, is more wide-ranging, but it remains an "intellectual" memoir to the extent that political practice, personal revelation, and scholarly documentation are all given short shrift.

In sum, virtually all the exciting research that has been applied to the Communist movement in recent decades has bypassed the Trotskyists. Hence it is now possible to give fuller and more serious answers to questions about the Communist tradition than the Trotskyist one.[33] Given this limitation, my purpose in the remainder of this essay is to raise questions that might be topics for research if their importance can be established, and to provide what light I can based on what is known at present.

Defining Trotskyism

One of the key problems in the theory and history of U.S. Trotskyism is the definition of Trotskyism itself. This problem immediately underscores the need for an analytical method based on perspectives and approaches, not absolutes and blueprints. It is, I think, fair and plausible to include within Trotskyism all those who declare themselves Trotskyists and exclude those who deny any such allegiance. Nevertheless, accepting any and all self-definitions is problematic, since some self-proclaimed Trotskyists are regarded by others as palpably fraudulent, and some groups refusing a Trotskyist identity have political views similar to Trotskyism. Thus, the "open-door" policy of determining who is and isn't

"Trotskyist," although it may be the only option, can force a discussion of Trotskyism into all sorts of byways and, necessarily, often into the very debates that have made it appear sectarian, ingrown, and cultist.

Yet a constructive 1990s discussion of Trotskyism, although it has an obligation to deal critically with sectarian offshoots that may well have done more harm than good to Trotskyism's legacy, has to keep its primary focus on the recoupable segments. One or another of the little groups that may be traced back to Trotskyist origins or that may consider itself the only "true Trotskyist" current may have produced an impressive analysis of this or that conjunctural event, or led a significant struggle here or there. However, in the end, one has to come back to the question of "impact" to determine one's priorities for focusing one's energies—the same question of "impact" that relegates Trotskyism as a whole to a vital element, but not the epicenter, of U.S. left-wing politics.

This issue of trying to define Trotskyism also raises the problem of explaining why there have been so many schisms and divisions in the U.S. Trotskyist movement, which parallels, although perhaps in more intensive form, the experience of the Left as a whole. The unfortunate result, as we all know, is that there now exists a plethora of different socialist and communist groups and grouplets, most of which are extremely hostile to one another. Many newly radicalizing students and workers can hardly tell the difference among the groups. Thus quite a few would-be socialists become perplexed if not discouraged by the state of disorganization on the part of the so-called organized Left. At the very least, this proliferation confuses the nonsocialist public as to the meaning of the word "socialism," let alone "Trotskyism." At worst, these divisions set the Left against itself precisely when it needs to unify against common enemies of racism, sexism, imperialism, and the exploitation of labor and the environment. Yet one finds that the subject of schisms on the Trotskyist Left is one that is rarely, if ever, treated with the seriousness, subtlety, and sophistication it deserves.

Most often, intra-Left feuding and the creation of what seems to be an endless list of new self-proclaimed vanguard parties bearing pretentious and redundant names and initials give rise to ridicule and cynicism on the part of those who either have abandoned or never took to heart a commitment to build a socialist movement. On the other hand, for those who are immersed in the difficult task of building socialist organizations, the subject is so complex, and the issues so volatile, that it is difficult to present an analysis with any semblance of objectivity or that at least achieves the simulacrum of a dispassionate statement of the two, three, ten, twenty, or fifty different positions that can and have emerged over this or that controversial political event.

Still, one has to say that, although one desires unity on the Left and has a vision of a broad, nonsectarian, internally democratic, multitendency, revolutionary socialist organization, it is pretty obvious that some of the divisions that have occurred on the U.S. Left have been necessary and important. To some degree, these divisions are the same divisions that have occurred within the international socialist movement of the last 150 years or so, and they reflect real differentiations in strategy, tactics, and even morality that cannot be overcome simply by goodwill. Here I am referring to the famous disputes between Marxism and anarchism, Marxism and revisionism (of the Bernstein type), bolshevism and menshevism, internationalism and social patriotism, workers democracy and bourgeois democracy, and Trotskyism and Stalinism.

Differences in these categories can be so momentous, can touch on such fundamental questions relating to the strategy and the very nature of social transformation, that I don't see how any "tactfulness," no matter how artful, or how any "conciliationism," no matter how magnanimous, can in the long run prevent differences of this order from erupting and necessitating a parting of ways. After all, if an interimperialist war breaks out and one faction in an organization wants to support "its" country's war and the other faction takes an internationalist position of urging all workers to refuse to fight, these factions cannot coexist in the same organization.

Likewise, there have been situations such as the war in Vietnam, where the French social democracy and later the U.S. social democracy refused to demand the complete withdrawal of the imperialist troops from the colonial country, and the revolutionary Left demanded "out now" and supported the right of the Vietnamese to self-determination. These are incompatible positions of historic magnitude. Such divisions occur not only in wartime; there have been relatively small strikes, such as the famous Ocean Hill-Brownsville teachers' strike of 1968, where different radical groups were on opposite sides of the picket lines: some supporting the union, and others supporting the Black community.[34]

Schisms of this character are subjects for highly detailed study; they are, in fact, the classroom for learning the "ins and outs" of politics. They should not be cause for dismay or demoralization in the sense that they

at least lend themselves to rational analysis, to the potential assimilation of certain methodological principles that ought to help prevent a
repetition. These are real and clear-cut distinctions. They are the kinds
of differences that resulted at certain past moments in the formation
of Communist parties, Socialist parties, Trotskyist parties, Leninist and
non-Leninist parties, and so on.

At the other extreme, and far more troubling, are splits and schisms
that seem less explicable. For example, there might be two Trotskyist
or Maoist factions of the same party that adhere to the same body of
theory yet go to war with each other over some passage in a document
that might seem obscure to the uninitiated. One faction ends up expelling the other, and perhaps even goes so far as to denounce the other as
counterrevolutionary. Here, there might be all sorts of possible explana-
tions. There could be genuine differences in the assessment of this or
that event, although the question remains why that should necessitate
such a brutal schism. Why shouldn't a socialist organization be broad
enough to contain a variety of opinions, with the factions and tendencies learning from one another?[35] Why not let the test of time resolve
such episodic controversies as long as there is agreement on the larger
questions? Clearly this is a reasonable perspective so long as one is not in
the situation of coping with provocations by police agents or a wrecking
operation by some external political group that has sent in or recruited
agents bent on destroying one's organization.

Yet one also has to be careful about relying on platitudes about
democracy and programmatic agreement that are likely to be violated the
moment one is faced with a real-life situation. The truth is that sometimes the kinds of schisms described above are going to occur whether or
not they are objectively justified. They may reflect internal power struggles for leadership of an organization, or severe personality conflicts, or
fits of subjectivity induced by conditions in the outside world. People
with socialist dreams still live in the same world as everyone else and are
subject to the same weaknesses as everyone else. Or an internal struggle that seems cryptic could actually be symptomatic of one faction or
another drifting in the direction of one of those historic dividing lines
that seem to necessitate separate organizations—that have always caused
a parting of ways, internationally and repeatedly, for a century and a half.

The list of schism-causing issues since the 1930s is unbelievably
long. There have been disagreements over the relationship of workers

to farmers; whether to work in existing trade unions or create new, revolutionary unions; whether to work within, without, or inside/outside the Democratic Party; whether to work with or against the trade union bureaucracy; whether to support or oppose the nationalism of oppressed minorities or condemn all forms of nationalism. Other debates occurred over the relation of politics to artistic and cultural work and the relation of socialism to feminism.

Moreover, it is necessary to realize that questions and disputes such as these have been played out against the very complicated social formation of the United States. Indeed, since the time of Marx and Engels a debate has raged over why the United States, with what appears to be the purest form of capitalism, has produced a working-class movement with a remarkably low level of socialist class consciousness in comparison not only to other advanced industrial societies but even to numerous dominated Third World nations. This debate has been recreated in many famous essays with variations of the title, "Why No Socialism in America?", which means, why have socialist class consciousness and mass organization been so limited? This could give a U.S.-specific framework to certain controversies, especially those around the most effective approach to the Democratic Party and to nationalist movements of people of color.

Such complications notwithstanding, the question remains, why are there so many splits, and what can be done about them? This cannot be answered by any formula and least of all by platitudes, pro-"pluralism" of all views, or pro-programmatic agreement. Formal guarantees of democratic rights and procedures for resolving disputes are absolutely essential, yet no one should have the illusion that these cannot be readily twisted, reworked, and refunctioned by majorities as well as minorities to justify almost any desired behavior. The answer will come only through studying examples and concrete experiences from all angles and, of course, through one's own engagements in analogous situations in the 1990s and after. No formula exists to protect socialists a priori from complex and painful developments. One can, however, seek to foster a long-term commitment to constructing a serious and democratic organization through collaboration with diverse individuals who are all pledged to a kind of collective political life, through which individuality is realized with, not against or apart from, one's cothinkers.

The big question nonetheless remains: can Trotskyism play a uniquely dynamic role in a current reconstitution of a revolutionary socialist

Left? The answer, I feel, will not be found in doctrine, by which I mean adherence to labels, programs, slogans, or theory. As with organizational "rights," the record now shows that all these can be interpreted far too variously. The answer can lie only in method. We have to go back and review the epistemological issues raised in Georg Lukács's famous essay that opens *History and Class Consciousness*, "What Is Orthodox Marxism?"[36] Lukács claimed that the essence of Marxism was method; Leninists, such as the Trotskyist George Novack, intelligently observed that a method that can exist for long periods of time without producing valid "programmatic conquests" must be highly suspect. Therefore, Marxism must be more than a method and embrace specific conclusions on historical experiences and political policy as well.[37]

By mid-1995, however, we can see for ourselves that reliance on the more specific kinds of "programmatic conquests" is also highly problematical, even if the more general propositions about class struggle seem to be confirmed over and over again.[38] Once a passage in a programmatic document begins to be applied in practice, all hell breaks loose. There are just too many divergent assessments of that application to enable socialists to crow about "programmatic conquests" with any certainty. The application of the "united front tactic" in the opinion of one Trotskyist is nothing but "slimey Popular Frontism" in the opinion of another; the defense of the principle of self-determination to one is merely "tail-ending petit bourgeois nationalism" to another, and so forth.[39] As a consequence, although not eschewing program entirely, we most return again to method—method as inseparable from program.

Method and Political Action

From this point of view, there are methodological aspects of Trotskyism that the twenty-five years since the height of "the sixties" have shown to be still necessary and valid. To be precise: in the 1960s, there was at the outset a salutary repudiation among New Left activists of both a pro-Stalinism that had illusions about the USSR and the so-called and-Stalinist Left that saw imperialism (euphemistically labeled the "free world") as the lesser evil to "Red totalitarianism." But this trend of thinking in the New Left was not based on the Trotskyist method of starting from the objective interests of the working class, regardless of the class's alleged relation to the state or any party ruling in its name.

In fact, the New Left's superficial rejection of Stalinism in the form of the USSR actually led many to a worship of Maoism, uncritical Castroism, and other trends that later brought sharp disillusionment and great losses. Trotskyism in the 1990s could contribute to correcting such errors in regard to future revolutionary developments in the Third World. In fact, some socialist activists from the Trotskyist tradition have already set a good example through their approaches to the Nicaraguan revolution and the El Salvadoran struggle, and they may make other contributions if they treat in a nondogmatic way the complex situations in South Africa, Haiti, and elsewhere.[40]

Still, so far as the United States is concerned, Trotskyism must be rejected as an autarkic revolutionary movement projecting its own hegemonic leadership, even with lip service to routine (although necessary) expressions such as, "of course, we don't have *all* the answers" (which usually means that we think we have *most* of them). Trotskyism in the United States has been proved too often to be an insufficient worldview, leading mainly to smug little groups that are more like extended families, splitting apart in bitter family quarrels.[41] A diverse and flexible revolutionary socialist group is quite an anomaly in the history of the U.S. Left in general and Trotskyism in particular; in fact, it is precisely this kind of group that the majority of self-proclaimed Trotskyists hate (as "soft," a "swamp"), define themselves against, and want to see destroyed in order to justify their own vanguardist existence.

If one's objective is to achieve a socialist movement with authority, based on real analytical cogency and power expressive of working-class agency, the pantheon of Trotskyist thinkers and "Great moments in Trotskyism" must not stand apart from or even above the rest of the Left. Despite the extraordinary talents and contributions at various times of Cannon, Shachtman, Dobbs, Draper, and C. L. R. James, no Trotskyist leaders can credibly be seen as "the" guiding lights of organizational strategy, political theory, and philosophy. Yet, within a broader context, many of the historic Trotskyist cadres can be appreciated as vital, stimulating, and serious contributors.

This issue is somewhat related to the famous charge of "Trotskyist sectarianism," a charge leveled frequently at Trotskyism by its various critics, although just as frequently by some Trotskyists against others. The charge is difficult to evaluate because, as my preceding analysis indicates, I think that there *is* considerable truth to it, but opinions vary markedly as to where the borders of sectarian behavior lie. From my experience, liberals and social democrats are quite capable of sectarian behavior equal to that of revolutionary Marxists, *Dissent* magazine being a good example in its hostile attitude and unfair caricaturing of almost everything to its Left. Moreover, it is possible to have very sectarian politics presented in a nonsectarian manner,[42] and nonsectarian views presented shrilly and aggressively.[43]

Nevertheless, Trotskyism has appeared to many people to be a politics largely devoted to criticizing the Communist and social democratic traditions for "betrayal." And this seems a rather preposterous if not counterproductive stance, not because Stalinism is what anyone wants, but due to Trotskyism's own comparatively poor showing in terms of practical achievements.[44] Moreover, a turn from the dogmas of Stalinism to the various theories of state capitalism, degenerated workers statism, and bureaucratic collectivism is unlikely to be the dominant trend we will see among the new generation of socialist activists.[45]

In truth, although the more sectarian Trotskyists get attention (including, sometimes, greater media notice due to their propensity to differentiate themselves from the rest of the Left), there are many other Trotskyists who work wholeheartedly for reform as a way of raising political consciousness and strengthening the positions of subaltern groups. But even this nonsectarian approach seems insincere to many independent radicals, because most Trotskyists regard only a tiny number of people—usually their group and affiliated organizations, and certain select movements from the past—as genuinely "revolutionary."[46] To be genuinely "revolutionary" means to adhere to particular policies (not just statements on paper, but interpretations of such statements), although the term "revolutionaries in action" is sometimes used for individuals who, without full political consciousness, nevertheless take action that is compatible with the theory. This latter label, however, seems to apply only so long as someone is committing certain positive acts, and it can quickly be rescinded when the actions are interpreted differently.

In any event, it is a dubious schema to regard someone selling a revolutionary newspaper at Columbia University or collecting membership dues in a downtown Los Angeles party headquarters as a bona fide revolutionary socialist, whereas a peasant occupying land in Latin America with the Bible as a guide may at best be considered a revolutionary in action if his or her struggle happens to provoke a crisis of the state that leads to a struggle for power. In my view, rather than operating with a category of revolutionary essence, it should be recognized that all individuals and groups have multiple aspects and identities as they evolve and contexts shift.

Again, the argument is not that it is impossible or undesirable to distinguish revolutionary from reformist theory or action. However, such a task is much harder to, carry out than it appears to those Trotskyists who spend so much of their time putting other groups and individuals into "boxes" (that is, liberal, reformist, centrist, revolutionary in action, and revolutionary) when the borders are always shifting. A group or individual may share features of several of these labels at once, or else be a "revolutionary" with zero impact on the class struggle or a "liberal" such as Martin Luther King who is a galvanizing force for social advancement.

Revolutionary socialists in the United States always have been and apparently always will be faced with problematic leaderships at the head of worthy struggles in far-off countries, whether the Sandinistas in Nicaragua, the African National Congress in South Africa, the Lavalas movement in Haiti, or the Cuban Communist Party. The approach of comparing these leaderships with mythical "true Bolshevik-Leninist parties" and then decrying them as bankrupt and treacherous is hardly more useful than uncritical adulation. In a way, both attitudes mirror each other by being based on simplistic premises.

The methodological objective required is one that obtains a balance between skepticism about political claims and sufficient belief in the possibility of amelioration to act in genuine solidarity.[47] My understanding of the history of the Left exempts no leaders from manifesting traits that are contradictory, including Lenin and Trotsky. Certain individuals appear at times to point the way: women and men who act as leaders in a community or in a factory. Yet, invariably, even the most extraordinary individual leaders eventually come up against real inadequacies in their capacity to lead, to understand, and to commit resources. The goal of socialist political cadres must be the development of a broad and democratically functioning team leadership, based on an organization's institutionalizing multiple tendencies and pluralism, that balances out strengths and weaknesses in order to sustain a movement diachronically as well as synchronically.

A big problem, of course, is that in an "individualist" culture, such as holds sway in advanced capitalist countries like the United States, very few individuals who achieve recognition for leadership talents are willing to subordinate their egos to a team, which has implications for revolutionary practice as well as for other activities. They desire recognition, gratification, and admiration, even if they are not directly motivated by monetary gains. Like many medical doctors who believe that years of grueling self-sacrifice in medical school entitles them to subsequent years of living well, not a few revolutionaries who have made genuine sacrifices for a cause will, after a period of time, think that this entitles them to various kinds of privileges. If removed from a national leadership body or an area of work where they have established a satisfying role for themselves, such individuals may, after a period of apparent acquiescence, suddenly undergo a kind of conversion and come up with a series of exaggerated political complaints against the organization—very often ones that are similar to those held by others who were driven out of the organization previously. Then, if those now making the complaints fail to win a majority, the organization is declared "undemocratic," even though it was regarded as "the most democratic in the world" just a few years earlier, when the individuals now in opposition were part of the majority.

Surely one of the most tragic features of the history of U.S. Trotskyism is the inability of individuals, who were once comfortable in an organization and then on the "outs," to recognize problems in theory, practice, and organization until "one's own ox is gored." Like those former Communists who believe that anyone who left the Communist Party by a certain date (usually when they themselves left) is all right, but those who remained afterwards are total dupes, many Trotskyists also put a "date" on the degeneration of the group from which they have broken. In most cases, this date roughly approximates the time that they were deposed, although some go too far the other way and write off the entire movement from start to finish. These responses reflect all-too-human traits that recur so frequently that they must be acknowledged and addressed; efforts to ignore, deny, or simply denounce them have proved inadequate.

The more one critically reads the oral histories and autobiographies of Trotskyist activists that do exist, mostly in unpublished form,[48] the more one sees that a crucial factor in many splits and disaffections has been the blockage of an individual's rise to a full-time leadership position. True, most political differences are real and are even necessary for hammering out a political orientation. Yet the transformation of a difference into the accusation of betrayal by the majority leadership can often be simply the construction of a pretext for an individual oppositionist and his or her circle to break away and set up their own political fiefdom wherein, although smaller, they will constitute the staff of generals. Sometimes, of course, the split is caused by the majority group in power in an effort to remove a potential future threat or distract the membership from objective problems by blaming internal enemies. Usually, however, the dynamic leading to a split occurs on both sides.

None of the above is by any means restricted to Trotskyist or Leninist or even socialist organizations. Anarchist groups and religious sects exhibit similar traits. The question is whether one should continue the Trotskyist tradition of lining up on historical factional sides, as if someone born in 1940 or 1950 or after was actually present as an engaged participant at the time of the "French Turn" or the "Auto Crisis." This relates to some of the controversies about the so-called "Cannon tradition." Is the proper appreciation of Cannon, who certainly represents a good deal of what is most recoupable in U.S. Trotskyist history, to be achieved by retrospectively reinscribing oneself as his right-hand man or woman in all the faction fights he ever waged? Is this the most effective way to combat vulgar and prejudiced anti-Cannonism? Might it not be more productive to step back and extract whatever is valuable from *all* points of view in such disputes to create a richer and more mature political culture that won't snap so quickly into raging factions, which at the first sign of serious disputation leads to crisis and split?

Clearly the rhetoric of "all-inclusiveness" and the abstraction of democracy don't work. They disorient and incapacitate as one deals with real-life situations, such as ultra-left elements in a coalition or an organization that really do disrupt and paralyze and that may even, under the most extreme conditions, have to be ejected for the sake of democratic, majority-rule functioning. But the older tradition, with its talk of political homogeneity and fidelity to a precise (rather than general) program, doesn't work either. The boundaries of what constitutes homogeneity are variously defined, as are the interpretations of the allegedly "historic program." The method required, then, must be based on approaches to problems and principles of analysis, and these must be derived from the relation to goals.

Conclusion

In sum, why not "drop" Trotskyism altogether? First, one shouldn't drop Trotskyism because politically active people need continuity if they are going to avoid repeating errors of the past. The problems telescoped in the Trotskyist tradition are hardly idiosyncratic; rather, they are an important variant of problems faced by the U.S. Left in all decades. Those who lived through the 1960s saw in the fate of Students for a Democratic Society (SDS) that one could not entirely escape program, coherent organization, and a theory of social formations. SDS's attempt to repudiate the Old Left, instead of critically building upon and advancing its legacy, only hastened the New Left's demise.

A second reason for coming to terms with and appropriating the best of U.S. Trotskyism—that is, putting it up on the reference shelf alongside the other potentially valuable traditions of class struggle, but perhaps letting it protrude a bit and dressing it in a brighter cover—is that there are recoup-able elements in its theory and tradition that are far superior to others available. The Theory of Permanent Revolution, of course, still remains to be verified, although the perspective of combining bourgeois-democratic and socialist demands seems the most plausible for liberation of the dominated countries.[49] However, the Trotskyist focus on workers' power—the assessment of strategy as well as the character of a social formation from the perspective of self-control by the producers—and the corollary arguments for separating party and state and the necessity of revolutionary pluralism, all of which are argued so compellingly in the Fourth International document "Socialist Democracy and the Dictatorship of the Proletariat," provide a crucial foundation.[50] So does much Trotskyist work regarding independent political action, nationalism, and self-determination.

However, because Trotskyism has had so little success in the United States, the attitude of Trotskyism historically has appeared to be, "if only we were in the leadership, we could set things right—because, if we were in the leadership, the class consciousness of the proletariat and its allies would have to be at a much higher pitch." In the famous case of Trotskyist policy regarding the Popular Front and World War II, for example, this stance is essentially the legacy that Trotskyism bequeathed—the truism that the only real solution is socialist revolution, and that that is obtained only by refusing to subordinate the interests of the working class to the program of liberal capitalism. But, Trotskyist or not, all reasonable people ought to be haunted by the questions: What if revolution were *not* possible then; what if the famous "crisis in leadership" (the failure of correct ideas to win out) were overdetermined by factors that simply could *not* be dislodged, even if Trotskyist organizations had memberships of tens of thousands? What if, in fact, the Popular Front did not, overall and in every case, facilitate the advance of reaction but was the best that could be produced in certain situations because socialist revolution was not then on the agenda?[51] As a new generation of revolutionary socialist activists emerges, they will have to go back and reconsider these issues in order to develop a theory and perspective on the course of world history that is genuinely produced and not a mechanical hand-me-down. If those from the Trotskyist tradition stand aside from such reconsideration or, even worse, participate only as "seasoned experts," it will only heighten their irrelevance; they must, of course, bring their experiences to bear, but also genuinely listen to people from other traditions and keep an open mind about the possibility of genuinely *new* issues arising.

Finally, in terms of future directions for research and theory, let me conclude by mentioning one area that has preoccupied me, personally, during the past decade, even before the "Crisis of 1989." In my view, the Trotskyist criticism of the U.S. Communist or "Stalinist" movement has been inadequate and reductive, which I discovered not only by reading the new scholarship but also as I conducted extensive empirical research based on about a hundred personal interviews and the examination of sixty or so new archival collections dealing with Communist Party activities. I raise this not as an academic question but because I find that young people and left-wing scholars in search of a U.S. radical tradition, especially one that is antiracist and rooted in the working class, return again and again to the Communist experience. I don't believe that this is only because at the height of the New Deal and during the "Grand Alliance" the movement had a kind of "power," because much of the scholarly interest also includes the Third Period of the late 1920s and early 1930s, as well as the Cold War era. I believe that it is because there is evidence that the struggles and impact of cadres of the CP-USA outdistanced by far those of any other organized socialist current. Even many who broke bitterly with the CP-USA went on to play admirable roles in struggles during the 1960s and after, and they frequently acknowledged the value of their years in the CP-USA.

Given this reality, the issue of a compelling and subtle theorization of the U.S. Communist movement also embodies the bigger question of how one critiques and relates to other more successful movements that one nonetheless believes to be profoundly flawed. Here it is significant to note that many features of the traditional Trotskyist critique of the Communist movement are far and away the most influential in scholarship on the Communist Party, outside of CP-USA circles themselves, of course. This was certainly the case after the end of the 1950s, when the low-level anticommunist Red-baiters such as Eugene Lyons faded from prominence. This Trotskyist critique, reworked to fit various political perspectives, was embodied mainly in Theodore Draper's early histories, Cannon's and Shachtman's writings, and in writings by Irving Howe, Lewis Coser, Phyllis Jacobson, Julius Jacobson, and Bert Cochran. The view was generally that CP-USA rank-and-file activists were decent people, not dupes of the USSR but dupes of their leaders, who, like the Soviet bureaucracy itself, covered up crimes and perpetrated lies out of self-interest (varying from monetary gain and power to more subtle psychological needs). Moreover, these leaders remained leaders mainly by fidelity to Stalin's shifting policies, in turn determined by Stalin's own need to maintain power in the USSR. Of course, revolutionary socialists like Cannon and the Jacobsons argued such analyses from an uncompromising anticapitalist and anti-imperialist perspective, whereas others, shading off into liberalism, combined features of this critique with very different politics.

However, in the mid-1990s, we see that much current scholarship on the CP-USA by leftists, most of whom are or were activists and "on the side of the angels," is in aggressive rebellion against this legacy. The main defender of Draper is Harvey Klehr, a neoconservative. This rebellion is not at all because many of these scholars, mostly middle-aged professors of history, have been in or around the CP-USA; actually, many of them had a connection with rival currents, including the C. L. R. James tradition, Maoism, and even Trotskyism. I won't repeat here what I've already published in reviews of the books by Paul Buhle, Maurice Isserman, Robin Kelley, and Ellen Schrecker.[52] What I think is crucial to emphasize here is that this scholarship on the CP-USA, although I disagree with much of it politically, has rendered the whole subject of U.S. Communism far more absorbing, useful, and relevant than ever before— and more than the study of Trotskyism has ever been. This is because these scholars have moved from a focus on documents, resolutions, and parallels with Soviet policy to paying attention to human dimensions and engaging gender and race issues. It is also because many of these scholars, although not eschewing the idea of commitment, have the ability to step back and examine a variety of perspectives on a problem somewhat dispassionately, according to the attitude popularly attributed to Lukács, "partisan but objective."

What this means is that those trying to sustain what is useful from the Trotskyist tradition need a less grandiose conception of Trotskyism's historic role. The view that the task of modern Trotskyists is to "reclaim a historic program" by using their publications to distinguish themselves from other political currents through defense of "the Trotskyist program" is far too simplistic. There are too many opinions about what constitutes "the real historic program" of Trotskyism, and, by incanting such mystical phrases, one will only end up confusing oneself with, not distinguishing oneself from, the discredited legacy of Trotskyist sectarianism. In the tradition of "American Trotskyism," much of this outlook flows from the belief held by James P. Cannon in the 1940s that the Socialist Workers Party was the already constructed vanguard, with its main objective being to win leadership of the masses. Although one has good grounds to believe that this kind of faith was necessary for Cannon and the SWP to survive the difficulties of the period, it surely must be rejected as a model for today, even though the basic idea appears in Cannon's otherwise inspiring "Theses on the American Revolution":

> The revolutionary vanguard party, destined to lead this tumultuous revolutionary movement in the U.S. does not have to be created. It already exists, and its name is the Socialist Workers Party. It is the sole legitimate heir and continuator of pioneer American Communism and the revolutionary movements of the American workers from which it sprang. . . . The fundamental core of a professional leadership has been assembled. . . .
>
> The task of the SWP consists simply in this: to remain true to its program and banner, to render it more precise with each new development and apply it correctly to the class struggle; and to expand and grow with the growth of the revolutionary mass movement, always aspiring to lead it to victory in the struggle for political power.[53]

This kind of thinking was not an aberration of the movement but flowed directly from the tradition of "American Trotskyism." Similar ideas appear in an article by Morris Stein, one of Cannon's most trusted supporters, who served as SWP national secretary when Cannon was imprisoned under the Smith Act:

We are monopolists in the field of politics. We can't stand any competition. We can tolerate no rivals. The working class, to make the revolution can do it only through one party and one program. This is the lesson of the Russian Revolution. That is the lesson of all history since the October Revolution. Isn't that a fact? This is why we are out to destroy every single party in the field that makes any pretense of being a working-class revolutionary party. Ours is the only correct program that can lead to revolution. Everything else is deception, treachery. We are monopolists in politics and we operate like monopolists.[54]

No doubt there are those who can sugarcoat and speciously "interpret in the appropriate context" such statements, or even try to minimize them in light of the fact that both writers (Cannon and Stein) modified their views as time went on. But the Trotskyist tradition has no hope of accomplishing anything more than the generation of small, sectarian groupuscules unless it breaks radically with the key features of this outlook. It must instead be recognized that *no* program or group of cadres or organization exists as "*the* heir and continuator" of the revolutionary tradition; that the programmatic task is *not* to render it more precise and apply it "correctly" but to profoundly revamp it in friendly interaction with rival perspectives, aimed at developing method more than precise policy; that leadership (even if united and to some degree centralized) is *not* something that should fall into the hands of a single group but should grow organically from the struggle with various kinds of political activists participating side-by-side with (and with veterans learning from) the participants more than "leading" them; and that one should be an *anti*monopolist in the field of politics, learning from and defending the rights of political rivals.

However, a repudiation of the strong elements of sectarianism, leader idolatry, hairsplitting, and so forth that have afflicted and disabled U.S. Trotskyism has nothing in common with the vulgar anti-Trotskyist views that the movement produced nothing of worth, that all forms of anti-Stalinism must lead to deradicalization or "objectively" aids reaction, that Trotskyism is simply Stalinism without power, and so forth.

To sum up: Trotskyism!!! is dead. Long live trotskyism.

Notes

I am grateful to several scholars and activists who gave me critical feedback on a draft of this essay: Steve Bloom, Paul Le Blanc, Peter Drucker, Christopher Phelps, Ellen Poteet, and Patrick Quinn. However, I alone am responsible for the analysis and any errors. An earlier version appeared in *Against the Current* 53 (November–December 1994): 29–32, 42; 54 (January–February 1995): 34–38; and 55 (March–April 1995): 33–37.

1.   The term "American Trotskyism" is the historic one for Trotskyism in the United States. Its use is problematic today when, increasingly, "America" is understood as a hemispheric entity.

2.   The most reliable information I have on membership numbers for the SWP comes from a series of letters I received from George Breitman on July 17, July 30, and August 9, 1985. His view is that the following figures, from convention records, are accurate: 100 in 1929; less than 200 in 1931; 429 in 1934; 1,520 in 1938; 1,095 in 1940; 645 in 1942; 850 in 1944; 1,470 in 1946; 1,277 in 1948; 825 in 1950; 758 in 1952; 480 in 1954; 434 in 1957; 399 in 1959; 413 in 1961; 441 in 1963; 420 in 1965; 385 in 1967; 500 in 1969; 791 in 1971; 1,125 in 1973; 1,125 in 1975; and 1,454 in 1976. Breitman noted that figures are difficult to compute for the fusion of the Communist League of America and Muste's American Workers Party (AWP); the former claimed 429 at that time and the latter less than 300, but some of the AWP members switched to the CP-USA or dropped out. Breitman estimates that between 500 and 600 actually entered the Socialist Party, and it is difficult to get precise figures because all factions were inflating their numbers by various means. Breitman was also dubious that one could come up with estimates for active sympathizers, or the proportion of inactive members, or even a general figure for how many individuals actually "passed through" the Trotskyist movement over the decades. After 1976, the figures for the SWP began to decline.

3.   This claim may be a weak point, since many careers have yet to reach their zenith. Moreover, it is still difficult to "name names" of individuals in midcareer who were once organizationally connected with U.S. Trotskyism, due to prejudice in our society, especially in the universities, against those who have held membership in revolutionary organizations. Eventually, however, this topic may be worthy of a full-scale study, comparing not only the two generations but comparing Trotskyist-influenced intellectuals of various countries and Trotskyist-influenced intellectuals with leftists from other traditions.

4.   Not "betrayal" in the sense of a personal sell-out; Trotsky's *The Revolution Betrayed* (1937) presents a materialist analysis of the social and historical conditions for the rise of the Stalinist bureaucracy.

5.   See my discussion of the comparative merits of some of these theories in *The New York Intellectuals* (Chapel Hill: University of North Carolina Press,

1987), pp. 186–92. Also, Paul Beilis's *Marxism in the U.S.S.R.: The Theory of Proletarian Dictatorship and the Marxist Analysis of Soviet Society* (Atlantic Highlands, NJ: Humanities Press, 1979), provides a useful survey of the theories of Trotsky, Shachtman, Burnham, Cliff, James, Dunayevskaya, and others.

6.   There are, of course, signs of nostalgia for the particular version of "October" associated with the rule of the bureaucratic elite, expressed by those associated with that elite who have mobilized some substantial demonstrations.

7.   *New York Times*, July 24, 1993, p. 4.

8.   See the collection of essays edited by Marilyn Vogt-Downey, *The USSR 1987–1991: Marxist Perspectives* (Atlantic Highlands, NJ: Humanities Press, 1993).

9.   Alex Callinicos, *Trotskyism* (Minneapolis: University of Minnesota Press, 1990), pp. 1–2.

10. As are many other topics treated in this essay, the "paradigm problem" is itself worthy of a separate study. For example, it is worth recalling that the "model" theorized by the experience of October 1917 itself involved a particular interpretation of earlier experiences, such as the Paris Commune of 1871. Thus it is not at all unlikely that future theorizations of revolutionary experience may reincorporate both of these in new forms. Moreover, any new paradigms will no doubt draw upon May 1968, the Sandinista revolution, and so forth, not to mention more recent cultural work based on previously underestimated thinkers such as Gramsci. What is perhaps most important to recognize is that much of Trotskyism overemphasized the Bolshevik experience more as a model to be emulated (albeit with "adjustments") than a paradigm for imagining revolutionary processes and anticipating their problems.

11. One part of the explanation for this failure may lie in the understandable choice that the Socialist Workers Party made to prioritize the building of a mass antiwar movement around the slogan, "Out Now." This led it to orient the bulk of its membership to working on the relatively elite white campuses and in coalitions with white liberals around the "single-issue" approach. Many Maoist groups contributed little to building a mass antiwar movement and oriented its cadres to communities and workplaces of people of color with more revolutionary-sounding demands. The Communist Party possessed a tradition of stronger links to communities of people of color and benefited from the Soviet Union's material aid to certain Third World liberation struggles. In addition, it might be noted that Maoist groups gave uncritical support to the Chinese revolution, and the Communist Party to the Cuban Revolution and the Communist Party of Vietnam. The various kinds of "critical support" offered by Trotskyist groups, though often quite justified, were frequently perceived by opponents as undermining the struggle or even as "racist."

12. I suppose that it is possible to object that neither of these groups, nor any of the other existing ones, are really carrying out the traditions of U.S. Trotskyism. Yet one is faced with a problem: Why is it that, with so many efforts to realize historic "American Trotskyism" (by groups such as the Spartacist League, Workers League, Revolutionary Workers League, and others), the results are

consistently so awful? Is the problem simply that "objective conditions" are preventing the "real" revolutionary program among these from getting a fair hearing, or is it something deeper and more strategic?

13. Today, these results are probably, at best, a dozen squabbling Trotskyist and former Trotskyist organizations of between twenty and 500 members (most of them closer to twenty) in a country of millions.

14. Indeed, among the next steps should be a comparative analysis of the situation of U.S. Trotskyism within the contexts of the United States as well as the international Left.

15. See my discussion of this in *New York Intellectuals*, pp. 193–99.

16. In 1991, an impressive study called *Community of Suffering and Struggle: Women, Men, and the Labor Movement in Minneapolis* by Elizabeth Faue was published the the University of North Carolina Press; yet she refers to Dobbs only twice in the book, whereas the Communist writer Meridel Le Sueur is cited at least thirty times.

17. A notable exception is Alice and Staughton Lynd, eds., *Rank and File* (New York: Monthly Review Press, 1990).

18. Two important exceptions to this are A. Belden Field, *Trotskyism and Maoism: Theory and Practice in France in the United States* (New York: Praeger, 1988), and Robert Alexander, *International Trotskyism* (Durham, NC: Duke University Press, 1991). Although both authors have their own political views, neither reshapes the subject dramatically in order to validate a factional obsession. On the other hand, both, at times, lack a "feel" for the reality of the Trotskyist movement, and both cast their nets so wide that their surveys of the historical experience in the United States are limited and partial. See a review of Field by Alan Wald in *American Historical Review* (April 1991): 473–4, and a review of Alexander by Paul Le Blanc in *Bulletin in Defense of Marxism* 102 (January 1993): 38–40.

19. One might hope that Callinicos would take to heart the thoughtful review by Paul Clarke in *International Marxist Review* 13 (Spring 1992): 127–43.

20. Christopher Z. Hobson and Ronald Tabor, *Trotskyism and the Dilemma of Socialism* (Westport, CT: Greenwood Press, 1988), p. xvii.

21. The eminent Canadian labor historian Bryan Palmer recently announced his intention to write one.

22. Of course, the writings of Cannon reprinted in that book can certainly facilitate one's learning more about U.S. Marxist strategy and tactics in the 1920s, but one would never have the slightest idea from the biographical essay or contents of that volume that Cannon was anything other than a political machine. Moreover, Cannon's political role in the period covered by the volume is almost always filtered through the lens of Cannon's memory decades later, with minimal independent verification. In addition, apparently due to factionalism, the editors take seriously Constance Ashton Myers's claim in *The Prophet's Army* (Westport, CT: Greenwood, 1977) that Max Shachtman died an admirer of Stalin. (It is not surprising, in light of the low level of her book,

that Myers mistook Shachtman's irony; but the editors of the Prometheus Research Library volume must have been looking mainly for a factional club against Shachtman.)

23.   Elizabeth Faue, at least, interviewed Marvel Scholl for *Community of Suffering and Struggle*, but the references are sparse, in accordance with her general lack of interest in Trotskyism. Among the few resource materials available from the Socialist Workers Party's publications are Dianne Feeley, "Antoinette Konikow: Marxist and Feminist," *International Socialist Review* 33, no. 1 (January 1972): 42–46, and "Socialist Women and Labor Struggles, 1934–1954: A Report by Participants," *International Socialist Review* 36, no. 3 (March 1975): 20–25, 36–38.

24.   Edgar Keemer, *Confessions of a Pro-Life Abortionist* (Detroit: Vinco Press, 1980). See also Charles Denby, *Indignant Heart* (Boston: South End Press, 1978).

25.   Bruce Lambert, "Vincent Copeland, 77, Is Dead; Led Anti-War Protests in 1960s," *New York Times*, June 10 1993, p. A16.

26.   Correspondence with Bruce Nelson, August 23, 1993.

27.   See Patrick Quinn, "In Memoriam: Phil Clark," *Against the Current*, n.s., 7 no. 4: 49.

28.   Letter from George Breitman to Alan Wald, March 14, 1985. Sam Gordon's recollections about Cannon's support of Stamm when Stamm was arrested for homosexuality tend to confirm Breitman's views. See Les Evans, ed., *James P. Cannon as We Knew Him* (New York: Pathfinder Press, 1966), p. 66.

29.   Telephone interview with Frank Fried, September 1993.

30.   Wohlforth must be especially praised for the generosity and balance of his portraits of numerous figures in the Trotskyist movement with whom he came in contact. However, his political conclusions do not strike me as anything new, as he claims, but largely a reversion to familiar pre-Leninist and anti-Leninist simplicities. I expressed my differences with Wohlforth on this matter in the article "In Defense of Critical Leninism," *Against the Current*, n.s., no. 6 (November–December 1986): 44–47. Wohlforth replied in "The Need for Post-Leninism," *Against the Current*, n.s., no. 8 (March–April 1987): 37–39.

31.   However, some of Cannon's personal letters toward the end of his life indicate an awareness of some of the dangers facing the SWP; see the pamphlet by Cannon, *Don't Strangle the Party* (New York: Fourth Internationalist Tendency, 1986).

32.   See the review by Wald, "Party Lines and Passing Factions," *Washington Post Book World*, January 14, 1990, p. 4, and the exchange in the *Post* between Glotzer and Wald, "Russian Histories," March 4, 1990, p. 15.

33.   Also lacking at this date is a theory for such a discrepancy, outside of the obvious observation that the Trotskyist movement was smaller. Among the factors that might be considered are the close connection between this movement and its exiled leader, who was assassinated in 1940—thus imparting a legacy that was largely based on a politics of survival apart from a center of power (note

the title of the third volume of Deutscher's biography, *The Prophet Outcast*) and that failed to address the dramatically new political world of the post-World War II era.

34. See the recent study by Jerald E. Podair, "'White' Values, 'Black' Values: The Ocean-Hill Brownsville Controversy and New York City Culture, 1965–75," *Radical History Review* 59 (Spring 1994): 36–59.

35. Of course, small groups usually do not have enough resources to try to do many things at once.

36. Georg Lukács, *History and Class Consciousness: Studies in Marxist Dialectics* (London: Merlin Press, 1971).

37. George Novack, "Georg Lukács as a Marxist Philosopher," in *Polemics in Marxist Philosophy* (New York: Monad Press, 1978), pp. 117–45.

38. However, even in regard to "more general propositions about class struggle," I would suggest that no alleged principle should ever be seen as "automatic." Thus the "principle" of never crossing a picket line or opposing a strike can be challenged if the strike is racist, just as the policy of never supporting the economic or military power of U.S. imperialism was modified when revolutionaries endorsed the U.S. economic embargo of South Africa and the use of federal troops to enforce school integration in the South. Although there are, no doubt, relevant analogies from the past, "general propositions" themselves must under new conditions be redefined and even questioned by experience.

39. For an example of this kind of sectarian polemicizing, see Fred Mueller, *SWP: Reform or Revolution* (New York: Labor Publications, 1972).

40. An outstanding example of this creative yet rigorous approach is Paul Le Blanc, *Permanent Revolution in Nicaragua* (New York: Fourth International Tendency, 1986).

41. The trend was first discussed by Max Shachtman in "Footnote for Historians," *New International* 4 (December 1938): 377–79, and elaborated by Daniel Bell in *Marxian Socialism in the United States* (Princeton, NJ: Princeton University Press, 1967), pp. 154–57.

42. The Trotskyist organization Spark frequently exemplifies this.

43. In observing the articulation of policy in the Socialist Workers Party, I frequently found the same basic analysis reasonable when presented by individuals such as George Breitman and Fred Halstead but shrill and simplistic when appearing in the *Militant* or presented by other leaders, including those who had graduated from the nation's most elite colleges.

44. Some Trotskyists try to strengthen their achievements by retrospectively taking credit for the Russian Revolution and other social transformations (Yugoslavia as an example of turning the antifascist war into a social revolution; Cuba as an example of "revolutionaries in action" carrying out an "unconscious Trotskyist" perspective; and so on). Today, of course, after 1989 and the assault on Bosnia, taking "credit" for October 1917 and Yugoslavia, even with the Trotskyist analysis of these societies' degeneration and deformation, appears even more tenuous than before.

45. Naturally the adherents of these theories don't believe that they are present-ing dogmas but the "true laws of motion" of these societies. As I have argued in *The New York Intellectuals*, pp. 188–89, none of these theories persuasively accounts for all aspects of these societies, and each seems to be based on one or more impressive points of analysis; therefore, a synthetic embodiment of these and other theories is the most useful perspective with which to work. Unfortunately, for most Trotskyists, absolute fidelity to their particular interpretation of a specific theory of Soviet-type societies is their political touchstone.

46. Actually, I favor using the term "revolutionary" with a great deal of caution. An individual with a revolutionary consciousness, such as a union official, may be operating in a structure that prevents revolutionary practice; likewise, a revolutionary-minded peasant may simply have no collective instrument to realize revolutionary action. What is offensive and destructive is the declara-tion made by adherents of tiny parties, which have no possibility of meaningful revolutionary action, that they themselves are "revolutionary" in distinction to those engaged in genuine social struggles but who lack the "revolutionary program."

47. This does not mean marching in a parade with signs and literature supporting the "masses" while denouncing their leaders as "criminal sell-outs."

48. Unpublished autobiographies exist in various forms by Carl Feingold, Milton Genecin, George Novack, Max Shachtman, Arne Swabeck, Stan Weir, and B. J. Widick.

49. See the valuable exposition by Michael Löwy, *The Politics of Uneven and Combined Development* (London: Verso, 1981). Nevertheless, it doesn't follow that this aspect of Trotskyist theory is unproblematic, especially from the per-spective of critiquing the "stagism" that has plagued virtually all of Marxist political analysis.

50. "Socialist Democracy and the Dictatorship of the Proletariat," *Special Supplement to Intercontinental Press Combined with Inprecor* (January 1980): 210–25.

51. Clearly there are *specific* examples in which Popular Front policy did facilitate the advance of reaction, such as the May–June 1937 events in Barcelona, drop-ping the fight for independence from Britain in India, and so forth.

52. The reviews of all but Kelley have been reprinted in Alan Wald, *The Responsibility of Intellectuals* (Atlantic Highlands, NJ: Humanities Press, 1992); the review of Kelley appears as "The Roots of African-American Communism," *Against the Current* 46 (September–October 1993): 33–36, and is reprinted in *Writing from the Left* (London: Verso, 1994).

53. James P. Cannon, *The Struggle for Socialism in the "American Century"* (New York: Pathfinder Press, 1977), p. 271.

54. *SWP Internal Bulletin* 6, no. 13 (December 1944): 10.

Appendix

George Breitman, whose essay "The Liberating Influence of the Transitional Program" is included in this volume, was one of the most highly respected figures produced by the U.S. Trotskyist movement. After his death, a memorial volume edited by Naomi Allen and Sarah Lovell was published under the title *A Tribute to George Breitman, Writer, Organizer, Revolutionary* (New York: Fourth Internationalist Tendency, 1987). The two items in this appendix are reprinted from that volume.

"George Breitman (1916–86)
More Than Half a Century of Revolutionary Dedication"

Editorial Board of *Bulletin in Defense of Marxism*

After almost thirty years of unremitting illness, George Breitman died on April 19. He was seventy years old. The immediate cause of death was a heart attack, but he had suffered from a wide variety of ailments, including rheumatoid arthritis, ulcers, and cancer, and had recently survived surgery on his stomach and a life-threatening abscess in his head and neck. Although he was in constant pain whenever he was not asleep, and grew progressively weaker over the past several months, he continued to spend much of his waking time in productive political work, dictating three letters from his hospital bed only two days before his death.

Founding Member of the SWP

Breitman joined the Spartacus Youth League in 1935, at the age of nineteen, and later that year the Workers Party of the U.S., a forerunner of the Socialist Workers Party. From that time until his death fifty-one years later he never wavered in his dedication to building the revolutionary socialist movement. He was a delegate to the founding convention of the Socialist Workers Party in 1937, and remained a loyal and dedicated member of that organization until 1984. In that year the present SWP leaders—who had developed profound political differences with the historical program of the party which Breitman continued to defend—shamefully expelled him and dozens of his comrades on trumped-up charges of "disloyalty." After his expulsion from the SWP Breitman immediately set out to organize the expellees and to try to save the party and its program. He helped to found the Fourth Internationalist Tendency and was an editor of its journal, the *Bulletin in Defense of Marxism*.

During his years in the SWP Breitman served in many capacities. He was a candidate ten times on the party ticket, for offices ranging from State Assembly in New Jersey to the U.S. Senate. He set such a good personal example with his election campaigns that James P. Cannon, the founder of the American Trotskyist movement, referred jokingly to his "perennial" candidacies and suggested that Breitman was going to be regarded as a chronic office seeker. In 1941 he began his first of several terms as editor of the *Militant*. Except for the two and a half years he spent in the army as a draftee during World War II, he served continuously on the party National Committee from 1939 to 1981, and was several times a member of its Political Committee. He took on the tasks of organizer, branch secretary, financial director, recruiter, educator, campaign manager, and writer, along with many others.

Perhaps his greatest strength was his ability to explain difficult ideas so that they could be understood by people who were unfamiliar or uncomfortable with movement terminology or jargon. He had a knack for seeing opportunities to apply the party's program to the day-to-day life of working people. And he had an informal, unpretentious style in writing and speaking that made it easy for his audience to understand him. These qualities made him an outstanding candidate for office in the party's election campaigns and a particularly effective speaker and educator.

Breitman also helped in many efforts of the party to defend itself or its members from victimization by the government. The most famous of these was the "Case of the Legless Veteran," James Kutcher. The Veterans Administration tried to fire Kutcher from his job as a clerk and take away his veteran's benefits during the witch-hunt years of the 1950s because of his membership in the SWP, despite the fact that he had lost both of his legs in Italy as a GI in World War II. Breitman, along with others, helped Kutcher in his political and legal campaign against the government's attack. After a long battle, the case was won. Breitman collaborated with Kutcher in writing his book about this experience, and the two remained lifelong friends. Kutcher was expelled from the SWP in 1983, after a terrible slander campaign against him.

In the 1960s Breitman made one of his best-known contributions to revolutionary Marxism when he helped develop an analysis of the profound revolutionary implications of Black nationalism in the U.S. In particular, he became an authority on Malcolm X and wrote *The Last Year of Malcolm X, the Evolution of a Revolutionary*, a book put out by Merit Publishers in 1967. He also edited, in whole or in part, many of Malcolm's writings and speeches for publication. These included the books *Malcolm X Speaks* and *By Any Means Necessary*, as well as the pamphlet *Malcolm X on Afro-American History*.

In the late '60s, the SWP and the Young Socialist Alliance began to gain members from the radicalizing youth on the campuses, in the anti–Vietnam war movement, the Black struggle, and the beginnings of the women's liberation movement. The party was looking for ways to educate its new recruits in revolutionary Marxism. Breitman proposed an extensive project for Pathfinder Press: to collect and publish the writings of Leon Trotsky, who was, with Lenin, the foremost leader of the Bolshevik revolution of 1917 in Russia. Breitman chose Trotsky for three reasons. First, because unlike the writings of other outstanding figures of revolutionary history, Trotsky's writings had never been collected and published in a systematic way. Second, Breitman considered Trotsky to be the greatest popularizer of Lenin's ideas, just as Lenin had been Marx's most oustanding interpreter. Trotsky could present the most important ideas of Marx and Engels and Lenin in a way that contemporary young radicals could appreciate. Moreover, Trotsky's own seminal contributions to the Marxist heritage—his theory of permanent revolution, the transitional program, his analysis of nationalism—were of paramount importance for the revolutionary movements of today.

Breitman took primary responsibility for the project of locating, selecting, translating from many languages, editing, and annotating the massive amount of Trotsky's writings, and shaping it into cohesive form. Ultimately this consisted of fourteen volumes in the series *Writings of*

Leon Trotsky, covering the years of Trotsky's last exile (1929–40). At the same time, he oversaw the work leading to the publication of several volumes of Trotsky's writings on specific countries and political themes—the Spanish revolution and civil war of the thirties, the rise of fascism in Germany, the French popular front, and many others. The result was that revolutionists now have an incomparable resource available to study the history and theory of revolution.

Youth and Family

George was born and grew up in a working class neighborhood in Newark, New Jersey. His mother was a houseworker for better-off families, and his father was an iceman who carried fifty-pound blocks of ice up six flights of tenement stairs in the days before refrigeration. When his father died at the age of forty, George's older sister Celia had to quit school to help support the family. She was one of the most important influences on George as a child. She became a member of the Young Communist League and combined her babysitting responsibilities with her political ones by bringing George to meetings while he was still quite young. It was as a baby brother that he attended a demonstration, with hundreds of Newark residents, to protest the execution of the Boston anarchists Sacco and Vanzetti in 1927.

As a youngster, George read voraciously. Mostly he read junk—the hundreds of adventure stories and pulp novels for boys that were the diet of a generation before television turned reading for pleasure into an obsolete activity. But he also read good novels and short stories. His hangouts were his neighborhood corner, which later became known to many as "Trotsky Square" because so many of his gang joined the Trotskyist youth, and the Newark public library. Fifty years later, George still spoke of the Newark public library with affection.

At the age of sixteen, in 1932, George graduated from Central High School during the depths of the depression, and joined the ranks of the unemployed. During the summer of 1933 he was often in a playground near his home playing baseball and editing some issues of the playground's mimeographed newspaper. The whole year after he graduated from high school he spent writing a novel about his neighborhood, which he later destroyed. In 1934 George went to Alabama as part of the Civilian Conservation Corps, a New Deal outfit intended to get unemployed youth off the streets. Here he received some copies of the *Militant* from a neighborhood friend.

Early Political Activity

After returning to Newark in 1935, Breitman joined the Trotskyist movement and turned his attention to mass work in the unemployed movement. He joined the organization of the unemployed, the Workers Alliance of America, which was thriving in New Jersey with several thousand members. He was soon in the thick of battles to protect the rights of unemployed workers and to gain higher pay on government-sponsored Works Progress Administration jobs. He was elected New Jersey state organization secretary of the Workers Alliance in 1936. In August of that year he was the youngest (at age twenty) of seven Workers Alliance leaders arrested, charged with "inciting to riot." They were organizing strikes and closing down WPA projects in Burlington County. Breitman spent a week in jail on that occasion. The charges were eventually dropped, the strikes were won, and the strikers got a five-cent hourly raise. This is only one incident in scores of such strikes in those years in which Breitman participated. He served as the state Workers Alliance secretary in 1936 and 1937, and then as Essex County secretary. During several of those years he was also editor of the news bulletin of the New Jersey Workers Alliance. He recruited many unemployed workers to the revolutionary movement.

In 1936 the organized unemployed occupied the state capitol in Trenton, forcing the state legislature to abandon the legislative chambers and begin negotiations for improved unemployment benefits. Breitman helped to organize the Trenton siege and later wrote a pamphlet about it.

The unemployed movement of the thirties was the main opportunity Breitman had to participate in the mass movement and to test himself and his politics in action. In 1941, eighteen leaders of the Socialist Workers Party, charged under the Smith Act with advocating the forcible overthrow of the U.S. government, were imprisoned on the day the U.S. entered the Second World War. The eighteen included Felix Morrow, editor of the *Militant*. Breitman was asked to take over as editor of the paper, a post he held until he was drafted in 1943 and sent to France.

In March 1946 he attended a pre-world congress meeting of the Fourth International in Paris as an observer. The meeting was broken up by the police, who arrested all the participants. The conference continued in a French jail, but Breitman was released in a few hours and shipped home.

On his return to the U.S. he again served as editor of the *Militant* from 1946–47 and 1951–53. In 1954 he moved to Detroit, where he worked as a proofreader for the *Detroit Free Press* and became a member of the International Typographical Union. He spent thirteen years as an active leader of the Detroit party branch, where he founded the Friday Night Socialist Forum which ran continuously from 1954 until 1967. When he left Detroit George returned to New York City where he remained for the rest of his life. He is survived by his wife, comrade, and companion of forty-six years, Dorothea.

A Tribute

ERNEST MANDEL[1]

With George Breitman, the Fourth International has lost the last survivor of the central cadre which founded the Socialist Workers Party and assured the continuity of revolutionary Marxism in North America for half a century, a mainstay of that continuity on a world scale, too.

Those who, like George, made up their minds in the thirties to support Trotsky against Stalin, to build new revolutionary parties instead of trying to operate through the traditional organizations of the working class, did not act because this was the easiest solution to the current problems of the class struggle, nationally and internationally. On the contrary; they were very conscious of the fact that they chose the difficult road, that they were swimming against the stream. Their opponents in the labor movement supported themselves on huge apparatuses, those of mass trade unions and of a mighty state, the USSR. They had tremendous material means at their disposal, all of which could not fail to exercise a power of attraction on many people. In addition, they had the political credibility of strength. They were leading masses. They were going places, or at least so many supposed.

---

[1] Ernest Mandel, an internationally recognized Marxist theorist active in the Belgian labor movement, sent the following remarks on behalf of the United Secretariat of the Fourth International.

There was only one little thing the matter with these mighty opponents. They didn't consistently act in the interests of the working class. At decisive moments of world history, they strangled the opportunity for the workers to make a leap forward towards socialism. They caused terrible defeats. They had done so in Germany in 1918–1919. They had done so in China in 1927. They had caused the terrible defeat of Hitler seizing power unopposed in 1933. They had prevented the American workers from building a labor party independent from the bosses during the rise of the CIO in the thirties. They would strangle the Spanish and French revolutionary possibilities in 1936. And the list would be stretched on and on, at the end of World War II, later in Indonesia, in May 1968 in France, then in Chile, in Portugal, in Iran.

Those who answered Trotsky's call for the Fourth International understood that it was necessary to challenge these misleaders of the working class. One had to challenge them on the field of program and theory. One had to challenge them on the field of action. There was nothing dogmatic or sectarian in that challenge. It meant acting side by side with millions of workers throughout the world, refusing to subordinate their ongoing struggles, their instinctive endeavors, their resolution and their hopes, to brakes and restrictions which in the last analysis express the interests of social forces alien to the working class. That is what people of George's generation started to understand. That is what history has proven ever since, again and again.

To build a new revolutionary party, a new revolutionary international against the stream, against the pressure of great bureaucratic machines, and against the disorienting and demoralizing effects of defeats caused by these machines, necessitated not only great lucidity and deep convictions regarding the future of the working class and of the socialist revolution. It also required great moral qualities: courage, resolution, patience, firmness of character and of willpower, the capacity to resist political and individual temptations. All these qualities George Breitman mustered to a high degree, rarely encountered in a single individual.

He was what all revolutionary cadres should strive to be: an all-round revolutionary, at home in the library as well as on the picket line, a gifted writer and an excellent organizer, great at organizing election campaigns and at helping others to develop theory, an outstanding editor and a real workers' leader. His qualities as educator and popularizer, which stemmed from a rare gift of perceiving the essential and expressing it in a clear and simple way so that many can understand it, did not prevent him from being at the same time a deep and independent thinker, one of the few in our movement who have made a genuine contribution to the development of theory, in his case in the field of Black nationalism, and more generally the nationalism of the downtrodden and the oppressed everywhere in the world.

I first met George when he was in Europe in the aftermath of World War II and assisted, as an observer, in rebuilding a functioning center for our world movement. As the youngest participant in that effort, I learned a lot from him. In fact, if I would want to single out the persons from whom I learned most during the years following the war, I would name two SWP leaders: Morris Stein and George Breitman. This collaboration established the basis for a friendship which would last nearly forty years.

It was interrupted once, after the 1953 split in our movement. George and I were in the opposite camps of that split. But right after that split we exchanged a series of letters which became public, the only correspondence which maintained a dialogue between the two sectors of the split movement. For sure we both hotly argued for our—at the time different—causes. But if one rereads these letters today, one cannot fail to feel that behind the arguments there was a sincere, even desperate wish to prevent all bridges from being burned, to keep open an avenue for healing the split. That's why the blind factionalists in both camps disapproved of that correspondence. That's why we both were so happy when the split was healed in 1962–63, and felt that in a modest way we had prepared that reunification through our initial dialogue.

When George and his comrades started to be harassed, pestered, and ostracized inside the SWP because they continued to defend the program of the Fourth International, the overwhelming majority of its cadre and militants had no difficulty in defending them and standing beside them in that ordeal and after their unacceptable expulsion. We owed that to our Leninist tradition of programmatic firmness and of defending workers' democracy, to start with, inside our own ranks. We shall continue to do so in the future.

George Breitman understood more than anybody else the importance of history, of historical continuity and historical causes for giving workers and the labor movement the drive and self-confidence necessary to realize the gigantic tasks they are confronted with. It is a great pity he had not learned before leaving us that we have just won a great historic victory: the complete rejection by the Chinese Communist Party of all the criminal slanders launched by Stalin and his henchmen against Leon Trotsky and his followers in the thirties.

This victory is symbolic for many others which will come to us. There is no future in this world for Stalinism, reformism, Social Democracy, labor fakers, or bourgeois nationalists. The future belongs to the working class, to revolutionary socialism, to the Fourth International! Forward in the footsteps of Jim Cannon and of George Breitman towards a revolutionary vanguard party of the American working class! Forward in the footsteps of Lenin and Trotsky towards a revolutionary vanguard international of the world proletariat.

Index

About Haymarket Books

Haymarket Books is a nonprofit, progressive book distributor and publisher, a project of the Center for Economic Research and Social Change. We believe that activists need to take ideas, history, and politics into the many struggles for social justice today. Learning the lessons of past victories, as well as defeats, can arm a new generation of fighters for a better world. As Karl Marx said, "The philosophers have merely interpreted the world; the point, however, is to change it."

We take inspiration and courage from our namesakes, the Haymarket Martyrs, who gave their lives fighting for a better world. Their 1886 struggle for the eight-hour day, which gave us May Day, the international workers' holiday, reminds workers around the world that ordinary people can organize and struggle for their own liberation. These struggles continue today across the globe-struggles against oppression, exploitation, hunger, and poverty.

It was August Spies, one of the Martyrs targeted for being an immigrant and an anarchist, who predicted the battles being fought to this day. "If you think that by hanging us you can stamp out the labor movement," Spies told the judge, "then hang us. Here you will tread upon a spark, but here, and there, and behind you, and in front of you, and everywhere, the flames will blaze up. It is a subterranean fire. You cannot put it out. The ground is on fire upon which you stand."

We could not succeed in our publishing efforts without the generous financial support of our readers. Many people contribute to our project through the Haymarket Sustainers program, where donors receive free books in return for their monetary support. If you would like to be a part of this program, please contact us at info@haymarketbooks.org.

Shop our full catalog online at www.haymarketbooks.org or call 773-583-7884.